curriculum & instructional planning & design
For Gifted Learners

DATE DUE

Joyce VanTassel-Baska
College of William and Mary

LOVE PUBLISHING COMPANY®
Denver • London • Sydney

Published by Love Publishing Company
Denver, Colorado 80222

Library of Congress Control Number: 2002105782

Printed in the U.S.A.
ISBN 0-89108-292-1

TO MY SPIRIT, ARIEL

CONTENTS

13 Toward Coherent Curriculum Policy in Gifted Education 257

Appendix: Sample Curriculum Units 273

Author Index 349

Subject Index 353

FIGURES

TABLES

ACKNOWLEDGMENTS

I would like to thank the staff and students of the Center for Gifted Education at the College of William and Mary past and present for their insightful contributions to my thinking about curriculum and instruction for gifted learners.

I am also grateful to Dawn Benson for her assistance with typing this manuscript and making revisions.

INTRODUCTION

P lanning is one of the basic human acts that distinguishes us as a species. We plan to solve problems, correct mistakes, and anticipate the future. The act of planning involves a complex set of mental and behavioral operations that deploy resources needed to attain desired goals. For educators with the task of planning curricula for the gifted, this concept of planning implies their need to focus on the task in an attentive way over time and to recognize its complexity.

A PLANNING MODEL

Friedman and Scholnick (1997) suggested that planning involves essential psychological components, such as representation, sequencing, attention, and self-regulation, which are moderated by expertise or a knowledge base and such motivational variables as values and coping skills. Also affecting planning, according to this model, are key aspects of the task itself, such as its complexity, coherence, familiarity, and whether it can be undertaken individually or in groups. Those aspects of planning are moderated by the environmental context, which determines the provision of resources, reassurance, and support and the existing norms affecting coordination of the plan. An adaptation of the Friedman and Scholnick model is shown in Figure 1.1.

For several reasons, this planning model provides a useful backdrop for educators planning curriculum experiences for gifted learners. First, it acknowledges the important role of *curriculum planners* and the knowledge, skills, and attitudes they must possess. Educators who engage in curriculum planning for the gifted must demonstrate the following characteristics, among others:

✓ Knowledge of gifted children, their nature, and their needs.

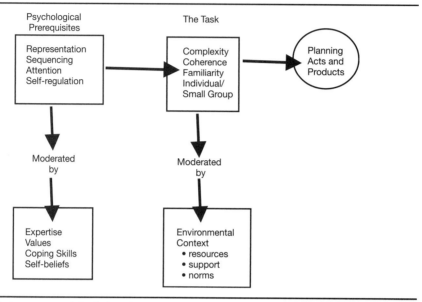

FIGURE 1.1   A Model of Planning

✓ Expertise in written lesson plan and unit development tasks.
✓ Ability to represent concepts and ideas in teaching and learning models.
✓ Strength in sequencing ideas and content for presentation.
✓ Capability to independently develop curricula.

Not all educators can be effective curriculum developers for gifted learners. Strong curriculum development and planning requires the attention of individuals with the knowledge and skill to undertake the task.

Second, the model highlights the importance of *task analysis* as an early step in any planning effort (Dick & Carey, 1996). Assessing how complex, broad in scope, and familiar the task is and determining the organizational frameworks required to complete the task are essential elements in curriculum planning for gifted learners.

The scope and complexity of the curriculum planning task may be determined by the levels of planning that will be involved. For example, building a K-12 curriculum framework, which involves primarily the levels of goals, outcomes, and assessment, is fairly complex in that it cuts across grade levels and subject areas and requires a strong team approach. Developing a unit of study on genetics for sixth graders may be conceived as narrower in scope and less complex with respect to target audience. In the latter example, coherence in the unit of study may be better achieved by one curriculum developer rather than several.

Third, the model recognizes the effect of the environment or climate of an educational institution on the curriculum planning effort. If the norms of an institution are for every teacher to develop his or her own curriculum, efforts to bring coherence to curriculum offerings will meet with resistance. And while the provision of monetary resources shows support for curriculum work, resources alone are insufficient for successful curriculum implementation (Henderson & Hawthorn, 1995). Administrative support also must be present, and a critical mass of the faculty— judged to be at least one third of the staff—must support the effort.

THE INSTRUCTIONAL DESIGN MODEL

The fundamental instructional design model employed throughout this text is illustrated in Figure 1.2. Systematic, yet with recursive elements, the model begins with

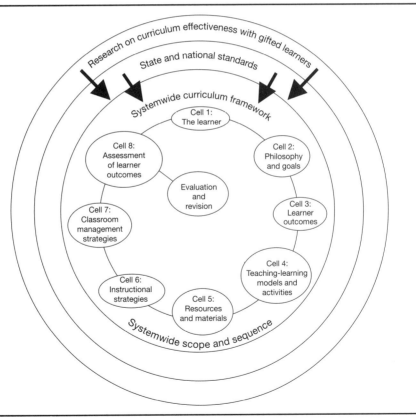

FIGURE 1.2　An Instructional Design Model for Gifted Curricula

an appreciation for the characteristics of gifted learners, how gifted learners are identified, and the basic curriculum dimensions necessary for serving them (Cell 1). The model then moves to an emphasis on philosophy and goals (Cell 2). At this stage, educators focus on clarifying the fundamental purposes of a gifted program, how the program fits with the regular program of study, and what broad areas of learning should be stressed. This phase of design has to be completed consensually, so that all relevant educators in the school district can agree with the outcomes of the planning effort.

Next, more specific learner outcomes (Cell 3) are derived from the identified student goals. Each outcome should be broad enough to cover the intent of a given goal yet narrow enough to allow assessment for determining the level and extent of student learning. As with philosophy and goals, learner outcomes should be developed consensually among teachers working at relevant levels in the program. In a framework document, outcomes can be specified across K-12; in a scope and sequence guide, outcomes may be clustered across proximate grade levels, with primary, intermediate, middle school, and high school outcomes treated separately. Further refinement by grade level may be done as needed.

Following the development of learner outcomes, the model focuses on classroom implementation via units and lesson plans (Cells 4–6). For this stage, archetypal activities linked to specific teaching models and resources that employ them may be a very helpful tool. No teacher has the time to develop curricula for the gifted from scratch, and no teacher should be encouraged to do so given the many good models and curricula that exist. Any teaching-learning models and activities, resources and materials, and instructional strategies used should be linked to the overall program goals and objectives. Educators can ensure this linkage by identifying one or two specific learning models for each goal, thereby providing a pathway for coherent translation into classroom practice.

Classroom management techniques (Cell 7) constitute the next focus of attention. Variables such as grouping, pretesting, and the use of contracts and individualized education programs (IEPs) contribute not only to the potential for successful implementation of a curriculum but also to the degree of flexibility employed in particular classrooms. Even a high-powered curriculum, if delivered the same to every student, will fail to account sufficiently for differences within the population. This is especially true for gifted students with special needs, for whom flexibility in curriculum implementation is essential for success.

The design model next turns to assessment of learner outcomes (Cell 8). At this stage, educators ascertain how well students learned what they were supposed to learn, how much they grew and matured in the goal areas identified, and how well various aspects of the curriculum and instructional design process worked. Student achievement, attitude, and teacher judgment all influence the effectiveness of the assessment stage. Newer approaches to student achievement, such as performance-based assessment and portfolios, can aid educators in judging how well a particular curriculum unit has been implemented.

Results of assessment should feed the final stage, evaluation and revision. At this stage, teachers and other educators carefully evaluate what has occurred as a result of implementing a particular instructional design module or unit of study. Decisions are made about the nature and extent of revision needed to improve the model and whether alternative models should replace it. Revisiting each cell in the design model is useful in deciding what revisions may be most appropriate. Results of this evaluation may suggest a need for more activities to support a learning outcome, for a more effective instructional strategy to teach a concept, for a broader array of resources, or for other action. Careful assessment of each possibly can help improve learning the next time around.

ROLES PERFORMED IN INSTRUCTIONAL PLANNING

Four essential roles must be performed during instructional planning for the gifted (Kemp, Morrison, & Ross, 1998). The roles are not overlapping; rather, each calls for a different type of expertise.

- ✓ *Instructional designer:* This person carries out and coordinates the planning work. He or she must be competent in managing all aspects of the instructional design process. In school districts, this individual could be a gifted curriculum specialist.
- ✓ *Instructor:* This person (or member of a team) helps to prepare and carries out the instruction being planned. He or she must be well informed about the learners to be taught, the teaching procedures, and the requirements of the instructional program. With guidance from the designer, the instructor carries out details of many planning elements. Following the planning phase, he or she tries out and then implements the instructional plan. In school districts, this individual would be an experienced teacher of the gifted.
- ✓ *Subject-matter expert:* This person provides information about content and resources related to all aspects of the topics for which instruction is to be designed. He or she also ensures that content is treated accurately in activities, materials, and examinations. In school districts, this individual could be a districtwide content specialist, librarian, or secondary teacher in a relevant subject area.
- ✓ *Evaluator:* This person assists the staff in developing instruments for pretesting and posttesting student learning. He or she gathers and interprets data when programs are initially tried out and determines the effectiveness and efficiency of programs when fully implemented. In school districts, this individual can be someone working in research and evaluation or an instructor from a nearby university.

Too frequently, gifted specialists have been expected to carry out all of these roles. Clearly such an expectation invites failure.

GROUP CURRICULUM PLANNING

Research on group decision making suggests several factors to consider in curriculum planning work. The research indicates that group planning should be effective if the group (a) has or gains task-relevant experience and skills, (b) uses effective group communication and decision-making skills, and (c) is not under excessive stress, such as that caused by time limits or fear of failure (Bodily, 1996; Scholnick & Friedman, 1993). Table 1.1 describes procedures that can be employed to increase the likelihood that these factors will be present. Broad-based groups are best suited for tackling many curriculum projects. However, such groups must effectively work through the issues and problems that may arise from their diversity if the result of their planning efforts is to be both high quality and consensual.

PLANNING AS GOAL-DIRECTED ACTION

As noted by Lachman and Burack (1993) and Skinner (1996), we plan in order to effect positive change. In schools, the fundamental goal of planning is to create learning communities in which teachers, students, and parents value and practice

TABLE 1.1   Factors Influencing Effective Group Decision Making

Requirements for Effective Decision Making	Procedures to Employ
Expertise of group members	• Select members with knowledge and ability • Train members on task-relevant skills • Include multiple members • Select for diversity in task-relevant knowledge and expertise
Use of effective group communication and decision-making skills	• Train members to seek additional information • Learn to identify which members have correct information • Train in effective group discussion behavior • Train members to evaluate with rigor all alternatives and proposed solutions
Absence of stressful emotions or excessive time pressure	• Eliminate stressors • Automatize needed repertoire of actions • Allow more time

learning as a lifelong endeavor. This goal, which is the overarching aim of the reform agenda, is central to the vision of planning curriculum outlined in this book, for it implies that the audiences for the curricula developed are broader than the students and that the outcomes of the curricula are more than cognitive. Curricula must be motivational if they are to trigger the desire for more learning. For gifted students, this implies the need for a sufficiently challenging curriculum.

All effective curriculum planning involves the following set of processes, which frame the major chapters in this text:

1. *Identifying the problem:* What is the curriculum issue to be addressed?
2. *Setting goals:* What are the goals of the curriculum for gifted learners? How do these goals differ from overall curriculum goals for all students?
3. *Initiating the planning process:* What specific curriculum products are necessary to achieve the desired goals?
4. *Building a strategy:* Who will develop these products, and how and when will they be developed?
5. *Executing the strategy:* How will the newly developed curriculum products be implemented?
6. *Monitoring and assessing outcomes and revising them based on data obtained:* How well were the curriculum outcomes realized? What changes will improve the outcome in the future?

PREMISES UNDERLYING THE INSTRUCTIONAL DESIGN PROCESS

Kemp et al. (1998) identified seven basic premises that should guide instructional design procedures. As they apply to gifted curriculum development, these premises are as follows:

Premise 1: *The instructional design process requires attention to both a systematic procedure and a specificity for treating details within the plan.* Curriculum planners must process a broad plan for the curriculum that incorporates the specific details for delivering effective teaching-learning activities.

Premise 2: *The instructional design process usually starts at the course development level.* Curriculum work is most coherent when it begins with goal development and then branches into specific areas of curriculum development.

Premise 3: *An instructional design plan is developed primarily for use by the instructor and planning team.* The initial documents should be created in user-friendly form for relevant teachers. Study guides for students can follow at a later time.

Premise 4: During the planning process, every effort should be made to provide for a level of satisfactory achievement for all learners. Because gifted students learn high-level material at different rates and levels of proficiency (VanTassel-Baska, Zuo, Avery, & Little, 2002), the instructional design plan must incorporate variation and flexibility.

Premise 5: The success of the instructional product depends on the accuracy of the information flowing into the instructional design process. Product refinement can result from several processes, including having the product critiqued by teachers early in the design phase and having teachers try out sample lessons in classrooms with designers present to observe where revision is needed.

Premise 6: The instructional design process focuses on the individual rather than the content. Characteristics of gifted learners in general should guide the curriculum development process. It should not be guided by a set notion of fixed content. Further tailoring of curriculum will have to occur for special needs students and the highly gifted.

Premise 7: There is no single "best" way to design instruction. Individual teachers and educators are idiosyncratic in their approaches to designing curriculum experiences. Although a common format is useful, different ways of achieving ends should be viewed positively.

ORGANIZATION OF THIS BOOK

This book describes the processes necessary for developing meaningful and sustained curriculum experiences for gifted learners. Its ideas are derived from 30 years of curriculum development experience in working with the gifted in schools, planning for them in other contexts, and working with their teachers and administrators.

The text is organized around the central design model described earlier in this chapter, which is crucial for developing lesson plans, units of study, and course syllabi. Thus, individual chapters address the philosophy and goals of a curriculum, learner outcomes, teacher-learning activities and resources, instructional and management strategies necessary to deliver curriculum, implementation strategies, assessment of learning outcomes, and evaluation and revision.

Aspects of this model are also necessary for creating the documents that guide gifted programs in school districts—namely, the curriculum framework that encompasses K-12 goals and outcomes and is linked to strategies for attainment and assessment approaches and the scope and sequence guide that represents the gifted curriculum over the span of years in which students are in school and covers all relevant areas of the curriculum. These macro-curriculum documents, which are described early in the book, are represented as a frame for the core instructional design template.

Also forming a frame for the template are the existing state and national standards in the various areas of the curriculum. These standards are addressed in this book as a basis for instructional adaptation by gifted educators seeking to honor their implementation and go beyond them as necessary for the population of interest. Thus, the goals, outcomes, and assessment procedures of the template are delineated by the standards, but the translation work of developing and aligning teaching-learning activities, strategies, and resources is not. Ideas for such translation and alignment are suggested in the chapter on standards.

A final frame for the instructional design template is formed by the existing research on curriculum effectiveness. Described in Chapter 2, this research provides information that should guide all curriculum planning and design work. Understanding what has been found to work and not work in curricula for the gifted is an essential starting point for curriculum planning and development. Although quite a few curriculum models currently exist in the field of gifted education, many have not been tested in the research arena, and others have a paucity of evidence suggesting effectiveness. Using the research knowledge base as a backdrop to comprehensive curriculum development for gifted learners in schools is crucial for success.

FORGING CONNECTIONS

Gifted education is at a critical crossroads in respect to its next stage of development. Since the mid-1970s, growth of the field at the grassroots and state level has been phenomenal. Even with a lack of federal visibility and support during the Reagan years, the field managed to grow in the area of direct service to gifted learners and in opportunities for training teachers and other school personnel. As we look ahead, however, what will make gifted education viable is highly dependent on its capacity to establish linkages with the existing structures in education, to form partnerships in key areas, and to take advantage of the best that general, special, and gifted education research and best practices have to offer.*

The field of gifted education historically has used the special education model as the basis for nascent efforts in program development. Identification and assessment practices, teacher training, and administrative program models have been derived from special education. Gifted education has also attempted to incorporate much of the special education rhetoric in its advocacy role for gifted children, speaking of the special needs of the population, appropriate placements, and categorical considerations. Use of these special education models has led to growth and development of the gifted education field. Yet the special education model may be limited

---

* In this text, *general education* refers to the educational curriculum practices used for the majority of students in our schools, including all basic and core curriculum requirements. *Special education* refers to the field of education that specializes in exceptionalities related to disabling conditions.

in the very areas in which gifted education is in greatest need of development—the areas of curriculum, instructional materials, and evaluation.

Thus, gifted education must relate to two educational worlds: (a) the special education world, representing the continuum of services necessary for exceptional learners, and (b) the general education world, representing the curriculum and organizational support structures that underlie schooling for all learners. Figure 1.3 depicts this concept and some program development issues in each realm. The task of gifted educators is to find ways to appropriately negotiate these worlds so that program development efforts for the gifted can move to a higher level of operation.

Gifted education program models for elementary school students have used almost exclusively the special education paradigm for development. In the push to build programs, curriculum intervention has frequently been the last consideration. At the secondary level, however, mild content acceleration and enrichment has been the point of departure in the scheme of program design, often thwarting development beyond the established honors concept in specific disciplines of study. This elementary-secondary split in gifted curriculum development illustrates the uncomfortable straddling of these educational worlds that gifted education has attempted.

If gifted education is to advance as a field, gifted educators will have to embrace the world of general education, its models, and its curriculum reforms while not

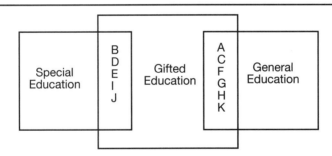

Program Development Issues in Gifted Education

A = philosophy and goals   G = materials and resources
B = identification and assessment   H = instructional processes
C = program approaches   I = teacher training
D = program administration   J = advocacy
E = grouping strategies   K = evaluation
F = curriculum

FIGURE 1.3   Key Linkages of Special Education and General Education in Program Development for the Gifted

forsaking the exceptionality concept that defines the nature of the gifted population. Sound curriculum practices for gifted learners must be built on a research base of the latest developments in teaching and learning, motivation, and child development, as well as on gifted education's own history of effective curriculum models.

SUMMARY

The age of educational reform and all of its trappings is clearly with us. The challenge is to find ways to adapt to its demands without compromising the entire enterprise of gifted education. The intent of this book is to provide a blueprint for curriculum planning that carefully considers the current climate of educational reform. Although this text does not supply easy answers, it does present curricular patterns that can make gifted programs more credible and stable than they currently are.

REFERENCES

Bodilly, S. (1996). *Lessons learned from New American Schools Development Corporation's demonstration phase.* Santa Monica, CA: RAND.

Dick, W., & Carey, L. (1996). *The systematic design of instruction.* New York: HarperCollins.

Friedman, S. L., & Scholnick, E. K. (1997). *The developmental psychology of planning: Why, how, and when do we plan?* Mahwah, NJ: Erlbaum.

Henderson, J. G., & Hawthorn, R. D. (1995). *Transforming curriculum leadership.* Englewood Cliffs, NJ: Merrill.

Kemp, J. E., Morrison, G. R., & Ross, S. M. (1998). *Designing effective instruction* (2nd ed.). Upper Saddle River, NJ: Merrill.

Lachman, M. E., Burack, O. R. (1993). Planning and control processes across the life span: An overview. *International Journal of Behavioral Development, 16,* 131–145.

Scholnick, E. K., & Friedman, S. L. (1993). Planning in context: Developmental and situational considerations. *International Journal of Behavioral Development, 16,* 145–167.

Skinner, E. A. (1996). A guide to constructs of control. *Journal of Personality and Social Psychology, 71,* 549–570.

VanTassel-Baska, J., Zuo, L., Avery, L. D., & Little, C. A. (2002). A curriculum study of gifted student learning in the language arts. *Gifted Child Quarterly, 46,* 30–44.

RESEARCH ON CURRICULUM MODELS IN GIFTED EDUCATION

Throughout the years, curriculum development for the gifted has been fraught with problems, just as the curriculum development for general education has been. The curriculum enterprise in general has suffered from neglect since the Sputnik-inspired research craze in the 1960s. Only with the recent national standards movement have we seen renewed interest in the issue of curriculum. This contemporary interest, however, has spawned concerns about whether to differentiate for gifted learners or raise the standards for all learners. Negotiating between responding to advanced learners as a group and providing high-level equitable access to all learners creates an interesting challenge for gifted educators.

The most successful curriculum models for gifted learners have been based on acceleration principles for advanced secondary students (VanTassel-Baska, 1998). The International Baccalaureate Program and the College Board Advanced Placement Program are perceived by many American school districts as representing the highest levels of academic attainment possible for secondary students and are thought to provide important stepping stones to successful college work. One approach to curriculum development for the gifted may therefore be a design-down model, where all K-12 curricula are organized to promote readiness for college and the process is both speeded up and shortened for the most apt.

Alternatives to this viewpoint abound, however, and tend to focus on learning beyond or in lieu of traditional academics. Most of the curriculum models cited in this chapter ascribe to an enriched view of curriculum development for the gifted, which addresses a broader conception of giftedness than the acceleration-oriented view, taking into account principles of creativity, motivation, and independence as crucial constructs to the development of high ability (Maker & Nielson, 1996a, 1996b; Renzulli, 1986). Proponents of enrichment approaches tend to see process skills such as critical thinking and creative problem solving as central to the learning enterprise and to view content choices as more incidental. Enrichment models also typically place high value on high-quality student products and performances.

Accelerative approaches to learning owe much to the work of Terman and Oden (1947), Pressey (1949), and early developers of rapid learning classes, which enabled bright students to progress at their own rate. Early educational examples of autodidacticism and tutorials also encouraged a view of learning that promoted independent interest and a self-modulated pace (VanTassel-Baska, 1995). Most of the enrichment-oriented approaches to curriculum development for the gifted emanated from the early work of Leta Hollingworth and her curriculum template for self-contained classes in New York City. Strongly influenced by Deweyan progressivism, Hollingworth organized curriculum units that allowed students to discover connections about how the world worked, to gain understanding of the role of creative people in societal progress, and to experience group learning through discussion and conversation about ideas (Hollingworth, 1926). In some respects, contemporary curriculum development efforts have not surpassed Hollingworth's early work in scope, purpose, or delivery.

Thus, current curriculum models are grounded in a history of research, development, and implementation of both accelerative and enrichment approaches. The early curricula typically were implemented in self-contained classes, where the level of content instruction could be modified based on the group, and chief differentiation approaches centered on differences between gifted and nongifted populations. One might argue that today's views of differentiation tend to center far more on individual differences among the gifted in respect to aptitudes, predispositions, styles, and experiences (Benbow & Stanley, 1996; Gardner, 1995; Lubinski, 1996; Snow, 1989) than on the group difference paradigm.

ANALYSIS OF CURRICULUM MODELS

As program activity for the gifted has focused more on curriculum, the following key criteria of viable curriculum models have gained prominence:

✓ The model provides a system for developing and designing appropriate curriculum for a target population and, as such, identifies elements of design and shows how they interact in a curriculum product.
✓ The model can be easily applied to all major areas of school-based learning.
✓ The model is flexible with respect to age-groups, such that the central elements work for both kindergarten-age children and high school students.
✓ The model has relevance in multiple locations and learning settings, such as tutorials and large classes.
✓ The model differentiates the particular needs of the target population for curriculum and instruction.

Each of the gifted education curriculum models discussed in the remainder of this section meets these criteria. The most researched and best-known models—the talent search model and the schoolwide enrichment model (SEM)—are described first. Not only have these models defined the major curriculum efforts of the gifted education field since the mid-1970s, but they also represent well the persistent programmatic division in the field between accelerative and enrichment approaches. Moreover, each is supported by more than a decade of research, development, and implementation. None of the other models described has enjoyed such longevity, widespread use, or research attention.

The Talent Search Model

The overall purpose of the talent search model is to educate for individual development over the life-span (Benbow, 1986; Benbow & Stanley, 1983; Stanley, 1991). Major principles of this model include the following:

1. Identification of students through a secure and difficult testing instrument that taps into high-level verbal and mathematical reasoning.
2. A diagnostic testing–prescriptive instructional (DT-PI) approach where students are taught in special classes with appropriate-level instructional challenge.
3. The use of subject-matter acceleration and fast-paced classes in core academic areas as well as advocacy for various other forms of acceleration.
4. Curriculum flexibility in all schooling (Daurio, 1979; Stanley & Benbow, 1983; Stanley, Keating, & Fox, 1974).

The model was developed and implemented at key university sites across the country, with some adoptions by local school districts that have established fast-paced classes.

The Study of Mathematically Precocious Youth (SMPY), which pioneered the use of the talent search model, was officially started in September 1971 at Johns Hopkins University and has been continued since 1999 at Vanderbilt University. Initially, the study searched for youth who reasoned exceptionally well mathematically (George, 1976; Stanley, 1976, 1977, 1978). Later, the search was extended to verbally gifted youth. Gifted students in seventh and eighth grade can participate in these talent searches by taking the College Board's Scholastic Aptitude Test (SAT) or the American College Test (ACT). Almost 150,000 gifted students do so every year. For those who score high enough, SMPY provides educational facilitation through acceleration or curricular flexibility and by developing fast-paced academic programs offered at university-based centers. Residential and commuter academic programs in several disciplines also are offered by the talent search centers and other universities and organizations to qualified students.

The research work of SMPY has been strong over the past 30 years, with more than 300 studies about the model published in articles, chapters, and books. Findings of these studies consistently have focused on the benefits of acceleration for continued advanced work in an area by precocious students (Kolitch & Brody, 1992; Stanley et al., 1974), the rationale for the use of acceleration in intellectual development (Keating, 1976), and the long-term positive repeated impacts of accelerative opportunities (Benbow & Arjmand, 1990; Hendricks, 1997). In addition to quantitative studies, case-study research has been undertaken to determine how acceleration affects individual students (Benbow & Lubinski, 1994; Brody & Stanley, 1991) and how students gain from fast-paced classes (Lynch, 1992; VanTassel-Baska, 1982). The SMPY model has been used extensively across the United States and in selected foreign countries.

Curriculum materials for the SMPY model have been developed by talent search staff at various sites and by teachers in the summer and academic-year programs. Especially noteworthy are the curriculum guides developed at Duke University's Talent Information Program (TIP) for teaching Advanced Placement courses. Strong use of articulated course materials is employed, followed by Advanced Placement courseware and testing in mathematics, science, and the verbal areas, the latter including testing in foreign languages. These materials have been reviewed by practicing professionals and content specialists.

Since its inception, the SMPY model has been very well received by parents and students who have been clients. Schools have been less receptive due to their generally conservative attitude toward accelerative practices for highly gifted students (Benbow, Lubinski, & Stanley, 1996; Benbow & Stanley, 1996; Lynch, 1990). As a result, the model has been difficult to implement in schools (Benbow & Stanley, 1996). It has been most successfully applied in afterschool and summer settings, where students complete the equivalent of high school honors classes in 3 weeks.

Although the model does not have a formal training component, the selection of teachers is a rigorous process carried out carefully in each university and school setting. Emphasis is placed on content expertise and prior work with highly gifted secondary students.

The SMPY model has proven to be highly sustainable, exhibiting strong replication capacity. Even in countries that do not conduct talent searches, students from those countries routinely attend summer programs at talent search universities.

Because the model is content-based, presenting core curricula on an accelerated and streamlined level, it aligns well with the National Content Standards, although some of the enrichment emphasis of the standards is overlooked in the model's implementation. The model is not totally comprehensive in that it addresses students in grades 3–12 who reason exceptionally well mathematically and verbally (Lupkowski & Assouline, 1993; Stanley, 1993). Some studies on spatially gifted students at those levels have also been conducted. The curriculum areas are comprehensive, including all 26 Advanced Placement course strands. Scope and sequence work has been articulated for grades 7–12 in some areas of learning. Northwestern University has developed a guide for educational options for grades 5–12.

Longitudinal data collected over the past 20 years on 300 highly gifted students have demonstrated the viability of the SMPY model with regard to the benefits of accelerative study, the early identification of a strong talent area, and expert assistance with educational decision making (Lubinski & Benbow, 1994; Swiatek, 1993; Swiatek & Benbow, 1991a, 1991b). A 50-year (1972–2022) follow-up study of 6,000 SMPY clients, currently in progress at Iowa State University, already exceeds Lewis Terman's longitudinal study of gifted students in regard to understanding the talent development process (Lubinski & Benbow, 1994).

The Schoolwide Enrichment Model

The schoolwide enrichment model (SEM) evolved from 15 years of research and field testing by educators and researchers (Renzulli, 1988; Renzulli & Reis, 1985). It combines the previously developed enrichment triad model (Renzulli, 1977) with a more flexible approach to identifying high-potential students called the revolving door identification model (Renzulli, Reis, & Smith, 1981). Since its establishment, SEM has been widely adopted throughout the country.

In this model, a talent pool of 15–20% of the above-average-ability/high-potential students is identified through a variety of measures, including achievement tests, teacher nominations, assessment of creative potential and task commitment, and such alternative pathways of entrance as self-nomination and parent nomination. High achievement test and IQ scores automatically include a student in the talent pool, which means that not only gifted students but also students who are underachieving in their academic schoolwork can be included.

Students identified for the talent pool are eligible for several kinds of services, including the following:

✓ Interest and learning style assessments.
✓ Curriculum compacting, where alternative work is substituted for portions of previously mastered content in the regular curriculum.
✓ Three types of enrichment experiences, which are defined in the enrichment triad model. Type I Enrichment consists of general exploratory experiences, such as guest speakers, field trips, demonstrations, interest centers, and the use of audiovisual materials designed to expose students to new and exciting topics, ideas, and fields of knowledge not ordinarily covered in the regular curriculum. Type II Enrichment includes instructional methods and materials designed to promote the development of thinking, feeling, research, communication, and methodological processes. Type III Enrichment, the most advanced level of the model, consists of investigative activities and artistic productions in which the learner assumes the role of a firsthand inquirer, thinking, feeling, and acting like

a practicing professional. The student pursues involvement in the activity at the most advanced or professional level possible given his or her level of development and age. These three types of activities are most appropriate for students with higher levels of ability, interest, and task commitment.

Heal (1989) compared the effects of SEM to other enrichment models or strategies. Other researchers conducted within-model comparisons (Delisle, 1981; Reis, 1981) or compared the SEM program to no intervention (Karafelis, 1986; Starko, 1986). However, because these studies did not use control or comparison groups of students participating in alternate or comparison models, results cannot clearly be attributed to participation in the SEM.

Evaluative studies have been conducted in 29 school districts on parent, teacher, and administrator perceptions of the model (Cooper, 1983; Olenchak & Renzulli, 1989; Reis, 1981). Positive changes in teacher attitudes toward the work have been documented.

Delcourt (1988) investigated creative behavior in 18 high school students who consistently engaged in SEM research on self-selected topics within or outside school. Similarly, Burns (1988) and Starko (1986) examined the effects of the schoolwide enrichment model on student creative productivity. Results of these studies indicated that students who became involved in SEM independent study projects more often initiated their own creative products in and outside school than did students in the comparison group. Further, multiple creative products were linked to higher levels of self-efficacy (Baum, Renzulli, & Hebert, 1995; Schack, Starko, & Burns, 1991).

Several studies examined the use of the model with underserved populations. Emerick (1988), for example, investigated effects of participation on underachieving high-potential students. Baum (1985, 1988) and Olenchak (1991) examined results for highly able students with learning disabilities, identifying both characteristics of these students and programmatic needs. All of these studies suggested positive effects of the model with the populations studied.

Studies of curriculum compacting have compared content-area knowledge scores of gifted students who rapidly progressed through regular school curriculum in order to spend time on Type III project work with scores for nonparticipating students. Results demonstrated participant knowledge scores being as high or higher on in-grade standardized tests than scores of noncompacted peers (Reis & Purcell, 1993).

Two SEM longitudinal studies have been conducted with 18 and 9 students, respectively. These studies showed that participants in the SEM sample maintained similar or identical career goals to the plans they had made in high school, remained in the major fields they had studied in college, and were satisfied with their current project work. Moreover, the Type III process appeared to serve as important training for later productivity (Delcourt, 1993, 1994; Hebert, 1993).

The SEM, in some form, is widely used in schools nationally and internationally. The University of Connecticut offers educators summer training on the model, reportedly training more than 600 individuals annually. The model is perceived by its developers as being closely linked to the core curriculum and as having the potential to be aligned with National Content Standards. The developers also offer a scope and sequence guide for Type II activities (Renzulli & Reis, 1994). Teachers and selected students are especially enthusiastic about the model.

The Autonomous Learner Model

The autonomous learner model was developed to facilitate growth in gifted and talented youth in grades K–12 by meeting their diverse cognitive, emotional, and social needs (Betts, 1991; Betts & Knapp, 1980). According to the developers of the model, as the needs of these students are met, they will develop into autonomous learners responsible for the development, implementation, and evaluation of their own learning. The model is divided into five major dimensions: orientation, individual development, enrichment activities, seminars, and in-depth study.

To date, no research evidence has been published concerning the impact of this model on student learning or its effectiveness over time with gifted learners. However, six curriculum units and curriculum guides have been produced as a result of the dissemination of the model's ideas. One article reviewed and described the model, presenting guidelines for developing a process-based scope and sequence as well as independent study programs for gifted learners (Betts & Neihart, 1986).

Despite the paucity of research, the autonomous learner model has received wide recognition and use in the United States and other countries (Betts, 1986). Teachers have commented positively on its implementation. Formal teacher training occurs in 3- and 5-day segments annually. In the model's design, a 3-year timeline is suggested for implementation. The model contains a degree of comprehensiveness in that it applies broadly to all curriculum domains and learner ages. However, it does not incorporate any features of accelerated learning, thereby limiting one aspect of its comprehensiveness.

The Multiple Intelligences Model

The multiple intelligences curriculum approach was built on the multidimensional concept of intelligence introduced by Howard Gardner in 1983. Gardner defined seven areas of intelligence in his original work—verbal-linguistic, logical-mathematical, visual-spatial, musical-rhythmic, bodily-kinesthetic, interpersonal, and intrapersonal. He added an eighth intelligence—naturalist—in 1995.

Several authors have reported research on classroom use of the multiple intelligences model (Latham, 1997; Rosnow, Skleder, Jaeger, & Rind, 1994; Strahan, Summey, & Banks, 1996). Most of the research, however, lacked control groups, making generalizations about the model difficult to infer (Latham, 1997). Longitudinal evidence of effectiveness with gifted students over at least 3 years has not been documented, although some research has been conducted on incorporating multiple intelligences theory with other curriculum models (Maker, Nielson, & Rogers, 1994).

Multiple intelligences has been used to guide the formation of new schools, to identify individual differences, to aid curriculum planning and development, and to assess instructional strategies (Fasko, 1992; Gardner & Hatch, 1990). Numerous curriculum materials have been produced and marketed based upon the model, which holds widespread appeal for many educators because it can be adapted for any learner, subject domain, or grade level. However, implementation is not easy and requires teacher training, financial resources, and time. The best-known project sites for the model are the Key School in Indianapolis, Indiana, and the Atlas Project in various states. Although the model has been readily adapted to curricula, it remains primarily a conception of intelligence applied broadly to school settings as a way to promote talent development for all learners.

Because of developer concerns about the application fidelity of the model's ideas and variability in implementation quality, a project has been designed to monitor the implementation of the model in U.S. classrooms in which positive impacts have been reported (Gardner, 2000).

The Purdue Three-Stage Enrichment Model for Elementary Gifted Learners and the Purdue Secondary Model for Gifted and Talented Youth

John Feldhusen and his graduate students at Purdue University in Indiana introduced the concept of a three-stage enrichment model as a course design for university students in 1973. The concept evolved into the three-stage enrichment model for elementary gifted learners by 1979 (Feldhusen & Kolloff, 1979). The model is primarily an ordered enrichment model that moves students from simple thinking experiences to complex independent activities (Feldhusen & Kolloff, 1986; Feldhusen, Kolloff, Cole, & Moon, 1988). Stage I focuses on the development of divergent and convergent thinking skills; Stage II facilitates development in creative problem solving; and Stage III encourages students to apply research skills in the development of independent study work.

The Purdue secondary model provides a comprehensive structure for programming services that support enrichment and acceleration options at the secondary level. Each of its 11 components, listed below, is designed to serve as a guide for organizing opportunities for secondary gifted students (Feldhusen & Robinson-Wyman, 1986). The components are as follows:

✓ Counseling services.

✓ Seminars.
✓ Advanced Placement courses.
✓ Honors classes.
✓ Math-science acceleration.
✓ Foreign languages.
✓ Arts.
✓ Cultural experiences.
✓ Career education.
✓ Vocational programs.
✓ Extra-school instruction.

Published research has documented gains in creative thinking and self-concept as a result of using the three-stage enrichment model with elementary gifted students (Kolloff & Feldhusen, 1984), and one study documented limited long-term gains derived from the Program for Academic and Creative Enrichment (PACE), an elementary application of the model (Moon & Feldhusen, 1994; Moon, Feldhusen, & Dillon, 1994).

Although research on the application and implementation of the elementary and secondary models is not conclusive, the models appear to be sustainable (Moon & Feldhusen, 1994; Moon, Feldhusen, Powley, & Nidiffer, 1993). Teacher training has accompanied site implementation of both the elementary and secondary models; however, it is difficult to ascertain the degree of application beyond Indiana. Neither model utilizes a scope and sequence guide, and neither may be viewed as a comprehensive model in terms of applying broadly to all areas of the curriculum, all types of gifted learners, or all stages of development.

The Grid Model

The grid model was designed by Sandra Kaplan to facilitate the construction of differentiated curricula. With the model, curriculum developers organize the curriculum components of content, process, and product around a theme. Content is defined as "the relationship between economic, social, personal and environmental displays of power and the needs and the interests of individuals, groups and societies (interdisciplinary)" (Kaplan, 1986). The process component includes productive thinking, research skills, and basic skills. The product component involves the translation of learning into a mode of communication.

Research evidence could not be found concerning the effectiveness of this model with a target population. Further, the quality of the curriculum products that are based on this model has not been reported. However, the approach has been extensively implemented at state and local levels.

Teacher training initially was conducted throughout the United States through the National/State Leadership Training Institute. Currently, training is offered independently by the developer. Thousands of teachers have developed curricula based on the model.

Although the Grid is intended to provide a developmental framework for curriculum planning for gifted learners, it does not contain a scope and sequence guide. Additionally, no provisions are explicitly made for accelerated learning.

The Matrix Model

The matrix model, which presents a set of descriptive criteria for use in developing classroom-based curricula, was developed to assist curriculum developers in categorizing the content, process, environmental, and product dimensions of an appropriate curriculum for the gifted (Maker, 1982; Maker & Nielson, 1996a). Recent work on the model, such as the Discover project, has primarily enhanced its problem-solving component. Offering a method for assessing problem-solving ability in multiple intelligence dimensions, the Discover project's problem-solving matrix incorporates a continuum of five problem types for use within each of the intelligences (Maker, 1993, 1996). Types I and II require convergent thinking. Type III problems are structured but allow for a range of solution methods and have a range of acceptable answers. Type IV problems are defined, but the learner selects a method for solving them and for establishing evaluation criteria for the solution. Type V problems are ill structured, and the learner must define the problem, discover the method for solving it, and establish criteria for creating a solution (Maker et al., 1994). The project typically is used by teachers for curriculum planning and assessing learners' problem-solving abilities.

Research is currently under way involving the use of the matrix in 12 classrooms in a variety of settings. To date, the results have not been published. A pilot study has shown that use of the matrix enhances the process of problem solving (Maker, Rogers, Nielson, & Bauerle, 1996). Studies to evaluate the long-term validity of the process are in progress.

School systems in several states have applied the matrix as a framework for organizing and developing classroom-level curricula. Teachers have been receptive to use of the matrix, and individual teacher-developed curricula have been reported. Some training is available for application of the matrix.

The sustainability of the matrix for at least 3 years is not known. Although the model is not comprehensive, it strongly emphasizes core subject domains.

The Structure of Intellect Model

The structure of intellect (SOI) model for gifted education is based on the structure of intellect theory developed by J. P. Guilford (1967). The SOI model describes 90 cognitive functions organized into a combination of content, operation, and product abilities. A test is associated with each combination, facilitating assessment and training.

The SOI model is definable as a system and applies broadly to all types of gifted learners at varying developmental stages. However, due to its comprehensiveness and emphasis on cognition, only a few sites have implemented the model (Meeker, 1985). Those sites have used it for identifying students or for training teachers to view intelligence as a non-fixed entity.

Research on the SOI model has not focused on effectiveness (Meeker, 1976); rather, it has primarily studied the use of the model for identification, for organizing information about a gifted child, or for assisting overall program design. According to this research, the SOI model has been used successfully in selected sites for the identification of culturally diverse learners (Hengen, 1983) and for preschool screening for multiethnic disadvantaged gifted learners (Bonne, 1985).

Although now somewhat dated, SOI offered a means for understanding students by delineating profiles of their intellectual abilities. It contained a teacher training component that used modules designed to instruct educators on one SOI ability at a time. Training materials included mini lesson plans for group teaching and self-help modules for individualized instruction with selected students (Meeker, 1969).

Models for Talents Unlimited, Inc., and Talents Unlimited to the Secondary Power (TU²)

In 1964, Taylor and colleagues (Taylor, Ghiselin, Wolfer, Loy, & Bourne, 1964), influenced by Guilford's research on the nature of intelligence, authored the multiple talent theory. This theory precipitated the development of Talents Unlimited, a model to be employed to help teachers identify and nurture students' multiple talents. Also based on Guilford's research, Talents Unlimited (Schlichter, 1986b) features four major components:

1. A description of specific skill abilities or talents, in addition to academic ability, such as productive thinking, communication, forecasting, decision making, and planning.
2. Model instructional materials.
3. An inservice training program for teachers.
4. An evaluation system for assessing students' thinking skills development.

Talents Unlimited, Inc., is the K-6 model, and Talents Unlimited to the Secondary Power is a model for grades 7-12 (Crump, Schlichter, & Palk, 1988; Schlichter, Hobbs, & Crump, 1988).

Research has documented gains in students' creative and critical thinking as a result of use of the model (Schlichter & Palmer, 1993). Additionally, research indicates that use of the model enhances academic skill development on standardized achievement tests (McLean & Chisson, 1980). To date, no longitudinal studies have been conducted.

Staff development and teacher training constitute a strong component of the model (Schlichter, 1986a; Schlichter et al., 1997), and teachers may become certified as Talents Unlimited trainers. Talents Unlimited has enjoyed widespread application across the United States and worldwide due, in part, to the strong emphasis on training and, in part, to funding by and membership in the U.S. Office of Education's National Diffusion Network.

The model has been used most effectively as a classroom-based approach with all learners (Schlichter, 1988). Therefore, it is less differentiated for the gifted in practice than some of the other models.

The Triarchic Componential Model

The triarchic componential model of curriculum is based on Robert Sternberg's information-processing theory of intelligence (Sternberg, 1981). The purpose of the model is to match student processing strength areas in analytic, synthetic, or practical dimensions to instructional approaches employed in teaching any content area. According to the model, three components must be present in the mental processes used in thinking:

✓ the executive process component, which is used in planning, decision making, and monitoring performance.
✓ the performance component processes, which are used in executing the executive problem-solving strategies within domains.
✓ the knowledge-acquisition component, which is used in acquiring, retaining, and transferring new information.

The model posits that the interaction and feedback between the individual and his or her environment within any given context allows cognitive development to occur.

A study by Sternberg and Clinkenbeard showed the triarchic model to be effective with students learning psychology in a summer program (Sternberg & Clinkenbeard, 1995). In more recent work using psychology as the curriculum base and employing larger samples of students, students continued to show growth patterns when assessment protocols were linked to ability profiles (Sternberg, Ferrari, Clinkenbeard, & Grigorenko, 1996). Primary to these studies is the validation of the Sternberg Triarchic Abilities Test (STAT) and its utility for finding student strengths in specific triarchic components. Other recent studies (Sternberg, Torff, & Grigorenko, 1998a, 1998b) focused on the use of triarchic instructional processes in classrooms at the elementary and middle school levels. Results suggest slightly stronger effects for triarchic instruction over traditional and critical thinking approaches.

Descriptions of teacher-created curricula and instructional instrumentation processes are limited but clearly are organized along discipline-specific lines of inquiry. Sustainability of the curriculum model beyond summer program implementation and pilot settings is not known.

The triarchic componental model does not have a packaged teacher training or staff development component, partially because the model is based upon a theory of intelligence rather than a deliberate curriculum framework. The model is systemic but not comprehensive, with applications in selected classrooms.

The William and Mary Integrated Curriculum Model

The integrated curriculum model (ICM) (VanTassel-Baska, 1986) was specifically developed for high-ability learners. It asserts that the needs of these learners are best met by advanced content, high-level process and product work, and intra- and inter-disciplinary concept development and understanding. With funding from the Jacob Javits Program, specific curriculum frameworks and underlying units in language arts, science, and social studies have been developed for this model.

Research supports the effectiveness of these curriculum units with gifted populations within a variety of educational settings. Specifically, students in experimental gifted classes using the developed curriculum units demonstrated significant growth gains in literary analysis and interpretation, persuasive writing, and linguistic competency in language arts as compared to students in gifted classes not using the curriculum units (VanTassel-Baska, Johnson, Hughes, & Boyce, 1996; VanTassel-Baska, Zuo, Avery, & Little, 2002). Studies have also shown that use of the problem-based science units embedded in an exemplary science curriculum significantly enhances students' capacity for integrating higher-order process skills in science regardless of the grouping approach employed (Boyce, VanTassel-Baska, Burruss, Sher, & Johnson, 1997; Gallagher, Stepien, Sher, & Workman, 1995; VanTassel-Baska, Bass, Ries, Poland, & Avery, 1998). Further, research has documented positive change in teacher attitude, student motivational response, and school and district curriculum (VanTassel-Baska, Avery, Little, & Hughes, 2000) following use of the William and Mary curriculum model over 3 years.

Teacher training is an integral component of the ICM. Training workshops have been conducted in 30 states, and the College of William and Mary offers training annually. Data collected on teacher change as a result of training in the William and Mary model suggest that teachers become significantly more proficient in using critical thinking and metacognition in the classroom after a 3-day training series (Avery & VanTassel-Baska, 2001).

Because the ICM curriculum units were developed using the national standards work as a template, the model establishes a strong relationship to core subject domains. Alignment charts have been completed for national and state standards work in language arts, science, and social studies.

The William and Mary units are moderately comprehensive in that they span grades 2–8 in language arts, science, and social studies. Newer language arts units developed in 1997–1998 offer K-11 coverage in language arts.

While high school level social studies units developed in 2001 offer material for grades 9 and 10, the ICM has been used for district curriculum development and planning. Evidence exists of broad-based application, but some questions remain about the ease of implementation of the teaching units and the fidelity of implementation by teachers (Burruss, 1997). Some districts use the units as models for developing their own curricula. One hundred school districts that are part of a National Curriculum Network use both the science and language arts units. The curriculum is reported to be used in 46 states. Internationally, the model is used in 18 countries, with systematic unit development occurring in two states in Australia.

Studies of effectiveness are ongoing. To date, data on student impact have been collected from over 300 classrooms nationally.

FINDINGS

Of the 10 models discussed, research studies have been conducted on seven. The research on six of those models employed comparison groups, allowing conclusions to be made about whether treatment might be attributed to the curriculum approach employed. Each of these models—the Stanley, Renzulli, Feldhusen, Sternberg, VanTassel-Baska, and Schlichter models—demonstrated some evidence of effectiveness with gifted populations in comparison to other treatments employed. Only the talent search model has amassed a comprehensive body of supportive literature. Although some evidence has shown effectiveness of the Talents Unlimited model, much of that research has been on non-gifted populations.

Evidence for the translation of these curriculum models into effective practice varies considerably. Seven models have training packages that provide for staff development; only four models explicitly consider scope and sequence issues. The autonomous learner model and the schoolwide enrichment model consider scope and sequence within the model itself. For the autonomous learner model, it is in the movement from one stage to another; for the schoolwide enrichment model, it occurs within Type II activities. Both the talent search and integrated curriculum models have developed scope and sequence charts linked to Advanced Placement work. The ICM has also developed alignment charts tied to the national standards projects and 15 state frameworks.

Data on curriculum and instructional practices with the gifted clearly favor accelerative approaches in the subject areas of language arts, science, and mathematics, although the approach to content acceleration may vary. Both the talent search and integrated curriculum models contain elements of acceleration, but only the talent search model has empirically demonstrated a strong impact of accelerative study on learning.

Curricula organized around higher-order processes and independent study have yielded few studies of student impacts, nor are the findings across studies consistent. Even longitudinal studies, such as those on the Purdue three-stage enrichment model and the schoolwide enrichment model, have produced limited evidence of outcomes related to clear student gains. Small sample size and other confounding variables such as lack of comparison groups also limit the credibility of the studies conducted.

SUMMARY

A strong body of research evidence exists supporting the use of advanced, accelerated curricula in core areas of learning for high-ability learners. Some evidence also suggests the effectiveness of enrichment-oriented models. These conclusions have not changed much in the past 20 years (Daurio, 1979). Moreover, recent meta-analytic studies confirm the superior learning effects of acceleration over enrichment in tandem with grouping the gifted (Kulik & Kulik, 1992). In comparison to strategies such as independent study, various modes of grouping, and problem-solving, acceleration also shows superior effects (Walberg, 1991). Despite the lack of convincing research to support their use, several of the enrichment models enjoy widespread popularity and are used extensively in schools.

Several implications related to research and practice in gifted education might be drawn from these findings. First, because research-based practice is critical to defensible gifted programs, practitioners must proceed carefully in deciding on curricula for use in gifted programs. The evidence strongly suggests that content-based accelerative approaches should be employed in any curriculum used in school-based programs for the gifted and that schools need to apply curriculum models faithfully and thoroughly enough to realize their potential impacts over time.

Second, the limited base of coherent studies that can make claims about the efficacy of enriched approaches to curriculum for the gifted implies that an important direction for future research would be to conduct curriculum intervention studies for these approaches. Testing the extant models as well as replicating existing studies would help to build a base of deeper understanding about what works well with gifted students in school programs.

Third, more research on differential student learning outcomes in gifted programs using discrete curricular approaches clearly needs to be undertaken. The field of gifted education has a long way to go before we will be able to say which intervention works best with which type of gifted learner at which stage of development. Future research efforts must define at a more discrete level the impacts of curriculum interventions on the multifaceted prototypes of gifted learners in our schools.

QUESTIONS FOR REFLECTION

1. Clinical practice in medicine focuses strongly on the effectiveness of different interventions as a basis for practice. What barriers preclude this model from being used as rigorously in education?

2. Individual differences can dictate the need for different educational practices. How adaptable are various curriculum models to such individual variations? How could they be strengthened in this respect?

3. What factors influence a school's choice of curriculum models? How appropriate are these influences?

REFERENCES

Avery, L., & VanTassel-Baska, J. (2001). *Changing teacher behavior: The struggle to provide gifted level instruction in the regular classroom.* Manuscript submitted for publication.

Baum, S. (1985). *Learning disabled students with superior cognitive abilities: A validation study of descriptive behaviors.* Unpublished doctoral dissertation, University of Connecticut, Storrs.

Baum, S. (1988). An enrichment program for gifted learning disabled students. *Gifted Child Quarterly, 32,* 226–230.

Baum, S., Renzulli, J., & Hebert. T. P. (1995). Reversing underachievement: Creative productivity as a systematic intervention, *Gifted Child Quarterly, 39,* 224–235.

Benbow, C. P. (1986). SMPY's model for teaching mathematically precocious students. In J. S. Renzulli (Ed.), *Systems and models for developing programs for the gifted and talented* (pp. 1–25). Mansfield Center, CT: Creative Learning.

Benbow, C. P., & Arjmand, O. (1990). Predictors of high academic achievement in mathematics and science by mathematically talented students: A longitudinal study. *Journal of Educational Psychology, 82,* 430–431.

Benbow, C. P., & Lubinski, D. (1994). Individual differences amongst the mathematically gifted: Their educational and vocational implications. In N. Colangelo, S. G. Assouline, & D. L. Ambroson (Eds.), *Talent development* (Vol. 2, pp. 83–100). Dayton, OH: Ohio Psychology.

Benbow, C. P., Lubinski, D., & Stanley, J. C. (1996). *Intellectual talent: Psychometric and social issues.* Baltimore, MD: Johns Hopkins University Press.

Benbow, C. P., & Stanley, J. C. (Eds.). (1983). *Academic precocity.* Baltimore, MD: Johns Hopkins University Press.

Benbow, C. P., & Stanley, J. C. (1996). Inequity in equity: How "equity" can lead to inequity for high-potential students. *Psychology, Public Policy, and Law, 2,* 249–292.

Betts, G. T. (1986). The autonomous learner model for the gifted and talented. In J. S. Renzulli (Ed.), *Systems and models for developing programs for the gifted and talented* (pp. 27–56). Mansfield Center, CT: Creative Learning.

Betts, G. (1991). The autonomous learner model for the gifted and talented. In N. Colangelo & G. A. Davis (Eds.), *Handbook of gifted education* (pp. 142–153). Boston: Allyn & Bacon.

Betts, G. T., & Knapp, J. K. (1980). Autonomous learning and the gifted: A secondary model. In A. Arnold, C. Arnold, G. Betts, D. Boyd, J. Curry, J. L. Fisher, V. Galasso, J. K. Knapp, A. H. Passow, I. S. Sato, M. Simon, T. C. Tews (Eds.), *Secondary programs for the gifted/talented* (pp.29–36). Ventura, CA: office of Ventura County Superintendent of Schools.

Betts, G. T., & Neihart, M. (1986). Implementing self-directed learning models for the gifted and talented. *Gifted Child Quarterly, 30,* 174–177.

Bonne, R. (1985). *Identifying multi-ethnic disadvantaged gifted.* Brooklyn, NY: Community School District #19.

Boyce, L. N., VanTassel-Baska, J., Burruss, J. D., Sher, B. T., & Johnson, D. T. (1997). A problem-based curriculum: Parallel learning opportunities for students and teachers. *Journal for the Education of the Gifted, 20,* 363–379.

Brody, L. E., & Stanley, J. C. (1991). Young college students: Assessing factors that contribute to success. In W. T. Southern & E. D. Jones (Eds.), *The academic acceleration of gifted children* (pp. 102–132). New York: Teachers College Press.

Burns, D. (1988). The effects of group training activities on students' creative productivity. In J. S. Renzulli (Ed.), *Technical report of research studies related to the revolving door identification model* (2nd ed., pp. 147–174). Storrs: University of Connecticut, School of Education, Research Report Series.

Burruss, J. D. (1997, April). *Walking the talk: Implementation decisions made by teachers.* Paper presented at the meeting of the American Educational Research Association (AERA), Chicago, IL.

Cooper, C. (1983). *Administrators' attitudes toward gifted programs based on the enrichment triad/revolving door identification model: Case studies in decision making.* Unpublished doctoral dissertation, University of Connecticut, Storrs.

Crump, W. D., Schlichter, C. L., & Palk, B. E. (1988). Teaching HOTS in the middle and high school: A district-level initiative in developing higher order thinking skills. *Roeper Review, 10,* 205–211.

Daurio, S. P. (1979). Education enrichment versus acceleration: A review of the literature. In W. C. Gregory, S. J. Cohn, & J. C. Stanley (Eds.), *Educating the gifted: Acceleration and enrichment* (pp. 13–63). Baltimore, MD: Johns Hopkins University Press.

Delcourt, M. A. B. (1988). *Characteristics related to high levels of creative/productive behavior in secondary school students: A multi-case study.* Unpublished doctoral dissertation, University of Connecticut, Storrs.

Delcourt, M. A. B. (1993). Creative productivity among secondary school students: Combining energy, interest, and imagination. *Gifted Child Quarterly, 37,* 23–31.

Delcourt, M. A. B. (1994). Characteristics of high-level creative productivity: A longitudinal study of students identified by Renzulli's three misconceptions of greatness. In R. Subotnik & K. D. Arnold (Eds.), *Beyond Terman: Contemporary longitudinal studies of giftedness and talent* (pp. 375–400). Norwood, NJ: Ablex.

Delisle, J. R. (1981). *The revolving door identification model: Correlates of creative production.* Unpublished doctoral dissertation, University of Connecticut, Storrs.

Emerick, L. (1988). *Academic underachievement among the gifted: Students' perceptions of factors relating to the reversal of the academic underachievement pattern.* Unpublished doctoral dissertation, University of Connecticut, Storrs.

Fasko, D., Jr. (Feb. 1992). *Individual differences and multiple intelligences.* Paper presented at the annual meeting of the Mid-South Education Research Association, Knoxville, TN.

Feldhusen, J. F., & Kolloff, M. B. (1979). A rationale for career education activities in the Purdue three-stage model. *Roeper Review, 2,* 13–17.

Feldhusen, J. F., & Kolloff, M. B. (1986). The Purdue three-stage model for gifted education. In J. S. Renzulli (Ed.), *Systems and models for developing programs for the gifted and talented* (pp. 126–152). Mansfield Center, CT: Creative Learning.

Feldhusen, J. F., Kolloff, M. B., Cole, S., & Moon, S. (1988). A three-stage model for gifted education. *Gifted Child Today, 11*(1), 14–20.

Feldhusen, J. F., & Robinson-Wyman, A. (1986). The Purdue secondary model for gifted education. In J. S. Renzulli (Ed.), *Systems and models for developing programs for the gifted and talented* (pp. 153–179). Mansfield Center, CT: Creative Learning.

Gallagher, S. A., Stepien, W. J., Sher, B. T., & Workman, D. (1995). Implementing problem-based learning in science classrooms. *School Science and Mathematics, 95,* 136–146.

Gardner, H. (1983). *Frames of mind: The theory of multiple intelligences.* New York: Basic Books.

Gardner, H. (1995). Reflections on multiple intelligences: Myths and messages. *Phi Delta Kappan, 77,* 200–203, 206–209.

Gardner, H. (2000). *Intelligence reframed: Multiple Intelligences for the 21ˢᵗ Century.* New York: Basic Books.

Gardner, H., & Hatch, T. (1990). *Multiple intelligences go to school: Educational implications of the theory of multiple intelligences* (Technical Report No. 4). New York: Center for Technology in Education.

George, W. C. (1976). Accelerating mathematics instruction for the mathematically talented. *Gifted Child Quarterly, 20,* 246–261.

Guilford, J. P. (1960). *Structure of intellect model: Its use and applications.* Los Angeles: University of Southern California.

Guilford, J. P. (1967). *The nature of human intelligence.* New York: McGraw-Hill.

Heal, M. M. (1989). *Student perceptions of labeling the gifted: A comparative case study analysis.* Unpublished doctoral dissertation, University of Connecticut, Storrs.

Hebert, T. P. (1993). Reflections at graduation: The long-term impact of elementary school experiences in creative productivity. *Roeper Review, 16,* 22–28.

Hendricks, M. (1997, June 3). Yesterday's whiz kids: Where are they today? *Johns Hopkins Magazine, 49,* 31–36.

Hengen, I. (Nov. 1983). *Identification and enhancement of giftedness in Canadian Indians.* Paper presented at the annual meeting of the National Association of Gifted Children, New Orleans, LA.

Hollingworth, L. (1926). *Gifted children.* New York: World Book.

Kaplan, S. (1986). The Kaplan grid. In J. S. Renzulli (Ed.), *Systems and models for developing programs for the gifted and talented* (pp. 56–68). Mansfield Center, CT: Creative Learning.

Karafelis, P. (1986). *The effects of the tri-art drama curriculum on the reading comprehension of students with varying levels of cognitive ability.* Unpublished doctoral dissertation, University of Connecticut, Storrs.

Keating, D. (1976). *Intellectual talent.* Baltimore, MD: Johns Hopkins University Press.

Kolitch, E. R., & Brody, L. E. (1992). Mathematics acceleration of highly talented students: An evaluation. *Gifted Child Quarterly, 36,* 78–86.

Kolloff, M. B., & Feldhusen, J. F. (1984). The effects of enrichment on self-concept and creative thinking. *Gifted Child Quarterly, 28,* 53–57.

Kulik, J., & Kulik, C. (1992). Meta-analytic findings on grouping programs. *Gifted Child Quarterly, 36,* 73–77.

Latham, A. S. (1997). Quantifying MI's gains. *Educational Leadership, 55*(1), 84–85.

Lubinski, D. (1996). Applied individual differences research and its quantitative methods. *Psychology,. Public Policy, and Law, 2,* 187–203.

Lubinski, D., & Benbow, C. P. (1994). The study of mathematically precocious youth: The first three decades of a planned 50-year study of intellectual talent. In R. Subotnik & K. D. Arnold (Eds.), *Beyond Terman: Contemporary longitudinal studies of giftedness and talent* (pp. 375–400). Norwood, NJ: Ablex.

Lupkowski, A. E., & Assouline, S. G. (1993). Identifying mathematically talented elementary students: Using the lower level of the SAT. *Gifted Child Quarterly, 37,* 118–123.

Lynch, S. J. (1990). Credit and placement issues for the academically talented following summer studies in science and mathematics. *Gifted Child Quarterly, 34,* 27–30.

Lynch, S. J. (1992). Fast-paced high school science for the academically talented: A six-year perspective. *Gifted Child Quarterly, 36,* 147–154.

Maker, C. J. (1982). *Curriculum development for the gifted.* Rockville, MD: Aspen.

Maker, C. J. (1993). Creativity, intelligence, and problem solving: A definition and design for cross-cultural research and measurement related to giftedness. *Gifted Education International, 9,* 68–77.

Maker, C. J. (1996). Identification of gifted minority students: A national problem, needed changes and a promising solution. *Gifted Child Quarterly, 40,* 41–50.

Maker, C. J., & Nielson, A. B. (1996a). *Curriculum development and teaching strategies for gifted learners* (2nd ed.). Austin, TX: Pro-Ed.

Maker, C. J., & Nielson, A. B. (1996b). *Teaching models in education of the gifted* (2nd ed.). Austin, TX: Pro-Ed.

Maker, C. J., Nielson, A. B., & Rogers, J. A. (1994). Multiple intelligences: Giftedness, diversity, and problem-solving. *Teaching Exceptional Children, 27*(1), 4–19.

Maker, C. J., Rogers, J. A., Nielson, A. B., & Bauerle, P. R. (1996). Multiple intelligences, problem solving, and diversity in the general classroom. *Journal for the Education of the Gifted, 19,* 437–460.

McLean, J. E., & Chisson, B. S. (1980). *Talents Unlimited program: Summary of research findings for 1979–80.* Mobile, AL: Mobile County Public Schools.

Meeker, M. (1969). *The structure of intellect: Its interpretation and uses.* Columbus, OH: Merrill.

Meeker, M. (Apr. 1976). *A paradigm for special education diagnostics: The cognitive area.* Paper presented at the annual meeting of the American Educational Research Association. (ERIC Document Reproduction Service No. ED 121 010)

Meeker, M. (Apr. 1985). *A partial compendium of SOI patterns on sub-groups of gifted people.* Paper presented at the annual convention of the Council for Exceptional Children, Anaheim, CA.

Moon, S., & Feldhusen, J. F. (1994). The Program for Academic and Creative Enrichment (PACE): A follow-up study ten years later. In R. Subotnik & K. D. Arnold (Eds.), *Beyond Terman: Contemporary longitudinal studies of giftedness and talent* (pp. 375–400). Norwood, NJ: Ablex.

Moon, S. M., Feldhusen, J. F., & Dillon, D. R. (1994). Long-term effects of an enrichment program based on the Purdue three-stage model. *Gifted Child Quarterly, 38,* 38–48.

Moon, S. M., Feldhusen, J. F., Powley, S., & Nidiffer, L. (1993). Secondary applications of the Purdue three-stage model. *Gifted Child Today, 16*(3), 2–9.

Olenchak, F. R. (1991). Assessing program effects for gifted/learning disabled students. In R. Swassing & A. Robinson (Eds.) *NAGC 1991 research briefs,* Washington, DC: National Association for Gifted Children.

Olenchak, F. R., & Renzulli, J. S. (1989). The effectiveness of the schoolwide enrichment model on selected aspects of elementary school change. *Gifted Child Quarterly, 33,* 36–46.

Pressey, S. L. (1949). *Educational acceleration: Appraisal and basic problems* (Educational Research Monograph No. 31). Columbus: Ohio State University Press.

Reis, S. M. (1981). *An analysis of the productivity of gifted students participating in programs using the revolving door identification model.* Unpublished doctoral dissertation, University of Connecticut, Storrs.

Reis, S. M., & Purcell, J. H. (1993). An analysis of content elimination and strategies used by elementary classroom teachers in the curriculum compacting process. *Journal for the Education of the Gifted, 16,* 147–170.

Renzulli, J. S. (1977). *The enrichment triad model: A guide for developing defensible programs for the gifted and talented.* Mansfield Center, CT: Creative Learning.

Renzulli, J. S. (Ed.). (1986). *Systems and models for developing programs for the gifted and talented.* Mansfield Center, CT: Creative Learning.

Renzulli, J. S. (Ed.). (1988). *Technical report of research studies related to the revolving door identification model* (2nd ed.). Storrs: University of Connecticut, Bureau of Educational Research.

Renzulli, J. S., & Reis, S. M. (1985). *The schoolwide enrichment model: A comprehensive plan for educational excellence.* Mansfield Center, CT: Creative Learning.

Renzulli, J. S., & Reis, S. M. (1994). Research related to the schoolwide enrichment triad model. *Gifted Child Quarterly, 38,* 7–20.

Renzulli, J. S., Reis, S. M., & Smith, L. (1981). The revolving-door model: A new way of identifying the gifted. *Phi Delta Kappan, 62,* 648–649.

Rosnow, R. L., Skleder, A. A., Jaeger, M. E., & Rind, B. (1994). Intelligence and the epistemics of interpersonal acumen: Testing some implications of Gardner's theory. *Intelligence, 19,* 93–116.

Schack, G. D., Starko, A. J., & Burns, D. E. (1991). Self-efficacy and creative productivity: Three studies of above average ability children. *Journal of Research in Education, 1,* 44–52.

Schlichter, C. (1986a). Talents Unlimited: An inservice education model for teaching thinking skills. *Gifted Child Quarterly, 30,* 119–123.

Schlichter, C. (1986b). Talents Unlimited: Applying the multiple talent approach to mainstream and gifted programs. In J. S. Renzulli (Ed.), *Systems and models for developing programs for the gifted and talented* (pp. 352–390). Mansfield Center, CT: Creative Learning.

Schlichter, C. L. (1988). Thinking skills for all classrooms. *Gifted Child Today, 11*(2), 24–29.

Schlichter, C. L., Hobbs, D., & Crump, W. (1988). Extending Talents Unlimited to secondary schools. *Educational Leadership, 45*(7), 36–40.

Schlichter, C. L., Larkin, M. J., Casareno, A. B., Ellis, E. S., Gregg, M., Mayfield, P., & Rountree, B. (1997). Partners in enrichment: Preparing teachers for multiple ability classrooms. *Teaching Exceptional Children, 29*(4), 4–9.

Schlichter, C. L., & Palmer, W. R. (Eds.). (1993). *Thinking smart: A premiere of the Talents Unlimited model.* Mansfield Center, CT: Creative Learning.

Snow, R. E. (1989). Aptitude-treatment interaction as a framework for research on individual differences in learning. In P. L. Ackerman, R. J. Sternberg, & R. Glaser (Eds.), *Learning and individual differences* (pp. 13–59). New York: W. H. Freeman.

Stanley, J. C. (1976). Youths who reason extremely well mathematically: SMPY's accelerative approach. *Gifted Child Quarterly, 20,* 237–238.

Stanley, J. C. (1977). Rationale of the Study of Mathematically Precocious Youth (SMPY) during its first five years of promoting educational acceleration. In J. C. Stanley, W. C. George, & C. H. Solano (Eds.), *The gifted and the creative: A fifty year perspective* (pp. 73–112). Baltimore, MD: Johns Hopkins University Press.

Stanley, J. C. (1978). SMPY's DT-PI mentor model: Diagnostic testing followed by prescriptive instruction. *Intellectually Talented Youth Bulletin, 4*(10), 7–8.

Stanley, J. C. (1991). An academic model for educating the mathematically talented. *Gifted Child Quarterly, 35,* 36–42.

Stanley, J. C. (1993). Boys and girls who reason well mathematically. In G. Bock & K. Ackrill (Eds.), *The origins and development of high ability* (pp. 119–138). New York: Wiley.

Stanley, J. C., & Benbow, C. P. (1983). Intellectually talented students: The key is curricular flexibility. In S. P. Harris, G. Olson, & H. Stevenson (Eds.), *Learning and Motivation in the Classroom* (pp. 259–281). Hillsdale, NJ: Erlbaum.

Stanley, J. C., Keating, D., & Fox, L. (1974). *Mathematical talent.* Baltimore, MD: John Hopkins University Press.

Starko, A. J. (1986). *The effects of the revolving door identification model on creative productivity and self-efficacy.* Unpublished doctoral dissertation, University of Connecticut, Storrs.

Sternberg, R. (1981). A componential theory of intellectual giftedness. *Gifted Child Quarterly, 25,* 86–93.

Sternberg, R., & Clinkenbeard, P. R. (1995). The triarchic model applied to identify, teach, and assess gifted children. *Roeper Review, 17,* 255–260.

Sternberg, R. J., Ferrari, M., Clinkenbeard, P., & Grigorenko, E. L. (1996). Identification, instruction, and assessment of gifted children: A construct validation of a triarchic model. *Gifted Child Quarterly, 40,* 129–137.

Sternberg, R. J., Torff, B., & Grigorenko, E. L. (1998a). Teaching for successful intelligence raises school achievement. *Phi Delta Kappan, 79,* 667–699.

Sternberg, R. J., Torff, B., & Grigorenko, E. L. (1998b). Teaching triarchically improves school achievement. *Journal of Educational Psychology, 90,* 374–384.

Strahan, D., Summey, H., & Banks, N. (1996). Teaching to diversity through multiple intelligences: Student and teacher responses to instructional improvement. *Research in Middle Level Education Quarterly, 19,* 43–65.

Swiatek, M. A. (1993). A decade of longitudinal research on academic acceleration through the study of mathematically precocious youth. *Roeper Review, 15,* 120–124.

Swiatek, M. A., & Benbow, C. P. (1991a). Ten-year longitudinal follow-up of ability-matched accelerated and unaccelerated gifted students. *Journal of Educational Psychology, 83,* 528–538.

Swiatek, M. A., & Benbow, C. P. (1991b). A 10-year longitudinal follow-up of participants in a fast-paced mathematics course. *Journal for Research in Mathematics Education, 22,* 138–150.

Taylor, C. W., Ghiselin, B., Wolfer, J., Loy, L., & Bourne, L. E., Jr. (1964). *Development of a theory of education from psychology and other basic research findings* (Final Report, USOE Cooperative Research Project, No. 621). Salt Lake City: University of Utah.

Terman, L. M., & Oden, M. H. (1947).Genetic studies of genius: Vol. 4. *The gifted child grows up.* Stanford, CA: Stanford University Press.

VanTassel-Baska, J. (1982). Results of a Latin-based experimental study of the verbally precocious. *Roeper Review, 4,* 35–37.

VanTassel-Baska, J. (1986). Effective curriculum and instructional models for talented students. *Gifted Child Quarterly, 30,* 164–169.

VanTassel-Baska, J. (1995). A study of life themes in Charlotte Bronte and Virginia Woolf. *Roeper Review, 18,* 14–19.

VanTassel-Baska, J. (1998). *Excellence in educating the gifted* (3rd ed.). Denver: Love Publishing.

VanTassel-Baska, J., Avery, L. D., Little, C. A., & Hughes, C. E. (2000). An evaluation of the implementation of curriculum innovation: The impact of the William and Mary units on schools. *Journal for the Education of the Gifted, 23,* 244–272.

VanTassel-Baska, J., Bass, G. M., Ries, R. R., Poland, D. L., & Avery, L. D. (1998). A national pilot study of science curriculum effectiveness for high-ability students. *Gifted Child Quarterly, 42,* 200–211.

VanTassel-Baska, J., Johnson, D. T., Hughes, C. E., & Boyce, L. N. (1996). A study of the language arts curriculum effectiveness with gifted learners. *Journal for the Education of the Gifted 19,* 461–480.

VanTassel-Baska, J., Zuo, L., Avery, L. D., & Little, C. A. (2002). A curriculum study of gifted student learning in the language arts. *Gifted Child Quarterly, 46,* 30–44.

Walberg, H. (1991). Productive teaching and instruction: Assessing the knowledge base. In H. C. Waxman & H. J. Walberg (Eds.), *Effective teaching: Current research* (pp. 33–62). Berkeley, CA: McCutchan.

3

STANDARDS OF LEARNING AND GIFTED EDUCATION

The importance of the standards movement in education cannot be underestimated. It represents the first time that policy makers from all sectors of U.S. public life have agreed upon a set of principles for the future direction of education in this country. For demographic, economic, and workforce reasons, this educational agenda, the goal of which is to enhance teaching and learning for all students in public and private schools, has gained a strong foothold in the national consciousness, and education has been forced to respond to the call for higher student achievement through implementing the national and state standards (O'Day & Smith, 1993). Gifted education must also be a strong voice in helping to improve student achievement for all while maintaining appropriate standards for gifted learners. The standards movement in general represents a new paradigm for the future of education, one that acknowledges postmodernism in all of its complexity.

THE POSTMODERN VIEW OF EDUCATION

Globalization, strengthened by the explosion of information technologies, has reshaped our thinking about curriculum and instruction in fundamental ways. We no longer can use just national standards to judge our educational systems; we must use international ones as well. We no longer can consider curriculum in schools as static but must consider it dynamic and evolving through the use of instructional technology that effectively connects learning to the "real world" of cyberspace.

The globalization and information technology forces are complemented by the major paradigm shift from modern to postmodern thinking. As modernists, we viewed education as discrete social progress over time that was aided by a mechanistic linear model of curriculum design and implementation. Purportedly rational and scientific, this model, we thought, could identify inputs and apply desired outputs, control the interaction of variables in intervention, and thereby improve education. The modernist approach dominated our thinking in public school education for the past century. Such terms as efficiency and effectiveness were primary in our vocabulary, and student outcomes as products of our labors were essential to the illusion that education was improving its products (i.e., the students) and its processes.

But soon cynicism and the reality of education as a chaotic enterprise set in, and we began to adopt a more postmodern view of education. With a focus on language to explain how the world works, we now look for themes and metaphors to explain what education is (Grover, Achleitner, Thomas, Wyatt, & Vowell, 1997). Dominant themes include cultural differences as perceived through unique "voices" heard in case studies of teachers, students, and classrooms and an analysis of irregularity as the norm in schools.

Assumptions for this postmodern view of education rest on the biological understanding of emergent, self-organizing systems. Capra (1982) described living systems as self-organizing, characterized by malleability, flexibility, and dynamic interaction with the environment. This relationship with the environment reveals itself in the coevolutionary growth of subsystems and systems. The systems perspective holds that dynamic movement is a requirement for survival. Members of systems and related subsystems interact and evolve as a whole.

Kelly (1994) explicated the concept of a system as a swarm that is adaptable, evolving, resilient, and boundless. According to this view, swarm systems embrace novelty and are nonoptimal, noncontrollable, unpredictable, nonunderstandable, and nonimmediate. For educators engaged in the process of making reform work, school systems may appear to behave in much the same way as swarms. Based on this understanding of how social systems behave in the real world, our comfortable notions that the educational enterprise can improve using a linear model may be greatly mistaken.

EDUCATIONAL REFORM AS A PARADIGM SHIFT

Although the call for educational reform is not new, the current standards movement represents a very different orientation to school improvement. This sudden shift supports Thomas Kuhn's (1996) contention that disciplines and fields advance and develop into maturity through a series of revolutions of ideas as opposed to responding to evolving discoveries in which scientists stand on the shoulders of their predecessors.

Kuhn's analysis of what constitutes a paradigm is also an instructive model for educators to consider. According to Kuhn, a paradigm occurs because of a problem or crisis in a field and typically constitutes an anomaly to existing practice. Paradigms thus constitute reconstructions of reality and claim to solve problems in new ways and with greater degrees of precision. Even though paradigms attract an enduring group of adherents, typically individuals who are new to a field or are young, they are often resisted by the existing scientific community. Rarely having solid supporting evidence, new paradigms are based on faith and are accepted by the assent of the community.

Operating within paradigms offers many advantages for fields and disciplines. For instance, paradigms provide a structure that allows for a commitment to common rules and standards. Because paradigms reduce divergency in a field, specific puzzles can be more easily solved by practitioners. Moreover, paradigms offer a focus and direction for new research efforts that link seminal ideas about a concept to ways of studying it. Paradigms, then, provide criteria for selecting problems for which solutions may be assumed and function as consensus-building agents within institutions.

The systemic reform movement in education displays many of the features just described. It causes us to reconstruct our reality based on new views of teaching and learning as well as new assumptions about the nature of learners. It calls for a coordinated response in schools to the major problems of student achievement and alienation. It suggests that schools have to be reorganized as collegial and collaborative learning communities and that classrooms have to focus on maximum competency standards designed to create competent adults in the society.

Such a view of education clearly marks a significant shift in how we carry out schooling. Some of the differences between the systemic reform movement and prior educational models are detailed in Table 3.1.

A RATIONALE FOR NATIONAL AND STATE STANDARDS

As described is the following paragraphs, national and state standards offer a variety of benefits to education.

1. *The standards will help to ensure that students learn what they need to know for high-level functioning in the 21st century.* National groups that were broadly representative of the professions and the educational community put more than 10 years of work into the development of the standards. The input of these groups was further shaped by public comment on multiple drafts of their work. Such thoughtful consideration for what America's students should be learning had not occurred since the 1960s (Vinovskis, 1996).

2. *The standards will help to ensure educational quality across school districts and schools within districts.* Every student has the right to a challenging curriculum and to the pedagogical supports needed to master it effectively. The new standards call for systemic implementation that leaves no one behind (Wang, Haertel, & Walberg, 1993).

TABLE 3.1   The Systemic Reform Movement as a Paradigm Shift in Education

Prior Educational Improvement Models	Systemic Educational Reform Movement
Progress occurs incrementally	Progress occurs simultaneously across dimensions
Minimum competency standards	Maximum competency standards (worldclass levels)
Subject-specific, based on bounded disciplines	Interdisciplinary work
Individual mastery of skills	Collaborative development of higher-order processes (e.g., communication)
Education viewed as a developmentally cumulative process (design up)	Education viewed as a process for creating competent, fully functioning adults (design down)
Outcomes assessed by a few external standardized measures	Outcomes assessed by multiple types of measures
Technology considered an add-on	Technology considered as an integrative learning tool
Grade-level and subject-area planning	Vertical and horizontal team planning
Lack of student success handled behavioristically, through remedial instruction in basic skills	Lack of student success handled constructivistically, through provision of multiple examples, a more conceptual focus, and attention to personal "style" and relevance
School organization hierarchical	School organization collegial

3. *The standards provide educators with guideposts to mark the way to providing students with meaningful work in education.* Because the standards are designed from the top down, the model of adult professional competencies is embedded in them, allowing educators to work on optimizing students' knowledge, skills, and attitudes through a focus on behaving like mathematicians, scientists, writers, or geographers.

4. *The standards provide a curriculum template within which teachers will be able to focus on instructional delivery techniques that work.* The United States is the only industrialized country in which teachers have been asked to develop, deliver, differentiate, and assess curriculum and to do so while managing inclusive classrooms. The sharper focus brought about by the standards will improve teaching and deepen learning for students.

THE STANDARDS AS CORE CURRICULUM FOR THE GIFTED

The curriculum reform movement requires gifted educators to embrace the traditional content dimensions as core areas of learning for the gifted in all grade levels rather than treating these areas as peripheral. Several valid reasons for moving to a content-based instructional model for the gifted are described in the following paragraphs.

At the school level, schools are organized by basic content areas, and so to deviate significantly from these areas puts gifted educators outside a predominant organizational pattern that aids communication on gifted issues within the school system. The content-based instructional model also provides a natural context for planning curricula, because school systems—those with self-contained programs for the gifted—are obligated to show mastery of basic skills for gifted students in these subject-matter areas. Moreover, because gifted students spend the majority of their instructional time working in the traditional subject-matter disciplines, the impact of programs for the gifted that ignore content is severely limited, as is the appropriateness of a significant amount of learning time.

At a social level, knowledge is organized in discipline-specific ways. We study disciplines in college. We organize our professions around key learning areas. Our knowledge producers clearly are content experts. Nobel prizes are given in physics, chemistry, and literature, not in the area of constructing an electrical car. Many significant products of civilization are discipline-specific such as novels, pieces of music, and paintings. In the following passage from "A Disciplined Approach to School Reform," Howard Gardner (1999) eloquently defends the role of the disciplines in shaping school curricula, suggesting its central authority in the enterprise:

> I do not believe that there is any definitive version of truth, beauty, or goodness; these virtues are consistently being defined and debated. I favor the greatest flexibility in how these "virtues" are presented to children and how their emerging understandings are probed and documented for purposes of accountability. However, only one group has been centrally committed to these topics: the scholars and practitioners who are truly expert in the several disciplines. They master the work of the past and they contribute to our future schemes of knowledge. To deny them the central role in the curriculum is to perform *Hamlet* without the titled personage. . . . The disciplines play the

central role in the endeavor. They are the chief determiners of which understandings are worth achieving, but more important, they furnish ways in which students can in the future approach questions, concepts, and theories. (p. 170).

Thus, society continues to organize learning and define societal progress around distinct knowledge bases or domains.

Finally, the current research base on conceptions of giftedness lends credence to a content-specific curriculum model. Gagné, Yekovich, and Yekovich (1993), Csikszentmihalyi (1996), and Bloom (1985) all conceptualized giftedness as domain-specific. Simonton (1994) pointed out that studies of eminent individuals speak to contributions in given areas of talent. In addition, research on teaching and learning suggests that wedding higher-level skills to content enhances transfer effect (Perkins & Salomon, 1989; Sternberg & Williams, 1998).

PROBLEMS WITH THE STANDARDS FOR GIFTED LEARNERS

Gifted education clearly is not exempt from the emphasis on standards-based reform. As gifted educators, we must view the standards movement as an opportunity to upgrade what we do, and we must go through the standards to do it, not around them. This section discusses some potential problems with the standards and gifted education. None of these problems is unremediable, but each may be difficult to handle.

One problem, found by Koshy and Casey (1998) in their study of the perceived effects of instructional standards on high-ability learners in Britain, is that teachers did not consider the standards helpful in differentiation for their most able students, even though they recognized that the standards were high level. This study and others suggest the need for translations of the standards into meaningful activities designed for bright learners. The time and energy constraints of individual teachers make widespread differentiation practices unlikely without the provision of exemplary curricula that can be used as a base.

Another problem is the perception that the standards are low level. Gifted educators complain that work on the standards narrows the instructional focus for gifted learners to the regurgitation of factual material. Countering this concern, however, are the realities that the standards are very broad, some are deep, and creative teachers have much latitude to implement the standards at appropriately high levels to satisfy the needs of their gifted students. Because gifted students may show mastery of many of the standards at an earlier stage of development than currently designated, testing-out mechanisms can and should be put in place to accommodate this reality (United States Department of Education, 1994). Moreover, teachers should reorganize strands across grade levels to streamline the curriculum.

A third perceived problem, mentioned earlier, is that the standards are content-based and therefore not appropriate for the gifted. Nothing could be further from the truth. Quality gifted programming has always been content-based. The hallmark high school Advanced Placement and International Baccalaureate programs are deeply grounded in the study of the disciplines. Historically, elementary models of gifted education have been similarly organized. Indeed, throughout the history of the gifted education field, educators have considered a strong content base as essential, not incidental, to strong curriculum and programming. Programs aimed at thinking skill development that are project driven but give no consideration to content are weak and unsupportable by available research. Many such programs already have died out as a result of their lack of effectiveness.

A fourth perceived problem with the standards concerns the assessment instruments typically used. Even though the standards represent high-level learning outcomes as replicated from the national standards project work, the assessments have been found to be narrower in orientation, less demanding, and tied more to factual material than to high-level thought. Recent critiques of several state assessment tests have noted their lack of scope, low level of task demand, and lack of consonance with the intent of the standards (Webb, 1999). Educators of the gifted can counter this problem by assessing gifted learners at higher levels through alternative assessment approaches that meet a standard of coherence. For example, specific performance-based instruments for assessment of student progress have been found highly suitable for use in gifted programs (Adams & Callahan, 1995; VanTassel-Baska, Johnson, Hughes, & Boyce, 1996).

Another problem concerns the amount of work required of teachers to implement the new standards, even under the best circumstances. This problem was noted by Cornell and Clarke (1999), who explored the feasibility of designing units of study around key standards in the state of Vermont. Following a yearlong effort working with 20 teachers and four university interns using the comprehensive school reform professional development model, the authors suggested that such alignment work is effective in raising student expectations for authentic learning but requires stronger teacher planning before instructional delivery and more effort in general for effective implementation. This tension between student benefit and the additional time and effort required of teachers constitutes a major issue in school reform.

More specific observations from the Cornell and Clarke (1999) study that relate to this issue are as follows:

1. *Less talking by the teacher in class requires more teacher preparation time.* When teachers became more facilitative in their work with students, they realized the amount of planning they needed to do to be responsive to student needs.
2. *Successful free-ranging student inquiry depends on a tight design structure.* Teachers realized that student creativity was heightened by greater structuring of activities.

3. *Higher challenges engage low-achieving students.* Teachers learned that a challenging curriculum is highly motivational for low-achieving students.
4. *Uniform standards elicit many different kinds of expression.* Teachers came to appreciate the range of individual differences in the classroom.
5. *One clear rubric opens many roads to achievement.* Teachers realized that once they set clear expectations for learning they could be flexible regarding how the expectations were met.

Even lead reformers become discouraged by the lack of infrastructure available to establish meaningful change. Lamenting the current stage of educational standards-based reform, Ted Sizer, the founder of the Coalition for Essential Schools, wrote: "One hopes that the current American educational leadership, currently paralyzed by their belief in the need for One Best Standard, will have the courage to admit that our conventional ways of 'curriculum building' and the 'assessment' that follows from it are profoundly flawed" (Sizer, 1999, p. 164).

ASSESSING THE NEED FOR DIFFERENTIATION OF STANDARDS

Any curriculum to be used with gifted learners should incorporate the following five elements: acceleration, complexity, depth, challenge, and creativity. An individual standard may contain only one of these elements. What is important is that the total curriculum in the area addresses the entire list. Often, standards contain several of the differentiation features listed. Figure 3.1 presents a checklist designed to provide educators with a means to quickly assess each curriculum standard for appropriateness for the gifted. Using this checklist, educators can ascertain how much modification of a standard may be necessary. The list can also facilitate translation of the standards into archetypal activities.

ADAPTATIONS OF STANDARDS FOR GIFTED LEARNERS

The following are strategies teachers might employ to implement the standards more effectively and efficiently with gifted students.

1. *Recognize that many of the standards focus on higher-level thought processes and that task demands for gifted learners may be developed directly from them.* For example, in the social studies standards, a strong emphasis is placed on historical analysis skills from primary grades through high school. These standards do not have to be changed to make them more appropriate for gifted learners. Rather, they should be translated into appropriate teaching-learning task demands. An example follows.

1. Acceleration
      a.   Fewer tasks assigned to master standards
      b.   Standards-based skills assessed earlier or prior to teaching
      c.   Standards clustered by higher-order thinking skills

2. Complexity
      a.   Used multiple higher-level skills
      b.   Added more variables to study
      c.   Required multiple resources

3. Depth
      a.   Studied a concept in multiple applications
      b.   Conducted original research
      c.   Developed a product

4. Challenge
      a.   Employed advanced resources
      b.   Used sophisticated content stimuli
      c.   Made cross-disciplinary applications
      d.   Made reasoning explicit

5. Creativity
      a.   Designed/constructed a model based on principles or criteria
      b.   Provided alternatives for tasks, products, and assessments
      c.   Emphasized oral and written communication to a real world
           audience

FIGURE 3.1   Differentiation Features Checklist

Example: Ask students to analyze a primary source document, such as the Declaration of Independence, using the following approach.

   a. Identify key words.
   b. State your feelings about the document.
   c. State key ideas contained in the document.
   d. Explain images or symbols contained in the document.
   e. Describe how the structure of the document enhances its meaning.
   f. Identify the context for the document, including who wrote it, when, and for what purpose.
   g. Summarize why the document is important today.

Students may complete this task demand through written homework, in-class discussion, or small-group work. The task demand is archetypal in that it may be used frequently as a tool for analyzing primary source documents in social studies instruction.

2. *Read and interpret individual standards carefully to discern their scope and intent.* One of the major problems with many of the standards, within and across subject areas, is their lack of easy translation into appropriate task demands. Particularly in the language arts and social studies areas, the standards are written at such a general level that interpretation is required before task demands can be developed. The following example illustrates this issue.

Example: Reading/Literature Strand, Virginia Standards of Learning (Commonwealth of Virginia, 1995)
The student will read and write a variety of poetry. (6.6)

✓ Describe the visual images created by language.
✓ Describe how word choice, speaker, and imagery elicit a response from the reader.
✓ Compare and contrast plot and character development in narrative poems, short stories, and longer fiction.

As can be seen from an analysis of this standard and its subcomponents, many different aspects of the standard must be worked with to ensure that the standard is adequately addressed. As with the social studies example, students may be provided with different reading selections and instructed to explore them according to the web criteria (see Figure 3.2). Moreover, writing assignments can be developed based on the web to enhance creativity. In the process of implementing the standard, teachers may ask students to create writing anthologies that employ different genres to illustrate the key aspects of language understanding addressed in the standard.

3. *Use the essence of the standards as a rubric for assessing student learning.* The more specific the interpretation of a standard is, the easier it will be to discern key features that students must master. In the example just provided for the language arts standards, the rubric presented in Figure 3.3 might be employed to assess how well students have handled the demands of the standard. Based on student scores, teachers may wish to reteach an aspect of the standard, meet with individual students to discuss an element of the standard, or provide additional applications for students to work through.

4. *Organize standards according to higher-order skills and then teach across subject areas.* For example, most state standards include a strand on reasoning within math and science, a strand on communication within language arts and math, a strand on research in language arts, which also is captured as the

Analyze the poem/short story using this literature web.
How are changes in plot and character similar? Different?

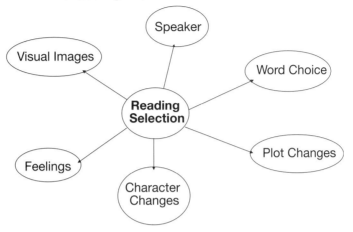

FIGURE 3.2   Sample Task Demand for Language Arts Standard

Circle appropriate response for each item.

The student is able to:	To a Great Degree	Adequately	Not at All
✓ Describe visual images.	3	2	1
✓ Describe effective word choice.	3	2	1
✓ Analyze reader response to language.	3	2	1
✓ Describe character development.	3	2	1
✓ Describe plot development.	3	2	1
✓ Analyze relationship between character and plot development.	3	2	1

FIGURE 3.3   Sample Assessment Rubric for Understanding of Language Arts Standard

scientific research process in the science standards, and a set of standards related to technology, which may be embedded or stand alone. These areas of the standards have relevance for all subject areas and could be used to organize direct teaching across subject areas. The following task demand example illustrates this strategy by incorporating science, math, language arts, and technology standards into a challenging student project.

Example: Design an experiment to test a question of interest to you. For example:

a. Do people prefer Product X over Product Y?
b. Are ants attracted to sugar?
c. Are girls more addicted to computers than boys?

Prepare and present a research report using technology applications. Be sure to address your hypothesis, data collection techniques, the data tables you used, your conclusions, and implications of the findings based on your research question.

As can be seen from this example, one task demand may address multiple standards across subject areas, thus reducing the need for separate student projects in each content area. Students benefit from understanding the interdisciplinarity encased in the project, and teachers benefit from the reduced instructional time required to implement the standards.

Another way to organize the standards at more challenging levels is to incorporate a specific cross-disciplinary teaching-learning model into the curriculum in all subject areas. Two models are particularly helpful in this regard: the Paul (1992) model of reasoning and the Taba (1962) model of concept development.

The Paul model of reasoning has been used in all subject areas and is highly flexible for use across grade levels. The model identifies eight elements of reasoning that may be applied to oral and written activities: framing an issue, identifying purpose, stating assumptions, defining central concepts, delineating points of view and multiple perspectives, collecting and interpreting evidence, making inferences, and drawing conclusions and implications. Figure 3.4 graphically displays these elements in relation to each other.

An analysis of these eight elements in respect to standards in the four core subject areas shows the model's cross-disciplinary power (Figure 3.5). By using the model, teachers can more readily address multiple standards and strands within standards. Thus, the repeated and systematic use of one thinking skills model from primary levels through high school can enhance learning within and among subject areas and economize instructional time.

With the Taba model of concept development, teachers integrate a higher-order concept, such as system, change, model, or scale, into relevant applications, categorical arrangements of applications, counterexamples, and generalizations across disciplines (Taba, 1962). This use of higher-order concepts provides students with

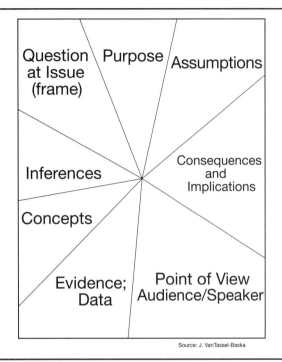

Source: J. VanTassel-Baska

FIGURE 3.4 Elements of Thought

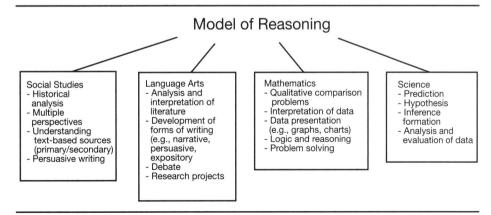

FIGURE 3.5 Applications of the Model of Reasoning in the Core Standards by Subject Area

scaffolding for understanding the demands of the standards. Figure 3.6 illustrates how key concepts work in a cross-disciplinary way across four separate subject area standards.

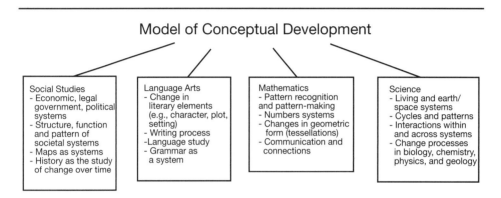

FIGURE 3.6 Applications of the Model of Conceptual Development for Systems and Change to the Core Standards by Subject Area

5. *Accelerate student work in the standards after carefully pretesting within strands and across levels.* Although many of the standards constitute higher-level work for the gifted, standards delineated for particular grade levels within subject areas may be too low level for gifted students in that grade. To determine if this is the case, teachers can pretest students using strands of standards across grade levels. In mathematics, for example, each strand could be pretested with gifted students to ensure appropriate-level work. In the area of research, when pretesting indicates that acceleration is in order standards across multiple grade levels may be collapsed to create a more meaningful instructional module for gifted students. The following example illustrates how the requirements of a research project for fourth graders could include the demands expected for fifth and sixth graders as well.

Example: **Research Strand, Virginia Standards of Learning**
The student will use information resources to research a topic. (4.9)

✓ Construct questions about a topic.
✓ Collect information about the topic using the resources of the media center.
✓ Evaluate and synthesize the information for use in writing.
✓ Use available technology.

The student will synthesize information from a variety of resources. (5.8)

✓ Skim materials to develop a general overview of content or to locate specific information.
✓ Develop notes that include important concepts; paraphrase, summarize, and identify important resources.
✓ Organize and record information on charts, maps, and graphs.
✓ Use available electronic databases to access information.
✓ Credit secondary reference sources.

The student will select the best sources for a given purpose, including atlases, dictionaries, globes, interviews, telephone directories, encyclopedias, electronic databases, and the *Reader's Guide*. (6.9)

---

6. *Select materials that address the intent of the standards, not just their content.* Most of the standards emphasize process skills and application, and the curriculum materials selected should have a similar emphasis. Careful attention to materials selection cannot be overstated, for materials typically constitute 95% of the curriculum in any classroom. One useful way to go about the selection process is to identify the key processes conveyed by the standards and then choose curriculum materials that address them directly. Table 3.2 shows the interplay of the science standards by topical area, identifying science curriculum materials found appropriate for use with gifted learners in each area.

These six strategies provide a pathway by which educators of the gifted may adapt state and national standards for their students. Yet these strategies are insufficient to address the core learning intent of the standards. Thus, an important consideration for implementing the standards, mentioned briefly earlier in this chapter, is the need to use effective teaching and learning models for translating the standards effectively over the years that students are required to address them. Models are particularly important for teaching students such areas of the curriculum as argument, experimental design, analysis, and interpretation of text and research. Because these skills are higher level and acquired over the lifespan, students will benefit from the scaffolds the models provide, which they may use over and over again.

TABLE 3.2   Selecting Science Resources: Relationship by Standards Topics to Exemplary Materials

Topical Focus in the Science Content Standards (K–5)	William & & Mary (W & M) Unit	Great Explorations in Math and Science (GEMS)	Science & Technology for Children (STC)	Full Option Science Systems (FOSS)
Physical Science 1. Students will develop an understanding of properties of objects and materials. 2. Students will develop an understanding of motions of objects.	What a Find (Grades 2–4): archeology/ civilizations	Investigating Artifacts (Grades K–6)	Soils (Grade 2) Rocks (Grade 3) Maps & Models (Grade 4)	Pebbles, Sand & Silt (Grades 1–2)
Earth and Space Science 1. Students will develop an understanding of earth materials. 2. Students will develop an understanding of changes in the earth and sky.				
Science and Technology 1. Students will be able to distinguish between natural objects and objects made by humans.				

References

Center for Gifted Education. (1997). *Acid, acid everywhere: A problem-based unit.* Dubuque, Iowa: Kendall/Hunt.

——. (1997). *Dust bowl: A problem-based unit.* Dubuque, Iowa: Kendall/Hunt.

——. (1997). *Electricity city: A problem-based unit.* Dubuque, Iowa: Kendall/Hunt.

——. (1997). *Hot rods: A problem-based unit.* Dubuque, Iowa: Kendall/Hunt.

——. (1997). *No quick fix: A problem-based unit.* Dubuque, Iowa: Kendall/Hunt.

——. (1997). *The Chesapeake Bay: A problem-based unit.* Dubuque, Iowa: Kendall/Hunt.

——. (1997). *What a find!: A problem-based unit.* Dubuque, Iowa: Kendall/Hunt.

Lawrence Hall of Science. (1990–present). *Full option science system (FOSS).* Chicago, IL: Encyclopedia Britannica.

Lawrence Hall of Science. (1990–present). Great explorations in math and sciences (GEMS). Berkeley, CA: University of California.

National Resources Center. (1991–present). *Science and technology for children (STC).* Burlington, NC: Carolina Biological Supply.

Another important consideration for implementing the standards for gifted students is the use of flexible grouping practices that allow students to be placed with like peers for high-level task demands. In all types of grouping situations, having students work in small dyads or study groups of three or four can intensify the learning experience. Such grouping strategies should be used frequently and varied depending on the assignment and subject area.

SUMMARY

From a postmodern perspective, educators must acknowledge the extent to which education constitutes a chaotic system in which only self-reformation will be effective. If the paradigm shift to a focus on educational standards is to be successful, it must penetrate deeply into classrooms and the teachers who orchestrate them. In the field of gifted education, deliberate strategies must be undertaken to align these standards with the best principles of differentiation for gifted learners.

At the level of a curriculum scope and sequence, strategies that accelerate and deepen student understanding of key skills and concepts are a central tool for accomplishing such alignment. At the level of individual classrooms and course syllabi, techniques that deliberately translate standards into differentiated tasks and products are advantageous in accomplishing such alignment.

Gifted educators will be able to defend their practice only when they thoughtfully implement a standards-based curriculum that is adapted and modified for gifted learners. When such action is taken, gifted education becomes a part of general education reform rather than an endeavor separate from it.

QUESTIONS FOR REFLECTION

1. What effects might emerge from standards-based reform over the next 10 years? What indicators did you consider most relevant for making your prediction?
2. What advantages do gifted educators gain by embracing standards rather than rejecting them?
3. In what ways might education still be viewed as modern rather than postmodern?
4. What evidence might convince gifted educators that their students are capable of exceeding the standards in selected areas at every stage of development?

REFERENCES

Adams, C. M., & Callahan, C. M. (1995). The reliability and validity of a performance task for evaluating science process skills. *Gifted Child Quarterly, 39,* 14–20.

Bloom, B. S. (Ed.). (1985). *Developing talent in young people.* New York: Ballantine.

Capra, F. (1982). *The turning point: Science, society, and the rising culture.* New York: Bantam.

Commonwealth of Virginia Department of Education. (1995). *Standards of learning for Virginia public schools.* Richmond, VA: Author.

Cornell, N. A., & Clarke, J. H. (1999, October). The cost of quality: Evaluating a standards-based design project. *NASSP Bulletin,* pp. 91–99.

Csikszentmihalyi, M. (1996). *Creativity: Flow and the psychology of discovery and invention.* New York: HarperCollins.

Gagné, E. D., Yekovich, C. W., & Yekovich, F. R. (1993). *The cognitive psychology of school learning* (2d ed.). New York: HarperCollins.

Gardner, H. (1999). A disciplined approach to school reform. *Peabody Journal of Education, 74,* 166–173.

Grover, R., Achleitner, H., Thomas, N., Wyatt, R., & Vowell, F. (1997). The wind beneath our wings: Chaos theory and the butterfly effect in curriculum design. *Journal of Education for Library and Information Science, 38,* 268–282.

Kelly, K. (1994). *Out of control: The new biology of machines, social systems, and the economic world.* Reading, MA: Addison-Wesley.

Koshy, V., & Casey, R. (1998). A national curriculum and the sovereignty of higher ability learners. *Gifted Child Quarterly, 42,* 253–260.

Kuhn, T. S. (1996). *The structure of scientific revolutions.* (3rd ed.). Chicago: University of Chicago Press.

O'Day, J. A., & Smith, M. S. (1993). Systemic reform and educational opportunity. In S. Fuhrman (Ed.), *Designing coherent education policy: Improving the system* (pp. 250–312). San Francisco: Jossey-Bass.

Paul, R. (1992). *Critical thinking: What every person needs to survive in a rapidly changing world.* Sonoma, CA: Foundation for Critical Thinking.

Perkins, D. N., & Salomon, G. (1989). Are cognitive skills context-bound? *Educational Researcher, 18,* 16–25.

Simonton, D. K. (1994). *Greatness: Who makes history and why.* New York: Guilford.

Sizer, T. R. (1999). That elusive curriculum. *Peabody Journal of Education, 74,* 161–165.

Sternberg, R., & Williams, W. (Eds.). (1998). *Intelligence, instruction, and assessment: Theory into practice.* Mahwah, N.J.: Lawrence Erlbaum.

Taba, H. (1962). *Curriculum development: Theory and practice.* New York: Harcourt Brace & World.

United States Department of Education. (1994). *Prisoners of time.* Washington, DC: U.S. Government Printing Office.

VanTassel-Baska, J., Johnson, D. T., Hughes, C. E., & Boyce, L. N. (1996). A study of language arts curriculum effectiveness with gifted learners. *Journal for the Education of the Gifted, 19,* 461–480.

Vinovskis, M. A. (1996). An analysis of the concept and uses of systemic educational reform. *American Educational Research Journal, 33,* 53–85.

Wang, M. C., Haertel, G. D., & Walberg, H. J. (1993). Toward a knowledge base for school learning. *Review of Educational Research, 63,* 249–294.

Webb, N. L. (1999). *Alignment of science and mathematics standards and assessments in four states.* (NISE Monograph No 18), Washington, DC: National Institute for Science Education and the Council of Chief State School Officers.

DEVELOPING SYSTEMWIDE CURRICULUM DOCUMENTS

he process of curriculum planning and development is complex, dynamic, and generative in nature, and gifted educators' approach to the task should reflect that reality. Emphasis must be placed on comprehensive planning of an appropriate curriculum for gifted learners in order to activate the curriculum development process on a large scale and to ensure its relevancy within a given school district. Such K-12 curriculum planning is a relatively recent phenomenon for gifted educators, who have historically focused on program development at more narrowly prescribed grade levels. Just as expert problem solvers spend more time on planning than on any other aspect of the problem-solving process, we in gifted education must become expert at planning and organizing a meaningful scope and sequence of curriculum experiences for our most talented learners.

ASSUMPTIONS ABOUT GENERAL CURRICULA

These assumptions, which form the foundation for the discussion, are as follows:

1. *General school curricula are inappropriate for gifted learners.* The needs of gifted learners are atypical in respect to rate of learning, capacity for in-depth learning, ability to manipulate conceptual schemata, and need for diversity and challenge in learning experiences (Benbow, Lubinski, & Stanley 1996; Gallagher & Gallagher, 1995; Sternberg & Williams, 1998). However, school curricula are nearly always organized around the needs of typical learners, where the spiral effect of incremental learning modules coupled with heavy doses of reinforcement around a given skill or concept is the pattern for basic text materials as well as the dominant mode for classroom instruction. One of the first issues to be addressed in developing curricula for the gifted, then, is

how to modify or adapt the general curriculum within core areas to better respond to the atypical needs of these learners. Clearly, if the core curriculum is to be meaningful for the gifted during their K–12 experience, accelerative, enriched, and conceptual reorganization must occur.

2. *Appropriate differentiation of the curriculum in one area and at one grade level affects all areas and levels. Thus, curriculum development for the gifted has to be viewed as a long-term process involving adaptation of the general curriculum, infusion of appropriate extant curricula for the gifted, and the development of new curricula.* Most curriculum work that has been done for the gifted has taken an isolationist perspective, being conceptualized and written with the idea that it would be "the curriculum for the gifted." Consequently, committees of writers struggled with key models and concepts as they strove to create "new" curricula that were appropriate only for the gifted in some special setting. That approach, however, fostered a fragmentation of curriculum experiences for the gifted, and frequently the curricula were organized based on a faulty understanding of the models and concepts they purported to convey.

   Some of the best curricula that exist for the gifted were not written for these students deliberately (VanTassel-Baska, 1998). The major curriculum projects of the 1960s in science, mathematics, English, and social studies (Man: A Course of Study (MACOS)) have proved highly useful with gifted populations even though they were not so intended. The Junior Great Books program and *Philosophy for Children,* both widely used curricula in gifted programs, were not developed expressly for the gifted. Yet the use of such tested curriculum materials can save districts the time and expense of trying to reinvent what would clearly be an inferior wheel. In addition, more effort should be expended in bridging the district core curriculum to appropriate adaptations for gifted learners. Curriculum development for the gifted is not a short-term activity. To conceptualize it as such is to misunderstand the nature and scope of the process that has to be undertaken.

3. *A curriculum plan for the gifted must be written down and communicated appropriately within a school district.* A curriculum has a recognizable shape or form only when it is written (VanTassel-Baska, 1995). What goes on in a classroom between teacher and learner is evanescent if the experiences are not recorded. What curriculum planning provides is a sense of purpose and direction in areas of educational value that both teacher and student explore. A curriculum for the gifted should give educational personnel and the community an understanding of what areas of investigation are valuable and why, how students will meet their learning objectives, and by what means students will be evaluated. The curriculum should emphasize purpose, means, and ends somewhat equally and in a manner that the lay public can understand. The obligation to communicate what is distinct about a program for the gifted is paramount, and the strength of that distinction derives from effective curriculum planning.

If we believe these assumptions to be true, we must advocate a curriculum planning effort that will allow for comprehensive and articulated curriculum experiences for gifted learners at all stages of their development. Unfortunately, many school districts have chosen to approach curriculum development at the level of unit development, where individual teachers organize teaching units on topics of interest and need in the gifted program. This work is termed "unfortunate" in that a great deal of teacher time and energy, as well as district financial resources, are required to consummate such curriculum products, and the school district typically ends up with idiosyncratic pieces of curricula that can be interpreted and taught only by the teacher who developed them. No real curriculum planning or development has occurred—only the random act of writing unrelated individual units.

Although working on individual units of instruction is a worthy task for teachers at the classroom level of instruction, this focus is inappropriate at the level of building an entire school-district effort. Rather, focus must be on developing a K–12 curriculum framework and scope and sequence. Such macro curriculum development work serves several interlocking purposes for a school district:

✓ It defines curriculum direction.
✓ It helps to define gaps in current curriculum practices and resources.
✓ It defines expectation levels for student work in curriculum areas. These areas, in turn, can be assessed for student learning.

A CURRICULUM FRAMEWORK MODEL

At the start of a discussion of the tasks associated with developing a curriculum framework and scope and sequence in curricula for gifted learners, the phrase "curriculum framework" should be defined. A *curriculum framework* is defined herein as a strategic plan for curriculum. It comprises the overall goals and outcomes of curriculum across all areas and grade levels and links those goals and outcomes to strategies for accomplishing them and assessment approaches that measure outcomes. A curriculum framework is a useful tool within a school district for several purposes. For example, it creates a consensus on what a gifted curriculum is supposed to be. Too often curriculum planning is fragmented by grade level and subject such that no one in the district sees the larger picture of K-12 curriculum for the gifted. Curriculum frameworks provide a specific tangible product that answers the question of what the district's curriculum for the gifted is. Another benefit of this document development effort is that it brings teachers and administrators into curriculum planning in a meaningful way. As noted by Gross (1997), curriculum design that is jointly and mutually derived has a strong motivational component for those involved.

A curriculum framework for a gifted program also represents a communication tool about the program for various stakeholder groups. Parents and students can gain insights into the curriculum much more quickly through reading a framework than through reviewing grade-level curriculum documents. The curriculum framework represents a shorthand way of representing the entire K–12 gifted curriculum model for a variety of audiences.

Finally, a gifted curriculum framework should capture those elements that represent the program's distinctive features and reveal its balance. Does the curriculum allow for acceleration? If so, in what areas and at what levels? Where is independent study valued? How much project work is expected at different stages of development? A curriculum framework should clarify questions such as these through the balanced scope of its presentation.

The following is an example of a center-based gifted curriculum framework that meets those criteria. Developed by principals, teachers, and specialists in gifted education in Fairfax County, Virginia, the document is highly consensual and reflects idealized practice in their center-based program. Moreover, the document has been incorporated into materials to be disseminated to parents about the program and thus will serve as a useful communication vehicle. Finally, it conveys the spirit of the curriculum at several sites by highlighting areas of strength, such as interdisciplinary work, affective development, and the teaching of thinking and problem-solving skills.

Fairfax County, Virginia, Curriculum Framework Document

Goal 1: To develop an understanding for systems of knowledge, themes, issues, and problems that frame the external world (i.e., "the big picture")

Outcomes:
Gifted students will be able to:

- ✓ Apply the tools, skills, techniques and perspectives of practicing professionals in the major knowledge domains (e.g., thinking like a scientist, using tools, habits of mind—questioning, skepticism, scientific method).
- ✓ Analyze various themes that frame the disciplines as they relate to a given area of learning (e.g., change: main generalizations about change are that it is pervasive, there are various types of change, and change occurs in different ways).
- ✓ Identify and evaluate current issues, consider varying perspectives (e.g., current events; politics; state, local, and national issues; historical issues [then and now]; pollution; environmental issues).
- ✓ Engage in problem-finding and problem-solving experiences that revolve around a real-world problem.

Strategies and Resources to Attain Outcomes (multiple approaches are enumerated):

- ✓ Use William and Mary problem-based learning units.
- ✓ Use *Future Problem-Solving* scenarios.
- ✓ Use concept lessons and strategies on teaching change from William and Mary language arts units.

✓ Use *Interact* materials.
✓ Use a thinking skills model (e.g., Paul's model of reasoning) to analyze current issues.

Assessment Approaches:

✓ Performance tasks (e.g., application of skills on a new task such as, in science, designing a circuit or designing own experiment to answer a question).
✓ Essay form (i.e., writing to a prompt that requires synthesis of ideas).
✓ Product assessment requiring demonstration of thinking skills in response to a problem.

Goal 2: **To provide for the mastery and enrichment of the core standards of learning in all curriculum areas, using appropriate resources, including technology, at a pace, depth, and intensity appropriate to the capacity of able learners**

Outcomes:
Gifted students will be able to:

✓ Apply and transfer new learning via the Standards of Learning (SOL) in a variety of contexts across disciplines within and outside the classroom setting.
✓ Analyze and evaluate key concepts in each discipline.
✓ Select and implement effective strategies for problem solving and continuous learning in and across all areas.
✓ Initiate new learning and acquire new skills collaboratively and independently by activating prior knowledge.
✓ Communicate learning effectively in oral, written, and interactive contexts.
✓ Access advanced learning opportunities within core areas as needed.

Strategies and Resources to Attain Outcomes (multiple approaches are enumerated):

✓ Use relevant core materials designed for high-ability learners or found effective with them (e.g., William and Mary language arts units, Junior Great Books, Great Explorations in Math and Science (GEMS).
✓ Use supplementary materials found effective with gifted students (e.g., William and Mary PBL units in science, TOPS, *Interact, Writing Source 2000).*
✓ Teach content-based models that reinforce SOL outcomes (e.g., historical analysis model, literature web, models of writing, experimental design model).
✓ Teach planning and assessing skills for all student-generated work.
✓ Provide reflection activities such as writing and debriefing.

Assessment Approaches:

✓ Pre- and posttests.
✓ Performance tasks with appropriate rubrics and exemplars.
✓ Multiyear portfolios.

✓ Multiyear learning logs.
✓ Virginia Standards of Assessment (required state testing).
✓ Stanford-9 (required state testing).

Goal 3: To develop cognitive and metacognitive skills that foster independent self-directed learning

Outcomes:
Gifted students will be able to:

✓ Apply the cognitive processes of application, synthesis, analysis, and evaluation.
✓ Apply basic argument forms.
✓ Reason logically using critical thinking models.
✓ Apply divergent thinking processes.
✓ Apply a variety of models of problem solving.
✓ Develop research skills.
✓ Evaluate the quality and appropriateness of arguments, lines of reasoning, and solutions.
✓ Develop criteria for self-evaluation.
✓ Develop self-monitoring behaviors to promote continuous learning.
✓ Make informed decisions about learning processes (e.g., selecting appropriate resources, selecting appropriate strategies for problem solving).

Strategies and Resources to Attain Outcomes (multiple approaches are enumerated):

✓ Use activities based on higher levels of Bloom's and Krathwohl's taxonomies.
✓ Use the creative problem-solving (CPS) model.
✓ Teach and encourage fluency, flexibility, elaboration, and originality in expression.
✓ Use the Hamburger and Dagwood models to teach reasoned argument.
✓ Use I-search and other tools for teaching research.
✓ Assign individual projects.

Assessment Approaches:

✓ Student thinking process logs.
✓ Assessment rubrics and checklists (self, peer, teacher).
✓ Reflection and discussion (informal observation by teachers, peers).
✓ Analysis of "scenarios."

Goal 4: To develop self-understanding

Outcomes:
Gifted students will be able to:

✓ Understand the characteristics, demands, and responsibilities of advanced intellectual development.
✓ Recognize, understand, and value their own strengths and relative weaknesses.

✓ Understand changing external circumstances and situations (time, place, people).
✓ Reconcile internal value conflicts to evolve a personal belief system.
✓ Apply personal belief system and reflection skills in making choices in life.

Strategies and Resources to Attain Outcomes (multiple approaches are enumerated):

✓ Use case studies and biographies of eminent people.
✓ Teach philosophical principles (e.g., using *Philosophy in the Classroom*).
✓ Teach metacognitive strategies.
✓ Use narrative writing models to encourage self-expression.
✓ Employ peer mediation activities.

Assessment Approaches:

✓ Student personal agendas.
✓ Student questionnaire at two key points (pre-post).
✓ Student products that display philosophy of life.
✓ Student-created goals with benchmarks and activities, courses, and projects (cocurricular, extracurricular).

Goal 5: To develop social skills that enable students to build their leadership skills, interpersonal skills, and ability to effectively relate to others in a variety of situations

Outcomes:
Gifted students will be able to:

✓ Demonstrate respect for others' ideas, perspectives, and needs.
✓ Communicate effectively through speaking, evaluative listening, and nonverbal cues in group situations (e.g., restating words of prior speaker, engaging in evaluative listening, and agreeing and disagreeing using respectful tone).
✓ Cooperate and collaborate in groups (e.g., establish goals, plan a course of action, assume a variety of roles, reach compromise or consensus, achieve goal[s], and evaluate group's success).

Strategies and Resources to Attain Outcomes (multiple approaches are enumerated):

✓ Use of inquiry-based discussions, using William and Mary units and Junior Great Books.
✓ Use of group project work.
✓ Use of simulations.
✓ Socratic seminars.
✓ Community service.
✓ Jigsaw method.
✓ Use of people resources (mentors, tutors, friendship group, resource personnel, aides).
✓ Class meetings.

Assessment Approaches:

- ✓ Student and teacher learning logs.
- ✓ Checklist of social behaviors.
- ✓ Group-processing assessment document.
- ✓ Anecdotal records of teachers.
- ✓ Scoring diagrams showing participation (similar to Junior Great Books (JGB) scoring device).
- ✓ Sociogram.
- ✓ Performance in standard problem situations.
- ✓ Use of videotapes (analysis of group work).

The process for delineating a curriculum framework is integrally related to the processes described in Chapters 6, 7, 9, and 12 of this book as well as to the process model for scope and sequence development described in the remainder of this chapter. Thus, no specific commentary on development will be provided here. However, the process of developing a curriculum framework, like all good strategic planning, should be consensual among relevant stakeholders and done with one eye on data representing the past and one eye on creating an idealized future. The completed framework should then be adopted by the school board and used as a central planning tool for the program.

A MODEL FOR SCOPE AND SEQUENCE DEVELOPMENT

Just as "curriculum framework" required definition, so too do the terms "scope" and "sequence." *Scope,* as used herein, refers to the expansiveness and comprehensiveness of a curriculum. Criteria to consider in deciding the scope of a curriculum for the gifted include the following:

- ✓ *What are the important knowledge, skills, concepts, and attitudes for gifted learners to master?* We can teach the gifted many things, but we have limited time. Given the parameters of time and developmental readiness, what are the broad areas of study to which these students should be exposed at the K-12 levels of schooling?
- ✓ *How broadly should various skills and concepts be presented?* We have to consider how we will treat the topics in a curriculum for gifted learners. Should we treat some topics at a survey level and others in greater depth? What decision criteria should guide our thinking?
- ✓ *What critical exposures to new content should the gifted learner have?* In a time of knowledge explosion, a curriculum for the gifted should promote opportunities for understanding whole fields such as biochemistry, systems analysis, and computer graphics. What will these opportunities be, and how will we systematically ensure that the content of the curriculum is continually updated?

✓ *How much time will be needed to engage in various topics in depth?* As we grapple with decisions of scope, we must be mindful of the interaction effect of time. Teaching fewer topics at a given stage of development may be preferable if the material that is covered is taught well and in depth. Brief coverage of many different topics may be far less meaningful.

✓ *Is the teaching staff capable of delivering the nature and extent of the proposed curriculum for gifted learners?* The more we expand curricula for the gifted, the more we stretch existing resources to handle the teaching task. Teachers of the gifted need to feel confident in their ability to deliver a particular type of curriculum before it should become a part of the plan. Staff development can help prepare staff, but it does not substitute for being well grounded in a curriculum area that one is expected to teach.

Sequence refers to the organizing and ordering of curriculum experiences to maximize learner effects (Kemp, Morrison, & Ross, 1998). Questions that curriculum planners need to ask about sequence include the following:

✓ *At what stages are gifted learners ready for certain curriculum experiences?* Most gifted learners show advanced development in key curriculum areas, so the idea of setting upper-level expectations by grade level is different for this population. We cannot really know what the appropriate upper limits might be without more experimentation. Thus, we need to carefully consider readiness issues for this population in each core area of the curriculum.

✓ *What are reasonable curriculum transitions for gifted learners from elementary to middle school to high school levels?* Curricula for the gifted shift dramatically as students move from one school context—elementary, middle, secondary—to the next. How can we smooth out these transitional points to allow for greater continuity and challenge in curricula for the gifted at each stage?

✓ *What is the desired cumulative effect of gifted learners' engagement in specified curriculum experiences?* We should be able to describe our outcome expectations for students who have been in specialized programs for 10–13 years. These expectations should be both greater than and different from those for students not participating in those experiences. The cumulative effect of gifted programs should be stated and used as a reference point for developing a reasonable sequence of curriculum experiences.

✓ *What contents, processes, and products constitute logical extensions of the gifted curriculum at key points in the schooling process?* When curricula are organized at high levels to begin with, it can be difficult to know what the next logical area of study might be. For example, should students move from one type of writing to another or become more proficient in one as they move from Grade 6 to Grade 7? Making decisions about this type of sequencing issue is difficult, yet it is central to determining how to continue to challenge gifted learners.

A Process for Developing Macro Curriculum Documents

The process for engaging in the development of macro curriculum documents entails the following steps.

1. *Conduct a curriculum needs assessment.* This initial step in the process provides a school district with basic planning information that can help direct the curriculum effort. Being able to articulate the current curriculum for gifted learners, how it differs from what is available for all learners, and where the gaps are is a key step in the process of developing meaningful curriculum products. Beyond discrepancy analysis, sources of data that can provide valuable input for curriculum development include the following:

   a. Gifted student performance on state and national tests (e.g., Scholastic Aptitude Test, Advanced Placement test, National Assessment of Educational Progress).
   b. Analysis of state standards and their impact on the curriculum development process for gifted learners.
   c. Longitudinal study data on gifted graduates, noting areas of deficiency in their education.

2. *Develop an overall curriculum framework of K–12 process and product goals.* Once a school district has determined what is currently in its curriculum for gifted learners, educators are in a better position to fashion what might be in the curriculum so that it is cohesive from kindergarten through 12th grade. At this stage of the process, product or outcome goals should be developed for gifted students, providing a clear set of expectations based on the students' participation in a program for 13 years. Process goals for teachers should also be developed detailing strategies that will enable teachers to help students reach the stated expectation levels. These goal statements should be translatable to content, process-product, and "great ideas" interdisciplinary curricula—all of which are necessary approaches in a comprehensive program for the gifted learner.

3. *Develop goals and learner outcomes for K–12.* After the framework has been conceptualized, goals and learner outcomes have to be delineated for all areas of the school curriculum. The general school curriculum should be used as a touchstone in this effort so that the resulting product circumscribes what is required for all learners but is reorganized and enriched for the gifted. Particular attention must be paid to the alignment process that links goals to learner outcomes in a coherent fashion and also links learner outcomes across grade-level clusters at increasing levels of complexity.

4. *Determine an appropriate coding format for representing scope and sequence work to various publics.* Once goals and student learner outcomes have been delineated, it is useful to consider how best to communicate scope and sequence work to various groups. Although many states require the learner outcome framework for their general curricula, some gifted educators may wish to depart from that format and take an approach that links immediately to classroom materials, activities, or teaching units.

5. *Write a K–12 outline for each major curriculum strand.* Many gifted programs use curriculum content that is not formally included in the general school curriculum. This content has to be well defined for each stage of student development and linked in a scope and sequence model. One of the central issues for sequencing content for an area such as thinking skills, for example, is the choice of paradigm to be used and the consistency of its use across grade levels. A second issue relates to the complexity of the assigned tasks at each stage. Deductive reasoning can be taught at increasing levels of difficulty, but some designation of the developmental process involved is necessary to understand that progressive challenge in that thinking skill area is going on.

6. *Align all goals and outcomes with exemplary activities, resources, and materials.* The next step in the scope and sequence process is to align learner outcomes to actual teaching units, resources, and activities. Only by including this step can educators be satisfied that the curriculum in the classroom reflects the general direction desired. At this level of alignment the ideal curriculum plan merges with the real classroom lesson plan.

7. *Identify areas within the scope and sequence that require curriculum unit development.* The scope and sequence process must also identify gaps in teaching units and curriculum materials. Typically, as one completes the alignment process, an imbalance between what should be taught and what will be taught becomes apparent. The reason for the gap is often a lack of "hands on" material. This issue can now be addressed systematically.

8. *Implement the scope and sequence model with staff and gifted students.* At this final stage of the process, several new initiatives must be carried out, for scope and sequence work now has to relate to the larger ongoing systems of staff development and evaluation in a given school district. Three major tasks might be identified:

   a. Hold staff development sessions to present the curriculum framework and scope and sequence work along with procedures for implementation.

   b. Monitor the implementation through classroom observations, teacher meetings and conferences, and focus groups with relevant stakeholders.

   c. Evaluate student progress via the assessment approaches delineated in the curriculum framework.

CURRICULUM ISSUES

Assessment of written curricula used in several districts suggests the need for more internal consistency in curricular products to meet the specific individual needs and interests of students. This assessment also reveals a number of critical issues to be considered in future planning and curriculum development:

✓ Providing for continuity and articulation in curricula for the gifted.
✓ Systematic planning to improve curricula for the gifted.
✓ Developing a comprehensive plan for curriculum development.
✓ Moving from the development of curricula at the micro level of unit development to the macro level of framework and scope and sequence development.

Curriculum Alignment

One of the major difficulties in developing written curricula for gifted learners is making curriculum documents relevant at two levels of the program simultaneously: First, the design model must reflect broad program goals and learner outcomes across the span of K–12. Second, the model must at the same time adequately represent and be aligned with what is actually taking place with gifted learners in the classroom. Thus, broad-level planning must be congruent with more specific planning at the level of classroom implementation. The following section suggests ways to approach this task.

Organization of Curriculum Products

Undue concern about the form a curriculum product takes can absorb valuable time and energy. Yet the shape of the product can predestine its usability within the school system. Because most states have developed statewide learner outcomes that local school districts are to adopt or modify, this framework seems reasonable for illustrating adaptations for gifted learners.

Even though individual teachers may prefer curriculum representation by activity clusters or key materials and texts, organizing by goals and specific learner outcomes is central to the curriculum development task. In an attempt to ensure curriculum alignment, however, documents should always be cross-coded to specific teacher activities at requisite grade levels, curriculum resource units used with the gifted program, "packaged" programs such as Junior Great Books, and key materials and texts. In that way, elements of the design process will be linked at all levels of the curriculum development process, from the learner characteristics and curriculum dimensions to classroom activities and materials and resources. The levels of specificity in curriculum alignment are depicted in Figure 4.1.

In preparing well aligned and articulated curriculum products, curriculum planners must ensure that teachers are involved in the curriculum work in various organizational patterns. Grade-level clusters should be identified according to natural

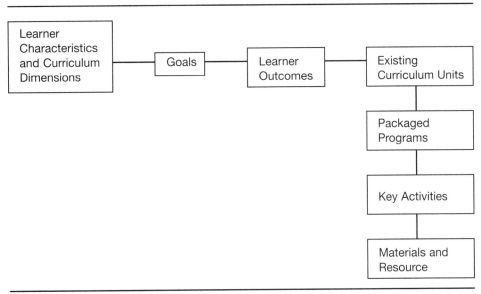

FIGURE 4.1   Levels of Specificity in Curriculum Alignment

grouping patterns in a given school district program. The following chart organizes the clusters into four levels, which are typical points at which to specify anticipated learner outcomes for the gifted. This organization also preshapes the levels at which student progress might be measured.

Level I	K–3	cluster defined by cross-disciplinary teaming and common core
Level II	4–6	cluster defined by cross-disciplinary teaming and common core
Level III	7–8	subject-specific classes in all core areas, special classes, interdisciplinary offerings
Level IV	9–12	subject-specific honors, Advanced Placement, and dual enrollment in selected areas; seminars; independent study options, and so forth.

The model shown in Table 4.1 summarizes the nature of the alignment process for the curriculum development stage of determining goals and learning objectives.

As noted earlier, many existing state and local scope and sequence documents are organized by key goals and learner outcomes for all learners. Thus, there is a need (1) to adapt this basic framework for gifted learners, and (2) to employ an

TABLE 4.1   Curriculum Alignment Model

Program Level	Alignment Needs & Issues	Classroom Level
Goals & learning objectives by Grade Level Clusters (K–3, 4–6, 7–8, 9–12)	Grade level objectives Sub-objectives Curriculum units Packaged programs Instructional processes	Activities Materials Resources Delivery Systems

alignment process that allows all classroom teachers at all grade levels to understand how their work with gifted learners fits into the larger schema. This alignment process also allows curriculum developers to spot weak links in the overall process, leading to the process of implementing changes such as the following:

1. Developing teaching units to help bridge where the program is to where it should be at the classroom level.
2. Incorporating existing packaged gifted programs to fill gaps in the model at the classroom level.
3. Selecting key materials to assist in carrying out the curriculum plan at the classroom level.

Through the process of alignment, one can more easily determine where curriculum needs may lie and make more intelligent decisions about how to meet them.

Numerous approaches might be employed in the alignment process. One approach is to analyze carefully the subcomponents of a given learner outcome. Figure 4.2 illustrates a learner outcome conceptualized for mastery by gifted students at the end of eighth grade. By breaking down the desired outcome into constituent parts, we can begin to see where individual grade-level emphasis might be.

EXAMPLE OF THE ALIGNMENT PROCESS

The following example of the alignment process is taken from the Gary Community School District language arts curriculum. It traces a learner outcome to sub-outcomes and then to specific teaching activities and resources. (An extended example is given in the Appendix to this chapter.)

By the end of Grade 3, students should be able to use appropriate texts such as fiction, nonfiction, poetry, letters, directions, and reference material to accomplish the various purposes for reading.

Learner outcome: By the end of Grade 8, students should be able to use appropriate texts such as fiction, nonfiction, poetry, letters, directions, and reference material to accomplish the various purposes for reading.

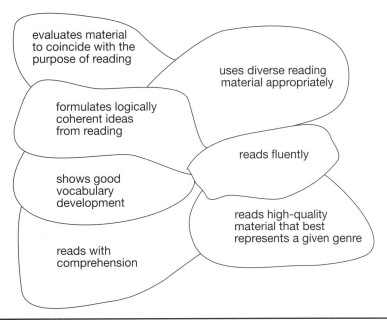

evaluates material to coincide with the purpose of reading

uses diverse reading material appropriately

formulates logically coherent ideas from reading

reads fluently

shows good vocabulary development

reads high-quality material that best represents a given genre

reads with comprehension

FIGURE 4.2   Analysis of the Subcomponents of a Sample Learner Outcome

Transition 1: Learner Sub-Outcomes
A. By the end of Grade 3, students should be able to use appropriate texts for reading aloud.
B. By the end of Grade 3, students should be able to use appropriate texts to learn new vocabulary.
C. By the end of Grade 3, students should be able to use appropriate texts to understand the meaning of what they read.

Transition 2: Learner Sub-Outcomes at Specific Grade Level
A. By the end of Grade 1, students should be able to understand directions and act on them appropriately.
B. By the end of Grade 1, students should be able to read children's literature and interpret meaning.
C. By the end of Grade 1, students should be able to read poetry aloud with expression and creative movement.

Learning Activities Needed to Support Grade 1 Sub-Outcomes
A.   Students will read and interpret various signs and symbols.
B.   Students will form literary groups to discuss selected children's literature.
C.   Students will conduct poetry readings and dramatize individual poems.

Resources Needed for Specific Grade 1 Sub-Outcomes:
Signs and Symbols Unit (teacher-developed)
Junior Great Books, Level 1
Poetry for Young Children, Tasha Tudor
Story and poetry tapes

This example and the one in the chapter Appendix illustrate alternative ways to ensure curriculum alignment as a part of the curriculum development process. They represent approaches to bring about the necessary linkages within grade levels and across grade levels when common resources such as key anthologies are employed.

Organizing for Curriculum Alignment

What is the best way to organize staff to accomplish curriculum alignment in school districts? One model, mentioned earlier, is to form grade-level cluster teams of teachers of the gifted so K–3 teachers, for example, could "work down" from the learner outcome conceptualized for mastery at the end of Grade 3. In like fashion, Grade 4–6, 7–8, and 9–12 teams can be organized. One major task for teams is to generate the necessary sub-outcomes, activities, and key resources at each level in order to align the outcomes for relevant content areas and special strands in the curriculum. A standard outline may be provided to ensure consistency in form. Another alignment task is to ensure levels of specificity across grade levels for sub-objectives, consonance of language, and comparable numbers of activities and resources across the clusters. A curriculum document created in this way will be perceived as somewhat standardized, even though different individuals developed pieces of it.

Other approaches also could work. For example, team leaders at the elementary level and department chairpersons at the secondary level could provide the alignment function. The individuals working with the curriculum alignment process must, however, understand the relevant components of the outcome and be sufficiently knowledgeable about what goes on in the classroom at each requisite level.

Teacher involvement with curriculum development is advantageous in that it sets the stage for greater acceptance and use of the curriculum developed. Teachers also must be integrally involved with writing down the alignment linkages, because the linkages represent the internal workings of the program that only they know. Teacher involvement in the process is crucial to its success.

ALIGNMENT TO THE GENERAL CURRICULUM

Another important alignment issue concerns matching the gifted program goals, outcomes, and activities and resources to those in the general curriculum. Admittedly, this task may be monumental, because many school districts do not have written curriculum guides that specify major learner outcomes by content areas. However, as each state has moved to develop learner outcomes, more uniformity and standardization around basic curricula are taking place. Every school district could use a state document of this nature as the foundation for aligning the gifted curriculum to the basic curriculum. One way to attempt this alignment process is to match, in a column model, the major goals and outcomes of the gifted and general programs within a given area for easy comparison. Table 4.2 provides an example in the area of reading. This approach visually allows even a casual reader to discern the differences between the focus of the gifted curriculum and that of the general curriculum in reading. The "match-up" conveys the necessary relationships between the two curricula.

Some school districts prefer to use a coding format that merely keys by number and letter the relationship of the gifted curriculum to the general curriculum. They might, for example, type column 1 of Table 4.2 and place a note beneath it that reads "Goal 2, Outcomes a–f," referring to the general curriculum. There is little substitution, however, for seeing the comparisons juxtaposed.

The explanatory note at the bottom of Column 1 in Table 4.2 is significant in that it describes how the two columns interface. Without it, a reader might assume that the basic skills of reading are not addressed at all in the gifted program and that accountability for mastery of these basic skills is missing. Relationships to the general or basic curriculum have to be made patent so that educators can understand the differences in educational focus between general education and gifted education in key content areas.

SUMMARY

In developing scope and sequence for gifted learners, educators have to assume that the general school curriculum is inappropriate for the gifted; that curriculum development for the gifted is a long-term process encompassing all areas and all grade levels; and that the curriculum plan must be written and understood throughout the school district. Scope and sequence development can serve as a planning tool, can define gaps in curriculum materials and resources, and can define student expectation that can be evaluated.

Curriculum alignment means making curriculum documents relevant across the entire K–12 span and adequately representing what is occurring in the classroom. Thus documents should be cross-referenced to goals, learner outcomes, and specific activities and resources at each grade level. This can be accomplished by generating sub-outcomes, activities, and key resources at each level to align the outcomes for

TABLE 4.2   Major Goals and Outcomes in Sample Gifted Program and
               Basic Education Program

Gifted Program Goal in Language Arts and Underlying Outcomes	Basic Education Goal in Language Arts and Underlying Outcomes
To develop critical reading behaviors*	To develop reading skills
The gifted learner will be able to:	The typical learner will be able to:
a. analyze material read from high quality children's literature and selected classical and contemporary adult literature	a. read with fluency selected material
b. interpret reading material in various genres	b. develop vocabulary at appropriate levels
c. evaluate authors' perspective and point of view	c. read with comprehension
d. draw inferences based on selected reading	d. use various genres of reading material appropriately
e. use deductive reasoning to understand arguments in written form	e. develop library reference skills
f. develop analogical reasoning skills based on reading	f. develop analytical and interpretive skills in reading

* Basic reading goal and underlying outcomes will be tested at each appropriate level in the gifted program to ensure mastery. The *emphasis* of the program, however, is best reflected in the outcomes that follow.

content areas and strands in the curriculum. Specificity can be encouraged through sub-objectives, consonance of language, and comparable emphases.

This chapter on developing curriculum framework and scope and sequence documents for gifted education has outlined key questions to ask in comprehensive curriculum planning and has provided a step-by-step process for undertaking the task. An example of a K–12 language arts scope and sequence of goals and outcomes is included in the Appendix to this chapter to illustrate an actual school district scope and sequence product.

QUESTIONS FOR REFLECTION

1. What might a curriculum needs assessment reveal in a school district? How might the needs assessment be used to encourage change?
2. What is your understanding of how curriculum decisions are generally made? How might this process be improved?
3. What are the benefits of developing a scope and sequence document for the K–12 gifted program?
4. What curriculum alignment procedures improve communication and understanding of the total curricular structure? How might teachers, administrators, and parents best be involved in the process?

REFERENCES

Benbow, C. P., Lubinski, D. J., & Stanley, J. C. (1996). *Intellectual talent: Psychometric and social issues.* Baltimore, MD: Johns Hopkins University Press.

Gallagher, J., & Gallagher, S. (1995). *Teaching the gifted child* (4th ed.). Boston: Allyn & Bacon.

Gross, P. A. (1997). *Joint curriculum design: Facilitating learner ownership and active participation in secondary classrooms.* Mahwah, NJ: Erlbaum.

Kemp, J. E., Morrison, G. R., & Ross, S. M. (1998). *Designing effective instruction* (2nd ed.). Upper Saddle River, NJ: Merrill.

Sternberg, R. J., & Williams, W. M. (1998). *Intelligence, instruction, and assessment: Theory into practice.* Mahwah, NJ: Erlbaum.

VanTassel-Baska, J. (1995). The development of talent through curriculum. *Roeper Review, 18,* 98–102.

VanTassel-Baska, J. (Ed.). (1998). *Excellence in educating gifted and talented learners* (3rd ed.). Denver: Love Publishing.

APPENDIX TO CHAPTER 4

A Scope and Sequence Document for the Gary, Indiana, Community School District Language Arts K–12 Curriculum

Language Arts Goals K–12

As a result of K-12 gifted programs, students will be able to:

1. Develop critical reading behaviors.
2. Develop critical listening skills.
3. Develop proficiency in grammar and usage.
4. Develop proficiency in oral communication.
5. Analyze and evaluate various literary forms (genres) and ideas (themes) in world literature.
6. Develop expository and technical writing skills.
7. Develop cross cultural understanding through studying the literature, art, and music of selected African, Oriental, Indian, and European cultures.

Goal 1
Develop Critical Reading Behaviors

By the end of Grade 3, gifted students should be able to:

A. Read fluently at least two grade levels above placement.
B. Comprehend stories read to them.
C. Understand character, plot sequencing, and setting in stories.
D. Interpret the meaning of stories and passages they read.
E. Write stories based on reading experiences.
F. Master vocabulary two grade levels above placement.
G. Participate effectively in literary discussion.
H. Manage independent writing.
I. Demonstrate proficiency in the skills of comprehension, application, and classification.

By the end of Grade 6, gifted students should be able to:

A. Read fluently at least two grade levels above placement.
B. Interpret the meaning of stories read.
C. Understand the literary structures of motivation, theme, climax, and story development.
D. Compare and contrast stories and passages read according to content and form.
E. Write essays based on original ideas.
F. Master vocabulary two grade levels above placement.

    G. Evidence skills in the inquiry process of discussion.

    H. Manage independent reading projects.

    I.   Demonstrate proficiency in the skills of analysis, synthesis, and evaluation.

By the end of Grade 8, gifted students should be able to:

    A. Comprehend advanced (adult) reading material on diverse topics.

    B. Analyze, interpret, and evaluate literature read.

    C. Recognize and understand characteristics of all literary forms and genres.

    D. Conduct debates and/or panel discussions on readings, using a thesis or key question.

    E. Critique selected readings orally and in writing.

    F. Make valid inferences based on reading selections.

    G. Demonstrate proficiency in recognizing and creating analogies.

    H. Generalize from specific data.

By the end of Grade 12, gifted students should be able to:

    A. Analyze and interpret adult reading material in any content domain.

    B. Synthesize ideas about an author's form and content.

    C. Master advanced adult vocabulary.

    D. Critique a reading selection according to a given set of criteria or standards.

    E. Develop an essay that compares key elements used by one author in several works to another author's work.

    F. Demonstrate proficiency in working with inference, inductive and deductive reasoning, analogies, assumptions, and evaluation of arguments.

Goal 2
Develop Critical Listening Skills

By the end of Grade 3, gifted students should be able to:

    A. Identify verbal and nonverbal cues to meaning.

    B. Identify different points of view in oral messages.

    C. Recognize cultural differences based on communication behaviors.

    D. Listen attentively to various media presentations of appropriate length.

    E. Use appropriate audience and listener responses.

    F. Follow multi-step oral directions.

By the end of Grade 6, gifted students should be able to:

    A. Identify relevant information, bias, and details from oral messages.

    B. Understand point of view in an oral message.

    C. Demonstrate ability to concentrate on listening, given a moderate level of distraction.

  D. Provide a summary of an oral presentation.

  E. Focus and sustain attention during an oral presentation of 30 minutes.

  F. Take accurate notes on underlying ideas presented orally.

By the end of Grade 8, gifted students should be able to:

  A. Identify criteria for evaluating oral presentations.

  B. Make valid inferences and judgments about an oral message.

  C. Demonstrate interactive listening skills.

  D. Provide constructive feedback at appropriate times in oral discourse.

  E. Focus and sustain attention during an oral presentation of 45 minutes.

  F. Develop a content outline of oral presentations heard.

By the end of Grade 12, gifted students should be able to:

  A. Analyze the content of oral presentations of varying lengths.

  B. Judge the effectiveness of an oral argument (debate) according to predetermined criteria.

  C. Evaluate purposes in oral messages.

  D. Analyze the effectiveness of various techniques used to present ideas orally.

  E. Demonstrate communication behavior consonant with purpose and intent.

  F. Demonstrate interactive listening skills in various settings.

  G. Focus and sustain attention during an oral presentation of 60 minutes.

  H. Analyze differing perspectives and points of view.

Goal 3
Develop Proficiency in Grammar and Usage

By the end of Grade 3, gifted students should be able to:

  A. Understand the various purposes of oral and written communication (e.g., describe, persuade, debate).

  B. Use correct symbols of capitalization and punctuation appropriate to level.

  C. Spell common words correctly.

  D. Correct errors in written and oral communication.

  E. Recognize nouns, verbs, and adjectives.

  F. Create simple, compound, and complex sentences.

  G. Use reference tools as needed for developing communication (e.g., dictionary, thesaurus).

  H. Design written and oral messages for a variety of purposes (e.g., to entertain, to express feelings, to share information).

By the end of Grade 6, gifted students should be able to:

  A. Write for various purposes and audiences.

B. Use correct symbols of capitalization and punctuation in all contexts.
C. Use all forms of words correctly.
D. Recognize and use all basic sentence patterns.
E. Correct common usage errors.
F. Write a coherent theme free of mechanical errors.

By the end of Grade 8, gifted students should be able to:

A. Write and speak using conventional forms of standard English.
B. Use multiple resources to develop communications.
C. Manipulate grammatical aspects of a theme to achieve a desired effect.
D. Expand and reduce sentence elements for either elaboration or clarity.
E. Analyze complicated sentence structure.
F. Analyze uncommon usage problems.

By the end of Grade 12, gifted students should be able to:

A. Proofread, edit, and revise written and oral communications.
B. Apply grammar and usage principles in the writing and oral presentation of coherent ideas.
C. Discriminate choice of style and content based on audience need and demand.
D. Evaluate effective word choice, sentence structure, and passage appropriateness in a variety of contexts.
E. Recognize usage errors in all forms of written and spoken communication.
F. Analyze the evolution of language syntax and usage within a culture.

Goal 4
Develop Proficiency in Oral Communication

By the end of Grade 3, gifted students should be able to:

A. Demonstrate poise when speaking before a group.
B. Organize an effective presentation of 5 minutes in length.
C. Use oral communication to create dramatic scenes and situations.
D. Express feelings about self and others in oral form.
E. Demonstrate appropriate language use when speaking.
F. Use voice and physical gestures to create a desired effect.
G. Send and receive oral messages in various forms (e.g., directions, information, ideas, actual and invented dialogue).
H. Use oral communication to enhance social interaction.

By the end of Grade 6, gifted students should be able to:

A. Use appropriate articulation, pronunciation, volume, rate, and intonation when speaking before an audience.

B. Adapt language usage to audience setting.
C. Use nonverbal cues to emphasize meaning and enhance oral presentations.
D. Use multiple media in an effective manner.
E. Demonstrate a variety of oral presentation purposes (e.g., to inform, to entertain, to feel, to imagine).
F. Organize an effective presentation of 10 minutes in length.
G. Use oral communication to enhance social relationships.

By the end of Grade 8, gifted students should be able to:

A. Use differing organizational patterns for oral presentations, based on purpose and audience.
B. Master parliamentary procedure.
C. Prepare an agenda and lead a group discussion.
D. Use multiple sources to support ideas in oral communications.
E. Demonstrate mastery of the fundamental rules of debate.
F. Use oral communication to express creative ideas and feelings.
G. Use oral communication to enhance social situations.
H. Analyze and evaluate oral presentations of peers.

By the end of Grade 12, gifted students should be able to:

A. Participate effectively in a debate structure.
B. Lead a group discussion on a self-selected topic.
C. Prepare and deliver a 15-minute oral presentation on a pre-assigned topic.
D. Create and act out an original dramatic scene expressing an idea, emotion, or event.
E. Demonstrate proficiency in extemporaneous speaking.
F. Analyze and evaluate the effectiveness of any example of oral communication.
G. Use oral communication to enhance social relationships and situations.
H. Participate effectively in a panel discussion.

Goal 5
Analyze and Evaluate Various Literary Forms (Genres) and Ideas (Themes) in World Literature

By the end of Grade 3, gifted students should be able to:

A. Identify the basic literary forms of drama, poetry, short stories, nonfiction, letters, myths and fables, biography, and autobiography.
B. Compare and contrast literary forms at appropriate levels.
C. Compare and contrast ideas from selections read.
D. Identify the literary structures of character, plot, setting, and theme in each literary form studied.

E. Compare and contrast literary devices.
F. Identify character behavior in selected literature.
G. Evaluate the effectiveness of alternative endings to selected pieces of literature.
H. Create a "literary piece" in a given form at the appropriate level.

By the end of Grade 6, gifted students should be able to:

A. Identify the literary devices important to each literary form (e.g., poetry—use of imagery, simile, metaphor, rhyme, alliteration, onomatopoeia, etc.).
B. Compare and contrast literary forms at appropriate levels.
C. Compare and contrast literary structural elements from two selections read.
D. Create a piece of literature in any form or style based on a given idea.
E. Infer ideas from literary works studied.
F. Analyze the use of symbols in selected pieces of literature.
G. Create a "literary piece" in a self-selected form at the appropriate level.

By the end of Grade 8, gifted students should be able to:

A. Analyze and interpret form and idea in "moderately difficult" literary selections.
B. Compare and contrast literary works from different periods based on a common theme.
C. Employ appropriate critical reading behaviors in encountering new reading material (e.g., finding the main idea, making appropriate inferences, evaluating data given, discerning author's tone).
D. Interpret character motivation in selected literature.
E. Compare literary structural elements from at least four selections read.
F. Create "literary pieces" in at least three different forms.
G. Demonstrate mastery of the creative problem-solving process as it applies to developing an independent or group project.

By the end of Grade 12, gifted students should be able to:

A. Analyze and interpret form and idea in "difficult" literary selections.
B. Compare and contrast disparate works of literature according to form, style, ideas, cultural milieu, point of view, historical context, and personal relevance.
C. Evaluate any new piece of literature encountered.
D. Create a piece of literature in a chosen form that successfully integrates form and meaning.
E. Evaluate the potential impact of selected literary works on individual or collective value systems and philosophies.
F. Create a "literary piece" in a self-selected form at a level appropriate for contest submission.

Goal 6
Develop Expository and Technical Writing Skills

By the end of Grade 3, gifted students should be able to:

A. Use at least five forms of public and personal writing (e.g., public—expository essay, report writing, narrative account; private—journal writing, letters).
B. Tailor writing for various audiences.
C. Write about a single event or idea.
D. Demonstrate an understanding of sequence in writing.
E. Illustrate ideas through word choice, graphic representation, and use of space on a page.
F. Exhibit ideational fluency in written form.

By the end of Grade 6, gifted students should be able to:

A. Use multiple sources in preparing research reports.
B. Develop a content outline for a report.
C. Prepare a bibliography and use footnotes appropriately.
D. Use descriptive details, reasons for an opinion, and concrete examples of a solution to a problem in written form.
E. Write in narrative, expository, descriptive, and persuasive styles.
F. Develop effective paragraphs that illustrate appropriate use of chronology, contrast, and cause-and-effect relationships.
G. Demonstrate basic competency in the writing process (pre-writing, writing, editing, revision).

By the end of Grade 8, gifted students should be able to:

A. Prepare a technical report of 10 pages that follows a standard format including, for example, outline, footnote, bibliography, multiple sources.
B. Prepare an expository essay of 250 words or more that shows proficiency in idea development, organization, and mechanics.
C. Use journal writing techniques for weekly entries.
D. Demonstrate mastery of punctuation, capitalization, grammar, and usage in the context of written work.
E. Use advanced vocabulary in the context of written work.
F. Use the workshopping technique with peers to improve individual pieces of writing.
G. Use appropriate techniques to facilitate the writing process (e.g., visualization, note taking, organizing).

By the end of Grade 12, gifted students should be able to:

A. Prepare a technical report of 20 pages that follows a prescribed format.

    B.   Prepare an expository essay of 500 words or more that reflects competency in the blend of form and idea.

    C.   Use journal writing techniques for a variety of purposes.

    D.   Demonstrate competency in the editing process.

    E.   Revise written work to meet the needs of various audiences and purposes.

    F.   Use peer review for improvement of individual writing.

Goal 7
Develop Cross-Cultural Understanding Through Studying the Literature, Art, and Music of Selected African, Oriental, Indian, and European Cultures

By the end of Grade 3, gifted students should be able to:

    A.   Discuss similarities and differences between stories, myths, or folktales representing two different cultures.

    B.   Re-create an artistic piece in the style of a given culture studied.

    C.   Create a musical composition reflecting the style of a given culture studied.

    D.   Cite similarities and differences in social customs, clothing, and beliefs of two cultures as depicted in their literature, art, and music.

    E.   Conduct research on key aspects of a given culture.

    F.   Create a "cultural exhibit" demonstrating one dimension of a culture.

By the end of Grade 6, gifted students should be able to:

    A.   Compare and contrast archetypal literature studied from African, Oriental, Indian, and European traditions.

    B.   Compare and contrast art forms studied from African, Oriental, Indian, and European traditions.

    C.   Compare and contrast musical compositions studied from African, Oriental, Indian, and European traditions.

    D.   Conduct research that compares two cultures on key criteria.

    E.   Compare and contrast language differences among the cultural traditions studied.

    F.   Create a "cultural exhibit" demonstrating two dimensions of two different cultures.

By the end of Grade 8, gifted students should be able to:

    A.   Analyze and interpret common themes and ideas found in the literature, art, and music of a given culture.

    B.   Conduct research on a key idea as it is reflected in the art, literature, and music of a given culture.

    C.   Analyze cultural artifacts to derive an elemental understanding of a culture.

    D.   Express similar ideas and feelings in two languages.

    E.   Analyze differences among artistic forms represented by at least three cultures.

F.   Create a "cultural exhibit" demonstrating multiple dimensions of two different cultures.

By the end of Grade 12, gifted students should be able to:

A.   Analyze and interpret key ideas represented by selected literature, art, and music of any given culture.
B.   Create a montage of literature, art, and music in the style of a given culture and period.
C.   Use an understanding of cultural "motifs" to enhance oral and written communication.
D.   Display oral and written proficiency in a second language that reflects a cultural tradition different from that of America.
E.   Demonstrate an understanding of global interdependence as evidenced by the similarities in cultural traditions, artifacts, etc.
F.   Use appropriate problem-solving strategies in focusing on world problems highlighted in literature read.

Sample Language Art Activities Keyed to Goals and Objectives by Level

Goals and Objectives	Goal Level
Write about your interpretation of the theme, mood or tone, author's style, descriptive language, and point of view in a book.	Goal 5A intermediate
Select a book to read and choose a special follow-up project to do (e.g., oral book report, taped book report, imaginary interview with the author or a character, a poster advertising the book, a skit about a favorite scene, a puppet show or a cartoon strip).	Goal 1H intermediate
Develop a group definition of literary criticism.	Goal 1E junior high
Research the time period, clothing, or customs of a book.	Goal 7E primary
Use a character's words and actions to write about a character's feelings.	Goal 6E intermediate
Relate causes and effects of a character's problems with problems of students.	Goal 5F primary
Make an outline or flow charts describing the plot of a book.	Goal 6D primary

Engage in role playing and creative dramatics to understand relationships.	Goal 4D high school
Visit an art museum.	Goal 7A high school
Attend various ethnic festivals.	Goal 7F junior high
Present skits or puppet plays.	Goal 4C primary
Listen to tapes to make comparisons, judge the qualifications of a speaker, evaluate what is being said, and judge for bias and methods of delivery.	Goal 2A intermediate
Listen critically to a variety of sources such as television, sociodramas, assembly programs, radio broadcasts, dramatizations, and dialogues to evaluate ideas and values transmitted.	Goal 2B junior high
Chart the characteristics of a good listener.	Goal 2C junior high
Keep a journal in which you write ideas about the events that occur in the world around you.	Goal 6C junior high
Make a list of feelings you've experienced today.	Goal 6C high school
Write your ideas of friendship and put them in a letter to a friend.	Goal 6E intermediate
Write an editorial showing the logic steps you used to reach a conclusion.	Goal 1G high school
Present choral readings.	Goal 4C primary
Stage radio and television broadcasts to satirize current shows.	Goal 4D high school
Write haiku and cinquain poetry.	Goal 5F junior high
Create rebus stories.	Goal 5G intermediate
Study the origins of the English language and its changes through the years.	Goal 3F high school
Play word classification games using the parts of speech.	Goal 3C intermediate
For art, paint prepositions as abstractions (e.g., across, under, down).	Goal 3C intermediate
Study adjectives by making a game of developing descriptive phrases.	Goal 3E primary

Make a "wordbook" in which you analyze the interaction
of different forms of words and their functions by
drawing cartoons or animated word pictures.   Goals 3C/D intermediate

Do an independent project on the authors, time
period, or cultural background of stories read.   Goal 1H intermediate

List events that happen in a story in the order in which
they are most important to you. Explain why.   Goal 6D primary

Resource Units

The following topical units have already been developed for use in Grades K–6 and
appear in the existing curriculum guide for the Gary Community School District.
These units are cross-referenced to each of the language arts goals delineated in the
preceding section of this document.

Unit	Goal
1. Oral language	4
2. Dictation	4
3. Journal writing	6
4. Choral speaking and rhythm instruments	2, 4
5. At the concert (listening skills)	2
6. Water animals	1, 2, 4, 6
7. Public speaking	4
8. Indian dunes	1, 2, 4, 6

Key Packaged Programs Used

Junior Great Books has been cited as a key resource for use at all levels of the gifted
program in elementary school and junior high. No other set of packaged materials
developed for use with the gifted learner has been cited.

5

THE NATURE AND CURRICULUM NEEDS OF GIFTED LEARNERS

Designing appropriate curricula for any target group requires an understanding of the group members' nature and needs as they relate to curriculum design. This is especially true for gifted learners, whose major characteristic of advanced development renders them at risk in school systems committed to rigid age-grade models of curriculum. This chapter will explore the characterological nature of gifted learners that renders them special need learners. It also will highlight basic definitions of intelligence and giftedness and identification approaches used in schools.

WHAT IS INTELLIGENCE?

Various views prevail in current thinking about intelligence. Perkins (1999) characterized intelligence in three broad areas: neural, experiential, and reflective. By *neural,* he referred to the psychometric views suggesting that intelligence is related to one's genetic potential for problem solving—the so-called general intelligence factor, or g-factor (Jensen, 1999). This view suggests that intelligence is malleable but only within limits. That is, we can stretch ourselves to handle difficult problems, but within areas where we lack expertise we will encounter limits to our effectiveness and efficiency.

By *experiential,* Perkins referred to domain-specific intelligence, or intelligence in an area in which one can develop expertise. Expertise comes with the development of highly specialized skills matched to the nature of particular endeavors, such as chess playing or writing an argument paper. The more we engage in these endeavors with expert instruction, the better we perform them. According to this view of intelligence, motivation, time, and practice may be the most important variables separating gifted individuals from others. This domain-specific view of giftedness has a long history and has been popularized by Gardner's multiple intelligence model.

Perkins' *reflective* view of intelligence mirrors the work of Robert Sternberg on the role of executive processing in intelligence. This view suggests that metacognition is central to understanding intelligent behavior and that the capacity to plan, organize, monitor, and assess one's situation is crucial to behaving intelligently and adapting to various kinds of environments. Sternberg and Williams (1998) studied these processes under the domain of practical intelligence, which they referred to as our way of coping with the world, adapting to its demands, and shaping its contours.

All three views of intelligence play a role in curriculum development for the gifted. Many districts still ascribe to an IQ model of giftedness, where students are identified for gifted program participation based on demonstration of high-level problem-solving abilities. Other school programs adhere more to the experiential, or domain-specific, view of giftedness, where students may be identified for participation in specialized programs in discrete academic or arts areas based on aptitude and achievement measures. Currently, no school-based programs use the reflective orientation to intelligence as a central force in shaping identification procedures, but reflective intelligence is a facet included in most multiple criteria approaches. Teacher recommendation forms frequently ask for work habits, motivational behaviors, and other signs that indicate that students have developed these metacognitive tools to a high enough level to be included in a gifted program.

WHAT IS GIFTEDNESS?

If intelligence involves the capacity to solve problems at higher levels, to develop high-level expertise in a discrete area, and to plan, monitor, and assess one's work in a reflective manner, then giftedness must be an appellation reserved for those students who perform these feats at very high levels in comparison to same age peers. At a simplistic level, then, giftedness may be considered evidence of advanced development across intellectual areas, advanced development within a specific academic or arts-related area, or unusual organizational power for bringing about desired results. Functionally, schools assess such development through the tools available to them, namely tests, inventories, checklists, and student performance.

HOW IS GIFTEDNESS IDENTIFIED IN SCHOOLS?

In school-based settings, giftedness is most frequently identified by a combination of three to five criteria. The tools most commonly employed are listed in Table 5.1. The increasing use of nontraditional tools demonstrates how dissatisfied the field of gifted education has become with using only traditional tools, which have not

TABLE 5.1   Overview of Commonly Used Identification Tools

Traditional	Nontraditional
Intelligence tests	Nonverbal ability tests
Achievement tests	Creativity tests
Aptitude tests (domain specific)	Student portfolios and performance by audition
Grades	Performance-based assessment
Teacher recommendations	Parent, peer, and community recommendations

yielded enough students of color, students of poverty, or students with uneven profiles. In recent years, both performance-based and portfolio approaches have gained favor and are included in several states' identification guidelines (Karnes, 2000).

THE DILEMMA OF IDENTIFICATION

Issues surrounding the identification of gifted children have long been debated in the field of gifted education. In the gifted education literature, more citations exist on identification than on any other topic. Identification remains one of the most common program development problems cited by school district personnel and state department coordinators administering programs and services to gifted children.

The difficult problems associated with identification of the gifted stem from a number of issues. One relates to whether giftedness should be thought of as absolute or relative. Because newer definitional structures are attuned to the idea of relativity, gifted educators today generally consider the context of the school, the nature of the student's background, and the demands of the program as they make decisions about individual learners. A second issue relates to the range of individual differences within the group of learners who might be designated gifted. As gifted educators, we tend to spend a great deal of time deciding who will be the last student in the program. However, cutting on a continuum of human ability is a risky venture that often is difficult to justify. And at the same time that such debates on identification rage, highly gifted students frequently lack extensive and intensive enough services because programs are far more likely to focus resources on the mildly gifted group, which may be larger and demand more attention. A third issue is the nagging concern that underrepresented groups are not adequately being assessed for inclusion in gifted programs. Thus, we make testing the proverbial messenger to be attacked and continue to search for a better instrument that may reveal greater parity in performance between underrepresented and mainstreamed groups.

Any one of these issues would put identification high on the list of concerns for local school districts' planning and implementing gifted programs. The three taken together guarantee that identification will always be a controversial topic.

Until our beliefs about identification change, we can make little progress in developing a system that resolves all of the issues noted. We must realize that our task is not to identify only the truly gifted but also to locate students who demonstrate undeveloped intellectual potential in specific areas, including academic, artistic, and leadership domains. We must also realize that our task is not to select students for all time but to select them for enhanced instructional opportunities that may benefit them at a given stage of development. Students in all gifted programs should be regularly reassessed for new opportunities and dropped from those that are not meeting their needs. Finally, we must realize that our task is not to be gatekeepers to exclude students but rather to be custodians of student growth by recognizing discernible strengths and working with the school community to enhance them, whether that is done through the gifted program or another medium. Establishing numerical cutoffs on relevant criteria may be less useful than gaining a holistic assessment of the students being considered and matching programs to the strengths of the particular population.

The following current understandings about the act of identification may help us deal with the difficulties inherent in the process:

1. *Giftedness is multidimensional.* Many studies and authors favoring newer conceptual definitions of giftedness acknowledge the multidimensionality of the phenomenon (Gardner, 1991; Sternberg, 1985). Some students are omnibus gifted, highly capable across many domains and areas. Yet the majority of gifted students have distinct profiles of strengths and relative weaknesses. Their abilities may be discerned by performance and not by paper-and-pencil tests. Their giftedness may not be evoked by the school environment but may shine in the context of community. Some may experience developmental spurts at key stages of development, revealing abilities that could not be discerned earlier. The interests of a student may be piqued at some stage, motivating him or her to develop abilities in relevant areas. All of these examples show that giftedness may be elusive in its manner and context of manifestation.

2. *Both genetic and environmental factors influence the manifestation of giftedness.* Individuals vary considerably in their ability to function effectively in various domains. Attention must be paid to the "rubber band" effect of human potential: Our genetic markers allow for expansive growth and development but not to an unlimited extent. We can stretch ourselves within a range that is based on the genetic potential we possess. The role of education is to provide the experiences that may stretch an individual's potential in his areas of greatest

flexibility for learning. This recognition of preexisting individual differences should help educators realize the folly of trying to find a "one size fits all" program of study or curriculum. As long as differentiated practices are reserved for labeled special populations, the spirit of individualized learning will be in jeopardy. Giftedness does not guarantee entitlement to educational privilege, but it does call for a flexible response by schools and other agencies to higher levels of functioning that is based on the individual, not just age.

3. *The concept of degree or extent of giftedness should be considered in developing identification processes and curriculum.* When I directed the talent search program at Northwestern University, teachers would tell me that seventh-grade students who were scoring at the 600 level in mathematics on the Scholastic Aptitude Test were not truly precocious in mathematics, even though their scores placed them in the top 2% of the age population. Only students scoring at the 700 level met that criterion. These teachers were noting the wide band of difference that exists within any gifted population, such that students at the bottom of a particular group may function very differently from those at the top. In psychometric language, this means that gifted students may vary among themselves by as much as three standard deviations in respect to mental functioning in one or more areas. Reading level in a fifth-grade gifted program, for example, could range from seventh-grade to college level. Thus, gifted educators must decide how broad a group might benefit from a particular intervention and then ensure differentiation of instruction in the delivery of that intervention such that students at the top of the group are adequately challenged and those at the bottom are not made unduly anxious. Wide ranges of abilities have to be tolerated in most gifted programs, because the context of delivery frequently requires sufficient numbers of students to justify the special intervention.

4. *The recognition of advanced behavior is the most critical variable in determining who can best profit from advanced work and instruction.* To deny services to students who clearly are advanced in reading, mathematics, the arts, or other domains because they have not been formally assessed calls into question a school system's capacity to respond to individual differences. Responding to advanced student behaviors is facilitated by the inclusion of teacher, parent, and community input in the identification process. Domain-specific checklists can be used to assess such behavior in context. Such checklists also contribute important insights into effective programming for individual children.

5. *Ability must be coupled with focused effort for success to ensue.* Work in talent development (e.g. Csikszentmihalyi, 1996; Simonton, 1999) has convinced most people in the gifted education field that ability alone may be insufficient to predict success in gifted programs, let alone in life endeavors. Nonintellectual factors such as motivation, personality, persistence, and concentration greatly influence creative productivity at particular stages of development and over the lifespan. Thus, identification processes should be sensitive to students whose

ability threshold is slightly lower than established cutoff scores but whose capacity and zeal to do work in a given domain is very high. Tapping into these nonintellectual strengths can best be accomplished through performance and portfolio-based assessment protocols coupled with careful observation of performance over time.

Currently, there is a call for a new paradigm for identification that takes into account the constructs of giftedness just described (Passow & Frasier, 1996). This new paradigm would recognize the different ways in which students display giftedness and would call for more varied and authentic assessment. Instead of relying solely on intelligence and achievement test scores for identification, multiple criteria would be used, including more nontraditional measures, such as observing students interacting with a variety of learning opportunities (Passow & Frasier, 1996). Many gifted educators believe that new conceptions of giftedness and a new paradigm for identifying and selecting students will help minority and disadvantaged students become more represented in gifted programs (Ford, 1996; VanTassel-Baska, Patton, & Prillaman, 1991).

Part of the process of nontraditional assessment involves trying to tap into fluid rather than crystallized abilities. The approaches assess cognitive abilities that often are not apparent when most forms of standardized tests are employed. One such approach, dynamic assessment, usually consists of a test-intervention-retest format, with the focus being on the improvement students make after an intervention as a result of learning cognitive strategies related to mastery of the tested task (Kirschenbaum, 1998).

Supporting the use of nontraditional assessment is research evidence suggesting that disadvantaged learners perform better on tasks that emphasize fluid over crystallized intelligence (Mills & Tissot, 1995) and spatial over verbal and mathematical reasoning (Naglieri, 1999). Employing an assessment approach that contains a strong spatial component may reduce disparities between scores for different socioeconomic status (SES) levels or ethnic groups (Bracken, 2000). Thus, assessment using such instruments as the Matrix Analysis Test and the Ravens Progressive Matrices may yield somewhat different populations of students than assessment with traditional intelligence tests that emphasize verbal tasks. The new Universal Nonverbal Intelligence Test (UNIT) also offers promise in this regard as a full-scale measure.

In addition, a two-stage process of screening and identification would help to ensure that appropriate measures are used in the selection of students for a gifted program. Simply using group achievement and intelligence test score data as the final arbiters for selection—say, by putting the cutoff at 98%—is not defensible. Many times, large numbers of students would qualify at 95%. When norm-referenced tests that are grade-level calibrated are used to make judgments about students at the top end, problems of ceiling effect occur. A better and more defensible strategy is to use off-level aptitude and achievement measures—such as the PLUS test, the School, College, and Ability Test (SCAT), and the SAT—to ascertain a true dispersion of the student scores in order to select the most able. Over the past 25 years, these instruments have demonstrated effectiveness and efficiency in discerning able students' range of functioning in critical domains (Benbow & Stanley, 1996).

The measures used must also be relevant to a program's emphasis. This is especially true for the identification stage of the process. Using verbal measures to decide who should be in a math program makes no sense. If a program's emphasis is writing, a writing sample should be included at the identification stage; if a program's emphasis is science, a performance-based science assessment or science project portfolio should be included. Such authentic assessment data help gifted educators select the most apt students for participation in carefully defined program areas (VanTassel-Baska, 1998).

Further, best practice calls for the use of identification protocols that are appropriate for the students' stage of development. Early childhood identification procedures, because of the children's age and lack of contact with the school, have to consider parental feedback more carefully, use testing data more judiciously, and consider advanced performance tasks more heavily. Identification procedures at the secondary level, dependent on the organizational context, have to focus on finding students in a broader range of talent areas. Domain-specific approaches based on departmental courses of study must also be considered.

Making placement decisions based on individual profile data is also considered best practice. This practice allows professional judgment to be exercised rather than simply relying on a numerical cut-off score on a matrix model to determine placement (Borland & Wright, 1994). Finally, the identification process must be equitable with respect to the selection, validation, and placement of students. Such fairness can only be obtained through the careful delineation and implementation of well understood procedures by conscientious educators.

SITUATING GIFTEDNESS INTO A CURRICULUM DESIGN MODEL

When considering the concept of giftedness through a curriculum lens, curriculum planners must analyze the characteristics and needs of gifted children and organize curricula that are responsive to them. Once a program is in place, teachers must be cognizant of the identification data on each gifted child and tailor the curriculum to ensure that student profiles are used in the classroom. Figure 5.1 illustrates the relationship between conceptions of giftedness and curriculum planning. Inputs to curriculum planning are derived from the conception of giftedness employed in a school district and the interplay of that conception with group and individual student characteristics and needs. Outputs from an appropriately tailored curriculum, instruction, and assessment system are gifted student creativity and productivity.

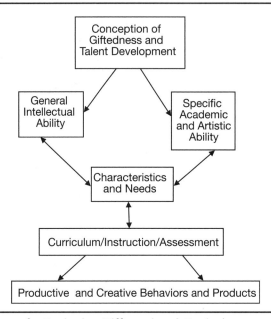

FIGURE 5.1   Context for Designing Differentiated Curricula

ASSUMPTIONS UNDERLYING SPECIALIZED CURRICULA FOR THE GIFTED

Curricula for gifted learners should be based on several assumptions. Although they are not commonly adhered to in practice, these assumptions are critical to ensuring that gifted students receive appropriate services.

1. *All children can learn, but they do so in different ways at different times in different contexts.* Educators of the gifted support this fundamental principle of the standards-based reform movement and applaud it as a necessary belief for improving schooling. Yet educators, in implementing the common standards, must recognize individual differences and accommodate them through flexible means.

2. *Some children learn more quickly than others.* This assumption has been demonstrated over and over again in research studies, yet the power of this difference in learning rate is obscured by age-grade notions of curriculum readiness. Gifted students can learn new material at least twice as fast as typical learners can. If the curriculum is reorganized into "larger chunks," learning rates often can increase exponentially.

3. *Gifted children find different curriculum areas easy to learn and therefore learn them at different rates.* Gifted learners vary as much from one another as they do from the nongifted population both in rate of learning and areas in which they may be ready for advanced learning.

4. *Intrinsic motivation for cognitive learning varies considerably among gifted learners.* The individual differences in motivation for learning, which may be related to cognitive capacity, tend to show up in critical ways as students attempt schoolwork.

5. *Not every student (or every gifted student) will attain a useful mastery of concepts and skills beyond a certain level of complexity and abstraction.* Many students, including some of the gifted, cannot handle advanced mathematics and science, both of which are highly abstract subject areas. Other gifted students encounter difficulty in interpreting complex passages of written text. Students who experience these difficulties may be encountering the maximal degree of abstraction they can handle at their stage of development.

6. *Learning should provide "a basic diet but also favorite foods."* One of the current assumptions of curricula for the gifted is that both specialization and opportunities for other modes of learning are important. Self-selected subjects, special project work, mentorships, and other activities provide opportunities for strong growth in specialized areas.

7. *Intra- and inter-individual variability is the rule in development.* For neither gifted students nor any other group of learners can learning be viewed as a group phenomenon. Rather individual differences coupled with the subtle dynamics of group classroom interactions determine the nature and extent of understanding at any given moment. As Dimitriou and Valanides (1998) observed, "Classrooms are developmental mixers in which each student's developmental dynamics constrain and are constrained by the developmental dynamics of every other student and of the classroom as a whole" (p. 195).

Thus, the beginning point for all meaningful curricula for the gifted must be the individual and group characteristics and needs of these students. Existing curricula found to be effective with the gifted have evolved primarily from this understanding (Maker, Nielson, & Rogers, 1994; VanTassel-Baska, 1995).

COGNITIVE CHARACTERISTICS OF THE GIFTED

Most effective approaches to gifted curricula rely on the introduction of advanced skills and concepts to students at young ages, thus tuning in to advanced cognitive development in specific domains. This approach demands sensitivity to the level and learning capacity of students at their given stage of development. Research by Sternberg, Ferrari, Clinkenbeard, and Grigorenko (1996) has documented the effectiveness of accelerating education in areas of strength. Studying the effects of teaching students a college-level psychology course based on the students' strongest cluster of learning characteristics, these researchers found that gifted students learn better when instruction is matched to learning characteristics.

Cognitive characteristics and needs, then, are not only important for identification of the gifted; they are also indispensable for curriculum design. A few of these characteristics are related to curriculum considerations in the following discussion.

Manipulation of Abstract Symbol Systems, Rapid Learning of New Material

Cognitively, gifted students' ability to manipulate abstract symbol systems much better than average-age peers obviates against a lockstep, incremental part-to-whole teaching-learning process, which is often the practice in the regular classroom. The rate and pace at which gifted students can learn material and their ability to process large amounts of information point to the need for advanced work early in their education. Indeed, many gifted students are early readers who operationally are 2–6 years ahead of their age peers. The power of gifted students' intellectual thought enables them to master concepts and systems of thought holistically rather than piecemeal, reducing the time needed to teach them any given topic. Their general quickness and alertness can be transformed into boredom and frustration when they are held back in a regular classroom situation or when they are submitted to a start-and-stop method of teaching, where, upon reaching a given point in a set of materials, they are told to wait until the rest of the class is ready to go on.

Affectively, many gifted learners are highly impatient. When appropriate pacing and what is actually happening in the classroom are disparate, their frustration is heightened. A greater degree of sensitivity, and even mild hyperactivity and central nervous system reaction, can cause gifted students to have an internal reaction against the "braking mechanism," or the process of not allowing students to move ahead at their own rate. Moreover, the socioemotional development of the gifted is impaired by lack of exposure to peers at their cognitive level. The only satisfactory balm for a gifted child who is ostracized in a typical classroom is to find "learning mates," even if they are imported from across a city or found two grade levels up.

Symbol system manipulation is probably first noticed in young gifted children who read early. Because language learning is a powerful key to other forms of learning, it becomes a good example of a crucial symbol system. The gifted tend to access this symbol system earlier and more intensely, and master it more rapidly, than typical learners do. They are also apt to rate reading as a favorite leisure-time activity during the secondary years (VanTassel-Baska, 1983). A curriculum design question regarding this characteristic is: Should we focus on this *one* symbol system primarily, allowing the gifted to advance and be enriched in all their reading and related language arts experiences? If the answer to this curriculum question is yes, the following elements would seem beneficial as staples in a reading program for the gifted at all levels (VanTassel-Baska, 1991):

✓ Off-level core materials.
✓ Literature program based on appropriate adolescent and adult literature.
✓ Writing program that encourages the elaboration of ideas from literature in building stories and essays.
✓ Emphasis on vocabulary development.
✓ Reading in the content areas and biography.
✓ Multicultural literature.
✓ Sustained foreign language opportunities.
✓ Emphasis on logic and critical-thinking behaviors.
✓ Diagnostic testing in reading skill areas, with instructional follow-up.
✓ Spelling work derived from both basal and literary reading selections.
✓ Storytelling, the reading of one's own stories, and discussion of stories read.
✓ Creation of one's own books, journals, and so on.
✓ Free reading based on student interests.

This list of reading program interventions with primary-level gifted learners exemplifies the role that key characteristics should play in setting the curricular pattern in all content areas. Although the overall emphasis of the program is whole-language experience with a strong emphasis on enrichment of the basic curriculum, the underlying issue of appropriate-level work is stressed through careful assessment of reading skill levels at various stages during the school year, through access to advanced reading materials, through basal, literary, and content dimensions, and through a requisite vocabulary and spelling program that responds to reading level.

Without this set of interwoven responses to the advanced reading level of a gifted child, progress would be limited. The child would be working with basal worksheets rather than receiving direct instructional intervention to produce sustained growth. Acceleration of content, then, is a key intervention for all gifted learners at each succeeding stage of development in each area in which they show advancement.

Mathematics represents another field of study where young gifted learners typically excel and show advanced behavior. Beyond assessment and intervention with basal materials at appropriate levels, the following should be considered in the curriculum:

✓ Attention to developing spatial skills and concepts through geometry and other media.
✓ A focus on problem-solving skills with appropriately challenging problems.
✓ An emphasis on the use of calculators and computers as tools in the problem-solving process.
✓ A stronger emphasis on mathematical concepts than on computation skills.

✓ A focus on logic problems that require deductive thinking skills and inference.
✓ Emphasis on real-world applications of mathematics through the creation of relevant projects.
✓ An emphasis on algebraic manipulations.
✓ Work with statistics and probability.

The components of an appropriate mathematics curriculum, like those of an appropriate reading curriculum, should be balanced between the early provision of advanced content and enrichment, so that skills, concepts, and requisite materials are presented at a challenging level for the child rather than being geared to grade level-considerations. The child's capacity to manipulate symbol systems should be recognized and responded to as a positive learning trait.

Power of Concentration, Diversity of Interests, Curiosity

The gifted tend to have high powers of concentration, wide diversity of interests, and strong curiosity. Gifted educators can manipulate learning time to promote these characteristics. They might focus on a topic for longer time periods but not every day. Or they might double the amount of time spent on advanced topics. In a secondary English program, for example, if more time and emphasis on composition are warranted, a double period twice a week could be scheduled.

Manipulation of time is only one variable of importance here. In addition, educators have to consider how to best nurture these characteristics. One way to make such a curricular decision is to ask students to make choices regarding tasks to be accomplished and topics to be studied. Then, the students could be engaged in independent and small-group investigations based on the area of interest they identify. These investigations typically follow a model of organization that stresses the processes of problem finding and problem solving and employs a project orientation. A typical student-generated project might consist of the following characteristics:

✓ Topic negotiated between teacher and learner.
✓ Work to be done planned by student.
✓ Contract written solidifying the learning to be accomplished.
✓ Student exploration of topic through multiple types of resources.
✓ Resultant product selected from a set of alternative options (written, oral, graphic, etc.).
✓ Higher-level thinking processes used to stimulate project development.
✓ Involvement of multiple media in product.
✓ Consideration of marketability in product generation.
✓ Product judged at a level of adult competence.

Research skills often are taught as a part of the background process for developing products. The following skills emphasize the level of intervention needed to have gifted students engage successfully in research: selecting a topic, issue, or problem to study, locating relevant resources, synthesizing information, interpreting data, and drawing conclusions based on data.

Affinity for Making Meaning, Good Perception of Relationships

The gifted have an interest in and capacity for constructing knowledge for themselves, which can be seen in their ability to generate new ideas and to creatively synthesize existing ideas. Of the characteristics of the gifted that have been described, this one may be the most powerful in any program in which gifted students are given the opportunity to explore an idea and make meaning out of it. Teaching-learning approaches that nurtue this characteristic include the following:

✓ Given the theme of alienation in much of modern literature and art, create a personal statement of that theme in some mode of expression (e.g., poetry, painting, film).

✓ Using art, music, dance, and literature, demonstrate the concept of "pattern" by:
   — Creating a skit.
   — Performing a play.
   — Making a film or video.
   — Developing an exhibit.

✓ Compose a short essay that discusses one of the following ideas about characters in literature:
   — They are blind to their faults.
   — They control their own fate.
   — They behave in foolish ways.

   Cite character examples from at least three different pieces of literature to support your point of view.

✓ Debate one of the following resolutions:
   — Studying extinct and endangered species is important for understanding life on earth today.
   — Studying our past will help us cope with the future. (Use multiple sources including surveys, interviews, and library sources.)

VanTassel-Baska (1998) compiled various cognitive characteristics of the gifted and corresponding needs and interventions (see Table 5.2). This list further explicates the relationship of characteristics of the gifted and implications for curriculum interventions, providing a blueprint for adapting curriculum opportunities for gifted learners at various stages of development.

TABLE 5.2   The Relationship of Characteristics, Learning Needs, and Curriculum for the Gifted (Cognitive)

Characteristic	Learning Need	Curriculum Inference
Ability to handle abstractions	Presentation of symbol systems at higher levels of abstraction	Reorganized basic skills curricula
		Introduction of new symbol systems (computers, foreign language, statistics) at earlier stages of development
Power of concentration	Longer time frame that allows for focused in-depth work in a given area of interest and challenge	Diversified scheduling of curriculum work
		"Chunks" of time for special project work and small-group efforts
Ability to make connections and establish relationships among disparate data	Exposure to multiple perspectives and domains of inquiry	Interdisciplinary curriculum opportunities (special concept units, humanities, and the interrelated arts)
		Use of multiple text materials and resources
Ability to memorize and learn rapidly	Rapid movement through basic skills and concepts in traditional areas; more economic organization of new areas of learning	Restructured learning frames to accommodate capacities of these learners (speed up and reduce reinforcement activities)
		New curriculum organized according to its underlying structure
Multiple interests; wide information base	Opportunity to choose area(s) of interest in schoolwork and go into greater depth within a chosen area	Learning center areas in the school for extended time use
		Self-directed learning packets
		Individual learning contracts

Source: From "Characteristics and Needs of the Gifted" by J. VanTassel-Baska, in J. VanTassel-Baska (Ed.), *Excellence in Educating the Gifted,* 1998, Denver: Love Publishing.

AFFECTIVE CHARACTERISTICS OF THE GIFTED

Just as we can delineate gifted students' cognitive characteristics and needs, we can attend in our curriculum planning to their affective needs. Some major benefits of gifted programs lie in the affective arena, including the opportunity to learn with others of like ability, interest, and temperament; the chance to be accepted for oneself and not perceived as a "nerd" or a "brain"; and the feelings of self-worth that accrue from developing good social relationships with others, perhaps for the first time. These affective issues can be addressed in a systematic way through a planned curriculum.

In analyzing the relationship of reading and writing processes to the counseling process, Bailey, Boyce, and VanTassel- Baska (1990) found many similarities. The use of books as cognitive therapy is a well-established strategy in counseling circles as well as in affective curricula for the gifted. Journal writing in particular has been found to be therapeutic for individuals in working through problems. Thus, the use of bibliotherapy and writing as curriculum interventions with gifted learners who have typical affective concerns and problems seems to be a way to define academic therapy. Table 5.3 delineates selected affective needs of gifted learners and suggests key aspects of the writing process and bibliotherapy that might specifically address them, illustrating how a curriculum might be used to enhance affective development.

One key affective characteristic of the gifted, for example, is a tendency toward perfectionism—that is, a need to perform at the top level in everything undertaken, to get all A's on a report card, to get 100% on all schoolwork. This tendency creates a fear of failure in the gifted, embodied in questions such as these: Can I keep my record in place? Will I slip if I take a particular class or approach a task differently? Concerns of this nature often lead gifted learners to confuse performance with the process of learning; they learn only to be able to demonstrate peak performance on some task demand rather than to engage in the riskier business of learning for its own sake.

The following are two curricular strategies that can combat the problem of perfectionism:

✓ *The use of a writing process model that values editing, revision, and open-ended approaches to assignments.* With this process, the gifted learner can begin to progress as a writer and a learner through the levels of reflection necessary for a quality product and experiences new learning along the way.

✓ *The use of carefully selected reading materials, whether biographies or novels, to engage gifted learners in identifying with a character or person who has experienced feelings of perfectionism.* Through guided discussion, gifted learners can understand a characteristic such as perfectionism as it is reflected in the lives of others and develop related coping strategies in their own lives.

TABLE 5.3   Addressing Affective Needs of Gifted Learners

Selected Affective Needs of Gifted Learners	Responsive Strategies of the Writing Process	Selected Books to Read and Discuss
Dealing with perfectionism • Fear of failure	• Focusing on process that stresses and rewards rewriting-editing • Assigning open-ended writing (in which format and content are not set—no standard for correct response)	Selected biographies of writers
Understanding giftedness • Feelings of being different • Coping skills • Need for risk taking	• Clarifying and articulating experiences • Publishing • Striving for excellence • Display of peer-group talent • Trying something new and different with writing techniques, ideas, format	John Updike's biography *Self Consciousness*
Developing relationships and social skills	• Conferencing and workshopping techniques with peers • Sharing your writing in a public forum or group setting • Developing a collaborative product (journal, newspaper collections of written stories)	*David Copperfield* by Charles Dickens
Introversion • Communication	• Allowing for individual expression of ideas in a protected environment • Promoting one-to-one sharing of ideas with teacher • Promoting reflection and introspection as part of the writing process • Providing opportunity to articulate thoughts, obtain feedback and test ideas and feelings against another's reality	*Hamlet* by William Shakespeare
Too high expectations of self and others	• Emphasis on improvement and development as an ongoing process rather than emphasis on the value of a single product	*The Old Man and the Sea* by Ernest Hemingway
Getting in touch with inner self	• Exploring experiences, feelings	*Catcher in the Rye* by J.D. Salinger
Sensitivity toward others • Tolerance	• Listening to another point of view • Sharing time	*Beloved* by Toni Morrison

Source: Bailey, J.M., Boyce, L.N., & VanTassel-Baska, J. (1990). The writing, reading, and counseling connection: A framework for serving the gifted. In J. VanTassel-Baska (Ed.), A Practical Guide to Counseling the Gifted in a School Setting, 2d. ed. Reston, VA: The Council for Exceptional Children.

CURRICULUM APPROACHES

The cognitive and affective characteristics of the gifted form the basis for the three major curriculum approaches used in developing programs for gifted learners.

1. *Content-based instruction* at advanced levels has been a staple of gifted curricula since the early years and has gained in popularity, particularly with middle school and secondary-level students through the national network of talent searches (Benbow & Stanley, 1983; Sawyer, 1982; VanTassel-Baska, 1985).

2. *Process skills as a basis for curriculum-making* for the gifted has been popularized through model curricula developed around higher-level thinking skills, creative thinking, and problem solving (Maker, 1982; Treffinger & Feldhusen, 1980). An emphasis on product development has emerged with curriculum models that stress independent learning for the gifted, the gifted as practicing investigators of real-world problems, and generative learning practices resulting in creative products (Betts & Knapp, 1981; Kolloff & Feldhusen, 1981; Renzulli, 1977, 1986; Treffinger, 1986).

3. *Concept- or theme-based curricula* for the gifted are derived from early work on the importance of students' understanding of the disciplines (Phenix, 1964; Schwab, 1964) and the later translation of these ideas to the field of gifted education (Ward, 1980). Theme-based curricula for the gifted also receive support from general education ranks through the ideas engendered in Alfred Adler's *Paedaeia Proposal* (1984).

In designing an integrated interdisciplinary curriculum for gifted learners, gifted educators must have a good understanding of the nature of the effort. Unfortunately, understanding has been hindered by the use of ambiguous terminology and a lack of helpful models to guide the development process (Davison, Miller, & Methany, 1995), despite the plethora of articles, workshops, and symposia devoted to the topic (Berlin, 1991). Moreover, evidence for the effectiveness of this type of curriculum is scant (VanTassel-Baska, 2000).

Table 5.4 explores some of the terminology, making important distinctions that may help to clarify the terms. One of the terms in the table—concept—may be defined as a large, overarching idea that has the power to connect disciplines, can assist students in understanding a given discipline more deeply, and has salience in the real world. An "interdisciplinary" curriculum may be defined as one that links two or more disciplines through a major theme or concept as well as the language and methodology of each discipline. An integrated curriculum, as explicated in the Integrated Curriculum Model (VanTassel-Baska, 1998), refers to an inclusive curriculum in respect to approaches employed, models used, assessment techniques, and the blend of general reform principles with gifted education pedagogy. Table 5.5 displays this integration pattern.

TABLE 5.4   A Comparison of Concept or Theme to Topic

Concept or Theme	Topic
Example is "scale."	Example is "large animals."
Scale is central to understanding measurement, estimation, patterning, and other mathematical topics.	"Large animals" can be contrasted with small animals, demonstrating size differences.
Scale is an important concept used in economics, the sciences, art, and music, among other disciplines.	"Large animals" is limited to low-level linkages, such as creating poems about large animals, making up stories about them, and drawing a large animal.

TABLE 5.5   Integration in a Curriculum for Gifted Learners

Dimensions of Connectivity	Features of Curriculum
Organization	Employs content, process, product, and concept opportunities
Models	Uses concept development, reasoning skills, and research models that transcend curriculum areas studied
Assessments	Performance-based and portfolio assessment are integrated into regular use
Reform elements and gifted education	Emphasis is on meaning-making through student-centered challenging activities

The three major ways to adapt curriculum for the gifted—content-based instruction, process skills emphasis, and concept-based instruction—are synthesized in Table 5.6. Each of the three models is delineated and described in respect to the manipulation process required for differentiation for gifted learners. Applications to curriculum context are provided to illustrate the process at work.

TABLE 5.6   A Comparison of Effective Curriculum Models for the Gifted by Differentiation Techniques Employed

Models	Differentiation Techniques	Description	Application
Content-based	Acceleration	Allowing students early access to advanced material and moving them through that material at a faster rate than the norm	Access to advanced reading and mathematics materials based on appropriate assessment.
	Compression	Using diagnostic-prescriptive techniques to ensure maximum new learning; minimal reinforcement of already mastered materials	Use of subject proficiency tests at the beginning of the academic year to determine areas of mastery and concentration needs.
	Reorganization	Organizing existing text material according to higher order skills and concepts (i.e., making the "bits" of learning larger based on the underlying system of the discipline of study)	Studying mathematical (+, -, x, -) operations simultaneously rather than individually <u>or</u> studying all types of addition together (1 digit, 2 digit, 3 digit)
Process/product-based	Infusion and Application	Using a cognitive skill paradigm as a central organizer for selected content.	Use of Guilford-Torrance model of creative thinking to employ in social studies content.
		Setting up novel projects for students to engage in that reflect internalization of the cognitive skill paradigm addressed	Use of the Parnes/Osborne creative problem-solving model as an organizer for a group project in ecology.
Concept- or Theme-based	Integration	Interrelating ideas within domains of inquiry	Studying prediction as an idea in the sciences with applications in geology, biology, chemistry, and medicine.
		Interrelating ideas across domains of inquiry	Studying prediction in the larger culture (astrology, tea leaves, social science models).

Another way to approach "differentiating" curricula for the gifted in the regular classroom involves appreciation of the ways in which gifted students differ from their age peers in the context of school-based learning experiences. These differential characteristics should underlie curricular differentiation. Consequently, appropriate curriculum experiences for this population should be based on the individual children's behavioral assessment profiles. In a model of behavioral assessment of gifted learners in the regular classroom, the curriculum has to be adapted to meet the behaviors manifest in these learners.

Table 5.7 delineates the correspondence of gifted learner characteristics to curriculum emphasis. The table shows the direct correspondence between observed behaviors and desired curriculum treatment.

While an understanding of key characteristics of the gifted learner is useful in making appropriate curriculum inferences, testing information and classroom performance tasks also are helpful in determining what is needed in a curriculum. Even though an underachieving child, for example, may not reveal her cognitive strengths in the classroom, testing information offers an understanding of her intellectual capacity for challenging curricula. Individual testing of gifted students provides a context for observing these behaviors not only through the test items themselves but also through one-to-one interactions with the child. Thus, careful individual testing

TABLE 5.7   The Correspondence of Observed Gifted Characteristics and Desired Curriculum Treatments

Gifted Learner Characteristics	Focus of Curricular Treatments
Ready manipulation of abstract symbol systems	Discipline-based systems of knowledge
Power of concentration Curiosity	Interest-based inquiry
Advanced learning rate	Accelerated learning opportunities
Affinity for making meaning	Issues, themes and ideas within and across knowledge areas
Perfectionism	Creative opportunities that encourage risk-taking
High expectations of self and others	Learning goals rather than performance goals

of children is highly desirable for assessing their strengths and diagnosing appropriate curricular interventions.

Another key issue to consider at this stage of the curriculum development process is the relative heterogeneity of highly gifted learners and the degree of intellectual power that they possess, which is well beyond that of more mildly gifted students. Strengths, interests, and a predisposition toward learning in this population call for special attention on the part of educators, as the general provisions for gifted learners are rarely sufficient in number or intensity for these students. Moreover, the highly gifted demand a more individualized approach to planning that may require at least one of the following procedures, if not a combination:

✓ Development of an individual learning plan that is mutually derived between school and home.
✓ Development of a mentor relationship with an older student or adult.
✓ Collaboration with universities that sponsor special programs or who offer dual enrollment opportunities.

SUMMARY

This chapter has identified key cognitive and affective characteristics of gifted students from which curriculum inferences may be made. It has also introduced the three major curriculum approaches used to address these characteristics: content advancement, process-product emphases, and concept- or theme-based models. Differentiation techniques for content-based instruction include acceleration, compression, and reorganization. Infusion and application are utilized in process-product-based approaches (creative thinking and problem-solving models). Theme-based curricula integrate ideas within and across domains of inquiry.

This chapter also discussed special considerations for linking assessment data to curriculum development. Value-added curriculum enhancements, such as mentors and university classes, were noted for highly gifted learners.

QUESTIONS FOR REFLECTION

1. How can student profile data be used more effectively as a basis for understanding the curriculum needs of the gifted?
2. How might educators systematically respond to the needs of the gifted for challenging curriculum experiences?
3. What major adaptations must be made in the core curriculum to respond effectively to gifted learners?
4. How can professional educators who are not gifted educators (e.g., classroom teachers, psychologists, curriculum specialists) help gifted educators plan effective curriculum experiences for the gifted learner?

REFERENCES

Adler, M. J. (1984). *The Paideia program: An educational syllabus.* New York: Macmillan.

Bailey, J. M., Boyce, L. N., & VanTassel-Baska, J. (1990). The writing, reading, and counseling connection: A framework for serving the gifted. In J. VanTassel-Baska (Ed.), *A practical guide to counseling the gifted in a school setting* (2nd ed., pp. 72–89). Reston, VA: Council for Exceptional Children.

Benbow, C., & Stanley, J. (1983). *Academic precocity.* Baltimore, MD: Johns Hopkins University Press.

Benbow, C. P., & Stanley, J. C. (1996). Inequity in equity: How "equity" can lead to inequity for high-potential students. *Psychology, Public Policy, and Law, 2,* 249–292.

Berlin, D. F. (1991). *A bibliography of integrated science and mathematics teaching and learning literature.* School Science and Mathematics Association topics for teachers series, no. 6. Bowling Green, OH: School Science and Mathematics Association.

Betts, G. T., & Knapp, J. K. (1981). Autonomous learning and the gifted. In A. Arnold, C. Arnold, G. Betts, D. Boyd, J. Curry, J. L. Fisher, V. Galasso, J. K. Knapp, A. H. Passow, I. S. Sato, M. Simon, & T. C. Tews (Eds.), *Secondary programs for the gifted/talented* (pp. 29–36). Ventura, CA: Office of Ventura County Superintendent of Schools.

Borland, J. H., & Wright, L. (1994). Identifying young, potentially gifted, economically disadvantaged students. *Gifted Child Quarterly, 38,* 164–171.

Bracken, B. (2000). *An approach for identifying under-represented populations for G/T programs: The UNIT Test.* Paper presented at graduate seminar, College of William and Mary, Williamsburg, VA.

Csikszentmihalyi, M. (1996). *Creativity: Flow and the psychology of discovery and invention.* New York: HarperCollins.

Davison, D. M., Miller, K. W., & Methany, D. L. (1995). What does integration of science and mathematics really mean? *School Science and Mathematics, 95,* 226–230.

Dimitriou, A., & Valanides, N. (1998). A three-level theory of the developing mind: Basic principles and implications for instruction and assessment. In R. Sternberg & W. Williams (Eds.), *Intelligence, instruction and assessment* (pp. 149–199). Mahwah, NJ: Erlbaum.

Ford, D. Y. (1996). *Reversing underachievement among gifted black students: Promising programs and practices.* New York: Teachers College Press.

Gardner, H. (1991). *Creating minds.* New York: Basic Books.

Jensen, L. (1999). *Developing mathematically promising students.* Reston, VA: National Council of Teachers of Mathematics.

Karnes, F. A. (2000). State definitions for the gifted and talented revisited. *Exceptional Children, 66,* 219–238.

Kirschenbaum, R. J. (1998). Dynamic assessment and its use with underserved gifted and talented. *Gifted Child Quarterly, 42,* 140–147.

Kolloff, P. B., & Feldhusen, J. F. (1981). PACE (Program for Academic and Creative Enrichment): An application of the three-stage model. *Gifted Child Today, 18,* 47–50.

Lonning, R. A., & DeFranco, T. C. (1994). Development and implementation of an integrated mathematics/science preservice elementary methods course. *School Science and Mathematics, 94,* 18–25.

Lonning, R. A., DeFranco, T. C., & Weinland, T. P. (1998). Development of theme-based, interdisciplinary, integrated curriculum: A theoretical model. *School Science and Mathematics, 98,* 312–318.

Maker, C. J. (1982). *Curriculum development for the gifted.* Rockville, MD: Aspen.

Maker, C. J., Nielson, A. B., & Rogers, J. A. (1994). Multiple intelligences: Giftedness, diversity, and problem-solving. *Teaching Exceptional Children 27(1),* 4–19.

Mills, C., & Tissot, S. (1995). Identifying academic potential in students from underrepresented populations: Is using the Ravens Progressive Matrices a good idea? *Gifted Child Quarterly, 39,* 209–217.

Naglieri, J. A. (1999). *The essentials of CAS assessment.* New York: Wiley.

National Research Council. (1989). *Everybody counts: A report to the nation on the future of mathematics education.* Washington, DC: National Academy Press.

National Research Council. (1996). *National science education standards.* Washington, DC: National Academy Press.

Passow, A. H., & Frasier, M. M. (1996). Toward improving identification of talent potential among minority and disadvantaged students. *Roeper Review, 18,* 198–202.

Perkins, D. (1999). The many faces of constructivism. *Educational Leadership, 57*(3), 6–11.

Phenix, P. (1964). *Realms of meaning.* New York: McGraw-Hill.

Renzulli, J. (1977). *The enrichment triad.* Wethersfield, CT: Creative Learning.

Renzulli, J. (Ed.). (1986). *Systems and models for developing programs for the gifted and talented.* Mansfield Center, CT: Creative Learning.

Sawyer, R. N. (1982). The Duke University program to identify and educate brilliant young students. *Journal for the Education of the Gifted, 5,* 185–189.

Schwab, J. (Ed.). (1964). *Education and the structure of knowledge.* Chicago: Rand McNally.

Simonton, D. K. (1999). *Origins of genius.* New York: Oxford University Press.

Sternberg, R. J. (1985). *Beyond I.Q.* New York: Basic Books.

Sternberg, R. J. (1999). Ability and expertise: It's time to replace the current model of intelligence. *American Educator, 23*(1), 10–13, 50–51.

Sternberg, R. J., Ferrari, M., Clinkenbeard, P., & Grigorenko, E. L. (1996). Identification, instruction, and assessment of gifted children: A construct validation of a triarchic model. *Gifted Child Quarterly, 40,* 129–137.

Sternberg, R. J., & Williams, W. M. (Eds.). (1998). *Intelligence, instruction, and assessment: Theory into practice.* Mahwah, NJ: Erlbaum.

Treffinger, D. J. (1986). Fostering effective independent learning through individualized programming. In J. S. Renzulli (Ed.), *Systems and models for developing programs for the gifted and talented* (pp. 429–460). Mansfield Center, CT: Creative Learning.

Treffinger, D., & Feldhusen, J. (1980). *Creative thinking and problem-solving.* Dubuque, IA: Kendall-Hunt.

VanTassel-Baska, J. (1983). Profiles of precocity: The 1982 Midwest Talent Search finalists. *Gifted Child Quarterly, 27,* 139–144.

VanTassel-Baska, J. (1985). The talent search model: Implications for secondary school reform. *National Association of Secondary School Principals Journal [Special issue], 69*(482), 39–47.

VanTassel-Baska, J. (1991). Identification of candidates for acceleration: Issues and concerns. In T. Southern & E. Jones (Eds.), *The academic acceleration of gifted children* (pp. 148–161). New York: Teachers College Press.

VanTassel-Baska, J. (1995). *Comprehensive curriculum for gifted learners* (2nd ed.). Boston: Allyn & Bacon.

VanTassel-Baska, J. (1998). *Excellence in educating the gifted* (3rd ed.). Denver: Love Publishing.

VanTassel-Baska, J. (2000). Curriculum policy development for secondary gifted programs: A prescription for reform coverage. *NASSP Bulletin,* 14–29.

VanTassel-Baska, J., Patton, J., & Prillamon, D. (1991). *Gifted youth at risk: A report of a national study.* Reston, VA: Council for Exceptional Children.

Ward, V. (1980). *Differential education for the gifted.* Ventura, CA: Office of Ventura County Superintendent of Schools.

6

Developing a Philosophy and Goals for a Gifted Program

Curriculum represents a critical interface between beliefs and action. In schools, curriculum decisions are based on constant, careful balancing of the authorities that underlie the various theoretical stances. Conflicts arise around the questions of whether the curriculum should be disciplinary or interdisciplinary; whether teacher flexibility and student interest or the demands of disciplines, professions, or societal expectations should drive the substance of curricula; and what role basic skills and standardized tests should play in a gifted program curriculum. Rogers (1999) cited several sources of authority that create tension in curriculum decision making, as described in the following paragraphs.

One of the primary sources of authority that acts on curriculum decisions comes from standards set outside the classroom, even beyond the school community. Standardized tests are a good example of this sort of authority. They shape curriculum by providing a map of material from which teachers draw to instruct their students. Another major external source of authority that is exerted on curriculum decisions is found in the scholarly disciplines, which constitute the most sophisticated articulations of knowledge that exist. Amid the power of the disciplines and standardized tests, the authority of those inside schools, such as teachers, is often ignored. Yet teachers can and do play a pivotal role in developing and carrying out curriculum. Their role may involve creating, designing, adapting, and fashioning what will be taught, how, and to what end.

Students' interests and needs also have acted as a powerful source of authority and influence on thinking about curriculum. This source of authority is the hallmark of progressives such as Dewey, who emphasized the "importance of studying the child to find out what kinds of interests he has, what problems he encounters, what purposes he has in mind" (1932, p. 4) in order to make basic choices of objectives, materials, and activities.

All four sources of authority—standardized tests and benchmark basic skills, the rules of the disciplines, teacher beliefs and knowledge, and students' interests and needs—must be taken into account in the process of making decisions about curriculum. Educators may balance these influences differently, emphasizing one source over another. Often, differences among curriculum approaches can be traced to different ways in which these sources of authority are balanced.

Squires (1995) suggested that although curriculum is usually thought of as a cognitive and academic plan for what will be taught in the classroom, its reach goes much further. He noted that the way learning is configured in the classroom, the way groups are used to support cooperation, the use of learning resources in the community, the discipline procedures, after-school activities such as sports, and the staff development agenda all have relevance to child development and learning within the social and organizational contexts of the classroom and school. As Squires wrote, "Curriculum, then, not only defines the intellectual architecture of the school, but the social and organizational architecture as well" (p. 5).

Because "human knowledge, and the criteria and methods we use in our enquiries, are all constructed," and social processes used to build knowledge are influenced by "power relations, partisan interests, and so forth" (Phillips, 1995, p. 5), our individual perspectives bear the distinct stamps of our experiences. When thought of in this way, the fundamental beliefs that provoke different curriculum approaches can be traced to differences in personal experiences, histories, and roles in society, and the clash of values around what to teach may be thought of as a clash among diverse ways of life, histories, and levels of opportunity. For this and other reasons, developing a philosophy to guide curriculum development must be considered a multilayered, nuanced enterprise.

A PHILOSOPHY OF CURRICULUM FOR THE GIFTED

Developing a philosophy of curriculum for the gifted is highly dependent on a school district's belief system about all learners and its value system regarding exceptional learners. A school district's general curriculum philosophy is a good point of departure to begin articulating a specialized philosophy for the gifted, keeping in mind three basic ideas fundamental to any statement of curriculum philosophy for the gifted:

✓ The gifted have a right to an appropriate education, one that is grounded in the recognition of individual differences and unique learning needs.

✓ The gifted need a curriculum that is responsive to their individual learning rate, style, and complexity.

✓ The gifted learn best in an instructional environment that encourages and nurtures inquiry, flexibility, and divergent thinking.

These ideas may be used to form the core of a differentiated philosophy for gifted learners, a philosophy that is concerned with a broad conceptual framework for developing curricula, not with the specific topics to include or the specific offerings to provide at given grade levels. A sample philosophy statement, taken from the Fairfax County, Virginia, gifted program reads as follows:

> We believe that all children have the right to an education commensurate with their ability to learn and should be challenged to attain their highest potential. Children who have demonstrated ability significantly beyond that of their age peers need differentiated programs and services designed to reach this goal. Special programs are essential for their appropriate education. By virtue of their more advanced development and interest, they need opportunities beyond those typically provided in the general education classroom.
>
> It is recognized that gifted children come from all cultural and socioeconomic backgrounds and have varying abilities and interests. The programs and curricula planned for them must be diverse, advanced, and complex enough to meet their needs. Academically advanced center-based programs provide opportunities for growth in intellectual, creative, socioemotional, and aesthetic domains. Appropriate educational opportunities take the form of accelerated content, provisions for in-depth study, meaningful product development as well as opportunities to accommodate diverse aptitudes and interests.
>
> Curriculum differentiation is planned so as to respect the unique needs of the gifted learner. Emphasis is on encouraging students to develop intellectual and scholarly skills and attitudes and to develop creative productivity. The school and the home collaborate to encourage gifted students to become productively engaged in the learning enterprise. (*Fairfax County, Virginia, Curriculum Framework,* 2000, p. 2)

In an attempt to design appropriate curricula, the question of purpose must be central to the planning effort. Tyler (1962) urged educators to consider goals in terms of the question: "What are the educational purposes that schools seek to attain?" Without a clear sense of purpose, curriculum efforts for the gifted will be fragmented and diffused. Goals provide a sense of focus and direction toward an ideal end. They should be visionary, reflecting the direction of maximum competency as opposed to reflecting concern for specific achievement. They also should reflect a balanced view toward the education of the gifted child in respect to implied approach and potential end state. Thus, goals should focus equally on such areas as the development of proficiency in core domains of knowledge, higher-order thinking skills, intra- and interdisciplinary concepts, and moral and ethical decision making. Figure 6.1 illustrates the interwoven characteristics of gifted program goals.

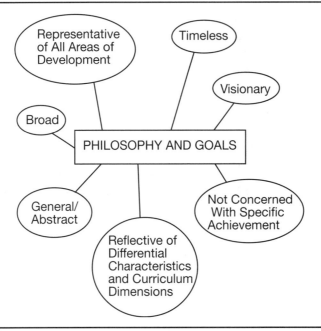

FIGURE 6.1   Key Features of Goals for Gifted Programs

DEVELOPING GOAL STATEMENTS

The development of appropriate goal statements for gifted curricula has received little attention in the field. DiNunno (1982) reported that goals are interpreted as processes around established programs rather than as desired student outcomes. The most common approach to goal development has been to take a list of differentiated principles regarding curricula and translate them into goals. Another approach has been to conduct a local needs assessment, based on identified needs of the gifted, to determine consensus on goal emphasis (VanTassel- Baska, 1998).

Student needs from which goals might be developed include the following:

A.   Basic cognitive skills

   1. Critical thinking
   2. Creative thinking
   3. Problem solving
   4. Research
   5. Decision making

B. Basic affective skills

   1. Tolerance of self and others
   2. Constructive use of humor
   3. Coping with being different
   4. Discriminating between the real and the ideal
   5. Use of high-level sensitivity

C. To be challenged by mastery-level work in areas of strength and interest
D. To be challenged by exposure to new areas
E. To be challenged by the opportunity to see interrelationships
F. To be challenged by experiences that promote understanding of human value systems
G. To be challenged through discussions with intellectual peers
H. To be challenged by activities at complex levels of thought
I. To be challenged through opportunities for divergent production
J. To be challenged by the opportunity for real-world problem solving

From a Delphi study of student goals in gifted programs, Hickey (1988) found that experts in the field converged on only three goals at the elementary level:

1. To provide a learning environment that will permit and encourage the capable student to develop to his or her individual potential while interacting with intellectual peers.
2. To establish a climate that values and enhances intellectual ability, talent, creativity, and decision making.
3. To encourage the development of higher-level thinking skills (analysis, synthesis, evaluation) and provide opportunities for using them.

Cahill and Cahill (1995) developed a broad set of educational goals that can be used as a resource for creating IEPs as well as gifted program goals. The authors began with goals for infancy and early childhood, including fine and gross motor skills, cognitive skills, and normal stepping stones for children, such as walking and using the bathroom. Skills in this range were broken down by months. Goals and objectives then progress through preschool, major content areas, physical development, hearing, skills used in employment, and other stepping stones. The book ends with specific goals and objectives for use throughout high school.

Using the design perspective set forth in this book, educators might derive a set of cognitive goals that correspond to each of the major curriculum dimensions described and then develop affective, social/behavioral, and aesthetic goals. An example of this comprehensive approach to goal setting follows:

A. <u>Cognitive</u>

   1. To develop high-level proficiency in all core areas of learning

2. To become an independent investigator
3. To appreciate the world of ideas
4. To enhance higher-level thinking skills
5. To encourage a spirit of inquiry

B. Affective

1. To enhance self-understanding
2. To develop effective coping strategies for being labeled gifted

C. Social/Behavioral

1. To develop appropriate social skills
2. To enhance understanding of relationships

D. Aesthetic

1. To develop an appreciation of the arts
2. To enhance creative expression

Delineating Subject-Matter Goals

When undertaken by individual teachers, defining goals is not always seen as a demanding task. In the context of a school district effort to plan effectively for gifted programs, however, it can be quite challenging because the success of any such undertaking lies in the ideas as they are shaped by the collective. *Vertical team planning* is essential to the success of goal setting. Articulated goals have to represent the thinking of the kindergarten teacher as well as that of the senior high school teacher. This requires "talking through" what a content-based curriculum should engender in gifted students.

Some part of the discussion must focus on how to handle the standards in the gifted curriculum. One approach is to keep the standards as they were written and translate them at the outcome level in a way that is appropriate for gifted learners. Another approach is to modify the standards' goals for gifted learners. Although the standards documents de-emphasize goals in favor of outcomes, rendering the goal strategies somewhat as an afterthought in the curriculum design process, the goal statements are critical frames for further development in curriculum design for the gifted. In many cases, philosophical differences about what a program should be are "battled out" at this level of analysis.

In developing content-based goals for gifted curricula, the following issues should be considered:

✓ A goal represents an ideal state to be worked toward but not necessarily attained. Thus, content-based goal statements should be written in a way that students can work toward them over 13 years of schooling.
✓ Content goals for gifted programs should be closely aligned with state standards but found to be more challenging, with a greater focus on advanced study,

higher-level thinking processes, and interdisciplinary opportunities. Even at this early level of curriculum development, aspects of differentiation should be discernible.

✓ All goal statements should convey meaning at all grade levels. That is, the translation power of each goal should be as great at the kindergarten level as at Grade 12.

✓ The goal statements should be comprehensive enough to subsume all worthy objectives and activities currently being addressed in the gifted program as well as those conceptualized as ideal.

✓ The goal statements should adequately represent the focus and direction of the actual program. Although goals are idealized representations of the program, they must also be seen as having operational potential.

The initial group session for reaching consensus on the goal statements can involve several hours of discussion. The tentative list that emerges from such a planning session should be reworked by the group's facilitator in light of differentiation factors, and the group should meet again for discussion of the recast goals. By the end of this second session, the group will often have delineated a set of goal statements that satisfy all criteria. The following is a sample list of goals in the language arts area taken from the William and Mary language arts curriculum goals (Center for Gifted Education, 1998):

1. Develop literary analysis and interpretation skills.
2. Develop oral communication skills.
3. Develop linguistic competency in grammar and usage.
4. Develop persuasive writing, technical writing, and narrative skills.
5. Develop high-level reasoning skills.
6. Develop an understanding of the concept of change in the language arts and other areas of study.

Note that the first four goals are content-based, the fifth is process-based, and the sixth is concept-based. Thus, all three dimensions of curriculum—content, process, and concept—are embedded in the teaching of language arts. A similar approach may be used in other subject areas as well.

Delineating Process Goals

The group that meets to define process goals for gifted learners should be cross-disciplinary. The fundamental question the group must answer is: Which higher-order skills in what areas do we want the gifted to develop through specialized programs? The answer to that question should be multidimensional, incorporating not only critical and creative thinking skills but also ethical decision-making skills, aesthetic judgment skills, and social skills. Thus, the matrix for decision making about process goals should highlight all four of these dimensions in some way. An example of such a matrix follows:

Dimensions	Process Goals of the Gifted Program
Cognitive	To develop critical thinking and logical reasoning.
	To develop creative problem-solving abilities.
Affective	To develop moral and ethical decision-making abilities.
Aesthetic	To develop aesthetic valuing and appreciation.
Social	To develop the skills of leadership.

Because the new standards include many of these process skill emphases, all process goals should be analyzed and aligned within specific standards.

Delineating Theme-Based Goals

Just as gifted programs require content and process goals, they also must have concept (or theme) goals. A myriad of universal themes are available from which to choose. The following discussion focuses on some that are currently used in gifted programs.

The Individual Progress Program (IPP) in Seattle, Washington, emphasizes three central themes in its gifted program: origins, change, and systems. These themes are woven into curricula from Grades 1–8 using a spiral model that revisits each theme every third year.

The Charleston, West Virginia, school district's social studies curriculum guide for the gifted articulates the following concept outcomes (*Charleston High School Scope and Sequence Guide,* undated):

By the end of Grade 12, students will be able to:

1. Understand how the United States is not a purely independent entity, but that its present condition is interrelated with the historic, social, and economic development of the rest of the world.
2. Understand how change results out of conflict, individual struggle, leadership, new ideas, and accidental occurrences.
3. Know the major periods of history, including the prehistoric, ancient, classical, medieval, early modern, and contemporary, why these periods are defined as such, what elements of each led to or inhibited the arrival of the next, and the important salient aspects that transcend these eras.

Just as the new standards address process goals, they also cover important themes and concepts. Identifying these concepts and aligning the curriculum for the gifted with them is helpful. As demonstrated in Chapter 3, the concepts of "change" and "systems" are embedded across all core areas of learning in the standards as large concepts worthy of study. To elevate these concepts to a prominent role in a gifted curriculum is helpful in teaching to the standards and beyond them.

Delineating Affective Goals

Many programs for the gifted emphasize personal development. Yet, programs frequently pay only lip service to affective development, never articulating the outcomes they hope will accrue to gifted learners in this area. One approach to decision making on affective goal development is to involve counselors and teachers as equal partners in reaching consensus on goals for this area. In some cases, the local context may dictate the specific goals derived. For example, a racially torn community may wish to institute the goal of developing an appreciation of individual and group differences. A community that has experienced a recent bout of teen suicide might set a goal of helping gifted students construct meaning in their lives. A sample set of affective goals compiled from several school districts follows:

By the end of the K-12 program, the student will:

1. Demonstrate effective social interactions.
2. Demonstrate understanding and application of coping strategies through the use of journal writing.
3. Demonstrate effective leadership in the context of peer teaching experiences.
4. Develop a long-range plan that encompasses future academic and career goals.
5. Demonstrate proficiency in the acquisition of independent learning habits.

Philosophy statements and goals set an important tone for curriculum development. By the end of this stage of designing curricula, a school district has a unified and consensual focus that directs the course for further curriculum development work. Strong goal statements are grounded in good practices of differentiation for gifted learners and yet are sensitive to more localized concerns. Moreover, they attempt to define key emphases the curriculum will take at a level that students, parents, and other educators can understand and accept.

COMMUNICATING THE MEANING OF GOAL STATEMENTS

An important step beyond goal delineation must be done by the planning group: The meaning of the goals must be communicated in a way that the lay community can understand. In gifted education, an idiosyncratic jargon of specialized terms has developed that mean different things to different educators. Curriculum planners must find a way to define terms such as "critical thinking," "creative thinking," and "research skills" so they can be interpreted the same by all who are involved.

Appendix A to this chapter reprints a course of study developed for use in Muskingum County, Ohio, by local and county directors of gifted programs (Muskingum County Board of Education, 1990). It provides an example of appropriate philosophy and goal statements for gifted programs and delineates transitional objectives to help teachers, parents, and students better understand what the goals would mean in classroom practice.

Appendix A illustrates one way of handling the definition of terms: to translate each major goal into underlying objectives that represent constituent elements of the goal. Another approach might be to develop a glossary of terms.

The goal phase of curriculum development is critical for the next stage of the design model—defining specific learning outcomes. It also provides educators with a sense of how to translate goals into classroom practice. One model for aiding in that translation involves delineating goals and then linking them to a small set of corresponding teaching-learning models that correspond to the intention of the goal. The following chart is instructive in that regard.

Curriculum Goal	Teaching Model
To develop critical thinking	Paul model of reasoning Questioning model
To develop creative thinking	Concept mapping Creative problem-solving model
To develop research skills	William and Mary research model Problem-based learning
To understand broad overarching interdisciplinary concepts	Taba model of concept development

Teachers can address these goals by selecting one of the scaffolds noted and then working out specific activities and resources based on the scaffold. In this way, curriculum design is moved forward beyond the stated goals.

Many school districts with strong gifted programs now incorporate content, process, and concept goals routinely into their curriculum frameworks. Appendix B to this chapter provides examples of goal statements from Fairfax County, Virginia, Virginia Beach, Virginia, Greenwich, Connecticut, and the South Carolina Consortium on Gifted and Talented.

SUMMARY

An operative philosophy and set of goal statements provide direction to curriculum development and create a consensual perspective among constituent groups regarding what the curriculum should be. Philosophy and goals should be translated into written statements of purpose for a gifted program. They should then be adopted by school boards, if possible, to give them the stature of policy.

There are different approaches to generating goals and different types of goals. From the student's perspective, the gifted have cognitive, affective, social/behavioral, and aesthetic needs. Along this needs dimension, educators might develop content-based goal statements, process goals, theme-based goals, and affective goals. The key to successful implementation of goals is to communicate their meaning to students, parents, and educators.

QUESTIONS FOR REFLECTION

1. What do curriculum goals communicate about a gifted program?
2. How can we create goals that balance concerns for cognitive and affective development, for aesthetic appreciation and leadership skills, and for creative productivity and proficiency in core areas?
3. How do values and beliefs shape thinking about curriculum goals in a school district?
4. How does the need to align curriculum goals with state standards advance the work of gifted educators in curriculum development? How does it impede this work?
5. How can a philosophy and set of goals be translated into action at the classroom level?

REFERENCES

Cahill, D., & Cahill, M. (1995). *Goal mine.* Fork Union, VA: IEP.

Center for Gifted Education. (1998). *Guide to teaching a language arts curriculum for high-ability learners.* Dubuque, IA: Kendall/Hunt.

Charleston High School Scope and Sequence Guide. (Undated). Charleston, WV.

Dewey, J. (1975). *Art as experience.* New York: Capricorn Books.

DiNunno, L. (1982). *Curricular decision making in program development for the gifted and talented.* Unpublished doctoral dissertation, University of Virginia, Charlottesville.

Fairfax County, Virginia, Curriculum Framework. (2000). Williamsburg, VA: Center for Gifted Education.

Hickey, G. (1988). Goals for gifted programs: Perceptions of interested groups. *Gifted Child Quarterly, 32,* 231–233.

Muskingum County Board of Education. (1990). *Muskingum County course of study for the gifted.* Zanesville, OH: Author.

Phillips, D. (1995). The good, the bad, and the ugly: The many faces of constructivism. *Educational Researcher, 24,* 5–12.

Rogers, B. (1999). Conflicting approaches to curriculum: Recognizing how fundamental beliefs can sustain or sabotage school reform. *Peabody Journal of Education, 74,* 29–67.

Squires, D. (1995). *ATLAS community's "break the mold" curriculum ideas.* Unpublished manuscript, ATLAS Seminar, Providence, RI.

Tyler, R. W. (1962). *Basic principles of curriculum and instruction.* Chicago: The University of Chicago Press.

VanTassel-Baska, J. (Ed.). (1998). *Excellence in educating gifted and talented learners* (3rd ed.). Denver: Love Publishing.

APPENDIX A TO CHAPTER 6

Muskingum County Course of Study for Gifted Students Position Statement

Gifted students have been identified as a population in our schools that requires a differentiated curriculum of greater challenge, more complexity and abstraction, and faster paced instruction. We recognize the diverse instructional levels of the individuals within the identified gifted population, and these differences make creating a common course of study a complex task. However, we believe that to ensure learning progress on a continuum and to avoid a hit-and-miss approach to instruction, a course of study for the gifted can serve as an invaluable document.

The areas included in this course of study are multidisciplinary in nature and reflect the essential content defined in the Ohio Rules for School Foundation Units for Gifted Children. This course of study reflects the common needs of gifted children in the Superior Cognitive, Specific Academic, and Creative Thinking categories. Gifted students must be given opportunities to develop competence in the areas of creative thinking, critical thinking, creative problem solving, higher level thinking (Bloom's taxonomy), logical thinking, research methods, oral and written expression, and social-emotional development. These essential areas are critical to enable gifted students to make full use of their capabilities and to enable them to perform at levels of excellence in their unique talent areas.

The purpose of this course of study is to guide and assist classroom teachers in serving the gifted child in the regular classroom. By including broad-based goals with sample objectives, teachers may use this document as a tool to develop challenging and appropriate curricula for the gifted at any level and within any core domain of inquiry. We support and encourage the teacher practice of prescriptive instruction, in which pre-assessment is used to determine the instructional levels of individual students. We also support the development of curricula for gifted students that progress at an appropriate pace and depth within a multidisciplinary framework based on the child's instructional level. The development of this curricula must be ongoing and allow for evaluation and revision when appropriate.

Goal 1:
The Student Will Develop Higher-Order Thinking Skills as Related to Bloom's Taxonomy.

Student Objectives:

1. The student will develop the cognitive process of *analysis.*
2. The student will develop the cognitive process of *synthesis.*
3. The student will develop the cognitive process of *evaluation.*

Goal 2:
The Student Will Think Critically in Response to Given Information.

Student Objectives:

1. The student will demonstrate the ability to *define* and *clarify* given information.
2. The student will demonstrate the ability to *judge* given information.
3. The student will demonstrate the ability to *infer/solve* problems and *draw* reasonable conclusions.

Goal 3:
The Student Will Reason Logically.

Student Objectives:

1. The student will demonstrate the ability to apply basic argument forms.
2. The student will reason logically using deductive methods.
3. The student will reason logically using nondeductive methods.

Goal 4:
The Student Will Develop Divergent Thinking Processes.

Student Objectives:

1. The student will develop *fluency.*
2. The student will develop *flexibility.*
3. The student will develop *originality.*
4. The student will develop *elaboration.*

Goal 5:
The Student Will Develop Competency in the Six Steps of Creative Problem Solving.

Student Objectives:

1. The student will use *mess* finding to solve real and fictitious problems.
2. The student will use *data* finding to solve real and fictitious problems.
3. The student will use *problem* finding to solve real and fictitious problems.
4. The student will use *idea* finding to solve real and fictitious problems.
5. The student will use *solution* finding to solve real and fictitious problems.
6. The student will use *acceptance* finding to solve real and fictitious problems.

Goal 6:
The Student Wil Develop an Understanding of, Learn to Appreciate, and Practice the Science and the Art of Oral Communication.

Student Objectives:

1. The student will recognize, prepare, and deliver the basic types of speeches.

2. The student will learn and demonstrate various forms of group communication (dyads, triads, etc.).
3. The student will understand and appreciate various aspects of drama.
4. The student will interpret and translate orally the meaning of selected works of art (linguistically, mathematically, musically, spatially, and/or kinesthetically).

Goal 7:
The Student Will Develop Written Expression Through Knowledge and Application of the Writing Process Model.

Student Objectives:

1. The student will learn and apply *pre-writing* techniques to generate and clarify ideas.
2. The student will transfer pre-writing experiences in *drafting* forms.
3. The student will achieve clarity and precision in composing by learning and using strategies of *responding.*
4. The student will achieve clarity and precision in composing by learning and using strategies of *revising.*
5. The student will learn and apply *editing* strategies for conformity to standard American English.
6. The student will prepare written products in forms to be *published* for real and varied audiences.

Goal 8:
The Student Will Learn and Apply Various Composing Strategies and Techniques.

Student Objectives:

1. The student will strengthen writing clarity and precision through the development of word meaning using formal and informal word study.

Goal 9:
The Student Will Develop Written Expressions Through Exposure to and Practice of the Various Forms Of Writing.

Student Objectives:

1. The student will learn and apply the techniques used in *personal writing.*
2. The student will learn and apply the techniques used in *functional writing.*
3. The student will learn and apply the techniques used in *transitional writing.*
4. The student will learn and apply the techniques used in *artistic writing.*

Goal 10:
The Student Will Become Actively Involved in Inquiry Into an Investigation of Student Selection and Design.

Student Objectives:

1. The student will select a research question to be investigated through a method appropriate to the content area/core domain:
   — scientific method
   — historical approach
   — case study approach
   — survey approach
2. The student will share the product with an appropriate audience, including presentations at academic competitions.

Goal 11:
The Student Will Demonstrate Facility in Using Various Sources of Information to Conduct Research.

Student Objectives:

1. The student will experience library/media that go beyond the regular public school library's offerings:
   — CD Rom
   — microfiche
   — ERIC system
   — audiovisuals
   — research journals
2. The student will refer to mentors and other experts for pertinent information.
3. The student will use computers when appropriate as tools for locating, organizing, storing, and analyzing information for use in the research process.

Goal 12:
The Student Will Develop Appropriate Self-Expectations.

Student Objectives:

1. The student will evaluate goals in terms of the student's personal abilities, performance, interests and personality.
2. The student will deal effectively with success or lack of success.
3. The student will be aware of the impact of self-expectations on himself or herself.
4. The student will distinguish between boredom and lack of familiarity.
5. The student will develop willingness to undertake tasks that have uncertain outcomes.

6. The student will recognize stress and possess awareness of stress reduction behaviors.
7. The student will develop the techniques for time management.
8. The student will recognize patterns of perfectionism and possess awareness of strategies for addressing perfectionism.

Goal 13:
The Student Will Develop and Maintain Positive Interpersonal Relationships.

Student Objectives:

1. The student will recognize the influence of peer pressure.
2. The student will develop empathy and sensitivity for the feelings of others.
3. The student will develop appropriate ways to interact with authority.
4. The student will accept and offer constructive criticism.

APPENDIX B TO CHAPTER 6
Sample Goal Statements

Fairfax County, Virginia, Goal Statements

Goal 1: To develop an understanding for systems of knowledge, themes, issues, and problems that frame the external world (i.e., "the big picture").

Goal 2: To provide for the mastery and enrichment of the core standards of learning in all curriculum areas, using appropriate resources, including technology, at a pace, depth, and intensity appropriate to the capacity of able learners.

Goal 3: To develop cognitive and metacognitive skills that foster independent self-directed learning.

Goal 4: To develop self-understanding.

Goal 5: To develop social skills that enable students to build their leadership skills, interpersonal skills, and ability to effectively relate to others in a variety of situations.

Virginia Beach, Virginia, Goal Statements

Goal 1: To develop an understanding for systems of knowledge, themes, issues, and problems that frame the external world.

Goal 2: To provide for rigorous, divergent content learning experiences in all areas of learning designated by the Virginia Beach Objectives.

Goal 3: To develop metacognitive skills that foster independent and self-directed learning.

Goal 4:   To develop critical thinking skills.

Goal 5:   To cultivate the creative process in a safe learning environment that promotes student confidence.

Goal 6:   To develop problem-solving skills.

Goal 7:   To develop research skills and methods.

Greenwich, Connecticut, Goal Statements

The program emphasis will be on the following goals:

✓ To provide appropriate-level instruction in reading and math.

✓ To promote critical thinking and higher-order reasoning skills.

✓ To develop creative problem-solving skills.

✓ To develop metacognitive skills that foster independent and self-directed learning.

✓ To foster a sustained commitment when faced with challenging learning situations.

✓ To provide access to advanced resources that will support the development of talent in math and reading.

South Carolina Consortium on Gifted and Talented Goal Statements

Goal 1:   To support mastery of core areas learning at a pace and depth appropriate for gifted and talented learners.

Goal 2:   To develop an understanding of the concepts, themes, and issues that are fundamental to the disciplines and an appreciation for interrelationships among the disciplines.

Goal 3:   To develop independent learning skills.

Goal 4:   To develop critical, creative thinking, problem-solving, and decision-making skills.

Goal 5:   To develop high-level communication skills.

Goal 6:   To develop aesthetic appreciation and creative expression.

7

DEVELOPING LEARNER OUTCOMES

The practice of stating learning objectives in American education has always been linked to a strong behaviorist orientation (Bloom, Hastings, & Madaus, 1971; Mager, 1962). Even today, thinking about curriculum considers stated learner outcomes* to be central to the teaching-learning enterprise (Gronlund, 1995; Kemp, Morrison & Ross, 1998; Shulman, 1987). Moreover, most states have instituted a set of standards that codify outcome statements for all learners from kindergarten through 12th grade. This has become the accepted form for expressing overall curriculum expectations. Gifted education has the task of translating these typically minimum outcomes into more appropriate ones for gifted learners.

Learner outcomes constitute perhaps the most crucial part of the curriculum design model, serving several functions in the curriculum (VanTassel-Baska, 1992):

✓ Learner outcomes delineate student expectations. They specify how much and in what areas gifted students will be educated at a particular level.
✓ Learner outcomes guide the assessment process by indicating what learning is valued and to what level of attainment students should aspire.
✓ Learner outcomes also guide the selection of key activities, materials, and strategies for use in classrooms with gifted learners. Without their specifications, curriculum for the gifted becomes a series of disconnected experiences, workbooks, and gimmicks.

These functions are shown graphically in Figure 7.1.

---

* The term *learner outcomes* is used throughout this chapter to mean the specific stated purposes that justify any given learning experience. This term is loosely synonymous with *learning objectives*. Differences reside in the emphasis on the student and his or her assessment in *learner outcomes*, in contrast to the process emphasis in the term *learning objective*.

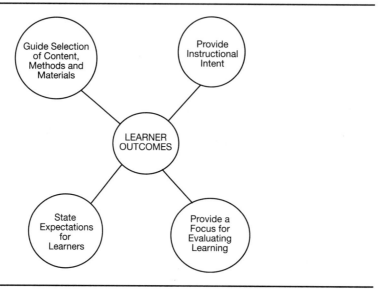

FIGURE 7.1   Functions of Learner Outcomes

Learner outcomes focus on outcomes or products rather than process. An important question to ask when formulating outcomes is, "What do I want gifted learners to be able to know and/or do after completing a study of this unit, topic, or course?"

Because learner outcomes specify student behaviors anticipated at a particular developmental point, they provide the basis for creating worthwhile learning experiences, setting appropriate expectations, and assessing the extent of learning attained. The following are examples of gifted student learner outcomes:

✓ Third-grade gifted students will prepare a science project using a scientific process—selecting a topic of interest, reading about the topic, designing an experiment to test a question of interest, completing the experiment, and communicating the results through a poster and oral presentation.

✓ Ninth-grade gifted students will conduct a community survey on a topic of interest and analyze the results using basic statistics.

Learner outcomes should be (a) appropriately challenging for gifted students at the requisite stage of development, (b) linked to specific areas of study within the general education school curriculum, (c) substantive and worthy of substantial instructional time and student independent time, and (d) assessable through authentic approaches.

THE BASIS FOR OUTCOMES

Outcomes are derived from goals and needs assessment data that suggest particular emphases necessary for enhancing student learning in a particular area. Thus, both goal analysis and needs assessment analysis should precede the derivation of learner outcomes. The following four-step process may be employed in carrying out the formulation of learner outcomes:

1. Identify essential knowledge, skills, and attitudes students must master to reach a goal or satisfy a need.
2. Cluster these lists of knowledge, skills, and attitudes by goal.
3. Write outcome statements that encompass the lists for each goal.
4. Write additional outcomes as required to address needs as they are identified. Then cluster the outcomes with the appropriate goals.

APPROACHES TO DEVELOPING LEARNER OUTCOMES

A Bottom-up Approach

A useful way to develop learner outcomes in districts that have ongoing gifted programs is for the teachers at each grade level to report what is occurring in the gifted program at their level, what materials are used, and what outcomes are expected for each goal statement. The curriculum writer then synthesizes the data across all necessary levels of the curriculum, frames learner outcomes by grade-level clusters within each goal statement, and returns the draft outcomes to the teachers for feedback. The teachers analyze the objectives to ensure that they accurately reflect the gifted program goals, are sufficiently challenging, and are broad enough in scope. A follow-up session is scheduled to talk through any discrepancies, issues, concerns, and misinterpretations. Subsequent to this session, a revised set of outcomes can be prepared. The schedule for this phase is given in Table 7.1. The same approach can be used to generate learner outcomes in all four core domains of learning.

The following example from a language arts scope and sequence document (VanTassel-Baska, 1988) illustrates a sequence of learner outcomes developed through this process. The example illustrates the relationship of a goal to its corresponding learner outcomes.

TABLE 7.1   Schedule for Developing Learner Outcomes

Task	Time Frame
Grade level teachers write key outcomes, activities and materials that address each goal statement.	1–2 months
Curriculum writer synthesizes all teachers' submissions and distills them into learner outcomes by grade-level clusters.	2 months
Grade-level teachers review work.	1 month
Grade-level teachers and curriculum writer meet to clarify issues and resolve misinterpretations and discrepancies.	1 day
Curriculum writer revises document based on mutual agreement with teachers.	1 month

Sample Language Arts Goal in Literature

As a result of K-12 gifted programs, students will be able to analyze and evaluate various forms and ideas in significant literature representative of different cultures and eras.

Sequence of Learner Outcomes

I. By the end of *Grade 3*, gifted students should be able to:
  A. Identify the basic literary forms of drama, poetry, short stories, nonfiction, letters, myths and fables, biography, and autobiography.
  B. Compare and contrast literary forms.
  C. Compare and contrast ideas from selections read.
  D. Identify the literary structures of character, plot, setting, and theme in each literary form studied.
  E. Compare and contrast literary devices.
  F. Identify character behavior in selected literature.
  G. Evaluate the effectiveness of alternative endings to selected pieces of literature.
  H. Create a "literary piece" in each form.

II. By the end of *Grade 6*, gifted students should be able to:
  A. Identify the literary devices important to each literary form (e.g., poetry; use of imagery, simile, metaphor, rhyme, alliteration, onomatopoeia, etc.).

B. Compare and contrast cultural differences revealed through the works of literature read.

C. Create a piece of literature in any form or style based on a given idea.

D. Infer cultural issues from the study of literary works.

E. Analyze the use of symbols in selected pieces of literature.

III. By the end of *Grade 8,* gifted students should be able to:

A. Analyze and interpret form and idea in "moderately difficult" literary selections.

B. Compare and contrast literary works from different cultures and eras based on a common theme.

C. Employ appropriate critical reading behaviors in encountering new reading material (e.g., finding the main idea, making appropriate inferences, evaluating data given, discerning author's tone).

D. Interpret character motivation in selected literature.

IV. By the end of *Grade 12,* gifted students should be able to:

A. Analyze and interpret form and idea in "difficult" literary selections.

B. Compare and contrast disparate works of literature according to form, style, ideas, cultural milieu, point of view, historical context, and personal relevance.

C. Evaluate any new piece of literature encountered.

D. Create a piece of literature in a chosen form that successfully integrates form and meaning.

E. Evaluate the potential impact of selected literary works on individual or collective value systems and philosophies.

A Top-down Approach

Another approach to delineating appropriate gifted learner outcomes across several years is to use state or locally derived learner outcomes as a point of departure and then adapt them to appropriate outcomes for gifted learners at key stages of development. The example in Table 7.2 is derived from the Georgia State Department of Education (1992) resource guide for secondary English teachers. The core curriculum outcome statements are given in the lefthand column; the corresponding outcome statements adapted for gifted learners appear in the righthand column, in which expectations for performance of gifted learners shift to a higher and more complex level.

TABLE 7.2   Example of General Outcomes Differentiated for the Gifted

Quality Core Curriculum for All Learners	Differentiation for Gifted Learners
• Uses literal comprehension skills (e.g., sequencing, explicitly stated main idea) • Uses inferential comprehension skills (e.g., predictions, comparisons conclusions, implicitly stated main idea, propaganda techniques)	• Demonstrates proficiency in working with inference, inductive and deductive reasoning, analogies, assumptions, and evaluation of arguments in literature read
• Identifies and comprehends the main and subordinate ideas in a written work and summarizes ideas in own words	• Analyzes literary themes as they are developed within and across authors
• Recognizes different purposes and methods of writing; identifies a writer's point of view and tone • Interprets a writer's meaning inferentially as well as literally • Identifies personal opinions and assumptions of a writer	• Discusses and synthesizes ideas about an author's form and content • Develops an essay that compares key purposes and methods of writing of two authors
• Comprehends a variety of materials	• Evaluates a given reading selection according to a set of criteria or standards
• Uses the features of print materials appropriately (e.g., table of contents, preface, introduction, titles and subtitles, index, glossary, appendix, bibliography)	• Creates a written product incorporating all major features of a novel, biography, autobiography, poetry, short stories, or book of essays
• Defines unfamiliar words by using appropriate word recognition skills	• Masters advanced adult vocabulary
• Is aware of important writers representing diverse backgrounds and traditions • Is familiar with mythology, especially Greek and Roman • Reads and compares world literature	• Compares and contrasts disparate works of literature according to form, style, ideas, milieu, point of view, historical context, and personal relevance

TABLE 7.2   *(Continued)*

Quality Core Curriculum for All Learners	Differentiation for Gifted Learners
• Develops effective ways of telling and writing about literature • Is familiar with the structural elements of literature, (plot, characterization, and so on)	• Creates a "literary piece" in a self-selected form at a level appropriate for contest submission, using appropriate structural elements and literary devices
• Judges literature critically on the basis of personal response and literary quality	• Evaluates any new piece of literature encountered according to key criteria such as use of language, unity of purpose, characterization, and credibility of main ideas
• Reads, discusses and interprets book-length works of fiction and nonfiction	• Analyzes and interprets form and idea in "difficult" literary selections
• Selects and uses a variety of print and nonprint resources to become familiar with and compare literature	• Using multiple resources, creates a critical essay comparing two pieces of literature
• Is familiar with the similarities and differences of various literary genres • Reads a literary text analytically • Sees relationships between form and content	• Creates a piece of literature in a chosen form that successfully integrates form and meaning
• Develops an understanding of the chronology of American literature • Develops an understanding of the effect of history on American literature, (e.g., literary movements and periods) • Reads and discusses representative works of American literature and American authors	• Analyzes and interprets key ideas represented by selected literature, art, and music of any given culture • Compares and contrasts the concepts of cultural identity, national identity, and global interdependence as evidenced by selected pieces of literature

A comparison of the two columns in Table 7.2 reveals several "differentiation" issues. The gifted learner outcomes consistently reflect the following features:

✓ *Greater focus on higher-level thinking tasks.* Choice of higher-level verbs such as "analyze" and "create" push the expectation for student performance higher.

✓ *More complex tasks.* Provision of more variables for students to manipulate increases the challenge level of the outcome demand.

✓ *Expectation of more sophisticated "products."* The product expectations routinely are higher in respect to complexity and depth.

✓ *Expectation that lower-level outcomes will be achieved more readily.* Typically, lower-level outcomes are subsumed by higher-order ones, implying that they are quickly mastered on the road to higher-level proficiency.

✓ *Promotion of creative responses to material.* Provision of opportunities for interpreting outcomes in multiple ways enhances the likelihood of creative response.

✓ *Broadened scope of learner experiences.* By incorporating multiple areas of learning, gifted outcomes promote learning breadth.

✓ *Emphasizes on multiple perspectives.* By promoting comparative analysis across authors and works, outcomes help students begin to grapple with profound differences in ideas and style.

✓ *Provision for thematic exploration.* Use of higher-order concepts and themes as organizers for discussion and follow-up application often deepens student understanding of how literature reflects the world.

Learner outcomes should be stated in relationship to a specific time frame for attainment. Teachers may wish to focus on a daily set of outcomes, a weekly set, unit outcomes over 9 weeks, an annual set of outcomes, or even multiyear outcomes. All of these time units are meaningful in curriculum implementation and correspond to the curriculum development "chunks" found in many gifted programs. Table 7.3 compares 6-week, 18-week, annual, and multiyear examples of outcomes for gifted programs.

More specific learner outcomes also can be developed, grounded in a particular topic or content piece. Curry and Samora, (1990) developed the following algorithm for creating these more specific learner outcomes, which are also highly product-based:

In a study of _____ , the students will be able to use what they have learned to _____ and will share their ideas through a _____ , a _____ , a _____ , or a self-selected product.

Example:

In a study of Shakespeare, the students will be able to use what they have learned to analyze famous Shakespearean women and will share their ideas through a performance, a videotape, an essay, or a self-selected product.

TABLE 7.3   A Comparison of Learner Outcomes by Time and Grade

Learner Outcomes	Time Unit	Grade Level of Outcome
By the end of the unit, gifted learners will be able to compare and contrast literary themes in selected short stories.	6 weeks	Upper Elementary
By the end of the unit, gifted learners will be able to evaluate the validity of an argument in written form.	18 weeks	Middle School
By the end of the year, gifted learners will be able to construct an argument supporting any given important issue.	36 weeks	9th Grade
By the end of four years, gifted learners will be able to analyze and interpret any given passage from classical or contemporary literature.	4 years	12th Grade

Behavioral Objective Format Versus Cognitive Objective Format

Learner outcomes can be written in behavioral or cognitive terms. An advantage to writing learner outcomes in behavioral terms is that criterion levels for evaluation are explicit. Two examples of this approach follow:

✓ By the end of the year, 90% of gifted learners will increase their ability to handle inference problems by at least 20% as measured by the Cornell Test of Critical Thinking.

✓ By the end of the program, 100% of the gifted learners will complete a satisfactory research paper as judged by receiving at least 80 out of 100 points on a predetermined assessment form.

However, the current emphasis on higher-level cognitive outcomes measured by performance and portfolio assessment suggests that cognitive outcome clusters may be a superior form of representing outcomes for gifted learners. Examples of this approach follow:

✓ *Finds selected information using the Internet*

1. Finds an article on a given topic.
2. Compiles a bibliography of related literature.
3. Identifies narrower and broader terms for a search.

✓ *Interprets a graph*

1. Determines the group that sold the most and the least.
2. Determines the groups that were below average.
3. Determines the mean, median, and mode of sales annually.

✓ *Conducts effective meetings*

1. Prepares an agenda prior to the meeting.
2. Arranges the room for effective communication.
3. States the intended outcomes at the beginning of the meeting.

SELECTING LANGUAGE THAT COMMUNICATES LEVEL OF EXPECTATION

Word choice frequently is crucial in constructing curriculum documents that must convey important aspects of differentiation to various audiences. The language of learner outcomes can be especially problematic, because it must reflect the intent of a broad goal yet be circumscribed by a specific time frame for measurement of student learning. Consequently, learner outcome language often requires more thought and effort than typically expended in curriculum development. Teachers tend to favor broader statements of student expectations that can leave too much room for student interpretation.

Verbs that are useful for shaping cognitive outcomes are listed in Table 7.4. Based on Bloom's taxonomic categories, the list provides a guide for selecting verbs that correspond to the higher-level thinking categories of application, analysis, synthesis, and evaluation.

LINKING LEARNER OUTCOMES TO ACTIVITIES

An aspect of curriculum design that is sometimes overlooked is the linkage system among the various levels of individual learner outcomes, which become more specific in stated form as the outcomes approach the level of activities. The linkage between an outcome and teaching activities is a critical one. Many times teachers have difficulty seeing the pathway between these two levels in the design process and may prefer to focus only at the level of teaching activities without developing an explicit statement about the desired outcomes for learners. Curriculum planners

TABLE 7.4   Verbs That May Be Used to Shape Cognitive Outcomes*

Knowledge (recall information)	Comprehension (interpret information in one's own words)	Application (use knowledge or generalization in a new situation)	Analysis (break knowledge into parts and show relationship among parts)	Synthesis (bring together parts of knowledge to form a whole and build relationships for new situations)	Evaluation (make judgments on basis of given criteria)
arrange	classify	apply	analyze	arrange	appraise
define	describe	choose	appraise	assemble	argue
duplicate	discuss	demon-	calculate	collect	assess
label	explain	strate	categorize	compose	attack
list	express	dramatize	compare	construct	choose
match	identify	employ	contrast	create	compare
memorize	indicate	illustrate	criticize	design	defend
name	locate	interpret	diagram	formulate	estimate
order	recognize	operate	differentiate	manage	evaluate
recall	report	practice	discriminate	organize	judge
recognize	restate	prepare	distinguish	plan	predict
relate	review	schedule	examine	prepare	rate
repeat	select	sketch	experiment	propose	score
reproduce	sort	solve	inventory	set up	select
	tell	use	question	synthesize	support
	translate		test	write	value

*Depending on the meaning intended, some verbs may apply to more than one level.

must find appropriate ways to express the relationship across these two levels. The model in Figure 7.2 illustrates alternative pathways that connect learner outcomes to teaching activities.

Linkage Through Sub-outcomes

As shown in the figure, one pathway is to create sub-outcomes that provide greater specificity and direction for activities. This transition often is helpful in gifted curricula, especially when the framing of learner outcomes is fairly broad and complex and spans multiple years of work. Sub-outcomes can clarify for grade-level teachers specific outcomes for which they are responsible, as illustrated in the following example for elementary-level language arts.

Sample Learner Outcome for Language Arts: By the end of Grade 3, students should be able to use appropriate texts such as fiction, nonfiction, poetry, letters, directions, and reference material to accomplish the various purposes for reading.

Transition 1: Learner Sub-outcomes

A. By the end of Grade 3, students should be able to use appropriate texts for reading aloud.
B. By the end of Grade 3, students should be able to use appropriate texts to learn new vocabulary.
C. By the end of Grade 3, students should be able to use appropriate texts to understand the meaning of what they read.

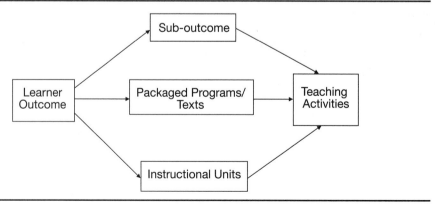

FIGURE 7.2   Alternative Linkages Between Learner Outcomes and Teaching Activities

Transition 2: Learner Sub-outcomes at Specific Grade Level

A. By the end of Grade 1, students should be able to understand directions and act on them appropriately.
B. By the end of Grade 1, students should be able to read children's literature and interpret meaning.
C. By the end of Grade 1, students should be able to read poetry aloud with expression and creative movement.

Learning Activities Needed for Grade 1 Sub-outcomes

A. Students will read and interpret various signs and symbols.
B. Students will form literary groups to discuss selected children's literature.
C. Students will conduct poetry readings and dramatize individual poems.

Resources Needed for Specific Grade 1 Sub-outcomes

A. Signs and Symbols Unit (teacher-developed)
B. Junior Great Books, Level 1
C. *Poetry for Young Children,* Tasha Tudor
D. Story and poetry tapes

Sub-outcomes can also be created that specify the layers of analysis necessary to achieve the outcome and thereby provide direction to the development of activities. Sub-outcomes that link objectives and activities in this way are shown in the following example.

Topic: Renaissance and Reformation

Goal: To understand the changes that took place in European civilization during the Middle Ages.

Outcome: The learner will be able to analyze and interpret the significant developments that led to a world view rather than a continental view.

Sub-outcomes: ✓ Distinguish economic developments that emerged in medieval Europe.
✓ Analyze the political, religious, social, and psychological forces that helped create the Reformation.
✓ Assess the intellectual accomplishments of the 12th century in comparison to the coming Renaissance accomplishments.

With sub-outcomes such as those in the example just cited, curriculum developers can see a clear pathway to specific curriculum development work yet not lose sight of the levels of analysis required.

Linkage Through Packaged Programs or Texts

A second pathway for connecting learner outcomes to teaching activities is through the use of packaged programs or textbooks that are already organized around the desired outcomes. Many programs for the gifted employ heavy use of text materials and packaged programs, yet the educators do not have a clear sense of how the materials might be adapted or used to highlight desired outcomes of the program.

Typically this pathway links multiple outcomes to teaching activities. The example that follows illustrates how the organization of a packaged program, in this case Junior Great Books, fulfills major elements contained in three language arts outcomes for the gifted learner. Individual discussion activities based on a preselected set of readings then provide the core teaching activities that complete the linkage process.

Using a Textbook or Classroom Program Approach

Learner Outcomes

1. By the end of Grade 6, students should be able to use appropriate texts such as fiction, nonfiction, poetry, letters, directories, and reference material to accomplish the various purposes of reading.
2. By the end of Grade 6, students should be able to read and enjoy selected American literature and literature from other countries.
3. By the end of Grade 6, students should be able to summarize the important ideas of the text and the important supporting details.

Major Transitional Approach: Junior Great Books Program

1. Provides exposure to and understanding of classical and contemporary literature of various genres.
2. Develops interpretive literary skills that stress comprehension, careful textual reading, and analysis.
3. Develops discussion skills such as listening, summarizing ideas, using social cues, question-asking, and taking responsibility for contributing orally.

Linkage Through Instructional Units

The third pathway for linking learner outcomes to teaching activities is through the use of special instructional units constructed by teachers or others that deliberately address major outcomes in a gifted program. An example follows:

Learner outcome:

Gifted students will be able to improve their skills in solving inference problems and analogies as measured by an appropriate pre-post instrument.

Teacher-constructed instructional unit:

A teacher may choose to develop an instructional unit on analogic and inference problems that provides short-term objectives and key activities, such as:

By the end of the unit, gifted students will be able to construct an argument using analogical reasoning.

1. *Students will engage in group problem solving of complex analogies and derive the decisions and rules for solution.*
2. *Students will conduct library research on a current topic of interest and develop a position paper regarding the topic.*
3. *Students will construct an oral argument using analogies to present their position.*

Each of these examples provides a linkage structure for connecting learner outcomes and teaching activities. Making explicit the stages of transition in this part of the curriculum design allows educators of the gifted to teach more precisely and thereby helps to ensure that outcome levels are as high as they might be. It also helps to expose the fallacy of thinking that outcomes are irrelevant and that only activities are important. A well-planned curriculum for the gifted has no substitute. Criterial questions to consider in developing outcomes for a gifted program include the following:

1. Are they appropriate for gifted learners at the requisite stage of development?
2. Are they substantive and worthy?
3. Are they measurable?
4. Are they clearly stated?

SUMMARY

Stating learner outcomes for gifted curricula is an essential part of the design task, for this process is central to being able to assess the impact of the curriculum on students. This chapter provided examples of short-term and multiyear learner outcomes. Several approaches to writing outcomes and multiple means of translating them into meaningful curriculum experiences for gifted learners were demonstrated. Moreover, the chapter delineated key distinctions between learner outcomes developed for all students and those developed for gifted learners.

QUESTIONS FOR REFLECTION

1. What are the stated learner outcomes for a given school district gifted curriculum? At what levels are they assessed?
2. How comprehensive are the learner outcomes for a given school district curriculum? Do they link back to goals and forward to activities?

3. Do you think it is possible to create a data bank of appropriate learner outcomes for the gifted based on student profile information? If so, how might such a bank be used?

4. Can appropriate expectation levels be set for gifted students' learning or does the nature of gifted learners defy such attempts? Explain.

REFERENCES

Bloom, B., Hastings, J., & Madaus, G. (1971). *Handbook on formative and summative evaluation of student learning.* New York: McGraw-Hill.

Curry, J., & Samora, J. (1990). *Writing units that challenge: A guidebook for and by educators.* Portland, ME: Maine Educators of the Gifted and Talented.

Georgia State Department of Education Resource Guide for Secondary Teachers of the Gifted. (1992). Atlanta: Georgia State Department of Education.

Gronlund, N. E. (1995). *How to write and use instructional objectives* (6th ed.). Upper Saddle River, NJ: Merrill.

Kemp, J. E., Morrison, G. R., & Ross, S. M. (1998). *Designing effective instruction* (2nd ed.). Upper Saddle River, NJ: Merrill.

Mager, R. (1962). *Preparing objectives for instructing.* Belmont, CA: Fearon.

Shulman, L. S. (1987). Assessment for teaching: An initiative for the profession. *Phi Delta Kappan, 69,* 38–44.

VanTassel-Baska, J. (1988). Developing a comprehensive approach to scope and sequence: Curriculum alignment. *Gifted Child Today, 11*(5), September–October 1988, 42–45.

VanTassel-Baska, J. (1992). *Developing learner outcomes for gifted students* (*ERIC Digest* No. E514). Reston, VA: Council for Exceptional Children. (ERIC Clearinghouse on Handicapped and Gifted Children No. ED 352 775)

8

DESIGNING ACTIVITIES AND SELECTING RESOURCES

onstructing activities for the gifted has received more attention than possibly any other aspect of curriculum development. Many current curriculum resources emphasize the importance of creating multiple menus (Renzulli, Leppien, & Hays, 2000) and developing tiered instruction that provides alternative levels of work to learners functioning at different levels in inclusive classrooms (Tomlinson, 1999). The demanding task of developing activities in the numbers required for a gifted program can be facilitated by employing an overarching set of strategies that reduces the teacher's workload of having to create myriad activities for gifted learners. This chapter begins, then, by delineating some key issues and related strategies involved in developing appropriate activities for the gifted. Important features of appropriate activities are illustrated in Figure 8.1.

The first issue is the importance of matching activities to a desired learner outcome. One way to ensure this process is to develop an "outcome cluster" that includes at least four activities to be used in developing student learning in a given direction. For an example, see the following cluster of activities based on the sample outcome given.

Learner Outcome:

The student will be able to demonstrate evidence of prejudice in news media presentations.

Activities:

1. Collect articles that reflect prejudice.
2. Trace placement of articles within the daily news.
3. Compare newsweeklies, opinion magazines, and newspaper reports to see how news is reported.

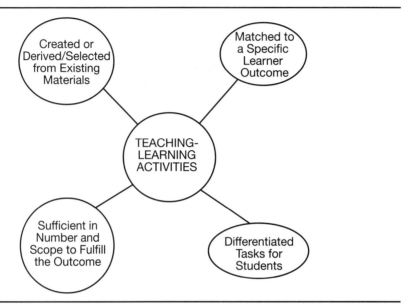

FIGURE 8.1   Key Features of Activities for the Gifted

4. Analyze the coverage of nightly television news programs, citing major stories, type of coverage, and potential biases.
5. Prepare a visual, written, or performance product that illustrates how prejudice operates in the news media.

Each activity relates to at least one aspect of the intent of the outcome, with the cluster fulfilling the parameters of the outcome. Creating such activity clusters is a useful strategy for developing a carefully articulated curriculum.

A second issue revolves around the question of how many activities and what types of activities are necessary to fulfill the outcome statement. If the outcome is sufficiently differentiated, and therefore complex, teachers must be careful to discern and address all the components of the learner outcome. Many times, as illustrated by the following example, a myriad of activities is necessary to fulfill such an outcome.

Learner Outcome:

Gifted students will be able to analyze form and meaning in selected multicultural literature.

Activities:

This objective implies the need for activities that address at least the following events:

1. Reading and discussion of key selections in multicultural literature, including experience with at least three cultural literary traditions.
2. Understanding of and experience with different literary genres.
3. Study of universal themes of literature.
4. Expository writing skills that support the capacity to synthesize ideas.

A third issue is that of differentiation. In developing activities, teachers are faced with the most specific manifestation of stating differentiated tasks for gifted learners. Key characteristics of differentiated tasks for this population include the following:

✓ Use of a variety of resources.
✓ No upper limit on expectations.
✓ Facilitation emphasis by teacher.
✓ Study of topics from multiple perspectives.
✓ More extended and involved.
✓ Higher-level thinking.
✓ Product alternatives.
✓ More open-ended (creative responses).
✓ More conceptual or abstract.
✓ More complex.
✓ More focused on analysis or interpretation.

A fourth issue concerns the source of activities for gifted learners. Though creating activities afresh may help gifted educators more fully understand the principles of differentiation, doing so on a regular basis is not practical. Thus, selecting or deriving appropriate activities from available resources becomes an important task. This task involves both identifying key resources and determining their quality.

DIFFERENTIATING APPROPRIATE ACTIVITIES FOR THE GIFTED

One way to approach differentiation of activities is to use a continuum model such as shown in Table 8.1 for the purpose of discerning activity appropriateness. At some stages of development for some gifted learners, a fairly standard activity may be appropriate. Often, however, some degree of differentiation is required based on the aptitude area of given students and their degree of giftedness. To label any activity as "inappropriate" for the gifted is probably short sighted. The use of a continuum model allows teachers to apply the principles of differentiation without losing the flexibility necessary to make decisions about using various activities with different gifted learners. Table 8.1 depicts a set of activities for secondary language arts students. The activities on the left are labeled "less appropriate" for gifted learners; the activities on the right are labeled "more appropriate."

In the literature example in the table, the more appropriate activity requires gifted students to analyze two classic American short stories in respect to the complex literary elements of motivation and theme. The less appropriate activity demands only a vague discussion of basic literary elements in one short story.

The writing example that is more appropriate for the gifted requires students to engage in a more sophisticated writing form (the essay), be able to apply universal literary themes to their own reading, and convincingly defend their choices of characters, works of literature, and themes. This activity demand contrasts sharply with the less appropriate one, which requires students to engage in simple descriptive writing about a character of choice using a simulation structure.

In the language example, the more appropriate activity requires students to master the linguistic system of form and function and apply it creatively in a self-generated written product. The less appropriate activity merely taps into students' ability to recall basic particularities of information related to a larger system.

The speaking example illustrates the appropriateness of the debate structure for engaging students in all forms of higher-level thinking, the issue approach to topics, and the need to perceive research as a broad-based and active enterprise. In contrast, the less appropriate speaking activity is vague about the structure of oral presentation, sets topics broadly, and defines research as library-based.

A second way to approach differentiation is to use strong teaching-learning models as a basis for developing activities. Models such as Taba's model of concept development, Paul's model of reasoning, and other models developed at the College of William and Mary (VanTassel-Baska, Johnson, & Boyce, 1996) contribute strongly to easy structuring of activities. The following example applies the Paul elements of reasoning to the development of a discussion lesson for students of any age. The purpose of the lesson is to have students determine why teaching thinking is important.

Issue: Should we teach students to think?

Purpose: Why do students need to learn to think?

Concepts: What concepts do you need to understand in order to think effectively?

Point of View: Who has a stake in students' learning to think? What is each stakeholder's position?

Assumptions: What assumptions are made by people who want students to just "learn the basics"?

Data/Evidence: What types of data support the teaching of thinking to students?

TABLE 8.1   Comparison of Less and More Appropriate Language Arts Activities for Gifted Learners

Less Appropriate Activities for the Gifted	More Appropriate Activities for the Gifted
Literature	*Literature*
Discuss plot, setting, and characters in the short story "A Rose for Emily".	Compare and contrast the plot, setting, character motivation, and theme of "A Rose for Emily" and "The Bear".
Writing	*Writing*
What if one of the characters we have read about were here? Write a description detailing what she looks like, how she behaves, and what kinds of things you would discuss with her.	Compose a short essay discussing one of the following ideas about characters in literature: 1) They are blind to their faults. 2) They control their own fate. 3) They behave in foolish ways. Describe characters from at least three different pieces of literature to support your point of view.
Language	*Language*
Identify basic parts of speech for key underlined words in a paragraph provided by the teacher.	Given a paragraph provided by the teacher: 1) identify form and function of underlined words, and 2) create a story using all of the basic sentence combinations found in the paragraph.
Speaking	*Speaking*
Choose one of the following topics, and prepare an oral presentation using at least four library references: 1) Shakespeare's World 2) The American Dream in Fiction 3) Science Fiction	Debate one of the following resolutions, using literary works, criticisms, historical treatises, etc., as evidence: 1) Humankind is on a path toward progress. 2) Studying our past will help us cope with the future. Use multiple sources including surveys, interviews, and library sources to support your perspective.

Inferences: What inferences about how thinking should be taught do you make from the data on thinking?

Consequences and Implications: Suppose thinking is taught. What are positive and negative implications? What if it isn't taught? What are positive and negative implications?

A third way to approach differentiation of activities is to employ prototypes such as case studies, simulations, or games that require both higher-level thinking and active learning on the part of gifted students. Simulations and dilemmas are particularly appropriate for gifted learners because they require higher-level thinking in a problem-centered context and use hypothetical situations for analysis that encourage relativistic thinking (see Perry, 1970). The example that follows illustrates a moral dilemma for use with gifted secondary students in science (Iozzi, 1984). It is adapted from Strunk v. Strunk, Court of Appeals, Kentucky, September 26, 1969, KY 455 SW. 2nd 145.

Needed: A New Kidney
Who Decides What?

Arthur L. Strunk, 54 years of age, and Ava Strunk, 52 years of age, of Williamstown, Kentucky, are the parents of two sons. Tommy Strunk is 28 years of age, married, an employee of the Penn State Railroad and a part-time student at the University of Cincinnati. Tommy is suffering from chronic glomerulus nephritis, a fatal kidney disease. He is now being kept alive by frequent treatment on an artificial kidney, a procedure that cannot be continued much longer.

Jerry Strunk is 27 years of age, incompetent, and through proper legal proceedings has been committed to the Frankfort State Hospital and School, which is a state institution maintained for the feebleminded. He has an I.Q. of approximately 35, which corresponds to the mentality of a six-year-old. He is further handicapped by a speech defect, and has difficulty communicating with persons who do not know him well. Therefore, visits with his family, and especially his brother Tommy, with whom he identifies closely, are a very important element in his life.

When it was found that Tommy needed a kidney, doctors considered the possibility of using a kidney from a live donor. His mother, father, and a number of relatives were tested. Because of incompatibility of blood type or tissue, none were medically acceptable as live donors. As a last resort, Jerry was tested and found to be highly acceptable. This immediately presented the legal problem as to what, if anything, could be done by the family to procure a transplant from Jerry to Tommy. Since Jerry is officially a ward of the state, the mother petitioned the county court for authority to proceed with the operation.

Should the court permit the transplantation to take place? Why or why not?

Activities based on this dilemma could proceed from either of the following sets of questions. In the first set, the clear emphasis is on the dilemma. Activities could be structured to begin as a role-playing situation, followed by group discussion.

1. What is the basic dilemma that the Strunks face?
2. What is the argument for Jerry's donating the kidney?
3. What is the argument against Jerry's donating the kidney?
4. Do you think Jerry's mental state should affect the decision?
5. If the situation were reversed, should the operation occur?
6. If you were the Strunks, what would you do? Why?
7. In your opinion, who should make the decision concerning the surgery?
8. How has scientific technology affected people's lives?
9. In your opinion, should we put greater emphasis on developing new technology or on working through the human consequences of current technology?

In the second set of questions, the focus moves to the dilemma only after the teacher emphasizes fundamental understanding of the scientific issues underlying the dilemma. Group problem solving may be an appropriate strategy for Level 3 deliberations.

Level 1: Knowledge

1. What is a kidney?
2. What does a kidney do?
3. What other organs perform some of the same functions as the kidney?
4. What is a tissue?
5. What is blood type?

Level 2: Application of Concepts

1. Why does each person have two kidneys?
2. What is the effect of receiving a kidney on the kidney that is already in the body?
3. What is diffusion?
4. How would diffusion be involved in dialysis?
5. Why test parents and siblings for blood type and tissue type?
6. Why not keep patients on dialysis over time?

Level 3: The Dilemma
1. What would be the benefits of the transplant? What might be the negative consequences?
2. The dilemma is concerned with the issue of human rights. What are the rights of each of the following in this case: the parents, the brothers, the courts?
3. Why do they have these rights?
4. Whose rights have priority?

A fourth way to approach differentiation of activities for gifted learners is to use a key resource or primary material as a basis for reading and then have students answer discussion questions and complete open-ended activities that build on the use of the resource. The two examples that follow illustrate this strategy. Reading and discussion become primary activities as well as a basis for deriving additional extension activities.

Activity Based on *If You Were a Writer* by Joan Lowery Nixon

This book describes the process of being a writer as viewed from the perspective of a child learning from her mother. It is rich in descriptive language and uses hypothetical situations to facilitate understanding of the writing process.

I.   Ideas for Using the Book
- ✓ Use this book to introduce a Young Author's project.
- ✓ Conduct an introductory brainstorming activity in which students list what they think the tasks of an author might be. Have students read the book and then list the writing activities mentioned in it. As a group, compare the list to the brainstormed list.
- ✓ Ask students to identify the thinking aspects of writing.
- ✓ Have students write ideas for a book.
- ✓ Use this book for a career education activity that is tied to a Young Author's product. After reading and discussing this book, students could research various careers and the types of tasks or skills required of that profession. Next, students could write a book entitled If I Were a _____. Share the books with the group and attempt some type of comparison or contrast of various professions through a listing, grid, or the like.

II.   Questions
A. Memory/Cognition
1. What are the names of the children in the family?
2. What steps did Melia's mother lay out for being a writer?
3. Where do words come from, according to Melia's mother?

B. Convergent
1. Why did Melia want to be a writer?
2. How does a writer determine his or her writing success?
3. How does the illustrator differentiate between reality and Melia's imagination?

C. Divergent
1. How would the story be different if Melia's mother had not been a writer?

2. What if Melia's brothers and sisters wouldn't listen to her stories?

3. Pretend you are Melia's career counselor. What elements do you believe are important for Melia to consider in thinking about a career?

D. Evaluative

1. In your opinion, is it good for children to follow in their parents' footsteps?

2. In your opinion, should Melia become a writer?

3. Which of Melia's story starters has the greatest potential for becoming an interesting story?

III. Follow-up Activity

Select one story starter and write a story.

Activity Based on *Come Away From the Water, Shirley* by John Burningham

This book, recommended for gifted children at the primary level, focuses on a family trip to the beach. Told primarily through pictures, the story centers on the contrast between Shirley's parents and their sedentary beach experience and Shirley's more active and imaginative experience.

I. Questions

✓ What do Shirley's parents do at the beginning of the story?

✓ How does Shirley's father spend his afternoon at the beach?

✓ Throughout the story, Shirley behaves differently to her parents' various responses. What are some of these behaviors?

✓ What do you think is going on in Shirley's mind when her parents advise her not to stroke the dog?

✓ Which of Shirley's imaginings were seeded by parental comments?

✓ In your opinion, which of Shirley's "imaginings" could be real and which could be only imagined?

✓ If you, like Shirley, were to find a chest full of treasures, what would be in it, and what would you do with it?

✓ Where do you think Shirley may have gotten the ideas for her adventure?

✓ Would you want to be Shirley? Why or why not? Would you feel "safer" at the shore *without* an imagination like Shirley's?

✓ Pretend you are Shirley. How would you react to her parents' concerns?

✓ If you were at the beach with your family, how would you behave differently from Shirley? Write, act out, or do both.

II. Activities

✓ Are there similarities between your life and Shirley's? List ways your life is the same as Shirley's and ways it is different.

✓ Divide into groups and dramatize another event in Shirley's life with her parents: at home, at the store, at a museum.

✓ Dramatize how Shirley may behave if she were the parent taking a child to the shore.

A fifth approach for constructing appropriate activities for the gifted is to build an interdisciplinary lesson around a current event. The lesson should require higher-level thinking and employ multiple approaches to learning. The following example, based on the recent war in Kosovo, illustrates this approach.

I. Purposes of lesson: To encourage student thinking about the relationship of contemporary issues and problems to the past; to demonstrate how history and poetry are linked

II. Standards Addressed: Language arts, English, and social studies

III. Activity:

✓ Pass out copies of the following chart. Have students fill in the names of the stakeholders of the current situation in Kosovo and their positions on the situation. Discuss the stakeholders' views.

State your initial position:	
Identify the stakeholder groups:	Describe each group's position:
State the issue: Macro issue: Should humanity be waging war? Micro issue: Should NATO be bombing Kosovo?	

✓ Have students fill in their own position on the micro issue. Conduct a discussion about their viewpoints.

✓ Ask students to discuss the larger issue: Should humanity be waging war? Discuss different student viewpoints.

✓ Ask students to read "Grass," a poem by Carl Sandburg. Discuss key vocabulary, reader response, themes, images and symbols, and literary devices.

✓ Based on the discussion of Kosovo and of the poem "Grass," have students explore the following questions.

IV. Questions:

✓ How does our contemporary view of war relate to Sandburg's view as portrayed in the poem "Grass"?

> ✓ What do the places named in the poem represent? Why does Sandburg cite them?
> ✓ What aspects of our view of war stay the same over time? What aspects change over time?
> ✓ In what way may history be defined as a series of wars? Examine appropriate historical sources to support your argument.

Hertzog (1998) advocated a sixth approach to curriculum differentiation, one centered in learner response to open-ended activities, and demonstrated the efficacy of this approach with young gifted children. Such an approach implies that self-differentiation may be the norm in gifted students given a challenging, open-ended activity format. The approach requires classroom teachers to develop high-level, well-designed activities from which a full range of learners can benefit. It also places demands on classroom organization and management, as teachers must demonstrate facility in varying differentiation response modes, times, and other logistical considerations.

BALANCE IN ACTIVITIES

Balance is another consideration in developing learning activities for the gifted. Teachers and curriculum developers should strive for balance in the types of activities used, as described in the following sections.

Active and Passive Activities

Gifted students are capable of absorbing large amounts of information in a short time. Using predominantly passive activities with these learners creates an imbalance and impedes more powerful learning opportunities that can accrue from lively interchange among the gifted, cooperative projects, and small-group problem solving. A good blend of active and passive activities is preferable so that students can learn from one another as well as from the teacher and themselves.

Oral and Written Activities

Teachers tend to prefer either the written or the oral mode for communication of student work. Gifted learners should have ample opportunities to participate in both types of activities. Expressive activities help them develop presentation skills. Written activities enhance thinking skills and precise use of language. Both are highly valued modes of communication in the world of professional work. Therefore, a strong balance in the use of these two modes is desirable.

Small-Group and Independent Activities

Gifted learners are often capable of working alone and, if unprompted, may frequently choose to work alone. But learning to collaborate with others in activities is an important skill. Project work for the gifted might be best served by alternating between individual and group assignments. Typically, culturally diverse groups and gifted girls prefer greater opportunities for working cooperatively. Attention to these special population distinctions also calls for a balance between the oral and written modes of learning.

Instruction and Self-Study

According to a popular myth, gifted students need only facilitation, never direct instruction, in learning. Actually, these learners do need direct instruction, though they may need less direct instruction than other learners, geared at higher levels and provided at different times and in different areas of the curriculum. As the myth implies, the gifted also have a strong capacity to take charge of their own learning. Thus, a balance between teacher-directed and student-directed activities is called for. One strategy for discerning the appropriate balance is mutual goal setting between the teacher and gifted learners.

Convergent and Divergent Thinking

As a field, gifted education has long promoted divergent thinking over convergent thinking as a process skill to be taught to gifted learners. In reality, both modes are essential for creating anything worthwhile, from musical compositions to essays. Deliberate emphasis on both styles of thinking should be incorporated into activities for the gifted. For example, ideational fluency activities can help students generate ideas in an exploratory context without outside judgment being imposed. By the same token, at a later stage of thinking, these ideas should come under closer scrutiny and be evaluated according to key criteria for facilitating the goal of learning. Such a balanced focus on creative and critical thinking skills is necessary to enhance creative productivity.

Reading/Reflection and Project Work

Gifted educators would do well to cultivate gifted learners who will become philosophers as well as those who will become marketing entrepreneurs. To that end, activities that reward reading and discussion of ideas should be given as much attention as those that result in tangible products. In many professional fields the "production" of a new idea brought about by discussion among a small group of people can cause a paradigm shift more readily than can a project report detailing what happened and why. The development of any meaningful theory requires both intellectual behavior and time to think as well as the conversion process to writing, speaking, or other forms of production. Gifted activities should reflect this balance, too.

Relative Emphasis

Another kind of balance that must be struck in the development and choice of activities for gifted learners concerns the relative emphasis given to one aspect of an activity over others. Table 8.2 outlines the major elements to be considered in developing language arts activities for the gifted and provides specific examples of each element to consider as choices. Although the examples are only illustrative, they represent an approach to ensuring that each element is given some consideration. Using this table, curriculum developers can strike a balance among content, process skill, product, and concept development.

Gifted educators may find the activity prototype checklist in Figure 8.2 helpful as a way to ensure that activities for gifted learners are sufficiently differentiated and appropriate. The checklist covers all of the major issues raised in this chapter regarding activities for the gifted.

RESOURCES FOR THE GIFTED

Appropriate activities are inextricably linked to appropriate resources. Both human and material resources are a vital part of curriculum design, development, and implementation.

Human Resources

Guest speakers, mentors, and community volunteers all represent viable avenues for potential assistance in a gifted program. Professionals such as practicing scientists, artists, and writers constitute a rich resource for programs across the country. In learning research skills, gifted learners should interview and interact with knowledgeable people in the area they are exploring.

This human side of resource utilization is fundamental to students' understanding of how knowledge is generated in the real world. Moreover, tapping into human resources adds the dimension of modeling: Here are individuals who directly engage in creative productivity from whom students can discern key qualities and skills necessary to function in a given field.

Material Resources

Materials of various types are essential to curricula for the gifted, and these must be selected carefuly. Many materials that are superb for gifted programs do not carry a

TABLE 8.2   Alternative Teaching/Learning Activity Elements in Language Arts

Activity Element	Alternative Examples
Themes	Patterns Change Space Signs and symbols Interdependence Systems Origins Reason
Topics	Colonial America Electricity Customs of France Fractions Popular composers Composition Poetry The brain
Content areas	Reading/Language arts Writing/Composition Math Science Social studies Art Music Foreign language
Literary genres	Poetry Short story Essay Novel Play Letter Biography Autobiography

TABLE 8.2   *(Continued)*

Activity Element	Alternative Examples
Literary devices	Characterization Plot Setting Theme Motivation Climax Openings Denouement
Content resources	*Ozymandias* (poem by Shelley) *The Lottery* (short story by Shirley Jackson) *Self-Reliance* (Emerson essay) *Old Man and the Sea* (novella by Ernest Hemmingway) *The Source* (novel by James Michener) *Self-Consciousness* (autobiography by John Updike) *Diary of Anne Frank*
Thinking skills (critical)	Creative problem solving Deductive reasoning Inductive reasoning Setting up hypotheses Making inferences Creating metaphors/analogies Finding similarities/differences or advantages/disadvantages Specific problem-solving heuristics
Thinking skills (creative)	Fluency (Name all of the _____ you can in the next 10 minutes.) Flexibility (How many different uses can you make of _____?) Elaboration (Add to the story/picture as much as you can.) Originality (Think of a _____ no one else has thought of. Represent it.)
Archetypal verbs for enhancing higher-order thinking	Analyze, compare/contrast, explicate, explain Set up criteria/standards Create, design, model, demonstrate Present, debate, write Evaluate, judge Critique, rate

TABLE 8.2   *(Continued)*

Activity Element	Alternative Examples
Archetypal activities	Read and discuss Practice/apply skill or concept Respond to structured stimulus, orally or in writing, or act out Build stimulus to react to Conduct experiment Represent idea in some form Organize work plan/product
Archetypal discussion questions	Who? What? Where? When? Why/how did _____ happen? What would happen if _____? Which is better or best ...? What are all the different ways that _____? What did you like best/least about _____? Why? What does the following quotation mean? What was the author's tone, attitude, feeling about _____? How do you feel about _____?
Discussion questions for the fine arts/ humanities	What is it? What's it made of? What does it say? How do you respond to it? How good is it? When was it created? What do you see? Make a list. What ideas are conveyed? What feelings are evoked? If you were to identify with a character or object, what would it be, and why? How might you represent all of your reactions to the poem/painting/music/photograph? Respond in your preferred form.
Archetypal product tasks for groups and individuals	Create a collage Evaluate best uses, products, processes Write a story/poem/play Design an ad Act out/dramatize a scene Create a slide presentation Debate an issue Build/construct a model

Yes	No	
_____	_____	1. Does the activity serve multiple purposes? Content purpose _____ Process purpose _____ Concept purpose _____
_____	_____	2. Does the teacher's role in the activity facilitative learning?
_____	_____	3. Does the activity promote critical thinking?
_____	_____	4. Does the activity promote creative thinking, problem-solving?
_____	_____	5. Does the activity promote product-oriented, generative thinking?
_____	_____	6. Does the teacher ask higher-level questions as part of the activity?
_____	_____	7. Does the activity contain an element of choice?
_____	_____	8. Is the activity interdisciplinary?
_____	_____	9. Is the activity sufficiently advanced and complex for gifted learners?
_____	_____	10. Does the activity promote opportunity for an open-ended response?
_____	_____	11. Does the activity encourage students to seek multiple sources for understanding?
_____	_____	12. Is the activity linked to a curriculum objective?

FIGURE 8.2   Activity Prototype Checklist

label identifying them as such, and many materials that do carry the label do not add anything of benefit to a curriculum plan.

Criteria in Resource Selection

Key criteria to consider in choosing resources for a gifted program include the following:

1. *The material addresses the major learner outcomes of the program.* Many times teachers are enamored of materials because they are attractive, contain the appropriate buzzwords, and emphasize hands-on activities. These criteria are insufficient, however, to use as a basis for selecting materials in a program for

gifted learners. The materials must address the desired learner outcomes, or they will not be helpful in attaining the goals of the curriculum.

2. *The reading level is appropriate for gifted learners at the given stage of development.* Too many texts in all subject areas are "dummied down," frequently written one to two grade levels below the stated level for which the material is intended. The result is low-level materials for the gifted. Gifted educators need to determine the reading level of all texts considered for the program so they can ensure challenging reading behaviors in the gifted.

3. *The material is organized by key concepts rather than by isolated skills.* Elementary materials tend to be organized by skills and not by ideas. Materials that offer a better balance of these two elements should be sought.

4. *The material includes ideas for discussion at higher levels of thinking.* A key feature that enhances materials used with the gifted is the inclusion of questions that tap into analytical, synthetic, and evaluative thinking.

5. *The material includes ideas for group and independent project investigations.* Materials that suggest self-generated activities for students are very useful, because they can guide students to various alternative project opportunities.

6. *Problem sets are organized from simple to complex and allow gifted learners to extend off-level as appropriate.* The structure of materials should allow for students to deal with more complex problems or issues than the entry level. Although skill-based materials often provide this developmental progression, materials geared only to the gifted often do not.

7. *The material offers diversity in learning, providing alternative means to attain ends within the curriculum framework.* Materials for the gifted should offer choices to activate student interest, such as suggestions for multiple activities that will lead to the attainment of a desired learner outcome. Moreover, materials should provide various modes of inquiry and options for student-generated work.

8. *The material provides extension opportunities to help students understand other domains of inquiry.* Good resources for gifted learners allow for student development of multiple perspectives in various disciplines. Materials should make these connections for students.

9. *The material provides opportunities for creative thinking, for challenging assumptions, and for offering alternative solutions.* Materials should be grounded in the inquiry approach and sensitive to problem-based learning strategies. They should lead students to think about what they are learning rather than merely accepting it.

10. *The material encourages gifted learners to consult multiple resources on given topics.* Material for gifted learners should encourage further exploration of ideas. Good bibliographies and resource suggestions in both print and nonprint form are important.

These criteria may be useful to gifted educators in choosing core text materials for gifted learners, as well as in referring to other resources of merit. Textbook adoption committees would do well to use such a list to ensure appropriate considerations for gifted students in districtwide adoptions.

Key Features of Curriculum

Regardless of target population, all good curriculum materials should contain the following features:

✓ rationale and purpose.
✓ goals and objectives.
✓ curriculum content outline.
✓ activities.
✓ instructional strategies.
✓ evaluation procedures.
✓ materials/resources.
✓ extension activities.

In addition, materials can be reviewed with respect to the content criteria that educators in the disciplines perceive as critical for an exemplary curriculum. Schmidt, McKnight, and Raizen (1996) viewed this task as vital for shaping the implementation of the standards, especially in science and mathematics. An example of such criteria from the discipline of science might include the following, based on the demands of the science standards (Johnson, Boyce, & VanTassel-Baska, 1995):

✓ presence of intra- and interrelations among scientific concepts.
✓ science research presented as practices in the real world of science.
✓ content base in key areas of science and technology.
✓ opportunities to hone scientific inquiry skills.
✓ opportunities for independent research.
✓ opportunities for collaborative work.
✓ presence of moral and ethical dimensions of science and technology.

Kulm (1999) focused on the importance of selecting appropriate text materials for teaching the math standards. To that end, he developed an analysis process that teachers and administrators can employ in district and state settings to ensure that curriculum materials adhere to the standards and their intent. He suggested that the substance and sophistication of the materials be examined, as well as whether they offer part or whole coverage of a standard. According to Kulm, analysis of math materials should include the examination of seven clusters of criteria, as shown in Table 8.3. The use of this approach by teachers in Kentucky suggested that the

TABLE 8.3   Selecting Mathematics Resources: Examination of Seven Clusters of Criteria

	Cluster 1: Identifying and Maintaining a Sense of Purpose	Cluster 2: Taking Account of Student Ideas	Cluster 3: Engaging Students	Cluster 4: Developing and Using Mathematical Ideas	Cluster 5: Promoting Student Reflection	Cluster 6: Assessment	Cluster 7: Other Features
Purpose		Prerequisite knowledge and skills	Variety of contexts	Building a case	Providing opportunities for students to express ideas	Alignment to goals	Teacher content knowledge
Activity purpose		Alerting the teacher to commonly held ideas	Quality of experiences	Introducing terms and procedures	Guiding student interpretation and reasoning	Application	Classroom environment
Activity sequence		Addressing commonly held ideas		Representing ideas Connecting ideas Practice	Promoting reflection and self-monitoring	Embedded Multiple formats	Welcoming all students

process does differentiate strong from weak curriculum materials and that teachers change their perceptions about materials and standards as a result of experiencing the process. The application of the process also revealed major changes in mathematics textbooks occurring following implementation of the standards. Many post-standard texts are more interdisciplinary, integrated, richer in applied problems, and reveal a stronger emphasis on problem-based learning approaches than texts written before the standards were developed (Kulm, Strati, & Bush, 1998).

Types of Materials

In the realm of material resources for programs for the gifted, several types are worth mentioning because they are so rich in challenging ideas for teachers and gifted learners alike. One group of such resources could be labeled "interdisciplinary and idea-based." This type of resource is typically organized thematically and provides a broad scope of examples drawn from many disciplines to illustrate a given idea. The following are excellent examples of this type of resource:

Boorstein, D. J. (1983). *The Discoverers: A History of Man's Search to Know His World and Himself.* New York: Vintage.
Boorstein, D. J. (1993). *The Creators: A History of Heroes of the Imagination.* New York: Vintage.
Bronowski, J. (1973). *The Ascent of Man.* Boston: Little, Brown.
Burger, D. (1965). *Sphereland.* New York: Harper & Row.
Burke, J. (1978). *Connections.* Boston: Little, Brown.
Burke, J. (1985). *The Day the Universe Changed.* London: British Broadcasting.
Hofstader, D. (1999). *Godel, Escher, Bach: An Eternal Golden Braid.* New York: Vintage.
Jacobs, H. (1982). *Mathematics: A Human Endeavor.* New York: W. H. Freeman.
Judson, H. (1974). *Search for Solutions.* Bartlesville, OK: Phillips Petroleum.
Sagan, C. (1980). *Cosmos.* New York: Random House.
Serra, M. (1989). *Discovering Geometry: An Inductive Approach.* Berkeley, CA: Key Curriculum Press.
Tamplin, R. (1991). *The Arts: A History of Expression in the 20th Century.* New York: Oxford University Press.

Also valuable for gifted programs are materials that annotate additional resources for the gifted learner and that provide multiple options for reading or doing activities. The following are excellent examples of this type of resource:

Baskin, B. H., & Harris, K. H. (1980). *Books for the Gifted Child.* New York: R. R. Bowker.
Halsted, J. (1994). *Some of My Best Friends Are Books: Guiding Gifted Readers from Pre-school to High School.* Dayton, OH: Ohio Psychology Press.
Hauser, P., & Nelson, G. A. (1988). *Books for the Gifted (Vol. 2).* New York: R. R. Bowker.
Polette, N. (1982). *3 R's for the Gifted: Reading, Writing and Research.* Littleton, CO: Libraries Unlimited.
Saul, W., & Newman, A. (1986). *Science Fare.* New York: Harper & Row.
Thompson, M. (1995). *Classics in the Classroom.* New York: Fine Arts Press.

With regard to fiction and nonfiction reading materials, Kolloff (1998) delineated the following set of criteria:

✓ well-written literature that is rich in vocabulary and images.
✓ complex, unusual plots or structure.
✓ imaginative illustrations that involve or challenge the reader.
✓ characters and situations with which the reader can identify.
✓ intellectually and emotionally challenging.
✓ appropriate, effective role models.
✓ realistic portrayals of people and events (nonfiction).
✓ accurate information (nonfiction).

The following are examples of good fiction and nonfiction:

Nonfiction

Nechita, A. (1996). *Outside the Lines.* Marietta, GA: Longstreet.

Sis, P. (1996). *Starry Messenger.* New York: Farrar, Straus, Giroux.

Biesty, S. (1992). *Stephen Biesty's Incredible Cross-Sections.* New York: Alfred A. Knopf.

Schlissel, L. (1982). *Women's Diaries of the Westward Journey.* New York: Schocken Books.

Fiction

Hoffman, M. & Binch, C. (1991). *Amazing Grace.* New York: Dial Books for Young Readers.

Brett, J. (1985). *Annie and the Wild Animals.* Boston: Houghton Mifflin.

Chesworth, M. (1994). *Archibald Frisby.* New York: Farrar, Straus and Giroux.

Henkes, K. (1988). *Chester's Way.* New York: William Morrow.

Bedard, M. (1992). *Emily.* New York: Delacort.

Nixon, J. L. (1988). *If You Were a Writer.* New York: Aladdin Paperbacks.

Cooney, B. (1982). *Miss Rumphius.* New York: Puffin.

Barton, E. (1993). *Peppe the Lamplighter.* New York: Lorthrup, Lee & Shepard.

Martin, A. (1992). *Rachel Parker, Kindergarten Show-Off.* New York: Holiday House.

Kaiman, M. (1989). *Sayonara, Mrs. Kackeiman.* New York: Penguin.

Isaacs, A. (1994). *Swamp Angel.* New York: Dutton.

Hopkinson, D. (1993). *Sweet Clara and the Freedom Quilt.* New York: Alfred A. Knopf.

Brett, J. (1992). *Trouble With Trolls.* New York: G. P. Putnam's Sons.

Fox, Mem. (1985). *Wilfred Gordon McDonald Partridge.* New York: Kane/Miller.

Konigsburg, E. L. (1976). *Father's Arcane Daughter.* New York: Dell.

Konigsburg, E. L. (1970). *(George).* New York: Atheneum.

Lowry, L. (1993). *The Giver.* New York: Bantam Doubleday Dell.

Bjork, C. & Anderson, L. (1985). *Linnea in Monet's Garden.* Stockholm, Sweden: Raben & Sjogren.

Enright, E. (1941). *The Saturdays.* New York: Dell.

Similar criteria have been used to select literature for the National Language Arts Project (Boyce, 1996). Such criteria would be useful for teachers and others to employ in selecting core reading for the gifted at any stage of development.

Another type of invaluable resource for use in gifted curricula is the "packaged" program—materials that have been prestructured for classroom use and come with excellent teachers' guides and often with videotapes, filmstrips, or other multimedia to help implement the program. These resources require less inventiveness on the part of individual teachers to create activities. Sample materials of this sort include the following:

Bank Street College of Education. (1984). *The Voyage of the Mimi.* New York: Holt, Rinehart & Winston.

Center for Gifted Education. (1998). *Problem-based Science.* Dubuque, IA: Kendall-Hunt.

Center for Gifted Education. (1999). *Language Arts for High-ability Learners.* Dubuque, IA: Kendall-Hunt.

Challenge of the Unknown. (1988). (Math program with video.) Bartlesville, OK: Phillips Petroleum.

Junior Great Books. (1967–2001). Chicago: Great Books Foundation.

LEGO TC Logo. (1987). Enfield, CT: Lego Systems.

MACOS (Man: A Course of Study). (1968). Washington, DC: Curriculum Associates.

Biographies and autobiographies are also materials of interest to the gifted. Studying individuals who engage in an area of interest to them provides gifted students with another whole dimension toward understanding a field of inquiry and relating to it as an individual. The following are excellent examples of these types of resources:

Baretta-Lorton, M. *Math Jobs.* Menlo Park, CA: Addison-Wesley.

Bell, E. T. (1965). *Men of Mathematics.* New York: Simon & Schuster.

Bruner, J. (1983). *In Search of Mind.* New York: Harper & Row.

Carey, L. (1991). *Black Ice.* New York: Knopf.

Carson, B. (1990). *Gifted Hands.* New York: Harper Paperbacks.

Dillard, A. (1987). *An American Childhood.* New York: Harper & Row.

Dillard, A. (1998). *Pilgrim at Tinker Creek.* HarperPerennial.

Feynman, R. (1985). *Surely You're Joking, Mr. Feynman.* New York: Bantam.

Fins, A. (1979). *Women in Science.* Skokie, IL: VGM Career Horizons.

Goodfield, J. (1981). *An Imagined World: A Story of Scientific Discovery.* New York: Harper & Row.

Keller, E. F. (1983). *A Feeling for the Organism: The Life and Work of Barbara McClintock.* New York: W. H. Freeman.

Krull, K. (1994). *Lives of Writers.* San Diego: Harcourt Brace.

L'Engle, M. (1986). *Circle of Quiet.* San Francisco: Harper.

L'Engle, M. (1989). *Two-part Invention.* San Francisco: Harper.

L'Engle, M. (1996). *The Summer of the Great-Grandmother.* San Francisco: Harper.

Nolan, C. (1987). *Under the Eye of the Clock: The Life Story of Christopher Nolan.* New York: St. Martin's Press.

Welty, E. (1995). *One Writer's Beginnings.* Cambridge, MA: Howard University Press.

All of these types of materials are invaluable in implementing an effective curriculum for gifted learners, for they provide a diverse set of opportunities for multiple activities and are responsive to the key issues cited earlier regarding qualities of good materials for the gifted. Above all, these materials stimulate teachers to improve and gifted students to learn.

SUMMARY

Teaching-learning activities should be matched to learner outcomes, should be geared to differentiated tasks, must be sufficient to fulfill an objective, and should be created or derived from existing resources. An ideal balance should be sought between active and passive, oral and written, small-group and independent activities. These activities should encompass both convergent and divergent thinking, reading/discussion and products.

Appropriate resources are both human and material. Human resources include guest speakers, mentors, community volunteers, and professionals in various fields. Criteria for material resources include appropriate reading level, organization by key concepts, inclusion of ideas for higher-level thinking, alternative means to attain ends (diversity), and opportunities for creative thinking, among others.

Basic types of materials are thematic and idea-based, those annotated for additional references, packaged programs, and biography/autobiography.

QUESTIONS FOR REFLECTION

1. How can teaching activities be organized so that gifted learners regularly experience reading, discussion, simulations, project work, creative opportunities, and affective experiences regardless of age or area of study?

2. How might educators ensure that all classroom activities contribute to the attainment of a stated objective?

3. If you were in charge of the gifted program in a school district, how would you organize the development of appropriate activities for the gifted?

4. What role should basal textbooks play in a gifted curriculum?

5. How can educators ensure that multiple and diverse resources are used with gifted learners?

REFERENCES

Boyce, L. (1996). In the big inning was the word: Word play resources for developing verbal talent. In J. VanTassel-Baska, D. Johnson, & L. Boyce (Eds.), *Developing verbal talent* (pp. 259–272). Boston: Allyn & Bacon.

Burningham, J. (1977). *Come away from the water, Shirley.* New York: Crowell.

Hertzog, N. (1998). Open-ended activities: Differentiation through learner responses. *Gifted Child Quarterly, 42,* 212–227.

Iozzi, F. (1984). *Dilemmas in bioethics.* New Brunswick, NJ: Rutgers University.

Johnson, D., Boyce, L., & VanTassel-Baska, J. (1995). Science curriculum review: Evaluating materials for high-ability learners. *Gifted Child Quarterly, 39,* 36–43.

Kolloff, P. (November 1998). *Selecting literature for gifted students.* Presentation at National Association for Gifted Children conference, Louisville, KY.

Kulm, G. (1999). Making sure that your math curriculum meets standards. *Mathematics Teaching in the Middle School, 4,* 536–541.

Kulm, G., Strati, D., & Bush, W. (1998). *Mathematics curriculum materials analysis: A textbook selection example.* Washington, DC: American Association for the Advancement of Science.

Nixon, J. L., & Degan, B. (1996). *If you were a writer.* New York: Simon & Schuster.

Perry, W. (1970). *Forms of intellectual and ethical development in the college years.* New York: Holt, Rinehart, & Winston.

Renzulli, J. S., Leppien, J. H., & Hays, T. S. (2000). *The multiple menu model: A practical guide for developing differentiated curriculum.* Mansfield Center, CT: Creative Learning Press.

Schmidt, W., McKnight, C., & Raizen, S. (1996). *A splintered vision: An investigation of U.S. science and mathematics education.* Boston: Kluwer.

Tomlinson, C. A. (1999). *The differentiated classroom: Responding to the needs of all learners.* Alexandria, VA: Association for Supervision and Curriculum Development.

VanTassel-Baska, J., Johnson, D., & Boyce, L. (Eds.). (1996). *Developing verbal talent.* Boston: Allyn & Bacon.

9

✓ SELECTING INSTRUCTIONAL STRATEGIES

T eachers employ certain techniques and delivery systems in the classroom to provide appropriate curricula to gifted learners. Most instructional strategies have some value in working with the gifted, but those strategies that allow for more open-ended, interactive, and generative learning behavior are probably most beneficial.

How do we know what strategies work? One way is to examine the strategies used in exemplary programs that reflect positive growth gains for gifted learners. Four programs that meet this criterion are the William and Mary language arts and science curriculum, Junior Great Books, *Philosophy for Children,* and *Man: A Course of Study* (MACOS). Students exposed to these programs have demonstrated growth gains in critical thinking and interpretation of written material (Lipman, 1988; Norris, 1985; Sternberg & Bhana, 1986; VanTassel-Baska, Zuo, Avery, & Little, 2002), and scientific research skills (VanTassel-Baska, Bass, Ries, Poland, & Avery, 1998). The common instructional strategy across these programs is *inquiry,* the use of questions to stimulate and expand thinking about what has been read, experienced, or seen. Thus, gifted educators typically promote inquiry and question asking as key elements in gifted programs.

Another way to ascertain effective strategies is to observe what exemplary teachers of the gifted do to facilitate growth in their students. Martinson (1974) developed an observational rating scale for recording the behaviors of gifted teachers. Subsequent adaptations to that scale have sought to extend our understanding of teacher behaviors based on general teacher education research as well as our understanding of what works with the gifted (VanTassel-Baska, 1995). The behaviors evaluated in teachers of the gifted in the Saturday and summer programs at the College of William and Mary consist of the following:

1. Plans curriculum experiences well.
2. Demonstrates understanding of the educational implications of giftedness.

3. Uses various teaching strategies effectively.
4. Selects questions that stimulate higher-level thinking.
5. Stimulates and models critical thinking skills in appropriate contexts.
6. Stimulates and models creative thinking techniques.
7. Stimulates and models problem-solving techniques.
8. Conducts group discussions well.
9. Encourages independent thinking and open inquiry.
10. Understands and encourages student ideas and student-directed work.
11. Synthesizes student assessment data and curriculum content effectively.
12. Provides for student extension activities outside of class.
13. Promotes a healthy teaching-learning climate.

Source: Center for Gifted Education, College of William & Mary, 1998.

Still another approach to examining effective strategies for the gifted is to focus on student outcomes and then identify the desired *teacher* behaviors that would facilitate those outcomes. Shulman (1987) cited the importance of linking teacher behaviors to student outcomes in his innovative assessment model. Table 9.1 demonstrates this process using common outcome statements from typical gifted programs.

GUIDELINES FOR CHOOSING APPROPRIATE STRATEGIES

Appropriate instructional strategies for gifted learners include all of the strategies deemed appropriate for other learners as well, and all teachers of the gifted should be comfortable using discussion, inquiry, small-group and individual consultation, and problem-solving approaches. But how does one choose the appropriate strategy in a given situation? Some principles to consider when planning instruction and choosing strategies for gifted learners are as follows:

1. *Strategies should relate to instructional purposes, curriculum, and setting.* The choice of a strategy depends, in part, on the purpose of a given lesson and the nature of the curriculum being taught. For example, inquiry teaching is appropriate in many situations, but if the instructional purpose is to provide an overview of key ideas on China in an hour, inquiry may not be the best choice. The interrelationship of strategy with purpose, content, and time frames must be carefully examined.

2. *Strategies should be diverse.* Research on instructional methods for the gifted currently points to the desirability of using a variety of techniques. Small-group cooperative learning strategies, independent learning models, and large-group instruction all have their place in the instructional pattern for the gifted. Striving for a good balance among these three instructional approaches may be optimal.

TABLE 9.1   Expected Student Behaviors Correlated With Teacher Behaviors

Outcome Statements	Teacher Behaviors
By the end of Grade 4, gifted students will demonstrate enhanced ability to think creatively as evidenced by appropriate pre-post measures.	1. Teacher employs brainstorming. 2. Teacher encourages flexible thinking. 3. Teacher asks students to elaborate ideas. 4. Teacher engages students in developing generative ideas and products.
By the end of Grade 6, gifted students will improve their problem-solving skills as evidenced by pre-post application of novel problem sets.	1. Teacher employs creative problem-solving model. 2. Teacher uses problem-solving heuristics in presenting ideas. 3. Teacher asks students to define problems in a question form.
By the end of Grade 8, gifted students will increase critical thinking skills in the areas of analysis and interpretation, inductive and deductive reasoning, and evaluation.	1. Teacher has students evaluate situations, problems, issues. 2. Teacher has students ask analytic questions. 3. Teacher has students generalize from concrete to abstract at advanced levels. 4. Teacher has students support generalizations in written and oral discourse. 5. Teacher has students interpret selected passages.

3. *Strategies should include several that are generative in nature.* Effective teachers of the gifted rely on strategies that involve the gifted as active learners who are capable of generating new ideas and products of various kinds. A few key strategies that all teachers of the gifted should have in their arsenal include inquiry, problem solving, and discussion via careful question-asking techniques. If these techniques are not applied in gifted programs, students are deprived of an important aspect of their learning.

4. *Strategies should provide a balance among active and passive activities.* Although having students work independently in the classroom has much value, it carries the potential problem of overloading students with passive types of

activities in which they are merely receiving information by doing work in isolation. Many of the best insights gifted students have are gained from interacting with one another and articulating ideas verbally. Consequently, educators of the gifted need to consider a balance among active and passive activities.

5. *Strategies should mesh with the cognitive style of both teacher and learners.* The individual learning styles of the gifted require a teacher's sensitivity to students' cognitive styles. At the same time, teachers need to know their own cognitive strengths and the instructional approaches they do best and try to capitalize upon them in classroom interactions. Teachers' recognition of their own and their students' cognitive styles, and their attempts to respond to those styles, maximize the outcome of learning.

6. *Strategies should be subordinate to educational purpose.* Occasionally the strategy, instead of what is taught, becomes the purpose. For example, brainstorming may become more important than the ideas being considered. When this happens, we have lost sight of *why* the technique is important to employ—namely as a way of exploring important ideas. Group process should not be an end in itself but, rather, must be tempered by relevant content for exploration.

PROGRAM STRATEGIES

Figure 9.1 identifies six strategies that promote open-ended, interactive, and generative learning in the gifted. These are described in the following sections.

Pacing

Activities must move at a rate that is comfortable for the gifted. I am often reminded of a student in my class many years ago. He was young for the seventh-grade class and had an annoying habit of going under his desk whenever the pace of instruction slowed to accommodate others. This went on for a few class sessions, with stern commentary from me regarding his appropriate physical placement in the classroom. Finally I made the connection between his behavior and the instructional pace. Once he was grouped with other learners also capable of moving more rapidly, he became a different learner before my eyes—rapt, interested in topics studied, and interactive with others.

Appropriate pacing also relates to limiting review of material already learned or providing only a quick summary of key points at the beginning of a new lesson. The gifted typically enjoy a rapid pace that matches their mental quickness.

Obviously, however, the pace should be deliberately slowed for some aspects of curriculum to allow more time for thinking about ideas and processing information. For some activities, such as writing, teachers must be sensitive to gifted students' individual capacities and allocate longer work periods as needed.

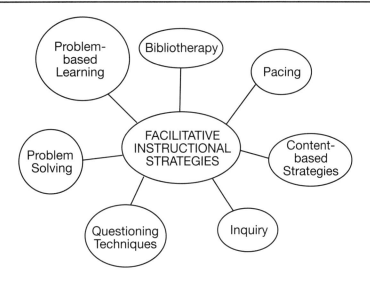

FIGURE 9.1   Key Strategies for Use With Gifted Learners

Inquiry

At the most expansive level, inquiry means creating a climate of mutual investigation into a problem, issue, or idea worthy of attention. Inquiry requires structuring a situation or activity in a way that elicits high-level thinking from learners. It involves asking open-ended and suggestive questions that lead the learner to think through a problem, issue, or idea in a deliberate way.

The use of inquiry techniques in gifted programs has long been supported in the literature as well as by enthusiastic teachers of the gifted who see its positive effects. Inquiry approaches work well with the gifted for several reasons. First, gifted learners usually can handle formal operational thought more readily than can other learners and thus grasp the discovery approach to learning more easily and quickly. The gifted have the insight to understand discrepant events in science, for example, within a class period, rendering this instructional approach extremely doable in most learning contexts.

Second, gifted learners generally have idiosyncratic knowledge of self. Because inquiry can honor many different ways of approaching and carrying out the learning task, it can be used to accommodate to the varying cognitive styles of the gifted.

Third, inquiry approaches work with this population because they are basically problem-centered. The gifted enjoy a good mystery, a puzzle, ambiguity, and paradox.

Inquiry provides a learning context in which the gifted learner's curiosity can roam unchecked, and it sets the stage for these learners to choose their own problems to be solved in future independent investigations.

A clarifying example may lead to a better understanding of the inquiry process.

A. *Stimulus Problem.* Each student is given a Japanese print that depicts a scene in nature. Some of the prints have human figures; some do not. The inquiry task is to study the picture and provide written commentary for each of the following questions:

1. What objects do you see in your picture?
2. What ideas does your picture convey?
3. What feelings does your picture evoke?
4. If you were to identify with an object in your picture, what would it be, and why?
5. Based on your impressions, thoughts, and feelings about your picture, can you synthesize your reactions to the picture graphically or in written form?

B. Each student shares the picture he or she viewed with two or three other students and discusses individual reactions. Each group then responds to the following questions in a discussion context:

1. What similarities and differences exist among your pictures?
2. Compare and contrast your individual reactions to each picture. What did you discover?
3. Based on your experience, what generalizations might you make about the pictures?
4. Based on your experience, what generalizations might you make about one another?

C. In the framework of group sharing, the total class engages in a debriefing of each group's perceptions. Pictures and ideas are shared across the five to six groups in the room. The total group then responds to the following questions:

1. Based on your experiences with these prints, what do you know about the Japanese culture (its philosophy, art, geography, religion, etc.)?
2. What did you learn about one another from this experience?
3. What important generalizations might you make about cultural understanding from this experience?

D. Key generalizations that might be derived from this inquiry lesson include the following:

1. A culture is represented in its art at a symbolic level.
2. Studying artifacts (e.g., Japanese prints) helps us understand ourselves as well as others.
3. Cultural understanding is dependent on understanding multiple perspectives.
4. Knowing other people's perceptions about a given situation or problem helps us appreciate rather than denigrate individual differences.

The inquiry lesson just described incorporates the nature of the activity, key questions, grouping arrangements, and anticipated outcomes of the lesson. The richness of the discovery, however, is left to individual gifted learners.

Questioning Techniques

Many educators of the gifted view effective questioning as employing a large number of higher-level questions. Other educators have successfully used techniques related to Socratic questioning, which force the student to think more deeply about the heart of an issue and explore it from many sides. From the teacher's standpoint, techniques related to Socratic questioning call for asking probing questions directed to central points.

The Junior Great Books Foundation, long a purveyor of key literature materials used in gifted programs, discourages teachers from asking either factual or evaluative questions. Rather, Junior Great Books recommends a focus on interpretive questions. It encourages the use of question clusters that direct the discussion along predetermined lines. Teachers are asked to read a story carefully and then single out the major aspect of interpretation, that area of the story that is intriguing to a reader because it has not been thoroughly explicated. The teachers then ask questions to help students explore this area. The following example helps to clarify the use of this technique.

In Shirley Jackson's classic short story, "The Lottery," the plot culminates in the stoning by her neighbors of one Mrs. Henderson, who drew the black spot on her paper in the lottery process. The story is intriguing because (a) there is no real reason the lottery is being held; only tradition and rituals keep it going; (b) the townspeople have no reason to punish one of their own, for no crime has been committed against their society; thus (c) the sheer horror of the act is overwhelming to the reader. What is horribly open to interpretation in this story is why the townspeople stoned an innocent woman and why this lottery ritual has been allowed to continue in the village. Thus, a question cluster for a 45-minute discussion with sixth-grade gifted student might be:

1. From the story, what do we know about Mrs. Henderson? About her husband? About others in her family?
2. Why, according to the author, does the town carry out a lottery?
3. What signs of foreboding are there in the story before the final act occurs?
4. What clues does the author provide that the ending of the story will be tragic?
5. Why do the townspeople carry out the stoning? What does this act reveal about their character?
6. A lottery usually represents "equality of opportunity"; in state lotteries, for example, people have equal opportunity to win prizes. How does Jackson treat this idea of "equality of opportunity" in the story?

In addition, many inquiry-based question paradigms have been developed. Sanders (1966) introduced several, and others including Barth and Shermis (1981) modified them for "goodness of fit" with a specific content domain. The Barth approach, as shown in the following chart, utilizes parts of the Guilford's structure of intellect model as the underlying organizer for developing a question set in social studies:

Question Type	Key Question
Memory/cognition	Who started the Civil War?
Convergent	Why was the conflict begun?
Divergent	What if the South had won the war?
	What might have occurred differently in the United States from 1865 to 1900 in this country?
Evaluative	In your opinion, who was the most impressive Civil War general? Why?

The Barth model also can be applied easily to language arts and literature, as can be seen in the following question set for the charming African folktale *Bringing the Rain to Kapiti Plain* by Verna Aardema.

Memory/Cognition
1. What caused the grass to turn brown?
2. What other things happened as a result of no rain?
3. What did Kipat do to solve the problem of no rain?

Convergent
1. What important qualities did Kipat have?
2. Why did Kipat think of using a feather?
3. How does this story show the relationship of cause and effect in nature?
4. Why did the author end the story with Kipat's son tending the herds?

Divergent
1. Pretend you were a herdsman in Africa at the time of the story. What obstacles would you face in carrying out your job?
2. What if the cows had died? How might the story have been different?

Evaluative
1. Why do you think Kipat waited as long as he did to get married?
2. What did you think of the way the author used rhyme to tell the story?
3. In your opinion, what is the best part of the story? Why?

Another effective questioning strategy has been used in the Great Books study program. This model is particularly effective with secondary-level gifted students. Students begin by reading a passage and responding to hypothetical situations. Next, they discuss the meaning of the passage, and they link ideas in that work to the real world of applications. The technique is shown in the following example.

Sample Reading Passage*

Can poverty in the United States be abolished within the limits of the welfare state? The answer is clear enough. The government's own figures demonstrate that the current antipoverty programs are basically inadequate. I do not, however, want to dismiss completely the government's antipoverty programs. Current serious discussion of poverty in this country is a gain which one owes in part to that program. But there is no point in pretending that a little more welfarism will do away with a national shame.

Today's poor are different from the pre–Second World War poor. The "old" poor lived at a time when economic opportunity was the national trend, when the net income from the growth of American manufacturing increased by 4,500 percent. It was the "old" poor, mostly Eastern European immigrants unified by language and culture, who created the big-city political machines and participated in the organization of unions and the political struggle for the New Deal. They had objective, realistic reason for hope.

An analysis of the first phase and second phase of the New Deal of the Roosevelt administration is quite relevant at this point. The first phase of the New Deal, supported by American business and dominated by the National Recovery Act, gave recognition to an old corporate dream—economy planned by business. The second phase of the New Deal (the source of today's welfare theory and antipoverty wisdom) moved away from the concept of planning and toward a "free market." The assumption was that in its intervention the government should not plan but should stimulate the economy and that the private sector and initiative would continue to be the mainspring of progress.

After the Second World War, the government started emphasizing training programs because some workers were not participating in the general economic advance. However, these training programs have missed the fundamental problem. The novelty of impoverishment today is that it takes place in a time of automation. The government offers education and training and at the same time admits that the jobs for its graduates are obsolete. Such hypocrisy reinforces the cynicism and resistance to organization which characterize poor communities.

It is therefore crucial that the federal government generate jobs and create an environment of economic hope. The essence of the "third phase" of the New Deal would be social investment, a conscious and political allocation of resources to meet public needs. This New Deal would be dependent upon a coalition, which would include but not be confined to, the poor, that would see to it that planning and social investment were extended in a democratic way.

Opening Questions
1. Propose a title for the passage. What is your title?
2. What audience would be interested in reading the passage? Why do you think so?
3. How would the President of the United States react to this passage? Why?

---

* Passage reprinted from College Entrance Examination Board (1983). *10 SATs.* New York: Author.

4. What public figures would agree with the perspective in the passage? Would any of our American presidents?

Core: Examining Central Points

1. According to the passage, is it possible for:

   Yes   No

   ____ ____   a. poverty to be abolished?

   ____ ____   b. America to return to pre–World War II levels of economic opportunity?

   ____ ____   c. poverty to be reduced in the current free market atmosphere?

   ____ ____   d. job training programs to solve the problem of poverty?

   ____ ____   e. America's poor today to have economic hope?

2. How would you rank order the following ideas for dealing with poverty in America, based on the perspective of the author of this passage?

   _____   Be more competitive in the world marketplace.

   _____   Stimulate the economy.

   _____   Create coalitions of support for social investment.

   _____   Return to earlier phases of the New Deal.

   _____   Let business plan the economy.

   _____   Reduce hopelessness among the poor.

   Which did you rank first? Why?

   Which did you rank last? Why?

Closing: Relating to the World
1. If fighting poverty requires "social investment," how might that approach be undertaken?
2. At what levels can this concept of "social investment" be employed? (neighborhoods, social community, states, at a global level)
3. How "marketable" is this idea in today's world?

These examples of questioning techniques represent some of the many approaches that are effective with gifted learners. Whatever technique is used, practitioners should consider the following when making decisions about questions to be asked:

1. What is the purpose of each question and of the string or cluster of questions? Do they individually and collectively contribute to greater student understanding of the work under study?

2. Are the questions interesting to *you?* Would you like to discuss them?
3. Do the questions encourage students to think more deeply about a story or event?
4. Do the questions encourage discussion and dialogue?
5. Do the questions raise issues, themes, and problems central to the story or event?
6. Will the questions carry a discussion for 45 minutes, without the need for teacher intervention?

All of the approaches cited here have to be preceded by students' careful reading of the assigned text material, for the questioning techniques are predicated on students' having sufficient knowledge and comprehension of the reading material to be able to discuss ideas intelligently. Questioning strategies can be effective only if students are prepared to engage in the inquiry process.

Problem Solving

Various forms of problem solving have been promoted for use with the gifted. One of the most frequently used has been the model of creative problem solving popularized by Parnes (1975) and Feldhusen and Treffinger (1979) and later refined by Treffinger, Isaksen, and Dorval (1994). This model places equal emphasis on the processes of problem finding and problem solving and allows students to develop a self-generated plan of action. Because the model is highly structured and moves from divergent to convergent inquiry with some regularity, it provides an excellent context in which to teach the importance of both types of inquiry for generating a worthwhile "product." The model is delineated as follows (Parnes, 1975):

Creative Problem Solving

1. *Fact finding: gathering data in preparation for defining the problem*
   ✓ Identify the problem by asking questions: Who? What? Where? When? Why?
2. *Problem finding: analyzing problematic areas in order to pick out and point up the problem to be attacked*
   ✓ Question: "In what ways might I . . . ?"
   ✓ Gather data
3. *Idea finding: idea production—thinking up, processing, and developing numerous possible leads to solutions*
   ✓ Put to other uses
   ✓ Modify
   ✓ Magnify
   ✓ Rearrange

✓ Combine

✓ Adapt

✓ Minimize

✓ Substitute

✓ Reverse

4. *Solution finding: evaluating potential solutions against defined criteria*

✓ Establish criteria

✓ Evaluate

✓ Verify

✓ Test

5. *Acceptance finding: adoption—developing a plan of action and implementing the chosen solution*

✓ Implement

✓ Prepare for acceptance

An activity using the creative problem-solving model for gifted students in a secondary English classroom might include the following guided inquiry:

I. *Problem Generation*

A. What are all the problems faced by characters in important American novels we have read? (brainstorm problems)

B. What are the most critical and general problems? (pick three, then one)

II. *Problem Clarification*

A .Where are illustrations of the problem?

B. What are things that cause the problem?

C. What are further problems caused by the problem?

III. *Problem Identification*

A .State the problem in light of Stage II discussion.

B. State the problem as a "how" question.

IV. *Idea Finding*

A .What could the character do?

B. Brainstorm solutions.

V. *Synthesizing a Solution*

A .Select the best elements from Stage IV.

B. Develop a comprehensive solution.

C. Does it fit the problem statement?

VI. *Implementation*

A .Who?

B. How?

C. What order of events?

D. State precautions, obstacles.

E. State how to overcome obstacles.

Problem-Based Learning

In problem-based learning, teams of four to five students work together to seek a solution to an ill-structured real-world problem that is relevant to a key area of school learning. The teacher facilitates their learning about the problem through providing heuristic tools, such as the three-part "need-to-know board" (used to ask: What do I know, what do I need to know, and how can I find out?), and posing probing questions about their understanding as it emerges. The teacher's instructional approach shifts throughout the problem episode depending on the support students need for various aspects of their work on the problem. Results from the use of this strategy with both elementary and secondary gifted students appear promising (Boyce, VanTassel-Baska, Burruss, Sher, & Johnson, 1997; Stepian & Gallagher, 1993).

Table 9.2 compares features of problem-based learning to those of creative problem solving (Parnes, 1975; Treffinger et al., 1994) and a more generic inquiry-based learning model (Joyce & Weil, 1996). All three models begin with a problem that is in some stage of disarray. In creative problem solving, the problem emerges from a discussion in which students identify that a problem exists, clarify the problem by providing illustrations and examples, and ultimately pose the problem as a question to be answered by further study. In general inquiry, students are presented with a puzzling situation and asked to derive meaning from it (Suchman, 1964). The problem may be real world or not and broad or narrow in its orientation. For example, students may be asked what a poem or a specific war in history means, or they may be asked what happened in a specific scientific demonstration. In problem-based learning, students are confronted with an ill-structured, real-world problem for which there may not be a clear-cut solution. Thus, the learner is drawn into a complex reality.

The role of the teacher varies in the three models. In creative problem solving, the teacher is clearly a facilitator of group process, for part of the learning to be achieved is related to the students' internalization of the heuristic steps in a collaborative group context. Newer versions of the creative problem-solving model stress the naturalistic processes employed by problem solvers in the real world and, thus, encourage a more flexible use of the specific steps of the strategy (Treffinger, 1995). In general-inquiry models, the teacher focuses on developing and posing open-ended, suggestive questions that encourage thought about the problem. The teacher typically arranges the questions in a careful hierarchy that assists students in exploring the subject at increasingly complex levels of thought. In problem-based learning, the role of the teacher is more complex. The model requires an ongoing, dynamic

TABLE 9.2   Comparison of Creative Problem Solving, Inquiry, and Problem-Based Learning

Dimension	Creative Problem Solving	Inquiry	Problem-based Learning
Nature of the problem	Starts with a discussion in which learners seek to understand the problem	Starts with the presentation of a puzzling situation	Starts with the presentation of an ill-structured, real-world problem
Role of the teacher	Facilitator of group process	Question poser	Metacognitive coach
Role of learners	Construct meaning through generating ideas	Construct meaning through questions, data collection, and analysis	Construct meaning through metacognitive and scientific heuristics
Application or transfer of learning	Application of plan to action	Application to conceptual	Application to real world

interaction between the teacher and individual learners and small groups of learners to assess their level of mastery related to both content and process considerations. Teaching interventions include but are not limited to questioning, developing group activities, initiating student self-study, and recommending a visit to a key resource person. Because of the broad purposes of this methodology, the instructional component tends to be diverse.

The role of the learner in all three models is to develop meaning. However, the means of constructing meaning and the nature and extent of the meaning derived differ among the models. In creative problem solving, meaning emerges from the manipulation of a prespecified and evolving process. In the more traditional inquiry models, meaning is derived from the careful examination of several perspectives sifted through a set of analytical and interpretive questions. In problem-based learning, the need-to-know board functions as the basic inquiry device. Students use it recursively to ask: What do I know, what do I need to know, and how do I find out? Meaning is derived through in-depth reiteration of the need-to-know heuristic as the inquiry process proceeds; thus, the approach represents a holistic and integrated method of self-learning that encourages depth and complexity of understanding.

A final point of comparison relates to the application or transfer of learning. In creative problem solving, the transfer of learning is to a plan of action that is worked out in detail to the level of citing potential barriers to implementing the plan and ways to overcome those barriers. In the general-inquiry framework, the application of learning is to conceptual understanding of a set of ideas or principles that influence an event or an artistic product. In problem-based learning, the application of learning is intended to extend beyond process and conceptual understanding to real-world utilization. Asking students, for example, to develop policy positions for real-world problems and then to articulate them to relevant adult audiences elevates the level of learning. Students have to consider the complexity inherent in real-world problem resolutions, not solutions, and the inherent conflicts of various stakeholders. Thus, the learning transfers directly to life.

The intent of this comparison is to convey the sense of sophistication of using problem-based learning as an overarching approach that can include creative problem solving and general-inquiry models. Because its perspective is broad and focused on developing self-directedness in the learner, problem-based learning can serve as an umbrella for other inquiry-based perspectives. For a relevance-based curriculum, problem-based learning is a highly valuable tool, for it competently engages the learner in constantly asking, "What makes this (learning) important to me and my life?"

In the William and Mary science units, problem-based learning provides an important catalyst for student learning in three major areas. *Conceptual learning about systems* was addressed by infusing the problem that was posed with opportunities for students to understand interrelated social, political, economic, and scientific systems in the real world. *The scientific research process* was learned through an emphasis on using experimental design techniques to tackle the scientific aspects of the problem. *Science-content learning* accrued through access to science resources that focused on specific, targeted learning. Thus, problem-based learning wrapped around a set of challenging outcomes. Preliminary studies of student learning resulting from employing the William and Mary units for at least 25 hours of instruction showed significant growth gains in the outcomes associated with integrated science process and demonstrated enhanced student and teacher motivation in science learning (VanTassel-Baska, Bass, Ries, Poland, & Avery, 1998).

When teachers were asked about unanticipated effects of using the units, they often reported increases in their own learning, especially of science content. One teacher remarked that she discovered that reading about archaeology was fun. Another said that she studied more than usual in order to effectively teach the units but that she liked learning new information. Equally important, teachers reported a new understanding of gifted learners. They commented on a greater appreciation of the problem-solving abilities of gifted learners and the need for a differentiated curriculum. The dynamic nature of problem-based learning resulted in true inquiry, with teachers learning alongside the students.

Bibliotherapy

The approaches discussed thus far relate to cognitive learning. Key instructional approaches also are valuable for working with the gifted in the psychosocial domain. These approaches can be used by both teachers and parents, who many times are in an excellent position to provide guidance to students in several areas of psychosocial development. The techniques often are integral to other teaching and learning activities that take place in the classroom. One of these approaches is bibliotherapy, the use of books to help learners reach important understandings about themselves and others. Deliberately choosing books that have a gifted child as a protagonist is an excellent way to help gifted students identify some of their own problems in others. Through discussion, these students can come to new awareness about how to cope with their problems. An example follows:

Problem identified: Understanding differences
Book: *Lord of the Flies*
Key questions (to be answered individually in writing and then discussed as a group)

✓ Why did the group ostracize Piggy?
✓ What might Piggy have done to prevent such treatment?
✓ According to the author, what happens to people who feel rejected?
✓ Can you think of a time when you have felt rejected? How did you respond or react?

How might you have changed your behavior to obtain more favorable results?

An excellent teacher reference for this type of activity is a book entitled *Some of My Best Friends Are Books* (Halsted, 2002).

A second area of psychosocial development that a teacher can help the gifted explore is their tendency toward perfectionism. By focusing on open-ended activities and leading students to engage in "safe" risk-taking behaviors, teachers can set a climate in which students are encouraged to accept that most situations in life do not have *one* right answer—rendering unimportant the standard the gifted often set to rate themselves and others on the way to "perfection." An example of an open-ended activity that promotes "safe" risk taking follows:

Pass out pictures (a different picture for each group of three students) that are linked to key pieces of literature by theme and impressionistic in style, and ask students to respond individually to these vital stimuli according to the following paradigm:

1. What did you observe in the picture? (Make a list of what you see.)
2. What ideas does your picture convey?
3. What feelings does your picture evoke?
4. If you were to identify with an object in your picture, what would you identify with, and why?

5. Now spend a few minutes synthesizing your observations, ideas, feelings, and reactions to your picture in whatever form you wish. You may choose, for example, to write a poem, draw a picture, or create a descriptive story.

After each student has responded to these questions and activities, have the members of each group discuss one another's perceptions of the group's picture. Then, if you wish, ask individual students to share their pictures and their reactions to them. Follow-up may include whole-group discussion of similarities and differences in the pictures and literature from which each was taken. This activity can also introduce a unit of study on cultural or individual differences.

A third area of psychosocial exploration with the gifted centers on the area of forming meaningful relationships and developing friendships. Books such as *The Bunny Who Wanted a Friend*, by Joan Berg, can be used as a key tool with primary-age students. The following example shows questions a teacher can ask to help elicit understanding of the strategies by which we gain friends.

---

1. What are all the reasons the bunny did not have a friend?
2. What was wrong with his method of making friends?
3. What was his "secret" to finally finding a friend?
4. What if you were the bunny? How would you have tried to make a friend?
5. Why were the bunny and the bird friends at the end of the story? List the reasons.

Both of these bibliotherapy strategies are viable for use with the gifted in both home and school settings.

Content-Based Strategies

The six instructional strategies that have been discussed have salience in many subject areas, but they clearly will not work well in all areas. For that reason, teachers of the gifted must also develop content-based strategies. Table 9.3 outlines specific content-based strategies for each of the major disciplines. As can be seen from a perusal of each column, many of these strategies are consonant with reform recommendations, emphasizing higher-level thinking, the use of technology, constructivist activities, and interdisciplinary learning approaches. Although these themes cut across the subject areas, each discipline also retains its own unique set of strategies pedagogically linked to the content area under study. Educators of the gifted need to develop a strong understanding of these strategies and implement them effectively within content-based programs.

TABLE 9.3   Content-Based Strategies for Improving Student Achievement

Language Arts	Mathematics	Science	Social Studies
✓ Incorporate extensive reading of varied kinds of material.	✓ Focus instruction on the development of important mathematical ideas.	✓ Utilize the learning cycle approach (exploration, invention, and application).	✓ Encourage thoughtful classroom climates that promote higher-order thinking.
✓ Foster interactive learning.	✓ Incorporate the use of calculators.	✓ Utilize cooperative learning for classroom and laboratory instruction.	✓ Utilize the jurisprudential approach.
✓ Extend students' background knowledge.	✓ Work with small groups of students.	✓ Use analogies for the development of conceptual understandings.	✓ Teach critical thinking skills and strategies in the context of content knowledge, with attention to their appropriate applications.
✓ Utilize skills and strategies that help create meaning, such as summarizing, questioning, and interpreting.	✓ Increase amount of time spent on mathematics.	✓ Allow wait time after asking questions.	✓ Support concept development by using definitions, examples and non-examples, exploration of relations to other concepts, and students' prior knowledge.
✓ Organize instruction into broad, thematically based clusters of work.	✓ Focus on number sense.	✓ Use student-generated and teacher-generated concept maps.	
✓ Teach critical reading and writing skills.	✓ Utilize concrete materials on a long-term basis.	✓ Incorporate computer simulations.	
✓ Emphasize discussion and analysis.	✓ Encourage students' intuitive methods for solving problems and allow for interaction and discussion in this process.	✓ Use computers to collect and display data.	✓ Incorporate effective phrasing, pacing, and distribution of questions and responses to students' answers.
✓ Stress the composing process.		✓ Employ systematic approaches in problem solving.	✓ Encourage cognitive prejudice reduction by developing students' reasoning skills so that students draw valid inferences about group differences.
✓ Provide balanced attention to different forms of reading, writing, and speaking.		✓ Encourage qualitative understanding of concepts used to solve quantitative problems.	
✓ Provide early intervention.		✓ Use a science-technology-society approach.	
✓ Expose students to varied kinds of literature.		✓ Incorporate real-life situations.	✓ Utilize computer data bases and simulations.
✓ Provide assessment that reflects the content and process of instruction.		✓ Use discrepant events to produce cognitive conflict.	✓ Encourage community service.
			✓ Incorporate constructive teaching strategies.

Source: From *Handbook of Research on Improving Student Achievement* by G. Cawelti (Ed.), 1995, Arlington, VA: Educational Research Service.

MEDIATING LEARNING THROUGH INSTRUCTION

Instructional processes mediate both the objective of any lesson and the receptivity level of students to that objective. Thus, the function of instruction, though not paramount, is critical to the enterprise of teaching and learning. It might be argued that the mode of instruction for gifted learners is less critical than for other learners, given the ability of the gifted to connect with content and their tendency to master it quickly and well. Yet, even the gifted need high-quality instruction to maximize their knowledge acquisition and minimize the time and energy taken up by lower-level work. If a teacher cannot mediate the knowledge acquisition process effectively for individual learners, the best curriculum plan and set of activities will go awry (Lebow, 1994).

How does one go about such mediation? Developing skills in areas such as discovery learning, inquiry, asking the right level questions, and using specific teaching paradigms is helpful, but merely manipulating process is insufficient for mediating curricula for the gifted. Gifted educators also must attend to manipulation of content in fundamental ways.

The alternative activity sets in Chapter 8, Table 8.1, help to illustrate this point. By way of example, consider the following activity set:

Discuss plot, setting, and characters in the short story "A Rose for Emily."	*Compare and contrast the plot, setting, character motivation, and theme of "A Rose for Emily" and "The Bear."*

The activity on the right, which is more appropriate for gifted students, engages learners in critical analysis as the foundational element of their manipulation of knowledge. Moreover, it seeks to have them use two stimuli to do so. Further, in addition to the basic elements of plot, character, and setting, it involves the more complex and abstract task of manipulating theme and character motivation.

If we agree that the activity on the right is more appropriate for gifted learners, what instructional mediation would enhance its use? A teacher of the gifted could:

✓ hold a discussion in which students demonstrate their capacity to complete the activity in oral form.

✓ have students develop an expository essay in class, and meet with students individually or in small groups to discuss their analysis.

✓ lecture on key elements of short stories, and use the activity as a seatwork application of information for quizzing students on their understanding.

✓ develop panel discussion groups that allow students to discuss and present as a group their critical analysis of the two stories.

✓ engage students in creating a representational visual product, such as a videotape, mobile, slides, or collage, that conveys their analysis of the stories.

✓ assign the activity as homework—a direct follow-up to a class lecture and discussion on short story elements.

Selecting the instructional process to use for this activity would depend on several factors:

1. *Instructional time.* Decisions about instructional process cannot be based solely on the relative importance of a given activity. They also must take time constraints into account. Some options are more time-consuming than others. If time is limited, a strategy that will work in the allotted time is most prudent.
2. *Mixing of instructional processes.* Choice of a process to accompany any activity is somewhat dependent on what processes preceded and will follow the activity. A variety of approaches works well with gifted learners.
3. *Student need for a particular approach.* The needs of gifted learners sometimes affect choice of instructional process. Perhaps students need more cooperative learning at a given point, or need to enhance expository writing skills, or need practice in orally articulating a perspective. Such needs then may become a criterion for choosing an instructional approach.
4. *Effectiveness of a given approach with gifted learners.* A meta-analysis of research on gifted learners demonstrated a high effect size for increased homework, a moderate effect size for active questioning and discussion, and a moderate effect size for inquiry-discovery teaching (Walberg, 1991). To make intelligent choices of strategies, we have to examine what we know about what works. For the three strategies cited, recognizing the role that each could play in delivering curriculum would be an important perspective to have.
5. *The nature of the activity itself.* The choice of activity may make the choice of instructional process easier, for many activities call for the use of particular strategies. For example, the critical analysis activity described earlier may be thought of as basically a reflective activity, one in which gifted learners need considerable time to think about the two stories in depth. Therefore, an instructional process that honors thinking time may be a better choice than one that emphasizes quick response or group interaction skills.

Instructional choice, then, can best be made after all factors have been considered. As in other aspects of this curriculum design model, the emphasis is on careful thinking and planning of what to do.

SUMMARY

Instructional strategies are crucial in delivering curricula for the gifted learner. No curriculum is likely to be judged effective with gifted learners without careful choices regarding strategies. Alternative strategies include small groups, individual consultation, inquiry, questioning techniques, pacing, and problem solving. Many educators cite the importance of linking teacher behaviors to student outcomes. Exemplary teachers plan curricula well, use various teaching strategies, select questions that stimulate higher-level thinking, foster critical thinking, creative thinking, and problem solving, encourage independent thinking and open inquiry, conduct group discussions well, promote student-directed work, and provide a healthy learning environment, among other behaviors.

Problem-based learning is a promising umbrella approach to employ with gifted learners in that it heightens both the complexity of the tasks and the motivation of the learners. Use of research-based, content-based learning strategies also enhances the teaching–learning process for these students.

Bibliotherapy—the use of books to further learning—is another strategy that is particularly effective with the gifted. Through books, gifted students can gain insight by identifying their problems in others, exploring their tendency for perfectionism, and learning how to develop friendships.

In selecting which instructional strategies to use, the teacher has to consider the amount of time required, a mix of processes, individual need and effectiveness of a given approach with that learner, and the nature of the activity itself.

QUESTIONS FOR REFLECTION

1. How can gifted educators find effective ways to monitor teacher behaviors in the classroom to ensure high-level instruction?
2. How might videotaping and peer coaching be employed to improve teaching strategies?
3. What combinations of strategies might maximize creative productivity for gifted learners?
4. How might we better organize classrooms to manage the instructional processes advocated in this chapter?
5. How would you respond to the statement, "Gifted education is just good teaching"?

REFERENCES

Aardema, V. (1997). *Bringing the rain to Kapiti Plain.* Boston: Houghton Mifflin.

Barth, J. L., & Shermis, S. S. (1981). *Teaching social studies to the gifted and talented.* Indianapolis: Indiana State Department of Public Instruction, Div. of Curriculum; Lafayette: Purdue University. (ED 212118).

Boyce, L. N., VanTassel-Baska, J., Burruss, J., Sher, B. T., & Johnson, D. T. (1997). A problem-based curriculum: Parallel learning opportunities for students and teachers. *Journal for the Education of the Gifted, 20,* 363–379.

Cawelti, G. (Ed.). (1995). *Handbook of research on improving student achievement.* Arlington, VA: Educational Research Service.

Center for Gifted Education. (1998). *A checklist of teacher behaviors in classrooms for the gifted.* Williamsburg, VA: Author.

College Entrance Examination Board. (1983). *10 SATs.* New York: Author.

Feldhusen, J., & Treffinger, D. (1979). *Creative thinking and problem-solving.* Dubuque, IA: Kendall-Hunt.

Halsted, J. (2002). *Some of my best friends are books.* Scottsdale, AZ: Great Potential Press.

Joyce, B., & Weil, M. (1996). *Models of teaching* (5th ed.). Boston: Allyn & Bacon.

Lebow, D. (1994). Constructivist values for instructional systems design: Five principles toward a new mindset. *Educational Technology Research and Development, 41,* 4–16.

Lipman, M. (1988). Critical thinking—What can it be? *Educational Leadership, 46*(1), 38–43.

Martinson, R. (1974). Martinson-Weiner rating scale of behaviors in teachers of the gifted. In *A guide toward better teaching for the gifted.* Ventura, CA: Office of the Ventura County Superintendent of Schools.

Norris, S. P. (1985). Synthesis of research on critical thinking. *Educational Leadership, 42*(8), 40–45.

Oakes, J. (1985). *Keeping track: How schools structure inequality.* New Haven, CT: Yale University Press.

Parnes, S. (1975). *Aha! Insights into creative behavior.* Buffalo, NY: DOK.

Sanders, N. M. (1966). *Classroom questions: What kinds?* New York: Harper & Row.

Shulman, L. S. (1987). Assessment for teaching: An initiative for the profession. *Phi Delta Kappan, 69,* 38–44.

Stepien, W., & Gallagher, S. (1993). Problem-based learning: As authentic as it gets. *Educational Leadership, 50*(7), 25–28.

Sternberg, R. J., & Bhana, K. (1986). Synthesis of research on the effectiveness of intellectual skills programs: Snake-oil remedies or miracle cures? *Educational Leadership, 44*(2), 60–67.

Suchman, J. R. (1964). Illinois studies in inquiry training. In R. E. Ripple & V. N. Rockcastle (Eds.), *Piaget rediscovered: Report of the Conference on Cognitive Studies and Curriculum Development* (pp. 105–108). Ithaca, NY: Cornell University Press.

Treffinger, D. J. (1995). Creative problem solving: Overview and educational implications. *Educational Psychology Review, 7,* 301–312.

Treffinger, D. J., Isaksen, S. G., & Dorval, K. B. (1994). Creative problem solving: An overview. In M. A. Runco (Ed.), *Problem finding, problem solving, and creativity* (pp. 223–236). Norwood, NJ: Ablex.

VanTassel-Baska, J. (1995). *Comprehensive curriculum for gifted learners.* Boston: Allyn & Bacon.

VanTassel-Baska, J. (1998). *Planning science programs for high-ability learners.* (ERIC briefs). Reston, VA: Council for Exceptional Children.

VanTassel-Baska, J., Bass, G. M., Ries, R. R., Poland, D., & Avery, L. (1998). A national pilot study of science curriculum effectiveness for high-ability students. *Gifted Child Quarterly, 42,* 200–211.

VanTassel-Baska, J., Zuo, L., Avery, L. D., & Little, C. A. (2002). A curriculum study of gifted student learning in the language arts. *Gifted Child Quarterly, 46,* 30–44.

Walberg, H. (1991). Productive teaching and instruction: Assessing the knowledge base. In H. C. Waxman & H. J. Walberg (Eds.), *Effective teaching: Current research* (pp. 33–62). Berkeley, CA: McCutchan.

10

EMPLOYING APPROPRIATE CURRICULUM MANAGEMENT STRATEGIES

Because teachers consider classroom management a significant variable in effective teaching and learning (Wang, Haertel, & Walberg, 1990), its relationship to classroom instruction strategies is important to consider. The beginning of this chapter explores various curriculum management strategies that enhance classroom control because effective classroom management is dependent on effective curriculum planning for the individual needs of learners.

A recent study by Kishar and Godfrey (1999) concluded that the use of teacher-developed instructional forms provides significant effects on student learning, suggesting that careful instructional planning and delivery can positively affect student behavior.

Trophy and Alleman (1998) described a well-managed classroom as one in which the teacher prepares a physical environment suitable for learning, develops rules of conduct, maintains student attention and participation in group lessons, and monitors student assignments and progress toward the desired learning outcomes. According to the authors, procedures for attaining these goals include the following:

✓ Establishing clear expectations at the beginning of the school year.
✓ Beginning and ending class periods smoothly.
✓ Making effective transitions between activities.
✓ Maintaining the flow of activities by stimulating involvement.
✓ Attending to the needs of individual students.

A basic principle of good classroom management is that it must support instructional goals. Another basic principle is that classroom planning should begin with the identification of outcomes that constitute the goals of instruction. Teachers need to ask: What knowledge, skills, values, and behavioral dispositions must students possess or acquire to engage in this learning activity most profitably?

Although a fine line separates instructional strategies from management techniques, Squires (1999) found that the marriage of instruction and school management occurs as five norms become stronger and begin to serve as the foundation for decision-making processes in the schools:

✓ A focus on students' instructional and developmental needs.
✓ The use of data to understand problems and evaluate solution implementation.
✓ A strong link between the central role of planning and staff development.
✓ The use of the group processes of consensus and collaboration.
✓ The role of leaders as process facilitators and guides.

A major aspect of classroom management is classroom organization. The following sections address fundamental ways that teachers of the gifted can organize classrooms to best accommodate their students.

CLASSROOM ORGANIZATION

Major curriculum management techniques include various grouping arrangements, diagnostic-prescriptive approaches, and individualized approaches including self-paced learning, independent study and specialized projects, and individualized educational programs (IEPs), as shown in Figure 10.1 and discussed in the remainder of this chapter. Several authors have focused on the importance of these techniques in planning curricula for gifted learners (Renzulli, Leppien, & Hays, 2000; Tomlinson, 1999; Winebrenner, 1999). Each technique offers opportunities for delivering a differentiated program of study to gifted learners.

Grouping Arrangements

In classrooms in which grouping strategies are not employed, much of the power of any differentiated curriculum or instructional plan is lost, for it is in the grouping arrangement that the gifted have the potential to fully respond to any curriculum. Key grouping strategies are cooperative learning groups, cluster grouping, dyads and triads, learning centers, and cross-age grouping.

Cooperative Learning Groups

Cooperative learning has become popular in recent years. With this strategy, students are divided into groups; all students in each group contribute actively to the problem under study; and group energy propels learners toward mastery of the material. To make cooperative learning effective for the gifted, students' ability and interest must be considered in establishing such groups since gifted students perform best with other gifted and high-ability learners (Rogers, 1998). Cooperative learning can be a powerful way, for example, to organize gifted learners for a project in which

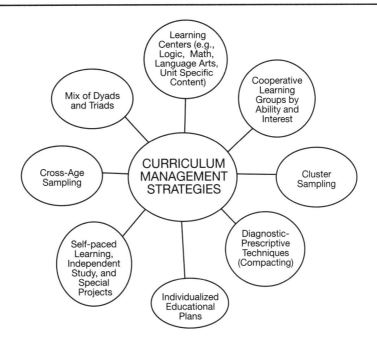

FIGURE 10.1   Types of Curriculum Management Strategies

each student has a role to perform. Examples of appropriate projects include the following:

✓ Writing skits.
✓ Performing a play.
✓ Developing an advertising campaign.
✓ Organizing a literary exhibit.
✓ Conducting research on immigration from a multiple source/multiple viewpoint perspective.

Cluster Grouping

In cluster grouping, all gifted students in a grade are assigned to the same teacher as part of a class of mixed-ability students. Thus, the gifted can be grouped and regrouped within the classroom to accommodate different instructional needs. For academic subjects, the gifted generally work in their cluster group on an accelerated instructional plan while other students in the room follow a different plan.

Dyads and Triads

This grouping strategy allows gifted learners to find one or two true peers in the classroom with whom they can work effectively. Sometimes these pairings occur naturally, and other times they are carefully nurtured by an insightful teacher. This approach to learning is ideal for initiating independent projects and for having students move ahead somewhat independently in parts of the curriculum. Rather than having isolated gifted students work alone on an enrichment project, two or three students can complete the assignments together, even if their ability levels are somewhat different. As long as the gifted learners are well motivated and interested in the learning task, some ability differences can be tolerated. This grouping approach encourages social development both in the classroom and beyond the classroom, in the form of study groups or less formal get-togethers.

Learning Centers

Many classrooms establish learning centers and have students actively participate in center activities according to a rotating schedule throughout the week. Gifted learners are typically accommodated by either (a) the provision of extended activities in each center geared to their level of need or (b) the establishment of a gifted center where all instructional activities are geared to their level. This approach provides instructional alternatives for all class members and enables students to develop responsibility for their own learning in selected areas of the curriculum. Sometimes the centers are organized in the school library rather than in individual classrooms. The important concepts are the student's freedom in choice of activities and voluntary movement toward desired learning opportunities.

Cross-age Grouping

Cross-age grouping allows gifted learners within two or three grade levels to work together in areas of strength and interest. Some high schools offer courses across grade levels. Others bring together groups of gifted students at predetermined times during the week. This technique is frequently used in small schools with few gifted children at each grade level.

All of these approaches should be considered in providing appropriate instructional options for gifted learners at the classroom level. Because even the most critical opponents of ability grouping voice support for instructional grouping (Oakes, 1985; Slavin, 1986), schools would be prudent to enhance their programs with variations of the grouping strategies discussed above. Without such provisions, the gifted have limited access to appropriate challenges in the context of elementary and secondary classrooms and programs.

The Diagnostic-Prescriptive Approach

In the diagnostic-prescriptive approach, each gifted learner takes a diagnostic pretest at the beginning of the school year covering subject matter to be studied that year.

Based on the information attained, the student's instructional range is determined both for grade-level skill development or content-based knowledge and for the level of capacity to engage in concepts and problem solving in verbal, mathematical, and scientific domains. The gifted students then are grouped in the configuration that best matches their instructional range and are provided opportunities to move at a rate in the curriculum consonant with their tested level of competency and their aptitude to engage in more challenging curricula.

Expectations for annual accomplishment in the area of a group's focus are determined for each group by the teacher, based on a differential starting point. Thus, a group of fifth graders conceivably could be studying algebra or probability and statistics as their core math program. For less precocious math students, pre-algebra mathematics could be accompanied by work in problem-solving heuristics and symbolic logic.

Pretesting aids in diagnosing and managing the needs of gifted learners in the classroom in several ways:

✓ It alerts learners to what they do and do not know about the topic and helps students and the instructor develop an understanding of students' readiness for the program.
✓ It indicates to both learners and the instructor the point at which to begin the curriculum work.
✓ It may motivate learners to study the topic by arousing their curiosity and interest.
✓ It informs learners of what will be covered during study of the topic, helping them to understand what will be required of them.
✓ It provides baseline data for determining growth in learning.
✓ It provides formative evaluation information that can help the instructor modify parts of the curriculum (adding or eliminating outcomes, activities, or both) so that the curriculum can start at the point of learner readiness.

Using pretesting data well is a staple of effective curriculum management. In the prescriptive aspect of this approach, instructors use pretesting data to guide curriculum modification by completing the following steps:

1. Identify the objectives of relevant curriculum.
2. Find and administer appropriate pretests.
3. Eliminate instruction in relevant areas for students who show mastery of the objectives (85th percentile criterion level).
4. Streamline instruction for the objectives students have not mastered but are capable of mastering more quickly than their classmates.
5. Offer challenging alternatives for students who show proficiency in core areas of the curriculum.
6. Document student progress.

Individualized Learning Approaches

Self-paced Learning

Self-paced learning has become a natural consequence of employing the diagnostic-prescriptive approach to a year's course of study with gifted students. Although "self-pacing" implies that each learner follows an individualized model of regulating his or her learning rate, very few classrooms employ the approach in this way. Rather, the general practice is for groups of advanced learners to collaborate on learning at a pace manageable to the group. Such a management strategy may impede the learning of the most able, but this disadvantage is compensated for by the advantages of the higher level of the work in general and the social dynamics created by having a study group.

Many school districts place artificial caps on self-pacing such that students can advance only the equivalent of half a year in mathematics, for example. Such an administrative decision defeats the purpose of self-pacing, which is to align learning rate with individual capacity without imposing a ceiling based on grade level. To be effectively employed at a school, self-pacing must be viewed as a continuous progress model that affects all grade levels and requires flexibility in instructional expectations and assessment schedules.

Independent Study and Special Projects

Managing independent study and special project opportunities for gifted learners is a challenging task. Decisions must be made about several key issues, including the following:

✓ independent versus group work.
✓ the number of independent projects in a given year.
✓ self-selected or mutually negotiated projects.
✓ targeted to a given subject area or interdisciplinary.
✓ topical or issue/problem-oriented.
✓ completed during school time or worked on as homework.
✓ the length of time anticipated to complete a study.
✓ the processes for conducting the study.

The overall goal of most independent study projects and other special projects for the gifted is to create autonomous learners. If gifted students are to engage successfully in these efforts, it may be argued that they must first be taught certain core skill areas. According to Boyce (1997), they represent important overlapping areas of learning for which gifted students require some degree of direct instruction.

1. Using information strategies to research an issue or problem
   Students will be able to:
   ✓ Access information sources

✓ Use information to research an issue
✓ Evaluate information

2. Researching an issue of significance
Students will be able to:

✓ Identify an issue or problem
✓ Explore an issue and identify points of view or arguments through information sources
✓ Form a set of questions that can be answered by a specific set of data
✓ Gather evidence through research techniques such as surveys, interviews, and experiments
✓ Manipulate and transform data so that the information can be interpreted
✓ Draw conclusions and inferences
✓ Determine implications and consequences
✓ Communicate results

3. Using reasoning skills during the research process
Students will be able to:

✓ Identify and use the elements of reasoning
✓ Exercise traits of the reasoning mind
✓ Apply standards of reasoning
✓ Demonstrate reasoning abilities

4. Using metacognition for independent and interdependent learning
Students will be able to:

✓ Plan a research project
✓ Monitor the progress of a research project
✓ Evaluate a research project

Independent study and special project work for the gifted should be carefully thought out and used in balance with other approaches to learning. For special project work, dyads may be more successful than students working individually, because partners have the opportunity to discuss and meaningfully collaborate on the process to be employed. Totally independent project work requires that students show basic competency with the skill areas noted earlier. Student-developed learning packages that provide guidance to mastery of a particular learning segment can be employed to assess students' capacity to learn effectively and efficiently in an independent mode.

Individualized Education Programs

Currently only 12 states require IEPs for gifted learners. However, such plans often are helpful, especially for students with dual exceptionalities who require specific modification to their educational program. IEPs are completed annually in consultation with relevant teachers, parents, and the student. In developing IEPs for gifted learners, all aspects of the learner must be addressed, including cognitive, affective, and expressive elements. The IEP should stress areas of student strength and strategies for augmenting the general school program for such students. Figure 10.2 presents a model for a gifted student IEP that provides for such balance in implementation.

Classroom teachers must monitor the progress of students with IEPs more regularly than they may monitor other students, and they must communicate with parents more often regarding student issues and problems. Too frequently, these procedures are not followed, and the IEP model is more honored "in the breach than the observance" to the detriment of the gifted learners' requiring these plans.

While multiple individuals are required to implement many IEPs, the classroom teacher typically is responsible for management of the overall plan. The use of a collaborative team model can help to ensure implementation at the school level.

SELECTING APPROPRIATE STRATEGIES FOR CLASSROOM USE

Relative strengths and limitations of major curriculum management approaches are addressed in the sections that follow. Decisions about strategy use should be made by balancing the purpose of a unit module against time restraints and population needs.

Lecture Method

Many members of the gifted community believe that the lecture method is inappropriate for use with gifted learners. However, evidence suggests that didactic instruction through direct teaching has an overall beneficial effect on learning for all students, including the gifted (Wang et al., 1990). Moreover, gifted students who are auditory learners respond well to well-crafted and delivered lectures. Visual learners also respond well if the lectures are complemented by visuals. Interspersed with questions, lectures can become an interactive conversation. These findings suggest that lecture clearly should be employed as a part of the instructional process in classrooms for gifted learners.

The effectiveness of lectures can be increased through three primary approaches: active interaction between instructor and listeners, note taking, and the use of well-organized handouts. A standard format for lectures includes the following components:

✓ Orient students to a topic with an outline, a story, or an overview.
✓ Review prerequisites.

INDIVIDUALIZED EDUCATION PROGRAM

Student's Name: Janet Doe   Age: 10   DOB: 6/22/91   Date: 8/15/01
School Division: Anywhere, USA   Grade: 5   School: Shepherd
Parent/Guardian: Mr. Lloyd Doe   Address: 325 Anywhere Lane
                                                 Phone: 525-6307
Date of Assessment: 6/1/01   Date of education program
                                                 (beginning/ending): 9/7/01–6/20/02

Overall Goals: Develop critical thinking behaviors
                  Enhance self-esteem
                  Promote opportunities for creative/artistic expression

Educational Program Emphases	Responsibility	Procedures for Implementation
Cognitive/Academic • **Verbal** – Develop vocabulary skills – Develop persuasive writing skills – Develop critical reading behaviors	Classroom teacher	– Use of William and Mary *Autobiographies* unit for first semester; use of Junior Great Books for second semester – Use of Word Within a Word program throughout the year
• **Quantitative** – Develop spatial reasoning – Develop logical thinking – Promote mathematical problem solving	Classroom teacher	– Use of Dale Seymour's Techniques of Problem Solving (TOPS) program all year – Use of Web Quests (select six per year) – Use of Geometry Sketch Pad all year
• **Nonverbal** – Develop experimental design skills	Science consultant/aide to the classroom	– Student to work through series of science experiments (e.g., Lim's *Invitation to Science Inquiry*) – Student to design an original experiment, based on interest area
• **Affective/Behavioral** – Develop understanding of strengths and areas of relative weakness – Develop the leadership skills of planning and organization	School counselor Advisor to relevant club or extracurricular area	– Administer and review aptitude, ability, and achievement tests and various inventories including those of values and interests over the course of the year – Student to plan and carry out responsibility for a special event over the course of 6 weeks
• **Creative/Aesthetic** – Develop expressive skills through acting in a play	Drama coach	– Student to practice and perform in a school or community-based play over the course of a semester

Signature of IEP Developer _____ Date _____

FIGURE 10.2   Model of Individualized Education Program for a Gifted Student

✓ Present the material in a clear, organized way. The lecturer should attempt to speak from an outline instead of reading verbatim.
✓ Ask questions.
✓ Provide independent practice for important concepts, procedures, or both.
✓ Review and preview.

The following are strengths and limitations of the lecture approach:

Strengths

1. Large numbers of learners can be reached at the same time. Thus, lectures are highly economical, limited only by the size of the room.
2. The instructor is in direct control of the class and in a highly visible position. For many teaching contexts, these factors support the achievement of learner outcomes.
3. Information can be presented that provides an overview of a topic or orientation to a new topic. Lectures can also be used to convey basic or essential information that provides a common background before learners engage in small-group or individual activities.
4. Good lectures can be motivating and interesting for students.

Limitations

1. Learning typically is passive, involving listening, watching, and taking notes, with little opportunity for the exchange of ideas.
2. Individual differences are not accommodated. Although it is commonly assumed that learners are acquiring the same understanding with the same level of comprehension at the same time, in reality this is not the case.
3. The lecture method is difficult for students who face difficulties with auditory learning.
4. High demands are placed on the lecturer to be engaging and challenging.

Long-Distance Learning

Few students prefer to learn at a distance, but the convenience of telecommunications sometimes outweighs this and other factors (Simonson, 1995). Listservs, e-mail, and web sites all provide means for instruction to be delivered through the Internet. Video teleconferencing is more expensive but is also an option. Recently produced curriculum resources provide exciting possibilities for using the Internet and CD-ROM sources effectively, especially for enhancing inquiry-based learning. Linn, Slotta, and Baumgartner's review of these resources (Linn et al., 2000) provides a helpful guide to simulations, on-line curricula and software programs that aid teachers in working with students in science.

The following are strengths and limitations of the long-distance learning approach.

Strengths

1. Students can participate without being present at the school.
2. Very large audiences, situated miles apart, can be served.
3. As in the traditional classroom setting, students experience instruction as it happens.
4. Students can interact with the instructor by asking questions and making comments electronically.

Limitations

1. Interactions between individuals are more constrained and less fluid than would occur if the individuals were in the same room.
2. The quality of video and audio transmission may be inferior to that in a regular lecture.
3. Distance learning is still a relatively expensive mode of education.

Self-Paced Learning/Independent Study

Self-paced learning methods frequently are used to accelerate the learning of basic material by gifted students. Usually the instructor selects the learning objectives and sets the requirements the learners must follow. Evaluations depend on what the students have completed in a given period of time, with learner mastery checked at relevant points. Students receive feedback for mastery of each objective. Evidence suggests that in many situations gifted learners participating in self-paced programs work harder, learn more, and retain more of what they learn, than do learners in conventional classes (Brody, 1992). Self-paced learning also is a feature of independent study project work, which is a frequently employed technique with gifted learners.

The following are strengths and limitations of self-paced learning approaches.

Strengths

1. Advanced learners can complete the instruction according to their own comfortable ability rate and under appropriate learning conditions.
2. Working independently builds self-reliance and personal responsibility.
3. The instructor spends more time working with learners in groups, consulting with individuals, and managing the learning environment.
4. Instructors are more aware of individual learning needs.

Limitations

1. Less interaction may occur between instructor and learners, or among learners, than with other approaches.

2. If a single-path lockstep method is followed, learning may become monotonous and uninteresting.

3. Open-ended projects may allow for too much divergence in what learners experience and accomplish.

4. Lack of self-discipline combined with procrastination can impede the completion of required study by some gifted learners.

Self-paced learning may be facilitated by the use of learner contracts, worksheets and textbooks, computer-based instruction, and multimedia packages such as CD-ROMs. Self-instructional modules also may be effective but require more time to prepare.

Small-Group Work in Various Settings

A number of techniques are available for providing interaction within small groups. These techniques include discussion, use of panels, role-playing, use of simulations and games, and cooperative learning. If group learning is used extensively with gifted students, careful controls must be in place for individual assessment. Gifted learners have come to resent the typical cooperative learning approaches employed in many classrooms because they carry the burden of the "group grade." Care must be taken to ensure that expertise levels are similar if gifted students are to benefit sufficiently from this mode of learning.

The following are strengths and limitations of small-group work:

Strengths:

1. Small group work can promote deeper understanding of content, because it allows individuals to discuss materials, share ideas, and problem-solve with others.

2. Learners strengthen communication skills by presenting and reacting to ideas.

3. Well-structured activities can promote active learning.

4. Learners strengthen social skills by working with others within a group setting.

Limitations

1. Thought must be put into group composition and development of group rules.

2. Groups require frequent feedback and prompting.

3. Individuals in groups must take responsibility for completing tasks.

4. Because students are not trained instructors, group activities should always be used in tandem with other forms of instruction.

5. The work a group completes may not indicate the learning of all group members. One individual often will do the majority of the work for the group, allowing others to shirk their responsibilities yet receive the same grade as the hard-working individual.

CLASSROOM MANAGEMENT TECHNIQUES FOR SPECIAL NEEDS LEARNERS

Special considerations must be undertaken in managing classrooms that include gifted students who have disabilities. Typically, the most common disabilities seen among the gifted are learning disabilities, attention deficit disorder (ADD), and attention deficit hyperactivity disorder (ADHD). Some gifted students have overlapping conditions that may require more adaptations.

In general, the following classroom adaptations have proven beneficial in working with gifted students with special needs.

1. *Increasing focus.* This modification can be accomplished by having these students sit in quiet, nondistractive areas, especially for seat work, quizzes, and tests. Placing clocks on the desks of these students can help the students keep track of time during tests and other timed work.

2. *Providing cueing.* Compared to other learners, students with these disabilities require more social cues from their environment for the reinforcement of desired behaviors. Developing a nonverbal cueing system with these students can be helpful in reminding them to settle down, stop talking, or get on with a task.

3. *Allowing classroom movement at key intervals.* Gifted students with these disabilities need to be able to move around the room at regular intervals and to take breaks from their work. Classrooms organized according to informal groups are advantageous for this adaptation, because the group structure promotes student movement.

4. *Making regular contact with parents.* Because the parents of gifted learners with disabilities often serve as the students' "case managers," they should be kept apprised of daily assignments and long-term projects. The use of e-mail and daily assignment sheets that parents must sign can be instrumental in allowing parents to be effective monitors of homework and class expectations.

5. *Providing visual and auditory reminders of classroom procedures and specific task requirements.* Because many of these students have difficulty following directions, posting reminders of major steps to be followed in the classroom and mentioning the procedures periodically can facilitate student follow-through on work assignments.

6. *Adjusting time requirements for tests, homework, and projects.* Students with these disabilities often need more time than their peers to finish work, especially when the work requires functioning in their area of disability. Because these students many times have difficulty working efficiently, time extensions may be called for with long-term projects.

7. *Allowing for alternative assignments.* Gifted students with these disabilities often prefer work that is conceptual and global in orientation, requiring them to synthesize ideas and create alternative ways of seeing the world or responding to situations. Thus, creative and open-ended assignments may help increase

their motivation to learn. Such techniques are important for all gifted students, but they are essential for keeping students with disabilities motivated and feeling successful with their schoolwork.

Managing gifted learners with special needs is best effected in self-contained gifted programs or classes. However, that ideal situation often is not the reality. Many of these students are found in other grouping arrangements, with or without a special education designation or a 504 plan. Thus, it is essential for classroom teachers to modify instruction to accommodate these learners in multiple settings.

SUMMARY

Managing classrooms to accommodate gifted learners requires flexibility and creativity on the part of classroom teachers. In selecting which management strategies to employ, teachers must consider the amount of time required, a mix of approaches, individual as well as group needs, and the constraints based on the nature of the activity to be implemented. These decisions are key to using classroom management to enhance learning.

The use of such key strategies as grouping, diagnostic assessment, and independent learning is crucial to promoting optimal learning in the gifted. Only through individualized and small-group techniques can gifted students learn most effectively.

QUESTIONS FOR REFLECTION

1. What type of arrangement would you use to group gifted students to design original experiments? To apply the concept of equations? To develop a newspaper? Why?

2. If you were a teacher of the gifted, how would you design a typical day's or week's schedule to accomplish a balance between group and independent work?

3. Given the relative advantages and disadvantages of using technology to deliver instruction, how would you advocate its use in your classroom?

4. Under what circumstances would you employ independent study as a major management strategy for the gifted? Justify your answer, given your understanding of the advantages and disadvantages of this classroom management tool.

5. What classroom provisions would you make for gifted learners with special needs? How do they compare with the management strategies described in this chapter?

REFERENCES

Boyce, L. (1997). *A guide to teaching research skills and strategies for grades 4–12.* Williamsburg, VA: Center for Gifted Education.

Brody, L. E. (1992). Mathematics acceleration of highly talented students: An evaluation. *Gifted Child Quarterly, 36*(2), 78–86.

Kishar, N., & Godfrey, M. (1999). The effect of information framing on academic task completion. *Educational Psychology, 19,* 91–101.

Linn, M., Slotta, J., & Baumgartner, E. (2000). *Teaching high school science in the Information Age: A review of courses and technology for inquiry-based learning.* Santa Monica, CA: Milken Family Foundation.

Oakes, J. (1985). *Keeping track: How schools structure inequality.* New Haven, CT: Yale University Press.

Parker, J. P. (1989). *Instructional strategies for teaching the gifted.* Boston: Allyn & Bacon.

Renzulli, J. S., Leppien, J. H., & Hays, T. S. (2000). *The multiple menu model: A practical guide for developing differentiated curriculum.* Mansfield Center, CT: Creative Learning.

Rogers, K. B. (1998). Using current research to make "good" decisions about grouping. *NASSP Bulletin, 82*(595), 38–46.

Simonson, M. (1995). Does anyone really learn at a distance? *Tech Trends, 40*(5), 12.

Slavin, R. (1986). *Educational psychology: Theory into practice.* Englewood Cliffs, NJ: Prentice-Hall.

Squires, G. (1999). *Teaching as a professional discipline.* Philadelphia: Farmers Press.

Tomlinson, C. A. (1999). *The differentiated classroom: Responding to the needs of all learners.* Alexandria, VA: Association for Supervision and Curriculum Development.

Trophy, J., & Alleman, J. (1998). Classroom management in a social studies learning community. *Social Education, 62,* 56–58.

Wang, M. C., Haertel, G. D., & Walberg, H. J. (1990). What influences learning? A content analysis of review literature. *Journal of Educational Research, 84,* 30–43.

Winebrenner, S. (1999). Shortchanging the gifted. *School Administrator, 56*(9), 12–16.

IMPLEMENTING CURRICULA FOR THE GIFTED

Too frequently educators view new curriculum projects as isolated from the ongoing school district institutional processes that they believe may have greater value than curriculum development itself or to which they attach greater significance. The central purpose of this chapter is to relate the critical factors of gifted curriculum implementation to existing structures in the school district that will ensure continued support for ongoing curriculum work. The proposed model for this process is illustrated in Figure 11.1.

Once curriculum has been codified systematically at all grade levels and in all content disciplines, many educators believe that the curriculum development phase is finished, and the implementation phase is about to begin. However, curriculum development is dynamic. Some of it is engaged at an implementation level of piloting, monitoring, and revising, while at the same time some of it is engaged in writing up and codifying curriculum—and each part of the process continuously feeds the other (VanTassel-Baska, 1993). Rather than being considered distinct, implementation should be viewed as a part of the overall curriculum development process that continues to impact written curriculum documents. Thus, the planning process for curriculum development must include elements for keeping the process going beyond the time of special funding and outside consultants.

The school district must recognize and accept the *centrality* of curriculum development to its overall enterprise of schooling. One way to encourage this understanding is to link the curriculum development process inextricably to existing efforts in the school district, such as school improvement initiatives, testing and assessment models, teacher evaluation approaches, and accepted staff development models. In this way, curriculum issues will continue to be addressed over time, and revisions based on new data can be made in written documents that have relevance to district priorities.

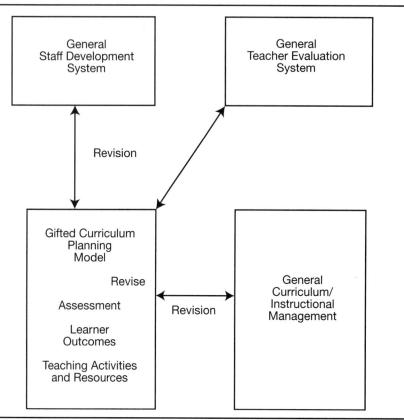

FIGURE 11.1   Interaction of the Curriculum Development Process With
Existing School District Model Systems

This attempt to institutionalize the gifted education curriculum development process should influence how curricula are viewed and reviewed for other learners as well. In that way, curricula for the gifted may filter down and have an impact on the general school curricula for all learners. Effective local planning in curriculum for the gifted should be able to provide such impact.

PROBLEMS WITH NEW CURRICULUM IMPLEMENTATION

Although the rhetoric associated with the current educational reform movement revolves around organizational reform and curriculum reform issues, much of the rhetoric has not been realized in practice. Adding to the problem, the major "reform" initiatives have been translated into a faddish emphasis on such administrative changes as heterogeneous grouping, cooperative learning, and site-based management. Without an underlying substantive base of change in classroom teaching and learning behaviors, this translation approach is doomed to be more ineffective than earlier models because it fails to account sufficiently for the role of learning. One can change organizational shells, but the activity of the organism inside still will dictate the nature and extent of productivity and desired results.

Muncey, Payne, and White (1999) analyzed the difficulties with curriculum innovation in a large school district. From their analysis, they drew the following conclusions:

1. Curriculum innovation must contend with high-stakes testing, which is a fact of life for schools. The state standards and assessment models drive the curriculum process. Moreover, the central office creates many mandates that individual schools have to follow to prepare for the high-stakes testing and for many aspects of daily school life, which interferes with new curriculum implementation.
2. Curriculum developers apparently are unable to use previous "successful" experiences with curriculum innovation to strengthen relationships and knowledge building between the curriculum project's local team site and the district.
3. Staff turnover and leadership changes, including shifts of key personnel at the school site, add to the difficulty.
4. Little effort is made to build on parent and community support.
5. The scope and scale of the work that has to be undertaken to implement the innovation are greater than project staff capacity.
6. Differences in views concerning curriculum emerge over time, causing problems with the fidelity of implementation.

Implementation of new curricula in the Javits projects, which focus on gifted learners from disadvantaged backgrounds, has encountered similar problems. From a meta-evaluation of several of these projects, Callahan, Gubbins, Moon, and Caldwell (2000) attributed problems in implementation to the following factors:

1. Lack of sufficient sophisticated teacher knowledge and skills to implement the curriculum deeply.
2. Lack of teacher autonomy or sense of autonomy to experiment with the new curriculum in the face of administrative pressure to prepare students for state tests.
3. Turnover in both teaching staff and principal leadership from year to year.
4. Insufficient or inconsistent administrative support for the innovation.
5. Competing ideas about what will improve learning, resulting in, among other things, the fusion of curriculum innovations based on different assumptions.

Until schools are willing to accept that several aspects of the educational enterprise must be changed simultaneously, there is little reason to think that educational reform will be meaningful. Among the simultaneous changes that must occur are the following:

✓ Profound changes in the development and use of curriculum materials.
✓ The use of instructional strategies that complement these changes and demonstrate effectiveness with a variety of gifted learners.
✓ Development of teacher attitudes and behaviors that accept the importance of curriculum and instructional change for the gifted and are capable of executing it.
✓ Development of models for understanding the conditions under which curriculum development, instructional strategies, and staff development work together to effect positive change for gifted learners.

IMPLICATIONS OF CURRICULUM PLANNING ON STAFF DEVELOPMENT

One of the first school district systems that should be affected by curriculum planning efforts is staff development, the major mechanism in schools for disseminating ideas for classroom implementation. Yet, many staff development models are haphazard, taking a shotgun approach to training in the belief that providing something for everybody is a viable avenue.

In summarizing the research on effective staff development, McLaughlin (1991) highlighted several key findings:

✓ Staff development programs influence teacher learning at reasonably high levels, but such learning does not translate automatically into changed classroom behavior without planned follow-up.
✓ Training that involves K-12 teachers who are competitively selected is more effective than mass training sessions for all teachers.
✓ Training that is initiated and developed through collaboration with universities and conducted by strong leaders is more effective than school-based training designed by potential participants.
✓ The most effective techniques used for teacher development have been observation of classroom practices, microteaching (i.e., presenting a lesson on which a teacher receives structured feedback), video/audio feedback, and practice.

These findings should be incorporated into staff development programs at local levels. The findings complement the curriculum planning model described in this text, in that they provide a solid backdrop for linking teachers to effective classroom implementation.

Moving teachers of the gifted from novice to expert status requires careful understanding of the sophistication of the skills needed to work effectively with these students. Understanding the nature and needs of the gifted, for example, is less sophisticated than being able to make appropriate inferences about curriculum experiences at a particular point in time. A model of staff development that considers these distinctions in planning experiences for teachers is superior to one that does not (VanTassel-Baska, 1998). Table 11.1 summarizes the relationship of a teacher's sophistication level and the competencies and skills required to implement a curriculum effectively with gifted learners.

The content of staff development programs that would support the curriculum planning model obviously should be derived from the major features of the developed curriculum, with particular emphasis on implementation strategies for helping students reach desired outcomes (Glass, 1992; Guskey & Sparks, 1996). Moreover,

TABLE 11.1   Teacher Sophistication Level and Related Competencies and Skills

Level	Competency or Skill
Novice	Plans curriculum experiences well
	Demonstrates understanding of the educational implications of giftedness
	Uses varied teaching strategies effectively
	Conducts group discussions well
	Provides for student extension activities outside of class
	Promotes a healthy teaching/learning climate
Intermediate	Selects questions that stimulate higher-level thinking
	Utilizes creative thinking techniques
	Utilizes problem-solving techniques
	Encourages independent thinking and open inquiry
	Understands and encourages student ideas and student-directed work
Expert	Promotes critical and creative thinking skills in appropriate contexts
	Synthesizes student assessment data and curriculum content effectively
	Responds to students' individual needs for curriculum adaptation and support
	Orchestrates instructional variability and curriculum challenge

staff development programs should provide time and opportunity for follow-up practice and feedback to participants after the planned activity has been conducted (Joyce, Weil, & Showers, 1992). For staff development to feed curriculum planning, the two systems must be viewed as interdependent. However, the curriculum planning model must be superordinate because the overall goal of staff development is to improve student learning, the outcomes of which are identified through effective curriculum planning (Sparks & Hirsch, 1997; NSDC, 1995).

Staff Development for Teachers in Differentiated Classrooms

Although the problems with educational reform are likely to be felt by all groups of students, those most directly impacted by the limited organizational translations of theory to practice will be the students needing the greatest amount of individual attention and learning plan adaptation; that is, the at-risk and the gifted. Because these groups tend to function farthest from the norm in a regular classroom, they tend to need more individualized techniques and processes. Yet, staff development programs have not addressed the key skills regular classroom teachers must use to help these groups receive an appropriate education.

Training programs for regular classroom teachers must teach skills that allow for the appropriate tailoring of curriculum experiences. Competencies that teachers must develop include the following:

1. *Ability to assess students' level of knowledge and appropriate instructional level.* Effective teachers engage in diagnostic-prescriptive techniques to develop an understanding of and address students' level of functioning in each subject area.
2. *Ability to select instructional materials that facilitate optimal challenge.* Effective teachers know how to access and select from multiple resources already judged appropriate for use with gifted learners.
3. *Ability to handle small- and large-group instruction and individual learning.* Effective teachers are flexible in employing different modes of instruction and try to balance modes appropriately, given the varying needs of students.
4. *Ability to accommodate different cognitive styles and special learning needs.* Effective teachers have developed the skills needed to deal with individual differences among gifted students in respect to rate of learning, attention span, special interests, and potential processing problems.
5. *Ability to employ various methods of advancement.* Effective teachers are knowledgeable about options for accelerated work and use them as needed.
6. *Ability to use problem-centered approaches and open-ended learning.* Effective teachers provide opportunities for students to take charge of their own learning and easily shift to the role of metacognitive coach.

7. *Ability to teach to varying learning modalities (i.e., auditory, visual, kines-thetic)*. Effective teachers employ different teaching styles to accommodate all learners.

Training for teachers in differentiated classrooms should also focus on instructional strategies, such as the following:

✓ *Pacing*. For gifted students, it often is appropriate to shorten time spent on instruction, provide less explanation, omit review, and limit drill and practice.
✓ *Question asking*. For gifted students, more time often is spent asking questions than providing explanations.
✓ *Use of open-ended questions*. For gifted students, open-ended questions often are more effective than closed questions. An example is, "If you were President Bush, how would you handle Iraq's defiance in the face of sanctions?"
✓ *Use of inquiry-based models*. For gifted students, hands-on, problem-solving, and discovery instructional strategies often result in high levels of learning.
✓ *Provision of access to advanced resources*, including materials, people, and places.

Whitla (1999) described the key to effective staff development work for teachers of the gifted in this way:

> Teaching that provides opportunities for students to develop rigorous thinking is different in kind from what we tend to see in American schools today. Such teaching also involves understanding how knowledge is created by the students themselves and making a commitment to teaching as the facilitation of that process. It thus involves sharing with students a profound curiosity about the subject, assessing the nature of students' understanding, and guiding inquiry and discussion. Such teaching requires [of teachers], first, changing [their] beliefs about the nature of knowledge and learning, then deepening and expanding their knowledge of what they teach, and third, reinventing their classroom practice from within the new conceptual frame (p. 152)

Developing Collaborative Skills

Ongoing collaborative planning is essential for ensuring that gifted learners are not left to stagnate in an unresponsive environment primarily geared to the needs of other groups of learners. Approaches for effecting collaborative planning include the following:

1. The use of teachers and specialists of the gifted as cooperative teachers in heterogeneous classrooms who focus on the needs of the gifted.
2. Regular meetings among educators to tailor the curriculum appropriately to the needs of the gifted and other special needs learners.

3. Staff development and training of general education teachers in adapting curriculum to individual needs, managing differentiated instructional plans, and using inquiry-based strategies.

4. The use of grouping and regrouping techniques within and across grade levels that honor individual differences in instructional learning level for key areas of the curriculum.

5. The development of a myriad of co-curricular opportunities from which students can select based on interest (e.g., learning centers, chess, theater, conceptual art).

6. Implementation of a system of curriculum and instructional monitoring that promotes better understanding of the impact of curriculum innovations on teaching and learning in the classroom.

7. A movement toward the use of multiple resources in the classroom, as opposed to a single text, allowing for greater student choice, alternatives in learning, and enhanced opportunities for interest-based inquiry projects.

8. The use of differentiated staffing so that teacher specialists in content areas can work with the most able learners in their areas of expertise in some model of instruction.

For each of these approaches, translations from theory to practice will provide the best view of helpful or harmful effects of innovations on any given group of learners. The most effective approaches will be revealed only if educators engage in various adaptations of collaborative planning and stay open to attempting the possibilities suggested.

Helping teachers develop both collaborative and instructional teaching skills appears to matter in enhancing student learning. From a recent analysis of over 100 staff development projects in mathematics and science, Kennedy (1999) found that only 12 of the projects showed gains in student achievement, and fewer than 20 attempted to assess those gains. The author identified the following key factors as crucial for staff development projects if they are to produce student achievement gains:

1. The use of pedagogically relevant strategies that teachers can implement easily in their classrooms to help students achieve better.

2. The use of team-building techniques to build collegiality for instructional change.

3. The treatment of teachers as professionals who can make good decisions for their students.

Borko, Mayfield, Marion, Flexer, and Cumbo (1997) found that teacher change was best effected when the "threat of testing" was removed and administrative support was strongly in evidence.

IMPLICATIONS OF CURRICULUM PLANNING ON TEACHER EVALUATION

Just as the staff development system must feed curriculum planning, the teacher evaluation system also must be interdependent with the model. Desired teacher behaviors emerge from a clear understanding of what outcomes are desired for gifted learners, and teachers should be evaluated on the presence of these behaviors. Table 11.2 shows the relationship between learner outcomes and teacher behaviors in teaching critical thinking. Principals could use behavioral checklists such as this to ensure that teachers are practicing the desired behaviors. Even four 40-minute visits

TABLE 11.2 Relationship of Student Outcomes to Teacher Behaviors in the Teaching of Critical Thinking Skills

Student Outcomes	Teacher Behaviors
Students will be able to:	Teacher:
1. Predict outcomes 2. Distinguish between fact and opinion	– encourages logical reasoning – encourages syllogistic reasoning – encourages student development of inference and evaluation of argument skills – utilizes inductive and deductive reasoning
3. Form hypotheses 4. Weigh evidence	– asks students to define problems in a question form – poses interpretive, open-ended, and evaluative questions for students – encourages student development of inference and evaluation of argument skills – utilizes inductive and deductive reasoning
5. Analyze information 6. Synthesize information	– asks analytic questions – encourages student participation in discussions – provides opportunities for students to summarize data in various forms – withholds own ideas and conclusions – encourages student development of inference and evaluation of argument skills – utilizes inductive and deductive reasoning

to a classroom during the year would yield important data regarding the use of criterial behaviors. The findings then might serve as a model for the development of more appropriate and targeted teacher evaluation systems in school districts.

IMPLICATIONS OF CURRICULUM PLANNING ON CURRICULUM AND INSTRUCTIONAL MANAGEMENT

The system by which a district maintains and changes its curriculum also represents a critical linkage to the curriculum planning model for the gifted. Frequently managed by a director of curriculum, or an assistant superintendent in smaller districts, this system controls the rate and nature of curriculum change and is fed by mandates from federal, state, and local boards of education. The power and control of district-level curriculum emphasis clearly are vested here.

Ironically, this system is given limited attention and resources in many districts, limiting its capacity to be effective. Regardless of its relative importance in a district, however, the curriculum and instructional management system must be open to the system of curriculum planning for the gifted so that the efforts of both systems move in the same direction rather than operate counterproductively. The following are foremost considerations in merging these systems:

1. The membership of all districtwide curriculum committees should include a representative of the gifted curriculum planning effort, ensuring ongoing communication between the two efforts.
2. Collaborative planning of all gifted curriculum development efforts should be undertaken by the gifted coordinator in concert with the director of curriculum and instruction and his or her staff in individual content areas.
3. The structure, format, and language used in planning curricula for the gifted should mirror the districtwide models. Although this issue may seem trivial, it carries enormous implications for communication to teachers, other educators, and the community concerning the relationship of gifted curricula to general curriculum practice.
4. Educators responsible for the superordinate system of curriculum management in the district must clearly understand and accept differential learner outcomes and assessment models. Points of convergence and divergence with the basic curriculum framework should be delineated and highlighted. In that way, important distinctions can be made between the gifted effort and the general curriculum effort without viewing the gifted curriculum as a totally separate enterprise.

These considerations are central to activating a meaningful curriculum system for the gifted that is not perceived as different from the mainstream business of teachers and learners for all students in schools. Gifted education has to be accepted into these generic systems if it is to become integrated into the basic functions of local education.

INSIGHTS FROM EXEMPLARY HIGH SCHOOLS TO GUIDE CURRICULUM REFORM

A discussion of general curriculum reform in schools may provide insights to guide curriculum work in gifted education. From her review of two exemplary high schools for curriculum change, Levy (1996) delineated characteristics that she believes contributed to successful reform. In her review, curriculum should be reconceived as a device for allocating resources on a *continual* basis rather than on an a priori basis, and teachers as well as students should be put in charge of much of the allocation. This reallocation process should create a state of slack, or a looseness that permits energetic bursts of work, timely targeting of efforts, and a genuine assumption of accountability. Levy noted that the school structure has to be amenable to change: Policies must be altered, contracts renegotiated, and ordinary assumptions overturned so that schoolwork happens across 8 hours rather than 6 hours and over 12 months rather than 10 months. Further, youth activities that are now relegated to the margins of the day—especially recreational and community-based activities— should be moved to the heart of the day.

Levy's analysis of the two high schools suggested that these schools have created an alternative custodial environment. They have cultivated an environment in which students share the responsibility for safety and caring. They have defined the work of teaching as including more than face-to-face contact with students; in these schools, teachers have responsibility for knowing a set of students roundly and well, maintaining close communication with the students' parents, intervening quickly when truancy or other threatening circumstances arise, keeping track of the students' progress toward graduation, and encouraging personal as well as intellectual growth.

According to Levy, exemplary schools for curriculum change also exhibit the following key characteristics. First, they achieve enough slack to manage a curriculum in which instructional leaders continually allocate resources to teaching and learning. Second, an important function of these schools is pastoral, such that school personnel can know students well and provide them with close care. Although the students may at any point be following an ordinary curriculum schedule (e.g., Spanish every morning, an internship on Thursdays), this schedule is secondary to a more fundamental arrangement, such as being part of the Alpha Team or being one of Mrs. Johnson's advisees. Third, the schools have a sense of self, with enough reflective capacity to coordinate efforts toward a given end. That is, the schools are mindful of their core purposes as a school and accountable for achieving those purposes.

Such schools also promote specific "habits of mind." They help students (a) learn to critically examine evidence, (b) be able to see the world through multiple viewpoints (i.e., to step into other shoes), (c) make connections and see patterns, (d) imagine alternatives (What if? and What else?), and (e) ask, "What difference does it make?" and "Who cares?"

CHALLENGES IN IMPLEMENTING CURRICULA

Factors that impact the process of curriculum development in many school districts and hinder the achievement of desired goals of curriculum implementation typically include the following:

✓ Traditional organizational patterns along elementary and secondary lines, which inhibit curriculum integration across grade levels.
✓ Limited communication, exchange, and cooperative planning between elementary and secondary divisions.
✓ Limited time available for teachers at the elementary and secondary levels to work together in planning and structuring curricular experiences for gifted learners.
✓ Lack of involvement, in the development process, of teachers who are responsible for implementing the curriculum.

Another factor, which is outside school district purview, that may impede curriculum development is the focus on program development rather than curriculum development. Because the emphasis in the development of gifted education opportunities has been on putting operative programs in place at all stages of development for the gifted learner, curriculum issues have been given much less consideration. What has emerged is a kind of potpourri of curriculum experiences for a given group of students identified as gifted at various grade levels. However, the recent national spotlight on educational reform and curricular change, coupled with a shift and refocusing at the state level from program development issues to comprehensive curriculum planning for the gifted, has caused a resurgence of interest in curriculum planning and development and a healthy climate for change.

Still another concern is that many teachers do not utilize gifted curricula to guide instruction. Rather, they often derive course content exclusively from adopted textbooks. Some teachers have indicated that they have used specific aspects of the developed curriculum to supplement the textbooks but not on a consistent basis. Their decisions about using the written curriculum typically reflected compromises they had made. Many believe they are prevented from effectively utilizing skills and concepts of an ideal curriculum for gifted students by administrators, mandated texts and tests, or subtle community pressures.

Another issue revolves around the commitment of time necessary to develop effective curricula. Sufficient time has to be scheduled for curriculum work during the school day rather than at the end of the teaching day. Further, time has to be provided during non-student attendance periods so that major writing, revisions, and recommendations might take place. The concentration of time available during the summer months makes that time period ideal for curriculum development work. These time segments taken in concert probably provide the most effective approach to keeping the curriculum development experience dynamic and meaningful.

Related to the time issue is the process for ensuring a team approach that allows for a continuous, flexible planning process and utilizes both teachers and content area experts in deciding the direction of curriculum work. Teachers selected for participation should have knowledge and experience in working with gifted learners in a variety of classroom settings, show an interest and aptitude for developing curricula, and have mastered the skills of adapting curricula successfully for the gifted learner. As members of the team, teachers have the role of providing critical pedagogical insights into the decision-making process for specific settings: what to include, what to exclude, and how to adapt and modify various learning experiences, strategies, and resources.

Teachers should receive training in this process by consultants who provide guidance in understanding conceptual and instructional designs of curricular models and developing appropriate and effective curricula for gifted. Content experts should supply key ideas and concepts in designing the curricular structure in specific domains of study and share major approaches to organizing courses. Moreover, district-level curriculum supervisors and gifted coordinators should provide the support and feedback necessary to keep the curriculum work going.

The organizing structure for curriculum work clearly is a major consideration in attaining success. Team representation by content disciplines and grade-level clusters is critical because the emphasis has to be on articulating the curriculum across K-12. Curriculum writing teams may be organized to represent every grade level in each of the major disciplines. This organizing structure is depicted in Figure 11.2.

CONDITIONS CONTRIBUTING TO SUCCESSFUL CURRICULUM DEVELOPMENT

Factors crucial to the success of broad-based curriculum efforts include the following:

1. *Conducting a comprehensive needs assessment to determine the actual and preferred status of the curriculum for the gifted.* This process sets the climate for change. Understanding needs and documenting them provides a necessary starting point for examining the curriculum and implementing change. It also installs a framework for effecting shared values and mutual support for the project. The needs assessment is instrumental in formulating a set of tentative goal statements, determining the acceptability of learner performance, and translating high-priority goals into plans.

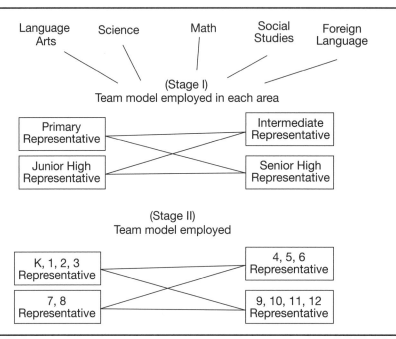

Language Arts   Science   Math   Social Studies   Foreign Language

(Stage I)
Team model employed in each area

| Primary Representative | Intermediate Representative |
| Junior High Representative | Senior High Representative |

(Stage II)
Team model employed

| K, 1, 2, 3 Representative | 4, 5, 6 Representative |
| 7, 8 Representative | 9, 10, 11, 12 Representative |

FIGURE 11.2   Organization of Curriculum Writing Teams at Two Stages of the Project

2. *Keeping central office staff (curriculum directors and content area supervisors) informed of the scope of the work and actively involving them in all stages of the project.* Providing opportunities for these administrators to assist and make recommendations is crucial to the process. Administrative support is instrumental to institutionalizing curriculum change.

3. *Assuring teachers that curriculum change does not mean throwing out all previous documents and replacing them with something totally new.* Teachers need to be informed that the results of needs assessments typically indicate that modification can be made based on previously developed materials. In knowing this, teachers generally will be more receptive to becoming involved in the process.

4. *Involving teachers in the decision-making process.* This is perhaps the most crucial aspect of the process from a personnel morale perspective. Informative sessions should be held to convey to teachers the overall process and the conceptual design of various curricular models to be used. Teachers should be given sufficient opportunities to voice concerns, raise questions, and offer suggestions regarding the plan. This type of involvement gives teachers a stake in the adaptation and curriculum development process and inspires acquisition of the skills and knowledge that will be needed for curriculum implementation.

5. *Marshaling staff members who are sophisticated in the principles of gifted education and committed to meeting the needs of students.* Staff with this knowledge and commitment are important assets in the curriculum planning process. Selected teachers also have to be sufficiently grounded in their disciplines to adapt and modify curricula for the gifted population in a given area. Many who become involved in the process come to view their involvement in curriculum development as one of their primary professional responsibilities.

6. *Enlisting the support of consultant resources (curriculum and subject matter specialists).* Consultants can assist in devising a comprehensive plan of action, supplying key ideas and concepts regarding content areas, and providing expertise outside the domain of the district. Utilizing university-based content consultants on an ongoing basis well into the implementation stage is helpful. Gary Community School Corporation in Gary, Indiana, uses content specialists year-round to assist teachers with the issues associated with curriculum development.

INHIBITING FACTORS AND BARRIERS

Factors representing potential problems in the overall implementation of a large curriculum effort are summarized here:

1. The emphasis on textbook adoption, state competency requirements, and state-mandated tests creates situations in which local curriculum objectives are driven by these priorities rather than by identified instructional needs of students in the district. When school districts become obsessed with standardization, individuals or groups that attempt to deviate from the prescribed pattern are likely to be vulnerable. Amazingly, though, common sense prevails in many districts if educators continue to stress the importance of curricula tailored to need.

2. Not all teachers working with the gifted are equally skilled or interested in the task of curriculum development. Consequently, at some grade levels and in some content areas, more effort will be needed to prod teachers into capturing curriculum experiences on paper and then implementing a tailored version of them. When resistance occurs, adapted curricula face political hurdles in classroom translation. Further, just as we do not want standardized curricula for the gifted, we also do not want standardized implementation if it implies reaching a goal in exactly the same way. In translation in the classroom, there is significant room for diversity and individual preferences. What should be held constant, however, is the shared consensus on overall learner outcomes. If the learner outcomes are not valued by all teachers working with the gifted, faithful implementation procedures will not be possible.

3. Difficulties in scheduling time when all relevant individuals in the curriculum development process can meet, plan, and write together will be ever present. Yet, the overall goal of "connected" curriculum is difficult to achieve if key

players are missing. Adding to the problem, the reality of schools is that unplanned events many times drive planned priorities. Building and classroom emergencies, bad weather, and individual needs can all hinder the timely implementation of a curriculum plan. The key to holding these disparate pieces together is the curriculum project manager, the individual in the school district coordinating the effort. This person must invest a significant amount of energy in pacing the entire project and ensuring that timelines are set and monitored and work is ultimately accomplished within appropriate time frames.

4. Staff turnover in a program can manifest itself in the "starting over" syndrome during a multiyear period. Each new teacher who becomes involved in the project during subsequent years has to become oriented to prior stages of the project, resulting in much time spent reviewing the evolution of the curriculum development process. Although change in staff can be a problem, it does reflect the reality of schools and must be addressed systematically.

Through careful planning within the district, school districts can avoid many of these problems as they undertake long-term curriculum projects. Even so, some difficulties may be inevitable in a curriculum development model that is driven by the consensus-building process.

SUMMARY

Curriculum development is central to schools, and it is dynamic, in a state of continual change. Implementation of the curriculum planning model should be done from a systems perspective so the effort becomes an ongoing part of school district operations. Curriculum planning has implications for staff development, in that teachers can be trained to become more sophisticated in the skills needed to work effectively with the gifted. Further, teacher evaluation should accurately reflect these behaviors. Curriculum and instructional management should be merged through collaborative planning, adherence to district-wide models, and an understanding of the distinctions between general and gifted efforts.

Potential problems may arise in a focus on traditional patterns, limited communication, scarce time, lack of teacher involvement in the development process, emphasis on program development rather than curriculum development, use of standardized materials as a basis, the need for training, and the lack of a team approach, among others. In contrast, successful curriculum development incorporates a comprehensive needs assessment, a well informed central office staff, prudent modification of existing materials, teacher involvement in the decision-making process, a committed staff, and the support of consultant resources.

QUESTIONS FOR REFLECTION

1. How can gifted educators influence existing school district initiatives to ensure that gifted education is on the list of priorities?
2. How might gifted educators develop a plan for ensuring the inclusion of curriculum development efforts for the gifted in the general staff development, teacher evaluation, and curriculum management systems at the district level?
3. What barriers may inhibit the training of all classroom teachers to work successfully with gifted students?
4. What approaches to curriculum monitoring might be implemented in an educational setting? Why would these approaches be more successful than others?
5. In addition to the issues described in this chapter, what other issues affect institutionalizing curricula for the gifted?

REFERENCES

Borko, H., Mayfield, V., Marion, S., Flexer, R., & Cumbo, K. (1997). Teachers' developing ideas and practices about mathematics performance assessment: Successes, stumbling blocks, and implications for professional development. *Teaching and Teacher Education, 13,* 259–278.

Callahan, C., Gubbins, J., Moon, J., & Caldwell, M. (2000). *Draft report: Evaluation of the Javits Gifted and Talented Students Education Program.* Washington, DC: U.S. Department of Education, Office of Educational Research and Improvement.

Glass, J. C. (1992). Components that promote transfer of learning to the classroom: Are they present in staff development activities for teachers? *Educational Research Quarterly, 15,* 35–44.

Guskey, T. R., & Sparks, D. (1996). Exploring the relationship between staff development and improvements in student learning. *Journal of Staff Development, 17,* 34–38.

Joyce, G., Weil, M., & Showers, B. (1992). *Models of teaching.* Boston: Allyn & Bacon.

Kennedy, M. (1999). Form and substance in mathematics and science professional development. *NISE Brief, 3*(2), 1–7.

Levy, S. (1996). *Starting from scratch: One classroom builds its own curriculum.* Portsmouth, NH: Heinemann.

McLaughlin, M. W. (1991). Enabling professional development: What have we learned? In A. Lieberman & L. Miller (Eds.), *Staff development for education in the '90s* (pp. 62–82). New York: Teachers College Press.

Muncey, D. E., Payne, J., & White, N. (1999). Making curriculum and instructional reform happen: A case study. *Peabody Journal of Education, 74,* 68–110.

National Staff Development Council & National Association of Elementary School Principals. (1995). *Standards for staff development: Elementary school edition.* Oxford, OH: National Staff Development Council.

Sparks, D., & Hirsch, S. (1997). *A new vision for staff development.* Alexandria, VA: Association for Supervision and Curriculum Development; Oxford, OH: National Staff Development Council.

VanTassel-Baska, J. (1993). Linking curriculum development to school reform and restructuring. *Gifted Child Today, 16*(4)34–37.

VanTassel-Baska, J. (Ed.). (1998). *Excellence in educating gifted and talented learners* (3rd ed.). Denver: Love Publishing.

Whitla, J. (1999). Curriculum in ATLAS. *Peabody Journal of Education, 74,* 146–153.

12 ASSESSMENT OF LEARNING AND EVALUATION OF CURRICULUM

ssessment of the impact of a gifted program curriculum on learners is one of the most important aspects in curriculum design work. This is the stage of analysis at which teachers can begin to understand the learner's level of comprehension and knowledge of what they had hoped to teach. At this stage teachers gain a sense of the learner's "learning receptivity" rather than "social receptivity."

The purpose of the assessment process is multidimensional. It provides insights into student progress in a curriculum and attempts to pinpoint future needs in a curriculum area for a learner. As such it is a critical tool for ongoing curriculum planning. Moreover, assessment data provide information about how well the planning and teaching of learner outcomes have fared. Under ideal circumstances, each stated learner outcome in a curriculum for the gifted will have a corresponding assessment technique so that each learning focus can be measured and evaluated. Figure 12.1 depicts these multiple purposes of assessment.

Because the emphasis of the educational enterprise with the gifted many times is different from that with typical learners in respect to contact time, delivery models, and learning levels, the match between learner outcomes and assessment approaches is all the more crucial. Yet, problems exist in assessing gifted learner outcomes and utilizing evaluation data.

Part of the problem lies with the evaluation methodology available to demonstrate effectiveness in gifted programs. Because of ceiling level effects, standardized tests normed on typical populations tell almost nothing about growth in learning for gifted populations unless they are used off-level. Any test used for evaluating the gifted must be carefully selected and piloted for potential ceiling effects. Often, alternative assessment tools such as performance-based assessment and portfolios are more useful in gauging the authentic level of performance in gifted students.

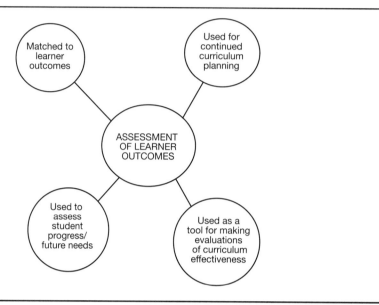

FIGURE 12.1   The Role of Assessment in Curriculum Design

Another problem concerns a lack of understanding of how to use evaluation results to improve programs for the gifted. Too frequently, evaluation reports are merely shelved. Indeed, problems with school district utilization of evaluation work have been noted in several studies (Avery, VanTassel-Baska, & O'Neill, 1997; Hunsaker & Callahan, 1993; Tomlinson, Bland, & Moon, 1993; Tomlinson & Callahan, 1994). These authors suggest that conceptualization of the evaluation process, the credibility of information, the timing, and the use of a follow-up action plan all affect the usefulness of evaluation data in gifted programs.

A new approach to conceptualizing evaluation studies for the gifted was delineated by Carter (1992), who used an ex post facto design in light of problems with establishing experimental conditions. Farrell (1992) advocated a process for analyzing lesson plans as a key way to assess the micro-level of curriculum efficiency. House and Lapan (1994) provided useful ideas for evaluating programs for disadvantaged learners, recommending multiple approaches including authentic assessment.

Approaches that should be used in evaluating gifted programs have also been delineated in the literature. In a recent review of published gifted evaluation studies over the past decade, Johnson (2000) summarized the recommendations for practitioners and evaluators as follows:

1. Select a trained evaluator.
2. Clearly define program outcomes and degrees of implementation.

3. Use evaluation not only for examining the program's effectiveness but also for improving it.
4. Use contrast groups in designing an evaluation.
5. Use multiple data-gathering methods, formats, and techniques.
6. Select quality instruments.
7. Allow diverse opinions to emerge.
8. Collect data over time.
9. Frame recommendations in a way that gives administrators flexibility in implementing them.
10. Allocate sufficient time for faculty and administrators to conduct and assess the evaluations.

If implemented, these recommendations represent an important step forward in evaluating gifted programs as a basis for program improvement.

GUIDELINES FOR BUILDING AN ASSESSMENT MODEL

The following principles should be considered in building an assessment model for gifted programs.

1. *The assessment model should use multiple measures and varied types of measures.* The most promising approaches in assessing gifted learner outcomes include portfolios of students' work, product evaluation, and observational checklists of student behaviors. (Sample forms that delineate key behaviors are included in Appendix A at the end of this chapter.)
2. *The assessment model should attempt to establish triangulation of perceived benefits.* Attempts to delineate student benefits from special curricula for the gifted should consider input from multiple sources. Parents, students, and teachers should be asked the same questions to establish triangulation of results from three different publics. Having three different groups concur on the outcomes derived froom the program helps take the edge off the subjectivity of the responses.
3. *The assessment model should work across three levels: curriculum validity, perceived benefit, and actual student outcomes.* Curriculum effectiveness can be analyzed at three levels, as depicted in Figure 12.2. At Level 1, content or face validity is established by subjecting initial curriculum development efforts to the scrutiny of trained curriculum specialists. At Level 2, attitudinal and perceptual data on effectiveness, are examined. At Level 3, the impact on student learning is measured more directly. Attention to all three levels ensures a systematic approach to revising curriculum efforts in such a way that desired changes are fed back into the curriculum design process.

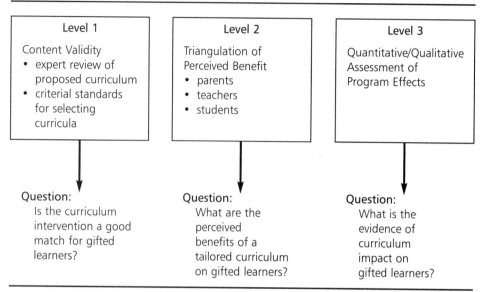

FIGURE 12.2   Levels of Analysis in Curriculum Evaluation

4. *The assessment model should incorporate long-term and short-term measures.* An interpretation of this principle that is familiar to most teachers suggests that a combination of frequent quizzes and less frequent tests is more desirable than the use of only one or the other approach. However, the principle has saliency for other types of evaluative tools as well. For example, the use of short-term projects combined with one long-term project reveals more of what has been learned than the use of only short projects or only one long-term one. This principle honors the concept of time series as a mode of assessment, as it shows how the learner has progressed incrementally as well as where he or she has ended up at the end of 32 weeks of intervention.

5. *The assessment model should incorporate multiple approaches to evaluation design.* A good combination might be pre-post, time-series, and product assessment. Because gifted learner outcomes are geared to higher levels than typical student outcomes are, relying on only one approach for evaluation of all students is problematic. Moreover, gifted curricula and programs frequently have outcomes that are incompatible with the use of any one design. Thus, a combinational approach is recommended. An overall assessment model for the College of William and Mary's Governor's School in Science and Technology, included in Appendix B to this chapter, illustrates well this issue of multiple evaluation design approaches.

6. *The assessment model should be developed early, preferably at the time learner outcomes are designed.* For each learner outcome in a curriculum for the gifted, a requisite outcome assessment approach should be delineated. It is much easier to delineate outcome assessment approaches while the overall planning process is evolving than after the instructional features have been delineated. Furthermore, the assessment approach should influence choices made in the instructional pattern. Appendix B to this chapter highlights this principle.

7. *The assessment model should be seen as a basis for making evaluative judgments about the effectiveness of the curriculum design elements singly or in combination.* Consider the following outcome and its assessment results:

> Ninety percent of gifted students at Grade 6 will increase their problem-solving abilities by 30% pre-post on a measure of mathematics and heuristic use. Only 40% of the students increased at the stated criterion level, whereas 50% of the students increased by 20%. For 30% of the students, no increases were noted. Yet the pre-post assessment also revealed that the 30% who showed no increase were already operating at the 75% or higher level on the pretest measure.

How should this assessment be interpreted? The standard interpretation would be that the outcome was not met, and therefore the teacher should work harder at this outcome another year. However, this interpretation of the assessment data is simplistic. Another interpretation, which is perhaps more valid, would be that the criterion level of 30% is inappropriate, given the nature of the outcome and the nature of the learners. The assessment results may be better evaluated by taking into account the relative difficulty in showing growth gains for a group already scoring very high on a pretest. For another year, the teacher may wish to alter the criterion level, change the substance of the outcome, or target activities to more sharply address the desired outcome. This decision must be based on careful consideration of all aspects of the design process, not just the end result.

Evaluation of student learner outcomes for gifted programs should be undertaken at least once each year. With some process outcomes, evaluation could occur less frequently, perhaps once every 3 years.

TOOLS FOR ASSESSING THE LEARNING OF GIFTED STUDENTS

Because traditional assessments are problematic in assessing the learning of gifted students, nontraditional approaches must be employed. Among those found to be most useful are rubrics, portfolio assessment, and performance-based assessment. These nontraditional approaches assess high-level performance authentically (i.e., in realistic contexts) and provide decision makers with credible evidence of student growth.

Rubrics

A recently developed and now frequently employed evaluation approach involves the use of rubrics to judge the quality of a product or performance. A rubric gives a more descriptive, holistic characterization of the quality of students' work than a conventional rating scale does. In designing and using a rubric, the concern is less with assigning a number to indicate quality than with selecting a verbal description that clearly communicates, based on the performance or product exhibited, what the student knows and is able to do. Thus, rubrics can be highly informative and useful for feedback purposes. However, developing distinct categories and meaningful verbal descriptions and scoring them reliably can be difficult.

Rubrics are much more informative about student skill levels than letter grades or numerical scores. They are also a helpful tool for enhancing gifted learners' understanding of expectations for specific assignments and the criteria by which they will be assessed. Many programs for the gifted engage students in the development of rubrics and in peer assessment processes for using them. Indeed, teaching rubrics to students as part of the overall learning of an instructional module is a common practice in strong gifted programs. Regular use of rubrics ensures that gifted students and teachers will grasp the importance of assessment as a fundamental part of the learning process, not something external to it.

Rubrics also may be used as part of other, more summative approaches to learning assessment. For example, they typically are employed in some way in both performance-based and portfolio assessment and can be used as a tool in pre-post design time-series analysis.

A sample rubric for use in judging student writing is shown in Figure 12.3. The rubric clearly describes each category, so that students and others can easily understand the ratings assigned.

Portfolios

Portfolios represent another form of authentic assessment. Tierney, Carter, and Desi (1991, p. 41) defined portfolios as "systematic collections by both students and teachers [that] can serve as the basis to examine effort, improvement, processes, and achievement as well as to meet accountability demands usually achieved by more formal testing procedures." As these authors noted, "Through reflection on systematic collections of student work, teachers and students can work together to illuminate students' strengths, needs, and progress." Portfolios also can illuminate strengths and needs in the instructional process. Teachers who use portfolio assessment often involve students in selecting samples of their work for their portfolios

Criteria	A	B	Other (no grade)
Organizational soundness	Paper is well organized, clear, and easy to follow	Paper is adequately organized but lacks clarity in sections	Paper rambles and is disconnected
Conceptual soundness, quality of insights and ideas	Ideas are insightful and explicate text and other sources well	Ideas are sound; text is explicated adequately	Paper lacks clear-cut presentation of sound ideas
Depth of under-standing of the selected topic	Topic is treated at a high level of depth, showing individual reflection on readings, class discussion, and experience	Topic is treated with some depth as seen by author ideas woven into commentary	Topic is treated shallowly with secondary sources being the total basis for shaping the discussion
Logical argument, persuasion	Argument is highly persuasive, with a strong thesis, reasons, and conclusion	Argument is convincing but weakened by limited examples or reasons	Argument is limited; lack of development of ideas
Use of relevant sources	Highly effective use of sources	Effective use of sources, although integration of sources into the argument could be improved	Limited use of sources
Form	Mechanical control is highly evident	Mechanical control is adequate	Mechanical control is insufficient

FIGURE 12.3   Rubric for Evaluating Student Writing

and have them update the portfolios over time so that improvements or changes in the quality of work may be noted.

Based on their instructional objectives, teachers must identify criteria for judging the work. Criteria for evaluating a portfolio of writing samples, for example, might include organization, elaboration of ideas, clarity, and correct mechanics. Teachers also must determine a mode for evaluating each piece in a student's portfolio. Rating scales (e.g., poor, average, superior) and comments (e.g., "shows good effort but lacks fundamentals") are the most frequently employed methods. Often, these ratings are converted to a numerical scale at the end of an instructional segment to facilitate the assessment of patterns of growth in key areas.

Just as there are different types of objective tests and rating scales, portfolios can take varied forms. Anderson (1994) described the following four formats, which she has used in working with elementary school children:

✓ *Showcase portfolio*—Presents the student's "best" work while emphasizing self-assessment, reflection, and ownership.
✓ *Evaluation portfolio*—Presents representative work to be evaluated on the basis of showing movement toward a specific academic goal.
✓ *Process portfolio*—Presents student reflections on work produced over time for the purpose of helping them develop points of view on their long-term learning process and subject synthesis.
✓ *Documentation portfolio*—Presents work that represents academic accomplishment for presentation to parents, other students, or school administrators.

Performance Assessment

Performance assessment is a form of assessment that requires students to construct a response, create a product, or perform a demonstration. Because performance assessments generally do not yield a single correct answer or solution method, evaluations are based on judgments guided by criteria.

Individuals who design these assessments must be creative, making decisions about content and scope, processes to be employed, and overall effect in respect to coherence. Important considerations in the design process have been outlined by Wiggins (1992). When the designers move to task development, they need to contextualize the tasks so that the situations are authentic to the field being studied and ensure that the tasks represent tests of knowledge in use, not drills made up of unrelated items.

Schulman (1996) noted the following key questions that developers of performance-based assessments must ask themselves to ensure that they institute appropriate task demands:

✓ What important concepts does this assessment task address?
✓ How can responses to this task inform instruction?
✓ How does the task allow for a variety of responses and modes of response?
✓ What references do students have for knowing what is expected of them in this task?
✓ What other sources of evidence exist to support inferences made from the assessment?
✓ How does this task fit with learning goals and procedures?

Designers of performance assessments must carefully consider the range of tasks given in the assessment. Direct assessments of the complex performances usually found in performance assessment do not tend to generalize well from one task to another, even within the same domain. For example, a writing assessment that uses only one prompt and one type of writing does little to assess how well a student is able to perform in the domain of writing. A wider range of tasks within a domain should be used. However, there also comes a point of diminishing returns, where more tasks or more raters do little to improve the reliability or validity of the assessment (Dunbar, Koretz, & Hoover, 1991).

Scoring and administration issues also need to be considered during task development. With regard to the former, the scoring rubrics must represent the traits being tested, instead of what is easiest to score. Administration issues include, among other things, making the constraints of the testing process as realistic as possible. Once the tasks are developed, templates of the tasks as well as exemplary tasks and design criteria should be pulled together to create a "tool kit" to facilitate the creation of tasks in the future. Finally, tasks should be piloted to determine any difficulties or problems for the students or assessors. After the piloting, revisions should take place based on the feedback received, and the tests should be tried again.

As performance assessment has moved from use by teachers in individual classrooms to large-scale assessment, quality control has become an important issue. In the individual classroom, the context of the assessment was known by the teacher doing the performance assessment, and the performance assessment constituted only one part of a student's evaluation for the marking period. With the current push to use performance assessments in larger contexts, such as in districtwide or statewide testing programs, that knowledge of context is lost, as is the opportunity for students, classrooms, and districts to be assessed in more than a singular manner.

Use of performance-based assessment with gifted students has yielded strong evidence of learning gains in specific areas within curriculum domains, including scientific research skills (VanTassel-Baska, Bass, Avery, Ries, & Poland, 1998), literary analysis and interpretation, and persuasive writing (VanTassel-Baska, Zuo, Avery, & Little, 2002). Care must be taken to ensure that tasks are sufficiently challenging to engage gifted learners to a high degree. Samples of a pre- and post-task demand assessment with actual gifted student responses follow. Also included is a sample scoring rubric (Center for Gifted Education, 1998).

Pre-Assessment, Student #2, Grade 5

Question: Do you think *Autobiographia Literaria* should be required reading for your grade?

Response: In my opinion this poem gives a good message because kids can relate to it. The first reason I say this is he wrights [sic] about a child and his feelings, which can relate to children. Second, this poem shows how much you can change in a lifetime, which teaches children. Finally, this will help [a] child who is feeling different to know that he is not alone.

Post-Assessment, Student #2, Grade 5

Question: Do you think *Where the Rainbow Ends* should be required reading for your grade?

Response: I really liked [the] poem "Where the Rainbow Ends" by Richard Rive. I think other kids my age would agree with me. I am concerned about racism mainly because I am Jewish and I know about the Holocaust. I totally agree with this poem. It's true that getting along together will be [important] to learn.

Most kids, no matter what their parents say, will play with whomever they like. I never ask my friends their religion, I just play with them. If these kids read this poem it will enforce positive beliefs that hopefully they will pass on [to] their children as well.

Because he uses the metaphor of music to explain a difficult idea, it makes it easier [for] kids to understand. The lines "There is no white music and no black music" make the idea that there is no difference between people very clear.

It is important for fifth graders to read a poem by a black poet and [for] them [to] see it is no different from one written by a white poet. This shows there is no white or black poetry—just poetry.

This is an excellent poem for a fifth-grade class. We should read words by writers from all different ethnic groups, the metaphor makes his point clear to everyone, and since most kids don't discriminate Mr. Rive's poem makes you feel you are right to think that way.

Persuasive Writing Scoring Rubric

Claim or Opinion

1   No clear position exists on the writer's assertion, preference, or view, and context does not help to clarify it.
2   Yes/no alone or writer's position is poorly formulated, but reader is reasonably sure what the paper is about based on context.
4   Meets expectations: A clear topic sentence exists, and the reader is reasonably sure what the paper is about based on the strength of the topic sentence alone.
6   Exceeds expectations: A very clear, concise position is given and position is elaborated with reference to reasons; multiple sentences are used to form the claim. Must include details that explain the context.

Data or Supporting Points

0   No reasons are offered that are relevant to the claim.
2   One or two weak reasons are offered; the reasons are relevant to the claim.
4   At least two strong reasons are offered that are relevant to the claim.
6   Meets expectations: At least three reasons are offered that are relevant to the claim.
8   Exceeds expectations: At least three reasons are offered that are relevant, accurate, convincing, and distinct.

Elaboration

0   No elaboration is provided.
2   An attempt is made to elaborate at least one reason.
4   More than one reason is supported with relevant details.
6   Meets expectations: Each reason (3) is supported with relevant information that is clearly connected to the claim.
8   Exceeds expectations: The writer explains all reasons in a very effective, convincing, multi-paragraph structure.

Conclusion

0   No conclusion/closing sentence is provided.
2   A conclusion/closing sentence is provided.
4   Meets expectations: A conclusion is provided that revisits the main ideas.
6   Exceeds expectations: A strong concluding paragraph is provided that revisits and summarizes main ideas.

This performance-based assessment protocol demonstrates the capacity for gifted students to grow and develop skills in a specific area of a domain. It also highlights the striking truth that many students come into a gifted curriculum with relatively low-level skills that need bolstering. The use of pre-assessment helps the teacher pinpoint areas of instructional need.

In general, teachers have used nontraditional assessments idiosyncratically. As for all other rating instruments, nontraditional assessments should be tried with a sample of two or three persons from the potential learner group or an equivalent group. This trial allows assessors to check for (a) each learner's understanding of the testing procedure, (b) the effectiveness of each part of the instruments, and (c) the required length of the testing period for each learner. If more than one teacher will use the scale, the procedure must be standardized so that each teacher grades similar performances equally. For interrater reliability (consistency) to be established, school administrators must establish uniformity in the development and implementation of these tools so that the process is equitably applied to students.

ESTABLISHING CONTENT VALIDITY OF CURRICULUM DOCUMENTS

The curriculum products developed for gifted learners must be judged appropriate before they are employed. Moreover, the design of the products must facilitate teaching to the specified outcomes. Having three outside experts review the curriculum documents is a good way to ensure this basic level of validity. The experts may be local program coordinators, experienced teachers in subject area and grade level for which the products will be used, content experts, or relevant university personnel. Review alone, however, is not sufficient. The feedback received from these individuals must be incorporated into the final documents to be used with students.

Too frequently, districts rush to finalize curriculum products without adequate review of the products developed. Such expediency is costly in the long run if a product is unsuccessful or not used because of faulty design. The Center for Gifted Education at the College of William and Mary has external curriculum reviewers complete the checklist that appears in Appendix B to this chapter. This checklist provides an example of key elements to consider in establishing content validity of a curriculum unit of study. The checklist also can be used by curriculum developers up front to ensure that key criteria are addressed appropriately in the design process. Moreover, packaged curricula can be assessed using the same criteria.

ESTABLISHING TRIANGULATION OF PERCEIVED BENEFIT OF CURRICULUM

Beyond assessing the face validity of curriculum materials for use with gifted learners at different stages of development, the materials should be piloted in classrooms as soon as it is feasible to do so. After a curriculum unit has been studied, students, teachers, and parents should respond to questions such as the following.

Student Questions

✓ What new learning did you acquire as a result of the unit of study just completed?
✓ What aspects of the unit were repetitive or focused on things you already knew?
✓ What in the unit was most interesting to you? Why?
✓ What aspects of the unit did you not enjoy?
✓ What activities had the greatest impact on you?
✓ If you were to experience this unit of study again, what one change would you like to see?

Teacher Questions

✓ What do you perceive to be the major benefits to your students from the unit?
✓ What activities did they find most motivating?
✓ What instructional strategies and management techniques worked the best in implementing the unit?
✓ What aspects of the unit did not work for you?
✓ What aspect of the unit did you enjoy teaching the most? Why?
✓ How would you change the unit the next time you teach it?

Parent Questions

✓ What do you perceive your child has learned from our unit study of _____ over the past ____ weeks?

✓ What aspects of the unit did your child find motivating and worthwhile?

✓ Did you see improvement in your child in any of the following ways as a result of studying the unit? (Check all that apply)

___ habits of learning

___ higher-level thinking

___ research skills

___ ability to work with others

___ deeper knowledge of subject

___ ability to see applications of the unit in everyday life

CONTENT-BASED APPROACHES FOR ASSESSING IMPACT OF CURRICULUM ON STUDENTS

Assessing learner outcomes provides a picture of the nature and extent of learning that has occurred in a special program. In gifted programs, for which there is a lack of good standardized assessment instruments, multiple and diverse ways of assessing student progress must be employed.

To provide an example, Table 12.1 identifies diverse approaches to evaluation according to major strands in a middle school language arts curriculum and corresponding learner outcomes. The table illustrates that both content area considerations and type of emphasis in the program dictate appropriate techniques for evaluation. For example, the oral communications outcome may best be evaluated by using a rubric, completed by teachers, peers, or both, to judge each student's presentation and complementing that assessment with a pre-post test on evaluative listening. In this way, the two major skills of oral communication—presentation and listening—are judged. In the area of reading/literature, assessment of analytical skills through essay writing can be complemented by teacher analysis of videotapes of class discussion and peer assessment of the discussions via a checklist. In writing, a rubric may be employed by the teacher and also used as a formative tool by peers to provide constructive feedback on early drafts. Further, a portfolio of final draft work may be kept and assessed on a trend line. The use of multiple and diverse ways of assessing gifted student learning, such as those described here for language arts, is essential for judging the nature, extent, and quality of learning. Several useful assessment methods are described in the following sections.

TABLE 12.1   Diverse Approaches to Evaluating Student Impacts

Speaking/Listening Development	Reading/Literature	Writing
(Gifted Student Outcome: Students will develop high-level oral communication skills.)	*(Gifted Student Outcome: Students will develop analytical skills in reading advanced literature.)*	*(Gifted Student Outcome: Students will be able to utilize expository writing skills in relevant assignments.)*
1. Rubric for presentations to be completed by teacher, peers, or both	1. Teacher-constructed essay tests	1. Rubric for assessing writing quality to be completed by teacher
2. Performance-based assessment of evaluative listening	2. Teacher analysis of videotapes of selected class discussions	2. Peer review based on use of workshopping model
	3. Peer evaluation checklist of student-led discussions	3. Portfolio of final-draft work

Teacher-Developed Essay Test

As noted earlier, one way to assess gifted student learning in the language arts is the essay test. Each of the following questions, adapted from College Board Advanced Placement language and literature examinations, would be appropriate for such a test for gifted middle school students. One question, well framed around the literature studied, would constitute a sufficient assessment of a gifted student's analytical skills at a given point in time. Each question would require a 45-minute in-class, written response.

Sample Essay Evaluation Questions

1. Setting is the physical environment in which action occurs. It includes time and place. In many novels and plays, setting is used significantly. For example, the author may employ it as a motivating force in human behavior, as a reflection of the state of mind of characters, or as a representation of the values held by characters. Choose a novel or a play in which setting is important and write an essay in which you explain the uses the author makes of it.

2. The struggle to achieve dominance over others frequently appears in fiction. Choose a novel in which such a struggle for dominance occurs, and write an essay explaining the purposes for which the author uses the struggle.

3. Choose a complex and important character in a novel or a play of recognized literary merit who might—on the basis of the character's actions alone—be considered evil or immoral. In a well-organized essay, explain both how and why the full presentation of the character in the work makes us react more sympathetically than we otherwise might.

4. In retrospect, the reader often discovers that the first chapter of a novel or the opening scene of a drama introduces some of the major themes of the work. Write an essay explaining how the opening scene of a drama or the first chapter of a novel you have read functions in this way.

5. A character's attempt to recapture or to reject the past is important in many plays, novels, and poems. Choose a literary work in which a character views the past with such feelings as reverence, bitterness, or longing. Write an essay in which you show with clear evidence from the work how the character's view of the past is used to develop a theme.

6. In some novels and plays, certain parallel or recurring events prove to be significant. In an essay, describe the major similarities and differences in a sequence of parallel or recurring events in a novel or play and discuss the significance of these events.

Peer Assessment of Student-Led Discussions

Figure 12.4 illustrates a peer-assessment checklist that students can use to judge the effectiveness of a student-conducted discussion. The checklist focuses on important aspects of providing leadership in this mode. Both the ratings and comments encourage reflection on the part of both peers and the discussion leader.

Student and Parent Comments

Another helpful qualitative approach for assessing curriculum impacts on students is to collect and review students' and parents' direct statements about the program. Avery et al. (1997) used this approach to assess the effect of a gifted program curriculum on student "quality of learning" indicators. The following representative comments made by parents of children in the program support the more quantitative data the authors collected:

> "The class creates a mutual competitiveness without the fear of failure or (more important) the embarrassment of being 'too smart.'"

> "She has renewed interest in school and her ability to learn. She has developed a true feeling of belonging and closeness with the other students in the class."

Rate the quality of the discussion on a 1–5 scale (using the following criteria) by filling in the number in the space provided.

Name of Discussion Leader: _____

	1	2	3	4	5
1. Questions were interesting and pertinent, illuminating the ideas raised within the work.					
2. Questions were clearly stated and effectively reworded when necessary.					
3. Questions directed me to a clearer understanding of the work or concept.					
4. Discussion introduced perspectives I had not already discovered.					
5. Leader was assertive and in control of the discussion, keeping it focused on that material and maintaining its coherence.					
6. Leader was well-prepared and able to answer questions and correct errors and misinterpretations.					
7. Leader was flexible, eliciting the expression of a variety of points of view.					
8. Leader effectively summarized the major points of the discussion					
9. Leader created and maintained an atmosphere conducive to the free exchange of ideas.					
10. Individual leaders shared time with one another and with students.					

AVERAGE RATING (add all numbers and divide by 10): _____

In the space below, write comments intended to help the discussion leader improve his or her discussion skills.

For the leader: In the space below, answer the following questions. What did you learn about the material, your skills, or the difficulty of the task? What would you do differently next time? What did you feel you did particularly well?

FIGURE 12.4   Peer Assessment of Student-led Discussion

"He has learned more responsibility. He has been academically challenged for the first time. Also his attitude toward school has improved. He hated it before."

Comments such as these provide another perspective on benefits to students of special programs. Clearly, for some audiences the directness of student and parent comments speaks more eloquently than quantitative assessment data of student learning and curricular impact.

LARGE-SCALE EVALUATION OF CURRICULUM WORK

Recent research attests to the need for school districts to proactively evaluate the programs they administer and the underlying curriculum structure that drives these programs. The research points to the following evaluation needs:

1. Regular and ongoing evaluation of all school-based programs to assess student learning impacts, perceived impacts by client groups, and implementation problems (Chase, Mutter, & Nichols, 1999).
2. Assessment of curriculum structure and design as a critical part of an overall evaluation (Lee, Croninger, & Smith, 1997).
3. Assessment of teacher belief systems and attitudes toward effecting student learning gains (Avery & VanTassel-Baska, in press; Yager & Weld, 1999).

School administrators would do well to develop a plan for such comprehensive assessments to be conducted by internal staff.

In an effort to assess the effectiveness of comprehensive educational reform projects, Wang, Haertel, and Walberg (1998) examined 12 nationally known programs with respect to research-based best-practice variables. The following programs were selected because of their focus on improving student learning in all subject areas through the use of a comprehensive improvement framework.

✓ *Accelerated Schools.* This program focuses on improving student learning through enriched curriculum and instruction, school climate, and organizational changes.
✓ *Coalition for Essential Schools.* The coalition was founded in and promotes nine principles that encourage students to think critically, help teachers facilitate learning, and foster the use of authentic assessment.
✓ *Community for Learning (previously known as the Adaptive Learning Environments Model).* This data-based, K-12 program focuses on promoting high academic achievement through schoolwide planning structures and coordination of instruction and related services.
✓ *School Development.* This program unites the resources of the school, family, and community to promote holistic child development.

The other eight programs, listed below, focus primarily on curricular changes:

✓ *Core Knowledge*. This curriculum develops students' cultural literacy, emphasizing content in history, literature, geography, math, science, art, and music.
✓ *Different Ways of Knowing*. This program emphasizes multiple intelligences and interdisciplinary studies to strengthen students' verbal, mathematical, logical, social, and artistic skills.
✓ *Foxfire*. This teacher network is learner-centered and promotes interaction with the community.
✓ *Higher Order Thinking Skills*. This pull-out program develops students' critical thinking skills through technology combined with Socratic teaching.
✓ *National Writing Project*. This program is designed to improve students' writing through the provisions of professional development opportunities for teachers.
✓ *Paideia*. This liberal arts program emphasizes developing students' minds through a classical curriculum, didactic instruction, Socratic questioning, and coaching.
✓ *Reading Recovery*. This pull-out program offers one-on-one tutoring to early readers with reading problems.
✓ *Success for All*. This reading and language arts program focuses on preventing academic deficiencies through one-on-one tutoring and small-group instruction.

Table 12.2 shows the breakdown the researchers found for each program with respect to classroom practices and curriculum and assessment practices. Local districts can use these findings about the best practices in large reform projects when considering efforts to improve curriculum, instruction, and assessment for any learner. Because the practices noted by Wang et al. exclude several that would be important gauges for gifted learners and include some that would not necessarily be highly effective with gifted learners (e.g., peer tutoring and cooperative learning), the checklist may need to be tailored to be as effective as possible in its application.

Another useful curriculum evaluation tool is a criterial checklist that addresses the major aspects of curriculum document design. Armstrong (1997) provided an excellent set of criteria for this type of checklist. The areas addressed include legitimacy of the documents, credibility of the developer, specification of intended learners, specification of intended users, specification of document purpose and coverage, clarity and usability of format and organization, and evidence of professional editing and reproduction. A rating form and rubric operationalize the criteria for each application. The criteria are also useful for curriculum developers as they plan and prepare documents.

SUMMARY

Determining the effectiveness of programs for gifted learners requires serious attention from curriculum planning to follow-up assessment. The evaluation of student

TABLE 12.2   Effective Practices Used by Educational Reform Programs

Program Practices	Accelerated Schools	Coalition for Essential Schools	Community for Learning	School Development	Core Knowledge	Different Ways of Knowing	Foxfire	Higher-Order Thinking Skills	National Writing Project	Paideia	Reading Recovery	Success for All
Classroom Practices												
High expectations for students	x	x	x	x	x	x	x	x	x	x	x	x
Frequent high-quality academic interactions between teachers and students	x	x	x	x	x	x	x	x	x	x	x	x
Metacognitive strategies		x	x	x		x		x	x	x	x	x
Student-directed learning		x	x	x			x		x		x	x
Direct instruction			x	x	x			x			x	x
Small-group instruction	x		x	x		x		x		x		x
Frequent high-quality social interactions between teachers and students	x	x	x	x		x		x		x	x	
Cooperative learning	x	x	x	x				x	x			x
Positive classroom climate	x	x	x	x		x	x					
Adaptive instructional strategies			x	x					x		x	x
Peer tutoring	x		x			x	x					x
Tutoring by teacher, teacher aide, or student			x						x		x	x
Curriculum and Assessment												
Alignment of curriculum and assessment	x	x	x	x	x	x	x	x	x	x	x	x
Curriculum and assessment tailored to student ability and academic background	x	x	x	x		x			x		x	x
Integration of content areas	x	x	x	x		x	x		x	x		
Curriculum and assessment tailored to student cultural background	x	x		x		x	x				x	x
Use of individual learning plans			x	x							x	x
Frequent assessments			x							x	x	x

Note: The 12 programs support these best practices to varying degrees, depending on the programs' goals and scope

learning in gifted programs must be multileveled and considered an ongoing part of the curriculum development process. Curriculum development is central to schools, and it is dynamic, in a state of continual change. Implementation of the curriculum planning model should be done from a systems perspective so the effort becomes an ongoing part of school district operations. Curriculum planning has implications for staff development, in that teachers can be trained to become more sophisticated in the skills needed to work effectively with the gifted. Further, teacher evaluation should accurately reflect these behaviors. Curriculum and instructional management should be merged through collaborative planning, adherence to district-wide models, and an understanding of the distinctions between general and gifted efforts.

Potential problems may arise in a focus on traditional patterns, limited communication, scarce time, lack of teacher involvement in the development process, emphasis on program development rather than curriculum development, use of standardized materials as a basis, the need for training, and the lack of a team approach, among others. In contrast, successful curriculum development incorporates a comprehensive needs assessment, a well informed central office staff, prudent modification of existing materials, teacher involvement in the decision-making process, a committed staff, and the support of consultant resources.

QUESTIONS FOR REFLECTION

1. What areas of gifted student learning would you want to emphasize each year in the classroom? Make a list, and think of appropriate approaches you might use to determine whether students have benefited from the experiences provided.
2. How might educators best assess theme-based or interdisciplinary learning in gifted programs?
3. If you were a school board member, what learner outcomes would you expect to see from a specialized curriculum for gifted learners? What approaches to measuring outcomes would you find most convincing? Why?
4. What mechanisms might schools employ to make assessment of learning easier to accomplish and more meaningful to ongoing curriculum development?

REFERENCES

Anderson, A. (1994). Mathematics in context: Measurement, packaging, and caring for our environment. *School Science and Mathematics, 94,* 146–150.

Armstrong, D. (1997, October/November). Rating curriculum documents. *The High School Journal,* 1–7.

Avery, L., & VanTassel-Baska, J. (in press). The impact or gifted education at state and local levels: Translating results into action. *Journal for the Education of the Gifted.*

Avery, L. D., VanTassel-Baska, J., & O'Neill, B. (1997). Making evaluation work: One school district's experience. *Gifted Child Quarterly, 41,* 124–132.

Carter, K. R. (1992). A model for evaluating programs for the gifted under non-experimental conditions. *Journal for the Education of the Gifted, 15,* 266–283.

Center for Gifted Education. (1998). *Autobiographies.* Dubuque, IA: Kendall-Hunt.

Chase, E., Mutter, D., & Nichols, W. R. (1999, August). Program evaluation. *The American School Board Journal,* 26–28.

Dunbar, S. B., Koretz, D. M., & Hoover, H. D. (1991). Quality control in the development and use of performance assessment. *Applied Measurement in Education, 4,* 289–303.

Farrell, B. G. (1992). Lesson plan analysis as a program evaluation tool. *Gifted Child Quarterly, 36,* 23–26.

House, E. R., & Lapan, S. (1994). Evaluation of programs for disadvantaged gifted students. *Journal for the Education of the Gifted, 17,* 441–466.

Hunsaker, S. L., & Callahan, C. M. (1993). Evaluation of gifted programs: Current practices. *Journal for the Education of the Gifted, 16,* 190–200.

Johnson, S. K. (2000, Fall). What the research says about accountability and program evaluation. *Tempo,* 23–30.

Lee, V. E., Croninger, R. G., & Smith, J. (1997). Course-taking, equity, and mathematics learning: Testing the constrained curriculum hypothesis in U.S. secondary schools. *Educational Evaluation and Policy Analysis, 19,* 99–121.

Schulman, L. (1996). New assessment practices in mathematics. *Journal of Education, 178,* 61–71.

Tierney, R. J., Carter, M. A., & Desi, L. E. (1991). Portfolio assessment in the reading-writing classroom. Norwood, MA: Christopher Gordon.

Tomlinson, C., Bland, L., & Moon, T. (1993). Evaluation utilization: A review of the literature with implications for gifted education. *Journal for the Education of the Gifted, 16,* 171–189.

Tomlinson, C. A. & Callahan, C. M. (1994). Planning effective evaluations for programs for the gifted. *Roeper Review, 17,* 46–51.

VanTassel-Baska, J., Avery, L. D., Little, C., & Hughes, C. (2000). An evaluation of the implementation of curriculum innovation: The impact of the William and Mary units on schools. *Journal for the Education of the Gifted, 23,* 244–272.

VanTassel-Baska, J., Bass, G., Avery, L., Ries, R., & Poland, D. (1998). A national pilot study of science curriculum effectiveness for high ability students. *Gifted Child Quarterly, 42,* 200–211.

VanTassel-Baska, J., Zuo, L., Avery, L., & Little, C. (2002). A curriculum study of gifted student learning in the language arts. *Gifted Child Quarterly, 46,* 30–44.

Wang, M. C., Haertel, G. D., & Walberg, H. J. (1998). Models of reform: A comparative guide. *Educational Leadership, 55*(7), 66–71.

Wiggins, G. (1992). Creating tests worth taking. *Educational Leadership, 49*(8), 26–33.

Yager, R. E., & Weld, J. D. (1999). Scope, sequence, and coordination: The Iowa Project, a national reform effort in the USA. *International Journal of Science Education, 21*(2), 169–194.

APPENDIX A TO CHAPTER 12

Sample Forms Delineating Key Gifted Learner Outcomes

FORM A
Essay Evaluation Form

Directions: Rate each student on a 1 (low) to 5 (high) scale for each item number listed.

Technical Qualities

_____ 1. Thesis
   a. Writer effectively expresses central idea in a clearly stated thesis.
   b. Thesis clearly arises from an analysis of/encounter with the assigned topic (rather than a thesis arbitrarily imposed upon a subject).
   c. Organization and development of essay are controlled by the focus and limits of the thesis.

_____ 2. Paragraph Unity
   a. Each paragraph contains only those ideas relevant to the topic of the paragraph.
   b. Sentences within each paragraph are sensibly ordered.
   c. Sentences are connected with clear transitions.

_____ 3. Developmental Flow
   a. Progression of paragraphs follows a sensible order.
   b. Transitions are used as needed to clarify relationships among paper's major points.
   c. Writer adequately develops major points with explanation, exemplification, and evidence. (Abstractions are made concrete; generalizations are supported with specific detail.)

_____ 4. Logic
   a. Writer has avoided conceptual errors [tautologies (circular reasoning), faulty cause and effect, contradiction, faulty identification—for instance, defining entities in terms of what they are not—unexamined, unsupported assumptions].

       b. Writer has avoided factual errors (misquotations, evidence out of context, misidentifications, insensitivity to or misappropriation of historical context).

       c. Writer has avoided syntactical errors (faulty parallel structure, excessive subordination or coordination, awkward shifts in grammatical structures).

_____ 5. Conclusions

       a. Writer brings essay to satisfying ending.

       b. Writer synthesizes main ideas.

_____ 6. Grammar and Mechanics

       Writer uses appropriate grammar and shows evidence of mechanical control.

_____ 7. Diction

       a. Writer consistently uses tone appropriate to audience addressed.

       b. Writer creates an authentic voice.

       c. Words chosen are precise and appropriate to context.

       d. Writer avoids needless repetition.

       e. Writer avoids wordiness and cliches.

FORM B
Sample Essay Evaluation Questions for Use in Literature Programs for the Gifted

1. Setting is the physical environment in which action occurs. It includes time and place.

   In many novels and plays, setting is used significantly. For example, the author may employ it as a motivating force in human behavior, as a reflection of the state of mind of characters, or as a representation of the values held by characters.

   Choose a novel or a play in which setting is important and write an essay in which you explain the uses the author makes of it.

2. "The struggle to achieve dominance over others frequently appears in fiction."

   Choose a novel in which a struggle for dominance occurs, and write an essay showing for what purposes the author uses the struggle.

3. Choose a complex and important character in a novel or a play of recognized literary merit who might—on the basis of the character's actions alone—be considered evil or immoral. In a well organized essay, explain both how and why full presentation of the character in the work makes us react more sympathetically than we otherwise might. Avoid plot summary.

4. In retrospect, the reader often discovers that the first chapter of a novel or the opening scene of a drama introduces some of the major themes of the work. Write an essay about the opening scene of a drama or the first chapter of a novel in which you explain how it functions in this way.

5. A character's attempt to recapture or to reject the past is important in many plays, novels, and poems.

   Choose a literary work in which a character views the past with feelings such as reverence, bitterness, or longing, Show with clear evidence from the work how the character's view of the past is used to develop a theme in the work.

6. In some novels and plays certain parallel or recurring events prove to be significant. In an essay, describe the major similarities and differences in a sequence of parallel or recurring events in a novel or play and discuss the significance of such events.

Source: Adapted from retired College Board Advanced Placement exams.

APPENDIX B TO CHAPTER 12

Composite Evaluation Form for Curriculum Units for Gifted Learners, Center for Gifted Education, College of William and Mary

General Curriculum Framework Elements	Yes	No
✓ Are the rationale and purpose of the unit clearly stated?	___	___
✓ Are the rationale and purpose substantive and worthy?	___	___
✓ Is the unit organized around a clear, well-developed concept?	___	___
✓ Are the unit outcomes and instructional objectives addressed systematically through the lessons and activities?	___	___
✓ Are the objectives measurable?	___	___
✓ Do the lesson outcomes or objectives emphasize high-level concepts, skills, processes, and ideas?	___	___
✓ Is a unit outline provided?	___	___
✓ Does the unit have a logical order and an integrated structure?	___	___
✓ Is the content substantive?	___	___
✓ Is the content developmentally appropriate?	___	___
✓ Does the unit demonstrate connections to national, state, and/or local standards?	___	___
✓ Do lessons include objectives, activities, questions, assessment, resources, and any other curricular elements needed for implementation?	___	___
✓ Is homework specified for a substantial number of the lessons?	___	___

Comments and clarification:

Activities	Yes	No
✓ Is there an appropriate balance of teacher-directed and student-directed activities?	___	___
✓ Do the activities explore, discover, clarify, and/or extend content?	___	___
✓ Are there opportunities for students to engage in worthwhile extension activities?	___	___

✓ Do activities allow students to discover ideas and concepts
more often than they are told ideas and concepts?
✓ Are activities developmentally appropriate?
✓ Do activities include hands-on exploration and active
student involvement?

Comments and clarification:

Instructional Strategies	Yes	No
✓ Are varied instructional strategies incorporated in the unit?		
✓ Are there varied approaches to grouping, including opportunities for small-group and independent work?		
✓ Do the instructional strategies engage students in problem finding and problem solving?		
✓ Do the instructional strategies engage students in sharing ideas and perspectives?		
✓ Do the instructional strategies engage students in practicing decision-making strategies?		
✓ Do the instructional strategies engage students in developing and asking thoughtful questions about what they are studying?		
✓ Does the unit include specific questions to ask students?		
✓ Are various types and levels of questions incorporated?		

Comments and clarification:

Assessment	Yes	No
✓ Is the assessment process comprehensive based on the outcomes?		
✓ Are assessment activities embedded in individual lessons?		
✓ Is authentic assessment employed?		
✓ Does the assessment process incorporate multiple types of assessment (e.g., portfolios, observational behavior checklists, product evaluation, and self- and peer evaluation)?		
✓ Does the unit employ pre- and post-assessments?		

✓ Is a means of overall unit evaluation suggested? ____ ____
✓ Are both student processes and products acknowledged
and assessed? ____ ____
✓ Does the unit include appropriate rubrics and other criteria
for student assessment? ____ ____

Comments and clarification:

Thinking Skills and Metacognition	Yes	No
✓ Does the unit incorporate techniques for enhancing thinking skills (e.g., teaching the steps of a specific reasoning process)?	____	____
✓ Does the unit include questions for discussion and writing that emphasize higher-level thinking?	____	____
✓ Does the unit emphasize instruction in thinking skills within the context of teaching content?	____	____
✓ Do the unit activities and questions engage the learner in various levels and types of thought?	____	____
✓ Does the unit employ a model or models of thinking that guide instruction in thinking skills (e.g., Bloom, Guilford, Paul)?	____	____
✓ Does the unit strategically engage students in thinking about their thinking strategies?	____	____
✓ Are clear directions for how to model metacognition included at relevant junctures in the unit?	____	____
✓ Does the unit engage students in planning, monitoring, and evaluating their progress on a project or activity?	____	____
✓ Does the unit engage students in reflecting on their performance and the process of learning?	____	____

Comments and clarification:

Communication	Yes	No
✓ Does the unit emphasize communication skills relevant to the content area?	____	____
✓ Does the unit engage students in active speaking and listening activities?	____	____
✓ Does the unit encourage students to respond to one another's presentations through questions, discussion, and critique?	____	____
✓ Does the unit provide relevant reading in the content area?	____	____
✓ Does the unit engage students in more than one type of written or spoken communication (e.g., technical, persuasive, creative communication) in the content area?	____	____

Comments and clarification:

Research	Yes	No
✓ Do students engage in research related to the content area?	____	____
✓ Are students directly taught a research model?	____	____
✓ Is student research issue-based, focusing on issues involving multiple perspectives and stakeholder groups?	____	____
✓ Are the opportunities to engage in research practices authentic to the discipline?	____	____
✓ Are the students encouraged to participate in the development of researchable questions?	____	____
✓ Is research work shared with multiple audiences?	____	____

Comments and clarification:

Technology	Yes	No
✓ Does the unit encourage students to use technological tools in conducting research (e.g., CD-ROM, e-mail, Internet)?	____	____
✓ Is the technology use relevant to the content and complementary to the instruction?	____	____

✓ Does the unit employ relevant software programs
(e.g., word processing, spreadsheet)?   ____ ____

✓ Does technology use provide access to resources
unavailable in other formats?   ____ ____

✓ Is technology used to actively engage students in
higher-order thinking skills and activities?   ____ ____

✓ Are activities that involve the use of technology
differentiated for various levels of technological competency?   ____ ____

Comments and clarification:

Interdisciplinary Applications	Yes	No

✓ Does the organizing concept or topic naturally bring
multiple disciplines together?   ____ ____

✓ Is the concept being studied demonstrated in at least
two other disciplines?   ____ ____

✓ Are there lessons that focus on making interdisciplinary
connections?   ____ ____

✓ Are interdisciplinary connections fostered at a conceptual,
abstract level?   ____ ____

✓ Are there opportunities for students to develop language
and reading skills in the content area?   ____ ____

Comments and clarification:

Materials and Resources	Yes	No

✓ Do the materials and resources included in the unit
support lesson activities?   ____ ____

✓ Do the handouts contribute to the enhancement of learning?   ____ ____

✓ Do the materials and resources pull from multiple types
of sources, including primary and secondary sources,
technical and creative material?   ____ ____

✓ Are resources that support student extension activities
identified or provided?   ____ ____

✓ Are resources to support teacher background knowledge identified or provided?   ____ ____

Comments and clarification:

Differentiation for Gifted Students	Yes	No
✓ Are the selected activities, resources, and materials sufficiently challenging for advanced learners?	____	____
✓ Is the organizing concept treated in sufficient depth?	____	____
✓ Are there opportunities for creative production?	____	____
✓ Are there opportunities for integrated higher-order processes?	____	____
✓ Are students given sufficiently complex issues, problems, or themes to explore?	____	____
✓ Are students given ample opportunities through unit activities to construct meaning for themselves?	____	____
✓ Does the content and instruction provide a sufficiently high level of abstraction?	____	____
✓ Is the reading material sufficiently advanced?	____	____
✓ Does the unit plan for different levels of ability?	____	____
✓ Is there adequate articulation of open-ended questions that encourage multiple or divergent responses?	____	____
✓ Are there appropriate opportunities for independent learning?	____	____
✓ Are there sufficient opportunities for meaningful project work?	____	____

Comments and clarification:

Language Arts	Yes	No
✓ Is the choice of literature or reading material based on intellectual, affective, and multi-cultural considerations?	____	____
✓ Does the unit emphasize expectations for advanced reading behavior?	____	____

✓ Does the unit provide activities conducive to developing and practicing critical reading skills? ____ ____

✓ Does the unit incorporate textual analysis of conceptually rich literature? ____ ____

✓ Is there a balanced perspective on at least three diverse cultures in the reading materials, classroom activities, and discussions? ____ ____

✓ Does the unit use concept mapping to teach outlining? ____ ____

✓ Does the unit emphasize persuasive writing? ____ ____

✓ Does the unit focus on strategies for developing a thesis statement, providing supportive evidence, and drafting a conclusion? ____ ____

✓ Does the unit promote the use of workshopping techniques and revision in the writing process? ____ ____

✓ Does the unit emphasize the development of word relationships, such as synonyms, antonyms, and analogies? ____ ____

✓ Does the unit include opportunities to learn appropriate-level vocabulary? ____ ____

✓ Does the unit encourage the development of linguistic competence in English, with emphasis on grammatical structure? ____ ____

✓ Does the unit include opportunities to learn about the history of language, etymology, and/or semantics? ____ ____

✓ Does the unit promote the use of persuasive speaking or debate? ____ ____

Comments and clarification:

Social Studies

	Yes	No

✓ Are important concepts in the social studies disciplines covered in sufficient depth? ____ ____

✓ Is there evidence of attention to multiculturalism or cultural diversity in the selection of reading materials? ____ ____

✓ Are the materials utilized with attention to multiple points of view and different stakeholder perspectives? ____ ____

✓ Is there an emphasis on the meaning and the process of the content area (e.g., history, geography) rather than isolated facts and events? ____ ____

✓ Is critical inquiry developed as an analytical tool for use by students?

✓ Are simulations or scenarios created that involve students in problem-solving opportunities?

✓ Is there sufficient utilization of primary source material?

✓ Is the breadth of social studies content sufficient for the instructional period allotted?

✓ Are some of the topics covered in enough depth to allow for deep understanding of illustrative content (i.e., depth rather than breadth of treatment)?

✓ Do learning opportunities or examples link content to current events or real-world problems?

Comments and clarification:

Mathematics

          Yes   No

✓ Are important mathematics concepts covered in sufficient depth?

✓ Does the content include the history of mathematical ideas, concepts, and mathematicians?

✓ Is the mathematics presented clearly and accurately?

✓ Does the content progress from the concrete to the abstract?

✓ Is problem solving an integral part of the curriculum?

✓ Do activities emphasize the oral and written communication of ideas and strategies?

✓ Do students communicate ideas and concepts in visual form, such as through graphs, posters, or diagrams?

✓ Is there an emphasis on relevant real-world mathematical connections?

✓ Is there an emphasis on connections between different areas of mathematics, such as measurement and geometry or number theory and algebra?

✓ Do activities provide opportunities for students to make conjectures and attempt to verify or prove them?

✓ Does the curriculum promote the habits of mind of mathematicians (e.g., curiosity, tenacity, collaboration, skepticism)?

✓ Do activities provide opportunities for divergent thinking
  and illustration of various thinking processes for a single
  problem?   ____ ____

Comments and clarification:

Science   Yes   No

✓ Are important science concepts covered in sufficient depth?   ____ ____
✓ Is the science content accurate and presented clearly?   ____ ____
✓ Are the topics linked to broad scientific concepts?   ____ ____
✓ Is there a balance of qualitative and quantitative information?   ____ ____
✓ Is there a balance of theoretical and practical science?   ____ ____
✓ Does the unit include considerations of the moral, ethical,
  and historical dimensions of science and technology?   ____ ____
✓ Are there opportunities for open-ended scientific
  investigation?   ____ ____
✓ Are the laboratory work and fieldwork integral to and
  integrated with the curriculum?   ____ ____
✓ Are there opportunities for students to work together to
  investigate real-world scientific technological problems?   ____ ____
✓ Does the unit include instruction on building and testing
  hypotheses?   ____ ____
✓ Does the unit allow for questioning of assumptions and
  diverse opinions on scientific topics and concepts?   ____ ____

Comments and clarification:

Source: Center for Gifted Education. (1999). *Curriculum composite evaluation form.*
Williamsburg, VA: Author.

13

Toward Coherent Curriculum Policy in Gifted Education

Policy development in gifted education has been limited primarily to state and federal initiatives linked to funding priorities and has focused extensively on identification and general programming features (United States Department of Education, 1993; Council of State Directors of Programs for the Gifted, 1998). Some attention to teacher training has been addressed through selected state certification and endorsement programs. Less frequently addressed in policy at any level have been curriculum issues. This chapter advocates for the institutionalization at state and local levels of curriculum policy initiatives for gifted learners that allow for compatibility with state standards and assessment mechanisms yet retain essential flexibility based on the nature of the learner. School districts that initiate such policies will encourage curriculum access by underrepresented groups (Ford, 1996) and be more likely to retain the best students rather than lose them to alternative schooling models.

RATIONALE FOR INSTITUTIONALIZING CURRICULUM POLICY INITIATIVES

The stance that curriculum policy on behalf of gifted learners is needed is based on three major assumptions about the role of curriculum in program development for the gifted. The first assumption is that curriculum is at the heart of what matters in gifted education. Without a challenging curriculum that is well delivered and appropriately assessed, a gifted program cannot be defensible. Seven of the 10 variables that Cox, Daniel, and Boston (1985) delineated as being representative of exemplary gifted programs were curriculum based, including a consensually derived philosophy and set of goals, clear expectations of learner outcomes, and challenge. Recent lists of research-based best practices for schools (e.g., Wang, Haertel, & Walberg,

1996) also stress curriculum issues, such as giving, grading, and returning homework; teaching to goals; direct teaching; and providing mastery learning for sequential skills. In both gifted and general education, curriculum and school improvement are inextricably linked.

The second assumption is that gifted education needs a coherent strategy for curriculum development and improvement of programs. Due to a lack of adequate resources, gifted education has always been a fragmented enterprise at the local level—a little pull-out program at the third- to fifth-grade levels, a small advanced math program at the sixth- to eighth-grade levels, a smattering of Advanced Placement courses at the high school level. In today's age of general educational reform, such an approach has no chance of success. Instead, gifted education must move through individualized sets of state standards, reorganizing, compressing, and adding as needed, to develop and maintain a coherent framework for gifted student learning. Commensurate with this strategy toward coherence, the field must employ a systematic approach to improvement that takes into account planning, implementation, evaluation, and a plan of action that is formulated on the results of studying what happened in implementation at the school level, where proactive improvement can best be observed.

The third assumption is that the development of curriculum policy will help to ensure long-term coherence in gifted student services in a school or district as opposed to ad hoc action for each separate problem. Curriculum policy can provide a kind of "standard notation" for research-based best practice, for it can serve, in many respects, as the glue that holds gifted programs together across elementary and secondary levels, subject areas, and organizational models. Clune (1993) noted the importance of policy development in sustaining an educational reform agenda. Appropriate curriculum for the gifted, which typically is an innovation in schools, should be treated in a similar vein, with the identification of policy goals, their components, the politics of implementation, and evidence of progress toward realizing the goals.

Although curriculum policy has been virtually absent in gifted education documents, curriculum issues have been the subject of much discussion. Ironically, the same issues have emerged repeatedly to plague program developers. Indeed, the following five issues have dominated the field for over 30 years:

✓ How do we handle acceleration of learning?
✓ What is real differentiation?
✓ Do continuity and connection to general education learning matter?
✓ What grouping model should we employ?
✓ How should teachers be prepared to work successfully with the gifted?

Perhaps the timing is right and the field sufficiently advanced for educational leaders to see the need for reaching consensus on these issues and converting them to policy initiatives that could serve as a template for program developers in the future. Rather than reinvent the wheel, practitioners would better support gifted learners by converting these five important issues into policy initiatives, such as those shown in Table 13.1. Three of these initiatives, or goals, focus on curricular considerations specifically, and two relate to the support structures essential to carrying them out successfully. The table displays these five goals, delineates their underlying components, and lists factors that would provide evidence of progress. Each of the goals is described later in this chapter, along with its relevant elements. It is hoped that such a template may offer a basis for cohesive practice in the field of gifted education.

THE POLITICS OF MAKING POLICY WORK

Theories about change abound (Fullan & Stiegelbauer, 1991; Senge, 1990), yet most writers agree that change is a complex process that involves top-down and bottom-up movement. Schools are difficult contexts within which to enact change for several reasons, including their resistance and entrenchment; their chaotic daily operation, which is more responsive than proactive to issues; teachers' lack of content and related pedagogical expertise, and hierarchical models of administration that may inhibit positive change. Based on these problems, identified in general education reform work, it is not surprising that institutionalizing gifted education curriculum practices is difficult.

Clearly, the task of successfully implementing curriculum innovation is daunting. Recent studies of reform projects in mathematics and science have exploded many myths about what works (Cohen & Hill, 1998; Kennedy, 1999). The studies indicate that such issues as contact hours, model of implementation, and even broad-based involvement of educational staff appear to be relatively unimportant in the process. Primary to the enterprise, however, is the emphasis on what students need to learn in a specific subject area and the strategies that best help them learn it. If these findings continue to hold up across new studies, they would influence both how schools organize for instruction and how they prepare teachers to continue being effective. Borko, Mayfield, Marion, Flexer, and Cumbo (1997) found that large reform projects needed to work with the same teachers intensively for 2 years to effect classroom changes and to treat these teachers as professionals without the "sword of tests" held over their heads. Such findings run counter to the current attitude of school administrators, bent on raising test scores at all costs. In many respects, however, successful policy implementation essentially rests on a foundation of policy development.

POLICY ON CURRICULUM FLEXIBILITY

One of the most important curriculum policy initiatives that school districts might enact on behalf of all students would address curriculum flexibility. Curriculum

TABLE 13.1   Curriculum Policies for Gifted and Talented Education

Research-based Goals	Components	Assessment of Progress
To provide curriculum flexibility at all levels of K-12 schooling	• Early entrance and exit at transition points • Content-based acceleration • Grade acceleration • Curricular telescoping • Diagnostic assessment of functional skill level in core areas (Modes: traditional and/or on-line)	• Adopted policy on curriculum flexibility • Evidence of implementation at all levels
To provide differentiated curriculum, instruction, and assessment opportunities for gifted students	• Curriculum that addresses advanced content, process, product, and concept dimensions • Instruction that addresses the use of inquiry, open-ended higher-level thinking, flexible grouping, and off-level task assignments • Use of appropriate materials • Use of off-level performance and portfolio-based assessment	• Adopted policy on differentiation • Evidence of classroom adaptations
To ensure curriculum articulation and alignment in core areas of learning	• K-12 scope and sequence prototypes for gifted learners in core areas • Alignment of gifted curriculum with state standards • Alignment of gifted curriculum with hallmark secondary programs	• Adopted policy on gifted curriculum alignment and articulation • Evidence of use in academic planning
To provide appropriate environments for advanced learning	• Flexible/cluster grouping in heterogeneous classrooms • Special classes • Independent learning contexts	• Adopted policy on appropriate learning contexts and range of delivery systems
To provide training for educators in relevant knowledge skills and attitudinal areas for successfully working with gifted learners	• Training on the nature and needs of gifted learners • Development of advanced knowledge and skills in subject areas and related pedagogy • Training on curriculum flexibility, differentiation, and articulation • Development of strategies and skills for facilitating advanced learning opportunities	• Adopted policy on educator preparation and staff development • Evidence of competencies through teacher evaluation system

flexibility assumes that different students of the same age are at different levels of learning within and across learning areas, thus necessitating the diagnosis of learning level and the prescription of curriculum at a higher level. The government document *Prisoners of Time* (National Education Commission on Time and Learning, 1994) reported the importance of recognizing time as the crucial variable in learning "If experience, research, and common sense teach nothing else, they confirm the truism that people learn at different rates in different ways with different subjects" (p. 4), an understanding that Bloom (1985) related more than a decade earlier. That student learning rate differs for different subject areas for students at different stages of development is a crucial understanding to school patterning of curriculum and instruction. For gifted learners, this flexibility translates into several forms of acceleration. For disabled learners, extensions of time for curriculum tasks, tests, and even whole courses of study represent appropriate forms of such flexibility.

Curriculum flexibility, however, has been one of the most difficult tasks for public schools to enact in responding to students with special needs. Special education mandates have called attention to the need for curriculum flexibility for the disabled, but no similar spurs exist in state and federal law to accommodate gifted learners, who frequently need a speeded-up curriculum.

Various components of a curriculum flexibility policy must be considered at the school district level. One component of the policy should allow for early entrance and early exit procedures for students at various stages of development. Early entrance to kindergarten and first grade, early entrance to high school, and early exit into college are all important stages for consideration. Many gifted children are academically ready for school before they reach the "magic age," and others develop more rapidly than same-age peers once they are in a schooling environment. Early access to high school eliminates the holding pattern of the middle school years that is so common in many contexts around the country. Early college entrance can be accomplished by those already academically proficient in high school subject matter (Olszewski-Kubilius, 1995). An advantage of the new standards movement is that it provides a clear way to document mastery levels in each area of schooling, thus allowing students who are ready to move forward to do so.

A second component of a curriculum flexibility policy should involve the offering of content-based acceleration practices at all levels of schooling and in all subject areas. In the past 20 years, schools have become more open to ideas of math acceleration but generally not to advancement in other subject areas. For gifted learners with precocious verbal, scientific, and artistic abilities, accelerated pathways are crucial to enhanced learning and development. Although many educators believe that only certain subject areas should be considered for accelerative practices and that the accelerative rate should be capped at 6 months or a year so students do not get too far out of step with the school curriculum or other students their age, both of these beliefs are faulty. Eighty years of research show the positive outcomes of such accelerative opportunities on enhanced learning, motivation, and extracurricular engagement of learners (Benbow, 1998; Swiatek & Benbow, 1991).

Several highly acceptable forms of acceleration are currently in operation at the high school level, including, the hallmark secondary programs of the College Board Advanced Placement (AP) Program and the International Baccalaureate (IB) Program. Both of these programs offer students the opportunity to engage in college-level work while still in high school and reward their diligence with college placement, college credit, or both, for work done during the high school years. Specific benefits to students from participation in AP programs include (a) flexible access to advanced course work in high school, (b) credit and/or placement at the college level for work done during high school, (c) motivation to continue taking challenging work, (d) the experience of a model for college expectations, and (e) the garnering of student awards. Benefits to schools include (a) the provision of advanced-level curriculum syllabi, meaning that teachers do not have to develop curricula from scratch, (b) the availability of curriculum-based assessment data for course and teacher evaluation, and (c) the resultant evidence of the implementation of high standards. Similar advantages may be perceived to accrue from IB programs as well.

The AP or IB program, or a similar model, should be made available to students at all stages of development, such that evidence of advanced work brings credit toward the next level of the educational experience. Such programs would help make learning more incentive-driven for bright students at all levels of the schooling process.

A third component of curriculum flexibility should involve simple grade acceleration for students who are advanced in all areas of the curriculum. Such acceleration may be handled through early entrance policies, but the practice should be broadened to consider stages of schooling beyond the naturally occurring transition years. For students showing more than 2 years' advancement in all school subjects, grade-level acceleration may be a good decision (Charlton, Marolf, & Stanley, 1994). Obviously, each case should be considered individually, but more concern is voiced about this well-documented and researched practice than is warranted. For our best students, grade acceleration at critical points of schooling can do much to counter boredom and disenchantment with school.

For secondary schools, a fourth component of a curriculum flexibility policy should involve dual enrollment courses at local community and 4-year colleges. This component would allow highly able students to sample college early without attending full-time. With dual enrollment, students may take one or two college classes away from their high school campus or, if arrangements are made, on-site at their high school. Currently, 22 states have dual enrollment policies, encouraging local districts to take advantage of the opportunity for students to gain access to higher education while still in high school. These courses are then banked for college and are automatically credited for a student attending a public college in the same state. Often, the equivalent of the freshman year in college may be credited. For students in small schools in rural areas, dual enrollment provides a strong alternative to AP and IB programs, which often are not possible to mount in these schools due to lack of interested faculty or insufficient numbers of students who might participate.

A fifth component to consider in a curriculum flexibility policy lies in the realm of telecommunications. Today, advanced courses can be provided technologically in ways not possible even a decade ago. School policy should reflect these new alternatives to teaching and learning, especially for advanced students, who can profit greatly from them. Several universities offer on-line courses, many of which are tailored to younger students, such as the Stanford Education Program for Gifted Youth (EPGY) computer-based program in mathematics and other subjects. Other universities, such as Ball State, beam advanced courses to rural schools through telecommunications links. High school students today can engage in independent study opportunities with university faculty, and research project work conducted globally can now be a part of student learning beyond the classroom. We have the technology, but the policy must be developed to regulate these newer forms of learning to the benefit of students capable of breaking out of traditional models of learning.

POLICY ON CURRICULUM DIFFERENTIATION

A second policy initiative for gifted curricula requires a statement on differentiation that recognizes the interrelated importance of curriculum, instruction, and assessment. A differentiated curriculum would be defined as one that is tailored to the needs of groups of gifted learners and/or individual gifted students, provides experiences sufficiently different from the norm to justify specialized intervention, and is delivered by a trained educator of the gifted, using appropriate instructional and assessment processes to optimize learning.

A major component of a differentiated curriculum policy for the gifted is curriculum design, because this process delineates key features that constitute the curriculum (Borland, 1989). A well-constructed curriculum for the gifted must identify appropriate goals and outcomes, addressing such questions as, "What is important for these students to know and be able to do at what stages of development?" and "How do planned learning experiences provide depth and complexity at a pace that honors the gifted learner's rate of advancement through material?" The curriculum must also be exemplary for the subject matter under study. That is, it should be standards-based and, thus, current regarding the thinking of real-world professionals, such as those who practice writing, mathematical problem solving, or science for a living (VanTassel-Baska, 1998b). Moreover, the curriculum should be designed to honor high-ability students' needs for advanced challenge, in-depth thinking and doing, and abstract conceptualization.

For the past 10 years, the Center for Gifted Education at the College of William and Mary has been involved in the review, development, field-testing, dissemination, and follow-up studies of specially designed language arts, science, and most recently social studies curricula for gifted learners at elementary and secondary levels. Each of these projects has been carefully calibrated to the national standards in each respective domain of learning. The research evidence to date suggests that differentiation policy for the gifted, given the new standards, requires increased attention to helping educators (a) develop advanced tasks that address the standards, (b) organize the standards across grade levels to ensure an emphasis on higher-level skills and concepts, and (c) provide opportunities for in-depth exploration of concepts across sets of standards (VanTassel-Baska, Bass, Reis, Poland & Avery, 1998; VanTassel-Baska, Johnson, Hughes, & Boyce, 1996; VanTassel-Baska, Zuo, Avery, & Little, 2002). Of less help is creating whole new courses or units that are outside the intent of the standards.

Curriculum differentiation policy should also address the need for careful selection of materials for use in classrooms serving gifted and high-ability learners. These materials should include a variety of texts as resources, provide advanced readings, present interesting and challenging ideas, treat knowledge as tentative and open-ended, and provide a conceptual depth that allows students to make interdisciplinary connections. Ideally, each classroom would also have high-quality technological resources that would meet the same criteria (Johnson, Boyce, & VanTassel-Baska, 1995).

Another component of curriculum differentiation policy should be instructional approaches that foster differentiated responses among diverse learners, including inquiry-based, open-ended instruction and approaches that employ flexible grouping practices. An example of an effective inquiry-based model is problem-based learning (PBL), where groups of learners encounter a real-world problem sculpted by the teacher from key learnings to be acquired in a given subject and then proceed to inquire about the nature of the problem, effective avenues for researching it, and sources for acquiring relevant data. The instructional techniques needed by the teacher for guiding the process to successful learning closure in a classroom include high-level questioning skills, listening skills, conferencing skills, and tutorial abilities. PBL also requires the use of flexible team grouping and whole class discussion. The PBL stage of problem resolution requires student-initiated projects and presentations that are guided by the teacher (Boyce, VanTassel-Baska, Burruss, Johnson, & Sher, 1997; Gallagher, Stepien, Sher, & Workman, 1995).

Although only PBL has been discussed here, other models are also effective. The curriculum differentiation policy must include a few core teaching models that successfully highlight the intended outcomes of the curriculum, and administrators must ensure that teachers have the opportunity to learn these models deeply and well.

Just as differentiation involves the careful selection of core materials and curricula that underlie them and the deliberate choice of high-powered instructional approaches, it also requires the choice of differentiated assessment protocols that reflect the high-level learning attained. High-stakes assessments such as the Scholastic Aptitude Test (SAT), Advanced Placement (AP) exams, and even state assessments provide a standardized means of showing how well students are doing in comparison to others their age. To be considered high quality, school districts must produce students scoring at the top levels on these nationally normed instruments. Yet, deep preparation for success on these tests must occur in individual classrooms. Even strong learners such as the gifted cannot do as well as they could without adequate preparation in relevant content-based curriculum archetypes. Thus, the use of standardized assessments as planning tools for direct instruction in each relevant subject area is a key to overall improvement in student performance. Administrators responsible for reviewing teacher lesson plans need to look at how these assessment models are being converted into work in classrooms. School-based teams and departments should spend time planning strategies for incorporating such elements. Because these assessments are a reality and are viewed by society as crucial indicators of student progress in school, gifted educators need to make the assessments work for them rather than against them in the public arena.

In addition to standardized measures being employed to assess student learning, performance-based tools must be employed to assess individual growth and development (Wiggins, 1996). In tandem with standardized measures, they provide a more complete picture of individual progress toward specific educational goals. For gifted learners, in particular, performance-based measures may provide a better indicator of mastery of skills and concepts than traditional paper-and-pencil measures. Gifted education has long favored performance- and portfolio-based approaches, because they align well with the goal structure of many gifted programs. For example, using a rubric to holistically assess a research project has long been a standard practice in strong gifted programs. When such assessments are used with gifted learners, care must be taken to measure real growth over time, revealed through careful pre- and post-assessment procedures, and to use pre-assessment results in instructional planning for individuals and small groups of students. Too frequently, students are assessed on what they already know or are not held accountable for reaching new thresholds of learning.

A final consideration in the use of alternative assessment approaches with gifted learners involves attention to teaching students the rubrics for assessment at the time an assignment is given, so that students can understand expectation levels required for the assignment at its conception. This approach also ensures that criteria for judgment are well defined by the teacher and well understood by the student.

POLICY ON CURRICULUM ARTICULATION

A third policy initiative necessary to create gifted program coherence deals with curriculum articulation and alignment. Gifted learners need to be assured early in their school careers that their advancement at earlier stages can continue and be supplemented by even more challenging offerings throughout their years in school (VanTassel-Baska, 1992). For this and other reasons, careful attention to scope and sequence of curriculum offerings coupled with alignment with existing curriculum structures must be a crucial aspect of curriculum policy development and implementation. Too frequently, lack of attention to these aspects of curriculum development results in fragmentation of program experiences and lack of consistent curriculum offerings.

Prototypes of K-12 options should be developed for each subject area so that districts can make decisions about the overall approach to be employed in developing the curriculum for discrete areas. For example, if the major approach to differentiating a mathematics curriculum is content acceleration by 1 or 2 years, the overall schema for this approach should be laid out so that appropriate options might be included at the senior high school level to ensure that students don't "run out of" mathematics. If a combined approach is to be employed, then delineating the connections between the components is an essential task. For secondary schools, an important function may be developing prototypes for Grades 6–12 if no models exist for the elementary program. Obviously, middle school models have to align well with high school options, and scope and sequence prototypes will direct the discussion about how to make that happen. Such prototypes also can provide a shorthand way to communicate the salient aspects of a gifted learner curriculum to parents and other educators.

In addition to the articulation of differentiated prototypes of subject area offerings, curricula must be aligned with state standards of learning. The alignment process clarifies the relationship between the gifted learner curriculum and the general education curriculum for students at given levels of development and in given subject areas. It shows the extent to which gifted student expectations exceed state standards and extend into areas beyond them. This core issue is central to communication about gifted curricula to various internal and external publics. Strong gifted curricula should be designed to ensure passages through state standards, not around them. Articulation documents provide a mechanism for helping educators and the lay public understand how the gifted learner curriculum is the same as well as different from the norm for all students.

A frequently voiced criticism is that state standards may hold gifted students back and severely retard their learning (Reis, 1999). However, after closely analyzing more than a dozen state standards documents, I find it difficult to understand this concern. The standards were developed based on the latest research on effective learning within each subject matter area and call for extensive use of higher-level skills by students. Strands such as research, historical analysis, literary interpretation, and experimental design all feature these skills at each stage of development within subject areas. Although gifted learners may master the skills sooner than more typical learners, even gifted students must practice the skills over time. Thus, the crux of the concern must rest not with the standards themselves but with how they may be translated by individual teachers. The key to effective implementation of the standards rests with the inferences teachers make about each student's level of functioning within each strand of a given subject. If no attention is given to diagnostic assessment or careful clustering of standards, gifted students may in fact be penalized.

Finally, the curriculum for gifted learners must align vertically with the hallmark secondary Advanced Placement and International Baccalaureate programs. Gifted teachers at all levels need to be aware of the highest-level skills that students will attain in subject matter areas before they leave a school district so that the core skills can be introduced and addressed early in the students' school experience. When core skills are taught later, it may be more difficult to bring students up to the rigorous levels required by the standardized exams in the AP and IB programs. Thus, an effective design-down process has to be developed to ensure continuity and reasonable levels of rigor at all stages of schooling.

POLICY ON GROUPING

Given the current research on the positive use of ability grouping with the gifted (Kulik & Kulik, 1992; Rogers, 1998), it is critical that school district policy attend to this facet of a support structure in evolving programs. Important components of such a policy would include attention to within-class flexible grouping and differentiated assignments as well as opportunities for special class and independent grouping options such as mentorships and internships.

Within-class grouping is critical at all levels of schooling. At the elementary level, where many classrooms are heterogeneous and inclusive, within-class grouping would allow for greater challenge for gifted learners (Lou, Abrami, Spence, & Poulsen, 1996). At the secondary levels, where the norm for honors and even Advanced Placement grouping is across high-ability and gifted ranges, the pace of the class and the opportunity for more in-depth work may be lost to gifted students as the teacher struggles to cover all of the material with everyone. Within-class grouping would, again, increase the level of challenge for gifted students. In-class grouping according to student capacity also provides teachers with alternative ways to handle certain aspects of learning. For example, differentiating paper assignments and readings by group allows advanced students more latitude and depth potential for their work. Similarly, more in-class writing practice may be given to groups already skilled at peer critique. All of these approaches to varying "within-group" work will help the teacher ensure that each student receives the appropriate level of instruction.

Another frequently used grouping approach is special class grouping. For gifted learners, special class grouping by subject area has historically been the most utilized approach to grouping at the secondary level, while pull-out by program focus has predominated at the elementary level (VanTassel-Baska, 1998b). Because special class grouping is so widely practiced in many school districts, the approach should be addressed in district policy. Special class grouping is one of the primary ways to deliver differentiated curriculum. Without such grouping arrangements, differentiated education is much more difficult to accomplish. Indeed, research has shown that 84% of the time in heterogeneous classroom settings is spent on whole class activities with no attention paid to differentiating for the gifted (Archambault, Westberg, Brown, Hallmark, Zhang, & Emmons, 1993). Moreover, special classes provide the context within which good acceleration practices for individual students can be applied, as the level of these classes, by necessity, is more advanced in content.

Many schools have provided special class grouping for mathematics and language arts but not for science and social studies. It is critical that grouping policy apply to all relevant academic subjects if the size of the school can allow for such clustering to be formed. Students who are advanced in any academic area need the opportunity to interact with others at their ability level and to proceed academically at a rate and pace consonant with their abilities. Such a situation typically can occur only in a specialized group setting.

A third critical component of grouping policy for gifted students at all levels is grouping for more independent types of work. Students in these groups may select among options geared at providing them with more personalized opportunities for intellectual growth, whether through a well-designed independent project, through work in a professional setting, or through an optimal match with an adult in an area of expertise and interest to the student. Each of these types of arrangements calls for schools to adopt a policy that allows for one-on-one interactions with the community at large as well as more individualized use of school time.

POLICY ON TEACHER DEVELOPMENT

The last support structure necessary for inclusion in a policy statement on curriculum should focus on a mechanism for ensuring teacher development that supports the components of policy already delineated in this chapter. Nurturing and socializing teachers to the demands of working effectively with gifted learners is a long-term process. This process is best accomplished within the framework of areas of content expertise, so that the incentive to grow in one's work with a particular group of learners is carefully embedded within overall job expectations. Rarely does a teacher work only with high-ability and gifted learners. Thus, the emphasis of teacher development has to be on modifying curriculum and instruction in an efficient and effective manner, given the limited time available for this task.

One important component of basic staff development is to provide understanding of the characteristics and educational needs of gifted learners. This understanding is essential for effectively manipulating a curriculum plan for these students as well as for teaching them. All teachers must take a course in understanding disabilities before they graduate from college, yet no analogue currently exists for providing understanding of gifted learners. State certification standards may be a viable way to ensure that all teachers to whom gifted learners may be assigned have received such education.

A second component of the staff development structural support is to ensure ongoing training in subject area content and its supportive pedagogy. Teachers who work effectively with gifted learners need to be highly knowledgeable about their content area and how best to convey it to learners. Such expertise is essential for helping students learn (Shulman, 1987). Workshops conducted nationally through College Board provide this mix of content and pedagogy in an effective manner, as do several sessions at national content conferences, such as those of the National Council of Teachers of Mathematics. School districts might also purchase subscriptions for teachers to such journals as *Mathematics Teaching* and *Science Scope.* As a field, gifted education has not actively promoted a teacher training model that merges content and pedagogical skill development, although such training clearly is needed.

Staff development policy must also attend to teacher understanding of aspects of gifted curriculum related to acceleration and articulation. Gaining familiarity with the school district and state gifted curricula at all levels of K-12 schooling constitutes an essential part of that education. Awareness of relevant standards and assessments to be employed provides teachers with a broader knowledge of their own curriculum area, even if they do not have direct responsibility for teaching many of these standards. Secondary teachers must also possess a working knowledge of the type of content tested in both Advanced Placement and International Baccalaureate examinations in their subject areas, as these assessments are considered the most rigorous secondary options through which gifted students may pass on their path to college. The level of task demand on these exams provides a good model for teachers of younger students to emulate, particularly in writing assignments for English and social studies and problem sets assigned in science and mathematics. Thus, the staff development approach must socialize teachers to exit expectations for high-ability learners at secondary levels.

Finally, curriculum policy should promote familiarity with a core arsenal of strategies that teachers will likely use with high-ability and gifted learners in the classroom. Because the goals of gifted programs so frequently stress research, higher-level thinking, and problem solving, teachers should be able to employ at least one teaching model that addresses each of these goals. Training, then, should include the use of a consistent model to teach research, a deliberate thinking model such as the Paul model of reasoning, and a problem-based learning or creative problem-solving model. Helping teachers link these models to relevant content is also essential to their being used effectively in the classroom.

SUMMARY

The need for coherent gifted programs calls for the development of policies that address curriculum flexibility, differentiation, and articulation issues. Support structures such as grouping and teacher education also must be considered. As the use of state standards and assessments intensifies, gifted programs at all levels of learning will find it necessary to use curriculum policies as the base for building a rich and complex set of options for gifted learners.

REFERENCES

Archambault, F. X., Westberg, K. L., Brown, S. W., Hallmark, B. W., Zhang, W., & Emmons, C. (1993). Classroom practices used with gifted third and fourth grade students. *Journal for the Education of the Gifted, 16,* 103–119.

Benbow, C. P. (1998). Acceleration as a method for meeting the academic needs of intellectually talented children. In J. VanTassel-Baska (Ed.), *Excellence in educating the gifted* (3rd ed., pp. 279–294). Denver: Love Publishing.

Bloom, B. S. (1985). *Developing talent in young people.* New York: Ballantine.

Borko, H., Mayfield, V., Marion, S., Flexer, R., & Cumbo, K. (1997). Teachers' developing ideas and practices about mathematics performance assessment: Successes, stumbling blocks, and implications for professional development. *Teaching and Teacher Education, 13,* 259–278.

Borland, J. A. (1989). *Planning and implementing programs for the gifted.* New York: Teachers College Press.

Boyce, L. N., VanTassel-Baska, J., Burruss, J. D., Johnson, D. T. & Sher, B. T., (1997). A problem-based curriculum: Parallel learning opportunities for students and teachers. *Journal for the Education of the Gifted, 20,* 363–379.

Charlton, J. C., Marolf, D., & Stanley, J. C. (1994). Follow-up insights on rapid educational acceleration. *Roeper Review, 17,* 123–130.

Clune, W. H. (1993). Systemic educational policy: A conceptual framework. In S. H. Fuhrman (Ed.), *Designing coherent education policy: Improving the system* (pp. 125–140). San Francisco: Jossey-Bass.

Cohen, D., & Hill, H. (1998). *Instructional policy and classroom performance: The mathematics reform in California* (Research Report No. RR-39). Philadelphia: University of Pennsylvania, Consortium for Policy Research in Education.

Council of State Directors of Programs for the Gifted. (1996). *The 1996 state of the States gifted and talented education report.* Longmont, CO: Author.

Council of State Directors of Programs for the Gifted. (1998). *The 1998 state of the States gifted and talented education report.* Denver, CO: Author.

Cox, J., Daniel, N., & Boston, B. (1985). *Educating able learners: Programs and promising practices.* Austin,: University of Texas Press.

Ford, D. (1996). *Reversing underachievement among gifted black students: Promising practices and programs.* New York: Teachers College Press.

Fullan, M., & Stiegelbauer, S. (1991). *The new meaning of educational change.* New York: Teachers College Press.

Gallagher, S. A., Stepien, W. J., Sher, B. T., & Workman, D. (1995). Implementing problem-based learning in science classrooms. *School Science and Mathematics, 95,* 136–146.

Johnson, D. T., Boyce, L. N., & VanTassel-Baska, J. (1995). Science curriculum review: Evaluating materials for high-ability learners. *Gifted Child Quarterly, 39,* 36–43.

Kennedy, M. (1999). Form and substance in mathematics and science professional development. *NISE Brief, 3*(2), 1–7.

Kulik, J. A., & Kulik, C. L. (1992). Meta-analytic findings on grouping programs. *Gifted Child Quarterly, 36,* 73–77.

Lou, Y., Abrami, P. C., Spence, J. C., & Poulsen, C. (1996). Within-class grouping: A meta-analysis. *Review of Educational Research, 66,* 423–458.

National Education Commission on Time and Learning. (1994). *Prisoners of time.* Washington, DC: Author.

Olszewski-Kubilius, P. (1995). A summary of research regarding early entrance to college. *Roeper Review, 18,* 121–125

Reis, S. M. (1999, Winter). Message from the President. *National Association for the Gifted Communiqué,* p. 1.

Rogers, K. B. (1998). Using current research to make "good" decisions about grouping. *NASSP Bulletin, 82*(595), 38–46.

Senge, P. M. (1990). *The fifth discipline: The art and practice of the learning organization.* New York: Doubleday.

Shulman, L. S. (1987). Knowledge and teaching: Foundations of the new reform. *Harvard Educational Review, 19*(2) 4–14.

Swiatek, M. A., & Benbow, C. P. (1991). A 10-year longitudinal follow-up of participants in a fast-paced mathematics course. *Journal for Research in Mathematics Education, 22,* 138–150.

United States Department of Education, Office of Educational Research and Improvement. (1993). *National excellence: A case for developing America's talent.* Washington, DC: Author.

VanTassel-Baska, J. (1998a). The development of academic talent: A mandate for educational best practice. *Phi Delta Kappan, 79,* 760–763

VanTassel-Baska, J. (Ed.). (1998b). *Excellence in educating gifted and talented learners* (3rd ed.). Denver: Love Publishing.

VanTassel-Baska, J., Bass, G. M., Reis, R. R., Poland, D. L., & Avery, L. D. (1998). A national study of science curriculum effectiveness for high-ability students. *Gifted Child Quarterly, 42,* 200–211.

VanTassel-Baska, J., Johnson, D. T., Hughes, C. E., & Boyce, L. N. (1996). A study of the language arts curriculum effectiveness with gifted learners. *Journal for the Education of the Gifted, 19,* 461–480.

VanTassel-Baska, J., Zuo, L., Avery, L., & Little, C. (2002). A curriculum study of gifted student learning in the language arts. *Gifted Child Quarterly, 46,* 30–44.

Wang, M. C., Haertel, G. D., & Walberg, H. (1996). *Educational practices and policies that promote achievement: Publication Series No. 7.* Philadelphia: Mid-Atlantic Laboratory for Student Success and National Research Center on Education in the Inner Cities.

Wiggins, E. (1996). Anchoring assessment with exemplars: Why students and teachers need models. *Gifted Child Quarterly, 40,* 66–69.

Appendix

SAMPLE CURRICULUM UNITS

The following curriculum units are based on the curriculum design model explicated in this book. They were developed by educators working with gifted learners at various grade levels and in various content areas. They provide concrete applications of the ideas outlined and, it is hoped, offer gifted educators a spark of motivation to engage in the curriculum development process at an individualized level.

Investigating Weather Folklore

Fourth Grade

William Chapman
Superintendent, Lancaster County School
Kilmarnock, Virginia

I. Curriculum Description
   Rationale and purpose: The ability to predict weather accurately has long been of economic and social importance. We may have progressed from weather folklore through weather balloons to satellites, but an understanding of the causes and indicators of weather change still has the power to enrich our lives and contribute to our understanding of the world surrounding us. The purpose of this unit is to study and evaluate the accuracy of selected weather folklore, which will require learning the causes and physics of weather and an understanding of tools for measurement and prediction.

II. Nature of Differentiation

    A. How has the unit been accelerated, compressed, and/or reorganized to accommodate gifted learner needs?

    A process/product approach will allow and provide for extensions of basic content through opportunities for student selection of projects and group activities. A pretest will determine which learners may advance beyond the basic approach (reading and discussion), which ones need a brief review, and which students may be accelerated and placed in individual and cooperative learning group projects. Teacher-directed activities will involve all students.

    B. How has the unit focused on higher-level process skills?

    The unit focuses on a body of knowledge (weather physics) as a means of enabling students to analyze and evaluate weather folklore. Emphasis is on problem solving requiring critical-thinking skills such as clarifying (identifying central issues, reasons, assumptions), judging information (determining relevance), and making inferences to solve problems (judging inductive conclusions, judging deductive validity, and predicting consequences of various weather elements).

    C. How has the unit engaged learners in meaningful product development?

    The unit emphasizes student projects and activities. Fourteen of the activities result in a product.

    D. How has the unit addressed key themes and ideas and related them to several domains of inquiry?

    Students will interact cognitively with the subject matter through problem-solving activities. Through solving problems, exploring concepts, conducting experiments, and discovering relationships, students will be involved in science, history, and language arts domains.

III. Content Outline (9 weeks)

    A. Major content topics.
        1. Elements of weather
           a. Temperature
           b. Water in the air (humidity, dew, frost, precipitation, clouds)
           c. Air pressure
           d. Wind
           e. Air masses, fronts, tracking weather formations
        2. Forecasting weather
           a. History of the Weather Bureau

           b. Weather instruments
           c. Weather maps
       3. Weather folklore
           a. Valid
           b. Invalid

  B. Organizational structure and order.

IV. Prerequisites
The whole class will be involved in the pretest. Those who score 80% or better on the pretest will advance immediately to independent reading and student-directed activities. The whole class will be involved in the teacher-directed activities.

Students will choose one activity from each of the four objectives. Students may volunteer for additional activities. Identified gifted students will be assigned to work together on activities demanding a superior amount/ level of production and a high degree of challenge in terms of mastery of knowledge of content. (Gifted students will also be assigned the most challenging individual assignments.)

V. Objectives
  1. Students will understand the causes of weather change (physics of the atmosphere).
  2. Students will develop a knowledge of basic weather instruments and how they help measure and predict weather.
  3. Students will become familiar with weather-predicting technology in use today.
  4. Students will attempt to prove or disprove the accuracy of selected weather folklore through observation and discussion, projects, and experiments.

VI. Sample Activities
Objective 1: Students will understand the causes of weather change (physics of the atmosphere).

  A. Teacher directed.
    1. The teacher will show films and videotapes illustrating the causes of weather changes.
    2. The teacher will invite a meteorologist to visit the class to explain how he or she predicts weather.
    3. The teacher will take the class on a field trip to visit a meteorologist at work and to see how weather maps are used to chart weather.

  B. Student directed.

1. The teacher will provide a variety of materials for each group of four students and ask each group to use the materials to demonstrate one or more of the following:
   a. Air has weight.
   b. Water vapor in the air changes to a liquid and forms tiny drops a certain temperature (dew point).
   c. Temperature causes differences in air pressure (weight).
   d. Moisture in the air can be measured.
2. Students may choose one or more of the following individual projects to present to the class:
   a. Next-day and long-range weather forecasts will be collected and compared to actual weather, and reasons for errors will be proposed (3-week project).
   b. Cloud formations will be videotaped and compared with weather data collected for a 3-week period.
   c. Students will compete against each other in forecasting various weather features such as temperature, precipitation, types of clouds, relative humidity, and barometric pressure for the next day at noon. Reasons for hypotheses must be explained.
   d. After researching weather maps and symbols, students will construct a weather map and explain how a cold front can travel across the country in several days and how the weather is affected in each area.

Objective 2: Students will develop a knowledge of basic weather instruments and how they help measure and predict weather.

A. Teacher directed.
   1. The teacher will display and explain real weather instruments, including a barometer, hygrometer, thermometer, rain gauge, and anemometer.
   2. The teacher will take the class on a field trip to visit a meteorologist at work to see weather instruments and communication devices used for predicting and recording weather (same trip as described in Activity 1).

B. Student directed. Students may choose one or more of the following projects:
   1. Students will research, construct, and attempt to calibrate weather instruments, including a hygrometer, rain gauge, barometer, and anemometer. Students may combine their instruments to form a weather station and to attempt weather predictions and measurement.
   2. Students will use their weather stations to issue "school weather forecasts" over the PA system during morning announcements for several weeks.
   3. Students will research and present an oral or a written report on the history of weather prediction efforts.

Objective 3: Students will become familiar with weather-predicting technology in use today.

A. Teacher directed.
   See Objective 2, A.2.

B. Student directed. Students may choose to participate in a mentorship with a meteorologist, designed to provide in-depth knowledge of weather-prediction technology in use today.

Objective 4: Students will attempt to prove or disprove the accuracy of selected weather folklore through observation and discussion, projects, and experiments.

A. Teacher directed.

   1. The teacher will provide a collection of weather folklore and will discuss samples representing scientifically valid and invalid lore, and the reasons why and why not.

      Example of valid folklore: "If the woolen fleece spread the heavenly ways, be sure no rain disturbs the summer day."

      Example of invalid folklore: "If the cat washes her face over her ear, 'tis a sign the weather will be fine and clear."

B. Student directed.

   1. Students may choose to form a team to interview residents of nearby retirement homes, farmers, and meteorologists in order to develop and publish an article on weather folklore for the local newspaper (showing respect for all viewpoints).
   2. Students may choose to form a cooperative learning team to attempt to prove or disprove the accuracy of selected weather folklore through analysis of the elements of the folklore and modern knowledge of weather, including knowledge of the physics of the air.
   3. Students may choose to form a cooperative learning group to research and present oral reports on the history and importance of weather prediction efforts and beliefs since pioneer days.
   4. Students may choose to attempt to prove or disprove the accuracy of weather folklore by participating in a debate presented to the student body as a culminating activity of the unit.
   5. Student teams may choose to document examples of valid and invalid weather folklore by preparing projects for the Science Fair.
   6. Using knowledge gained earlier from the unit, student teams may choose to create valid and invalid "modern" (funny) weather folklore to be published in the school newspaper.

7. Students may choose to form a cooperative learning group to demonstrate weather phenomena (physics of air) involved in selected weather folklore, using self-made and professional weather instruments as a focus.

VII. Major Instructional Strategies Employed

    A. Problem solving.

The focus of the unit is to solve the problem of how to differentiate between valid and invalid weather folklore. Proving and/or disproving the accuracy of selected weather folklore will require problem solving through observation, discussion, experiments, and projects.

    B. Inquiry.

The unit emphasizes inquiry-based activities relative to predicting weather and proving/disproving the validity of weather folklore. A certain amount of research methodology (the scientific method) is required in order to reach such conclusions.

    Meteorologists will interact with students as practicing scientists and mentors. The latest technology having to do with weather prediction and tracking will be shared with gifted students to provide challenge and depth of knowledge for further study and research.

    C. Grouping approaches.

The unit will be taught to a heterogeneously grouped class, with a cluster group of six gifted students. All students will be involved in the pretest and all teacher-directed activities.

    Students who score 70% or higher on the pretest will advance immediately to independent reading and student-directed activities. Others will be grouped for teacher-directed study in the science text, featuring more traditional reading assignments, discussion, tests, and re-teaching, prior to moving into student-directed activities.

    Identified gifted students will be grouped together for student-directed activities. Highly challenging activities are identified for choice-selections by gifted students/group.

    Gifted students may opt to participate in more than the one-activity-per-objective, for extra credit, or may opt to create their own activity, with teacher approval.

    D. Questioning techniques.

Teacher-directed activities will emphasize discussion and the use of questioning techniques. To challenge and motivate gifted students, memory/

cognition-type questions will be deemphasized in favor of the following types:

(1) Convergent: analytical in nature, tend to begin with "why" or "how." Examples: "Why did people formerly think that 'lightning sours milk,' or 'thunder curdles cream'?" "How does a barometer help predict weather?"

(2) Divergent: hypothetical in nature, no right answer, frequently begin with "What if" or "Pretend." Examples: "What if there were no clouds?" "Pretend you are a meteorologist the day before the Fourth of July. How important would you be? What other occasions would be especially crucial for a meteorologist?"

(3) Evaluative: calls for judgment or opinion, begins with "In your opinion . . ." or "Which is best?" Examples: "In your opinion, what will our weather be tomorrow if the cold front passes through tonight?" "Which weather instrument is best for predicting long-range weather change?" "Which weather folklore was the most commonly accepted and yet without scientific basis?"

VIII. Evaluation Procedures
A. Pre/post assessments.

A pretest will be used for initial teaching decisions for the unit. A posttest will be given to assess unit learning. The posttest grade will be averaged with the project grade 50-50. Projects will be evaluated according to teacher and student-developed criteria.

B. Observational approaches.

The teacher will monitor the activities, observing and recording anecdotally the levels of effort, creativity, critical thinking, and mastery of concepts and understandings. Anecdotal records will be shared with students and student teams during a post-unit evaluation discussion session. Difficulty level of activities will be taken into consideration when deciding grades, as well extra-credit activities.

INVESTIGATING WEATHER FOLKLORE

Pretest

1. What causes weather to change?
2. What is meant by the term "dew point"?
3. Define the term "relative humidity."
4. What causes dew to form?
5. What is the purpose of a "hygrometer"?
6. Name and describe three types of clouds.

7. How is hail formed?
8. Describe briefly the way a barometer measures air pressure.
9. What causes wind to blow?
10. Define the following terms:
    a. Air mass
    b. Front

Posttest

Analyze the validity of the following weather folklore in terms of your scientific knowledge of weather physics:

1. "If the sun sets clear on Friday, it will storm on Sunday."
2. "When the leaves show their backs, it will rain."
3. "Rain long foretold, long last;
   Short notice, soon past."
4. "Evening red and morning gray
   Sets the traveler on his way;
   Evening gray and morning red
   Brings down rain upon his head."
5. "Lightning is attracted to mirrors."

What factors cause weather to change?

Which weather instruments are most helpful in *predicting* weather?

Which weather instruments are most helpful in *measuring* weather?

How has modern technology made weather prediction more accurate?

MATERIALS/RESOURCES

Bibliography of Teacher Materials Used in Preparation and Execution of the Unit

Books

Bates, D. (1959). *The earth and its atmosphere.* New York: Basic Books.
Cable, G. K., & Crull, P. (1959). *The physical sciences.* Englewood Cliffs, NJ: Prentice Hall.
Forsdyke, A. (1970). *Weather and weather forecasting.* New York: Grosset & Dunlap.
Sloane, E. (1963). *Folklore of American weather.* New York: Hawthorne Books.

Other Media

Films: "Synoptic Weather, Earth Science for Teachers," Virginia State Film Library, Richmond, VA.
Audiovisual instructional materials for Virginia's public schools: No. 22170, Richmond, VA: "Weather Forecasting;" 39605 "Weather—Understanding Storms;" 64190, "What Makes the Weather;" 67008, "Weather Scientists."

Computer Software: Carolina Biological Supply, Burlington, NC: "Water and Weather Services," "Forecast," and "Weather or Not."
Videotapes: "Understanding Weather and Climate," Educational Audiovisual, Pleasantville, NY. "Weather: Come Rain or Shine," National Geographic, Washington, DC.
Filmstrips: "Rain and Clouds," "The Atmosphere, Climate, and the Weather," Clearview Company, J. S. Latta, Distributor, Huntington, WV.
"Forecasting the Weather," National Geographic Society, Washington, DC.
Kits: "What Air Can Do," "Why Does It Rain?" National Geographic Society, Washington, DC.

Student Bibliography

Barufaldi, L., & Moses, A. (1981). *Health science*. Lexington, MA: D. C. Heath & Co.

Bodin, S. (1978). *Weather and climate in color*. Dorset, England: Blandford Press.

Hardy, R. (1982). *Weather Book*. Boston: Little, Brown.

"How to Make Weather Instruments." Santa Barbara, CA: Learning Works Enrichment Series.

Lambert, D., & Hardy, R. (1987). *Weather and its work*. New York: Macdonald and Company.

Lehr, P., Burnt, R., & Zim, H. (1957). *Weather*. New York: Golden Press.

Ross, F. (1965). *Weather*. New York: Lothrop, Lee, & Shepard, Inc.

Rubin, L. (1970). *The weather wizard's cloud book*. Chapel Hill, NC: Algonquin Books.

Thompson, P. (1968), *Weather book*. Boston: Little, Brown.

Whipple, A. (1968). *Planet earth — Storm*. New York: Time-Life Books.

Wigginton, E. (1972). *The foxfire book*. New York: Anchor Books.

Time Line:
A Scientist's History of the World

Fourth to Sixth Grades

Beverly Sher
Science Teacher, Saturday Enrichment Program
College of William and Mary

I. Curriculum Course Description

   A. Title of unit: Time line: A Scientist's History of the World

   B. Grade levels: 4–6

   C. Rationale and Purpose:

      This course has been designed to provide students with a variety of hands-on scientific experiences in the context of the history of the planet Earth. Each session focuses on a different time period in the planet's history. Experiments from different areas of science that are directly relevant to events occurring during that time period are included in each session, as is teacher-directed discussion of the scientific importance of events of the time period. Students also are encouraged to relate the events of the time period under study to events occurring in the present. The purpose of the course is to help the student develop an understanding of the interrelationships of different scientific disciplines and their relevance to the world around him or her.

II. Nature of Differentiation for Gifted Learners

   A. How has the unit been accelerated, compressed, or reorganized to accommodate gifted learner needs?

      The unit includes a great deal of material that the students would not ordinarily encounter until much later in their scientific educations. Although students are not expected to retain every detail of the material presented, it should stimulate their curiosity, challenge them, and encourage them to learn more on their own.

   B. How has this unit focused on higher level process skills?

      The laboratory portions of the course require the student to use the scientific method and critical thinking skills to study a variety of scientific phenomena. In-class discussions require the students to assess the relevance of different scientific phenomena to events of the past as well as processes occurring on the planet Earth at present; they are thus required to judge information, make inferences, make predictions, and so on.

C. How has the unit engaged learners in meaningful product development?

Several of the laboratory activities result in a permanent product (for example, model meteorite craters, recovered fossils, and records of human tracks). Even though other laboratory activities create no lasting product, setting up an experiment, letting it run, and recording the results constitute product development. It's a little like performance art.

D. How has the unit addressed key themes and ideas and related them to several domains of inquiry?

The unit focuses on two major processes: biological evolution and geologic change. A variety of scientific disciplines are called upon to explain the mechanisms underlying these processes.

III. Content Outline

A. Major content topics to be addressed in eight 2½-hour sessions:

1. Geological change
   a. Weathering.
   b. Processes of rock layer formation.
   c. Vulcanism.
   d. Plate tectonics.

2. Biological change
   a. Chemical evolution and the origin of life.
   b. Biological evolution.

B. Organizational structure and order

Each session has two foci, one a specific period in the Earth's history, and the other a specific scientific topic relevant to that time period. These are:

1. Session I: Time period: 5 Bya - 3.5 Bya
                   Scientific topic: geologic change
2. Session II: Time period: 3.5 Bya
                   Scientific topic: the chemistry of life; chemical evolution
3. Session III: Time period: 3.5 Bya - I Bya
                   Scientific topic: early life forms; microbiology
4. Session IV: Time period: I Bya - 500 Mya
                   Scientific topic: life in the early oceans
5. Session V: Time period: 420 Mya - 200 Mya
                   Scientific topic: adaptation to life on land; ecology
6. Session VI: Time period: 65 Mya
                   Scientific topic: dinosaur evolution and extinction

7. Session VII: Time period: 65 Mya - 5 Mya
                     Scientific topic: mammalian evolution
8. Session VIII: Time period: 5 Mya - present
                     Scientific topic: human evolution; human
                     impact on planet Earth

IV Prerequisites

No special knowledge is required; however, students with a good scientific background (e.g., sixth graders) probably will get more out of it than children who have had little exposure to science.

V. Objectives

1. Students will demonstrate an understanding of the processes and time scale of geologic change.
2. Students will demonstrate an understanding of the processes and time scale of biological evolution.
3. Students will demonstrate an understanding of the scientific method.

VI. Sample Activities

A. Session 1: Formation and prebiotic history of planet Earth.

1. Class discussion and demonstration: time scales

a. Human history: Get children to supply events happening 1, 10, 100, 1,000, 2,000, 10,000 years ago; teacher can fill in the gaps.

b. Biological time scale: do in lifetimes.

(1) E. coli: 30 minutes
(2) Butterflies: weeks to months
(3) Mouse: 1-2 years
(4) Cat: 10-20 years
(5) Human: around 100 years
(6) Galapagos tortoise: up to 150 years
(7) Redwood tree: up to 1,000 years
(8) Bristlecone pine: 5,000 years

c. Geological time scale.

(1) 1 Mya: Great Ice Age (mammoths, Cro-Magnon man)
(2) 10 Mya: first hominids
(3) 65 Mya: dinosaur extinctions
(4) 400 Mya: first life on land
(5) 1 Bya: multicellular life
(6) 3.5 Bya: life begins

(7) 4.5 Bya: Earth coalescing into a planet

(8) 12-18 Bya: Big Bang

d. To better illustrate the geologic time scale, build a time line with the kids. Use a large ball of string to represent time. Fasten it securely to a lamp post and pace backward in time (I found steps of 50 million years convenient), attaching labels to significant time points with tape. Remind the kids of how little time human beings have really been around compared to the lifetime of the planet.

2. Major events in formation of the planet

a. Planetary accretion and the role of gravity

(1) Gravity is a weak force between little things but a strong force between big things; the bigger something is, the harder it pulls on other things. This can be easily demonstrated: Two books don't move closer together, but the earth pulls a book to the floor quite nicely.

(2) Briefly outline the history of Earth's formation.

b. Meteoric impacts

(1) Meteors as a source of water, carbon dioxide, and nitrogen for Earth's atmosphere.

(2) Experiment: Modeling impact craters

Before class, melt paraffin and pour it carefully into plastic plates, one per student, to a depth of $\frac{1}{4}$"–$\frac{1}{2}$". Allow it to harden. Collect a supply of gravel. In class, take the kids outside and space them about 6–8' apart. Have them throw gravel at the paraffin until the surface of each student's plate is heavily cratered. Bring them back inside; discuss their results.

(3) Why does Earth lack evidence of the heavy meteor bombardment that Moon still has? Answer: Earth has an atmosphere and liquid water on its surface and thus undergoes weathering. This neatly introduces the next topic . . .

c. Gradual geologic change: rock formation and breakdown (1) How do rocks break down?

(1) To help answer this, take the kids outside. Point out frost damage in rocks or bricks; erosion caused by wind or water; chemical damage caused by pollution and oxidation.

(2) How do rocks form?

First, list the three different types of rock (igneous, metamorphic, sedimentary). Pass around samples of each type. Next, start some crystals growing (many books are available with recipes for crystals, some of which take only an hour or so to work). This experiment can be designed to illustrate the effects of environmental conditions (for example, ambient temperature, presence or absence of convection currents, presence or absence of chemical impurities) on the formation of rocks.

    d. Large-scale geology

        (1) Discuss the formation of the current planetary structure (nickel-iron core, mantle, crust).

        (2) Talk about plate movements and their consequences: moving continents, earthquakes, volcanoes (the kids will have heard most of this before).

        (3) Finish off with a videotape that illustrates the effects of continental drift (we used the first tape in David Attenborough's *Living Planet* series).

B. Session II: Chemical evolution and the origin of life

    1. Basic chemistry

To understand anything meaningful about the origin of life, the kids have to know a bit of chemistry first.

    a. Everything is made of atoms.

        (1) How big are they?

Object	*Size*
human	1–2 meters
little finger	a few centimeters (10^{-2} meters)
bacteria	a few microns (10^{-6} meters)
atoms	Angstroms (10^{-10} meters)
atomic nucleus	(10^{-12} meters)

(You may have to explain scientific notation to them, but the kids who haven't seen it before catch on fast.)

        (2) What do they look like?

Basically they look like little billiard balls. Pass around a STEM picture or two (for example, one of the pictures of gallium arsenide crystals from the February 1990 issue of *Scientific American*).

        (3) How many different kinds are there?

Give each kid a copy of the periodic table. Most of them will have seen it before. Mention that there are probably even more kinds than are listed but that we just haven't been able to make them (or observe them in nature) yet. Also mention that only a few elements are really important for life: carbon, oxygen, nitrogen, phosphorous, sulfur, hydrogen, sodium, and potassium; most of the rest are needed in only small amounts, if at all.

(4) Atoms combine to form molecules.

Talk about the different ways in which atoms can combine to form molecules.

    (i) Covalent bonding: Use water as a sample structure; mention valence; discuss the energy needed to break covalent bonds. (Light a match to demonstrate.)

    (ii) Ionic bonding: NaCl. Dissolve some salt in water to demonstrate the breakage of ionic bonds.

    (iii) Hydrogen bonding: ordered structure in water and ice. Mention that hydrogen bonds constantly break and re-form in liquid water.

    (iv) If there's extra time, you could give the kids a list of valence rules for C, O, N, and H and some molecular models, and ask them to come up with structures of familiar things such as carbon dioxide, ammonia, ethanol, and benzene.

b. Macroscopic chemistry: Chemical properties of substances

(1) List a few; for example: color, state at room temperature, boiling point, freezing point, reactivity with other chemicals (for example, oxidation); mention the two that are most important for biology: acid-base behavior and hydrophobicity.

(2) Miscibility with water (hydrophobicity/hydrophilicity)

Demonstrate this as follows:

— Have the kids mix cooking oil with water (hydrophobicity).

— Have the kids mix rubbing alcohol with water (hydrophilicity).

— Have the kids add some soap to the oil/water mixture. What happens? Mention that soap is an amphipathic molecule, one part of which is hydrophobic and the other, hydrophilic; ask them how this mixture might look at the molecular level.

(3) Acid-base chemistry

— Talk briefly about the pH scale (i.e., numbers 0-14, with 0 being the most acidic and 14 the most basic).

— Pass out the acid/base chemistry lab worksheet; after the kids read it, have them do the lab.

2. Chemical evolution

a. What happened 3.5 Bya, and how do we know?

(1) Composition of the early atmosphere.

(2) Urey-Miller experiment.

(3) Chemical fossils (terpene worksheet, if time, or handout for later fun at home).

(4) All living organisms share the same fundamental chemistry, based on DNA, RNA, and protein. Briefly explain what DNA, RNA, and proteins are and what their functions are in the cell:

    (i) DNA: the software, encoded in units called genes.

    (ii) RNA: the floppy disk that carries the software to the part of the cell that can read it.

    (iii) Proteins: the machines that run the cell and the structural components that give it shape, motility, and so on; each protein is directly encoded by a single gene.

    (Mention to the kids that the detailed chemical structures of each type of molecule are in their copies of *The Daily Planet,* if they are interested. Some of them probably will be, but not all.)

b. Exercise: Decoding DNA

Pass out the sample gene sequence handout and have the kids translate it into a protein sequence using the genetic code dictionary in *The Daily Planet.*

C. Session III: Microorganisms

1. What is life? Get the kids to define it. Definition should include reproduction, growth, and use of external energy/nutrient sources.

2. What was first life like?

a. Show them pictures of microfossils.

b. Show them pictures of modern-day bacteria.

c. Diagram the parts of a bacterial cell. Mention that the inner membrane is made of amphipathic molecules that effectively form a greasy barrier around the cell and keep the liquid phases inside the cell and outside the cell from mixing, just as the very first cellular membranes must have done.

d. Show them yogurt under the microscope; it's solid lactobacilli.

3. Given that the DNA of the first bacterial cell only contained instructions for making more bacterial cells, how is it that Earth has other life forms today?

a. DNA can change through a process called mutation.

b. Although most mutations are deleterious, a few improve the organism's chance of survival—natural selection.

c. Biological evolution occurs through a process of mutation followed by natural selection.

4. The biggest change in the first billion years or so of life on this planet: the evolution of photosynthesis.

    a. Define it; give the simplified chemical reaction (CO_2 + H_2O + light energy = O_2 + sugar or starch).

    b. Photosynthesis resulted in the first major life-induced change in the planet—namely, creation of free oxygen in the atmosphere. Discuss the oxygen crisis (well reviewed in the Sara Stein *Evolution* book). Point out that we're *not* the first organism to have changed the chemistry of Earth's atmosphere.

5. Evolution of eukaryotes—engulf and symbiose.

    a. Discuss the typical structure of aeukaryotic cell, paying particular attention to the mitochondria and chloroplasts (if any). Mention that these organelles have their own DNA and make some of their own proteins without relying on the cell's nucleus; mention the endosymbiont hypothesis.

    b. Experiments with simple eukaryotes:

        (1) Make simple French bread dough, involving the kids in mixing, measuring, and kneading it. Have each kid place a small piece in a transparent plastic cup. Have the kids flatten the top of the dough and mark with a felt-tip pen the position of the top of the dough on the side of the cup. Have them cover the cup with a tissue and mark the position of the top of the dough every 20 minutes (designate one kid as timekeeper so everyone will remember all the time points). At the end of class, ask the kids what happened.

            — Why did the dough rise? (They will have seen fermentation in action at this point, so they should be able to answer this.)
            — How long did the dough take to collapse?
            — How big were the air bubbles in the dough when it was at its highest? When it had collapsed?
            — Why do bakers punch down dough when it has just doubled in bulk, and then allow it to rise again?

        (2) Look at yeast under the microscope.

        (3) Run yeast fermentation/gas evolution experiment. Discuss the results.

        (4) Discuss other uses for eukaryotic fermentation (making soy sauce, wine, etc.).

    c. Evolution of oxidative phosphorylation

        (1) Mention that using oxygen allows organisms to extract even more energy out of their food; that's what mitochondria are for; they are also of endosymbiont origin. Give them the simplified chemical reaction (fermentation products + oxygen = CO_2 + H_2O + energy).

(2) Mention that you can tell when your muscles switch from oxphos to fermentation—build-up of the fermentation product lactic acid (which happens when your muscles aren't getting enough oxygen) makes them ache; resting and letting them break down the lactic acid with oxygen the blood carries to them makes the aching stop.

D. Session IV: Multicellular life; life in the oceans

1. Discuss briefly the evolution of multicellular life (what came when and why).
2. Discuss the first forms of life to make up macroscopic fossils; include gastropods, tube-dwelling worms, and bivalves in particular.
3. Take the kids down to the fossil bed on campus. Have them fill large Ziploc bags with fossils; take them back either to the classroom or to a flat, sunny place outdoors and have the kids clean them out as best they can (a good source of running water that won't become clogged by dirt and an assortment of tools for scraping dirt out of crevices would be useful here). Have the kids line up their cleaned finds and decide how many different types of animal life they have found; identify as many as possible (we found scallops, clams, and worm tubes). Discuss the lifestyles of these organisms and help the kids figure out what the environment in which these beds were formed must have been like. This discovery process can take up to 1½ hours.
4. Provide a selection of modern mollusks for the kids to observe. As a teacher demonstration, dissect a mussel for the kids. I tried having the kids dissect their own, but they were disgusted by the process (elementary school kids are pretty tenderhearted).
5. The second videotape in David Attenborough's Living Planet series has an excellent description of the evolution of early life forms in the sea, along with footage of modern-day mollusks in their own habitats. Play as much of this as possible at the end of the session.

E. Session V: Life comes up on land

1. Briefly discuss the first organisms to colonize the land. Some of these will be familiar to the kids; be sure to include modern-day equivalents and provide actual samples (pieces of lichen, moss, and so forth).
2. Discuss the constraints posed by a land-based lifestyle and the adaptations to these constraints that were made as life colonized the land. Have the kids supply as many of these as possible (for example, thick skins that reduced evaporation, root systems for plants, hard seeds that resist drying, and so forth).

3. Introduce the concept of the ecosystem and relationships between the organisms within it. Define the following:
   a. Predator/prey
   b. Symbiosis
      (1) Commensalism
      (2) Mutualism
      (3) Parasitism
   c. Competition

4. With the kids supplying names of organisms and their relationships to each other, describe the suburban ecosystem as completely as possible. Be sure to include humans. We diagrammed it on the board using different colors of chalk to represent the different relationships. It rapidly became a colorful, convoluted mess, which convinced the kids of the complexity of the ecosystem and of the interdependence of the organisms within it.

5. Define the concept of niche, using a couple of the organisms from Part 4 as examples. Talk about specialist niches versus generalist niches. Point out that the human is the ultimate generalist.

6. Take the kids on a nature walk. We went through the wildflower refuge at the college. Have them list the organisms they find and think about their niches (for example, millipedes are found in decaying logs but not on the branches of trees; wolf spiders are found on the forest floor and seem to patrol their own territories; moss is found in damp shady places but not dry sunny ones). Try to help the kids appreciate the vast variety of niches and of organisms adapted to fill those niches. The longer this takes, the better.

7. If time allows at the end of the session, discuss the peculiar niche of the Monarch butterfly. This is appropriate because insects were among the first organisms to colonize the land; it is also interesting because of the specialist nature of the Monarch's niche. The videotape "Pretty Poison," while somewhat sensationalistic, does a nice job of describing the migration of the Monarchs and the increasing human threat to their existence.

F. Session VI: Dinosaur evolution and extinction

1. Discuss biological classification.
   a. Define the following: kingdom, phylum, class, order, family, genus, species.
   b. Give the kids the following mnemonic to help them remember the order: King Philip comes over for giant slugs.
   c. Go back to the species definition. A key component of this is that two animals belonging to the same species can mate and produce

fertile offspring. Illustrate this with the example of mules (the result of mating a male horse and a female donkey). But how do you determine whether two fossil animals were members of the same species? Point out that Chihuahuas and St. Bernards might not be classified as belonging to the same species by an alien paleontologist looking only at their skeletons.

2. Discuss the evolution of large organisms on land. I used the book *The Dinosaur Heresies,* by Robert Bakker, extensively here, as he summarizes the major evolutionary themes quite clearly.

3. Discuss the differences between the lifestyles of warm- and cold-blooded animals. Discuss the evidence that at least some of the dinosaurs were probably warm-blooded.

4. Fossil footprints have given us a great deal of information about dinosaur lifestyles and behavior. To illustrate the kinds of information that can be obtained from footprints, do the following (quite messy) experiment:

Have the kids paper the (preferably tile) floor with large sheets of newsprint that have been securely taped down. Fill disposable aluminum baking dishes with a thin layer of somewhat dilute tempera paint. Have several colors available. Have the kids (volunteers only - two of the wildest boys in the class were too fastidious for this) take off their shoes and socks, roll up their pants legs, and carefully step into the paint. They then can try the following:

a. Walking.
b. Running.
c. Walking as a group.
d. One person following another.
e. "Funny walks" (crabwalk, walking on all fours, walking backward, and anything else they can dream up).
f. Walking while carrying a heavy object.

For each kind of walk, have them:

— Measure the length of the stride.
— Determine the angle between the long axis of the foot and the direction of motion.
— Observe which parts of the foot made contact with the surface and which didn't.
— Observe the degree of pressure made on the surface with each part of the foot.

Have them compare the different kinds of walking/running. Based only on the footprints:

— Which looked most strained?

— Which looked most efficient?
— What were the differences between the patterns of people walking in a group?
— Was it possible to tell the difference between the prints of two people who had just happened to walk over the same area and those of one person actively pursuing another?
— What kind of information about human skin texture can be obtained from a footprint? Is every footprint equally informative?

5. Discuss theories that attempt to account for the mass extinctions at the end of the Cretaceous.

   a. List what died and when.
   b. Review the evidence for the gradual decline of dinosaur diversity at the end of the Cretaceous; discuss the declining shallow seas hypothesis (covered quite well in Bakker's book).
   c. Discuss the evidence for meteoric impact and the effects the impact of a large meteor (or, more likely, meteors) would have on Earth. I found David Raup's *The Nemesis Affair* quite useful (although the periodicity effect he discusses is almost certainly nonexistent); in addition, the Larry Niven novel *Lucifer's Hammer* and the Gregory Benford novel *Shiva Descending* have quite nice descriptions of the effects of a large meteor strike on the Earth of the present. Mention nuclear winter here as well.

G. Session VII: Mammals

   1. Discuss high points in mammalian evolution:

      a. Therapsids.
      b. Monotremes.
      c. Marsupials.
      d. Placental mammals.
      e. Primate evolution.
      f. The effect of continental plate movements on the pattern of mammalian evolution (existence of marsupials in Australia, decimation of South American marsupials once Central America formed and placental mammals moved in).

   2. Discuss mammalian features:

      a. Hair and its varied uses.
      b. Evolution/formation/function of the placenta.
      c. Milk (with emphasis on the different characteristics of milk from different species of mammals).
      d. Heavy parental time and energy investment in the young—evolutionary advantages and disadvantages.

3. Show at least the first half of the videotape "Songs of the Whales, Signs of the Apes." Use it to make the point that our nearest relatives, the great apes, are really quite close to us in their intellectual abilities as well as in their morphology. Also bring up the point (from King and Wilson's genetic studies) that we are 99% genetically identical to chimpanzees.

4. Discuss the ethics of human uses of animals. Ask the kids to list all the ways we use animals (including food, fur, pets, medical research). With the kids' assistance, draw up a list of guidelines for the ethical uses of animals, focusing particularly on "higher" forms. Questions to bring up include:

   a. What are the tradeoffs between animal life and human life? Is it ethical to sacrifice 100 mice to possibly save one human life? 1,000 mice? 1,000,000 mice? Would it be less ethical in these cases if we were sacrificing larger mammals (rabbits or cows, for example)?

   b. When is it ethical to use members of a threatened or endangered species (chimpanzees, for example) for medical research? For example, chimps are the only other species that can become infected with the AIDS virus. Is it ethical to use chimps in AIDS research?

   c. Is it ethical to injure animals to test substances involved in nonessential products (for example, cosmetics)? Describe the Draize test.

   d. Is it ethical to use pound animals in research? To train medical students?

   e. If you disagree with a particular way in which animals are being used, is it ethical to break the law to "rescue" the animals? Describe the actions of PETA and ALF.

H. Session VIII: Human evolution and impact on planet Earth

   1. Discuss trends in human evolution.

      a. Physical changes.
         (1) Posture.
         (2) Height.
         (3) Cranial capacity.

      b. Cultural changes.
         (1) Improving tool technology.
         (2) Use of fire.
         (3) Agriculture.
         (4) Religion.

      c. Effects on the environment.
         (1) Extinction of animals such as the mammoth.
         (2) Modern anthropogenic changes (get kids to make the list they know most of them).

2. Discuss the human population size over time and the reasons for the current exponential growth of the population. Discuss Malthus's theories.

3. Have the kids do the thought experiment of removing humankind from the ecosystem. Each kid should do it individually; then, after they have all handed in their versions, the class should discuss it, as there will be a wide variety of opinions on the subject.

4. Discuss the future of the planet. Include topics such as:

   a. What's the worst we can do to the planet?

   b. Will humans become extinct?

   c. What can we do to reverse or ameliorate anthropogenic changes?

   d. What will the continents look like in the future?

VII. Major Instructional Strategies Employed

A. Problem solving

The laboratory sections of the course emphasize problem solving, as do hypothetical questions the teacher poses during class discussions.

B. Inquiry

The laboratory sections of the course emphasize use of the scientific method to examine various natural phenomena. Much of the material discussed in class is the direct result of scientific inquiry. The evidence for the assertions made in class will be discussed so students can get a better feeling for the strategies scientists use to inquire into natural phenomena. In addition, extensive reading lists are provided at each session, and students are encouraged to pursue more information on topics of interest outside of class.

C. Grouping approaches

For the most part, activities were pursued either as a whole class or individually. Small-group activities didn't seem to be needed as the class consisted of only nine students.

D. Questioning techniques

Teacher-led class discussions emphasized student participation. Students were encouraged to volunteer information that helped build a better picture of the topic under discussion and to answer (and pose) hypothetical questions. Their opinions and judgment were elicited repeatedly, and they were required to support their statements with logical arguments. Many questions required them to propose an experiment to elucidate a scientific point.

VIII. Evaluation procedures

Evaluation of student performance was primarily anecdotal: I tried to see that all of them got a chance to participate in class discussions so I could tell whether they had understood the point under discussion. In addition to anecdotal assessment, the thought experiment in Session VIII provided a post-course assessment opportunity, as many of the concepts required for sophisticated answers to the questions posed in the experiment required application of the concepts covered in class.

IX. Materials/Resources

  A. Teacher bibliography

   1. For current information on scientific topics, see:

     — Tuesday Science section of *The New York Times.*
     — News and Views section of *Nature.*
     — News and Comment and Research News sections of *Science.*
     — Recent issues of *Scientific American.*

   2. Bibliography of materials used to prepare the unit:

Bakker, R. T. (1986). *The dinosaur heresies: New theories unlocking the mystery of the dinosaurs and their extinction.* New York: Morrow.

Birdsell, J. B. (1975). *Human evolution.* Chicago: Rand McNally.

Dickerson, R. E., & Geis, I. (1969). *The structure and action of proteins.* Menlo Park, CA: W. A. Benjamin, Inc.

Eiger, M. S., & Olds, S. W. (1987). *The complete book of breastfeeding.* New York: Workman Publishing.

Frye, K. (1986). *Roadside geology of Virginia.* Missoula, MT: Mountain Press Publishing.

Gould, S. J. (1989). *Wonderful life: The Burgess shale and the nature of history.* New York: W. W. Norton.

Johanson, D., & Edey, M. (1981). *Lucy: The beginnings of humankind.* New York: Simon and Schuster.

Keeton, W. T. (1972). *Biological science* (2nd ed.). New York: W. W. Norton.

Lehninger, A. L. (1975). *Biochemistry* (2nd ed.). New York: Worth Publishers.

Mahan, B. H. (1975). *University chemistry* (3rd ed.). Reading, MA: Addison-Wesley.

Pelzcar, M. J., Reid, R. D., & Chan, E. C. S. (1977). *Microbiology* (4th ed.). New York: McGraw-Hill.

Pyle, R. M. (1984). *The Audubon Society handbook for butterfly watchers.* New York: Charles Scribners' Sons.

Raup, D. M. (1986). *The nemesis affair: A story of the death of dinosaurs and the ways of science.* New York: W. W. Norton.

Redfern, R. (1983). *The making of a continent.* New York: Times Books.

Scott, J. A. (1986). *The butterflies of North America.* Stanford, CA: Stanford University Press.

Silver, D. M. (1989). *Earth: The ever-changing planet* (Random House Library of Knowledge). New York: Random House.

Stein, S. (1986). *The evolution book.* New York: Workman Publishing.

Strickberger, M. W. (1976). *Genetics* (2nd ed.). New York: Macmillan.

Watson, J. D. (1976). *The molecular biology of the gene.* Menlo Park, CA: W. A. Benjamin, Inc.

Videotapes:

Planet Earth. (1989). John D. and Catherine T. MacArthur Foundation Library Video Classics Project. New York: BBC/Time-Life Films.

The Living Planet. (1984). John D. and Catherine T. MacArthur Foundation Video Classics Project. London: BBC/Timc-Life Films.

Nova: Signs of the Apes, Songs of the Whales. (1984). John D. and Catherine T. MacArthur Foundation Video Classics Project. Boston: WGBH.

Lorne Greene's New Wilderness: Pretty Poison. (1987). A Greene and Dewar New Wilderness Production. Los Angeles: Prism Entertainment.

B. Student bibliography

For appropriate readings for students, *please see* the "Recommended Reading" section of the Weekly Planet handouts.

C. Handout material

X. Extension Ideas

In addition to the suggested reading material, you could suggest appropriate museums to visit (for example, the Smithsonian Institution and the Virginia Living Museum). It also would be worth watching the television schedule for appropriate nature and science programs.

Building the Caduceus *(LESSONS 1–5)*

Fifth to Seventh Grades

Christopher Fischer
Norfolk Public Schools
Norfolk, Virginia

RATIONALE AND PURPOSE

This unit has been designed to introduce fifth- through seventh-grade students to the concepts of evolution and knowledge in the context of the development of Western medicine. It introduces advanced historical content in a conceptual approach, consistently relating relevance of topical content to unit generalizations that emphasize the nature of knowledge and its evolution.

The unit is a marriage of enriched content and accelerated reasoning skills. It requires the application to historical content of the critical thinking skills enumerated in Paul's reasoning model. Students are expected to develop proficiency in critical analysis of historical sources and persuasive writing ability as a result of the accelerated curriculum. The application of Paul's reasoning model to advanced historical content allows the students to hone their historiographical and communication skills, while the concepts of knowledge and evolution provide students with an analytical framework for future disciplinary study.

APPROPRIATENESS FOR GIFTED STUDENTS

The advanced historical content and the accelerated thinking skills curriculum will provide the building blocks for productive thinking in a relevant context. The accelerated thinking skills curriculum is based on Paul's reasoning model. Students will employ the eight elements of reasoning when working with primary and secondary source material. The elements are not a hierarchy but an interdependent progression of qualities that should be present in the critical thinking process. The unit requires that students employ the elements of reasoning to historical material and transfer their understanding of the material into persuasive writing. The conceptual framework (i.e., knowledge and evolution) on which the unit is organized provides a relevance to the content and facilitates the transfer of the skills honed during the unit to other academic disciplines.

ASSESSMENT

Each lesson includes an assessment instrument in the form of a rubric based on a four-point scale. The highest criterion represents a standard above and beyond the benchmark for gifted students. The unit includes a pre-assessment that measures content and process (critical thinking) fluency so that appropriate differentiation measures can be taken. Final assessment takes place in the closing lesson and is both traditional and authentic in nature.

UNIT GOALS

Content Standards

Goal: Through curriculum and instruction, students will develop an understanding of the evolution of knowledge in the field of medicine.

1. Students will develop a basic understanding of epistemological concepts (i.e., types of knowledge, types of thinking).
2. Students will understand the evolution of medicine from antiquity to the present.

Concept Standards

Goal: Students will develop an understanding of the concept generalizations.

1. Students will demonstrate an understanding of the following generalizations:
   ✓ Logic is only as good as the premises it is based upon.
   ✓ Knowledge evolves by building upon existing knowledge.
   ✓ Knowledge evolves through a process of eliminating prior misconceptions.
   ✓ Misconceptions, when recognized, are positive building blocks toward understanding.
   ✓ Knowledge is not static but changes.
   ✓ Knowledge is subdivided into specific academic disciplines where it develops unique tools, approaches, standards, and traditions that contribute to the deep understanding of the discipline. This deep understanding leads to application in interrelated disciplines.

Process Standards

Goal: Through curriculum and instruction, students will develop and demonstrate critical thinking skills in a historical context as described in Paul's reasoning model. Students will be able to:

1. Identify purpose, issue, and position present in source documents.
2. Identify existing and potential multiple perspectives and assumptions on a given issue.

3. Check for validity and reliability of sources by classification (primary/secondary) and through analysis of a source's author and legacy.
4. Examine evidence present in a source document and identify inferences drawn by the author.
5. Identify implications and consequences behind a line of reasoning in a persuasive piece of writing.
6. Acknowledge references to the concept in source documents.

Goal: Through curriculum and instruction, students will develop and demonstrate fluency with the Hamburger model of persuasive writing. Students will be able to:

1. Identify the parts of a persuasive essay.
2. Outline a plan for a persuasive essay.
3. Write a persuasive essay including all of the facets of the hamburger model.

Goal: Through curriculum and instruction, students will develop and demonstrate fluency with the William and Mary research model. Students will be able to:

1. Identify the steps in the research process.
2. Complete research on an issue following the procedures described in the William and Mary research model.

CONTENT OUTLINE

I. Basic Epistemology

   A. Types of Knowledge

     1. Knowledge How

     2. Knowledge That

     3. A Priori Knowledge

     4. A Posteriori Knowledge

   B. Types of Thinking

     1. Inductive

     2. Deductive

II. Ancient Medicine

   A. Egyptian Medicine
   (Hamburger Model Introduced)

     1. Imhotep and Superstition

     2. Egyptian Papyri

   B. Greek Medicine
   (Research Model Introduced)

     1. Homer, the Iliad, and
       Pre-Hippocratic Medicine

     2. Hippocrates and Humoral Theory

     3. Healing Cults

   C. Roman Medicine
   (Reasoning Model Introduced)

     1. Galen and the Taboo of Dissection

III. Medieval Medicine

   A. *Canterbury Tales* General Prologue

   B. Vesalius, Dissection and Anatomy

   C. The Black Plague

IV. Classical Medicine

   A. Jenner and Smallpox

   B. Pasteur and Germs

   C. Koch, Anthrax and Immunology

V. Civil War Era Medicine

   A. Surgery During the Civil War

VI. Modern Medicine

   A. Issues and Controversy

VII. Homeopathic Medicine

   A. Acupuncture

Concept Emphasis

✓ Evolution and knowledge introduced and examined

Content and Process Emphasis

✓ Paul's reasoning model
✓ Hamburger model
✓ Research model

Concept and Process Emphasis

RESOURCES

Teacher Resources

Paul, R. W. & Binker, A. J. A. (Eds.). (1992). *Critical thinking: What every person needs to survive in a rapidly changing world.* Sonoma, CA: Foundation for Critical Thinking.

Pre-assessment Resources

Congressional Record. (1906). Cong. 1 session, p. 7801, in Bailey, T. A. & Kennedy, D. M. (1994). *The American spirit: Vol. II, United States history as seen by contemporaries* (8th ed.). (pp. 639–640). Lexington, MA: D. C. Health.

Sinclair, U. (1906). *The Jungle.* New York: Amsco Literature Series.

Lesson Resources

Lessons 1–4

Antiqua Medicina: From Homer to Vesalius. [On-line]. Available: http://www.med.virginia.edu/hs-library/historical/antiqua/anthome.html

Beyond Science? (videotape). Scientific American, November, 1998.

Mastermind board game, Milton Bradley.

Vincent, P. F., & Hester, J. (1987). *Philosophy for young thinkers.* Monroe, NY: Trillium Press.

Lessons 5–9

Colarusso, C. (1995). *The presocratic influence upon Hippocratic medicine* [On-line]. Available: http://www.perseus.tufts.edu/GreekScience/Students/Chad/pre-soc.html

Magner, L. (1992). *A history of medicine.* New York: Marcel Dekker.

Mayeaux, E. J. (1989). History of Western medicine and surgery [On-line]. Available: http://lib-sh.lsumc.edu/fammed/grounds/history.html

Online Classics Archive http://classics.mit.edu/

Philips, E. D. (1973). *Greek medicine.* London: Camelot Press.

Lesson 10

Dietz, D. (1960). *All about great medical discoveries.* New York: Random House.

Galen http://www.systemajo.com/scientific1.html

History of Western Medicine and Surgery 1989
http://lib-sh.lsumc.edu/fammed/grounds/history.html

Lesson 11

Chaucer, G., & Cohen, B. (Ed.). (1988). *The Canterbury tales* New York: Lothrop, Lee, & Shepard.

Chaucer, Geoffrey
   http://federalistnavy.com/poetry/GEOFFREYCHAUCERcahall/wwwboard.html

Medical Source book
   http://www.fordham.edu/halsall/source/grtschism2.html

Medieval medicine http://www.geocities.com/Athens/Forum/8923/medieval.html

Lesson 12

Eaton, L. (Producer). (1989). *The black death: March 27, 1361.* [Videocassette]. Culver City, CA: Zenger Video.

Plague and Public Health in Renaissance Europe
   http://jefferson.village.virginia.edu/osheim/intro.html

Wisnia, Cory M. The Black Plague: A Hands-on Epidemic Simulation
   http://www.mcn.org/ed/cur/cw/Plague/Plague_Sim.html

Lesson 13

Dietz, D. (1960). *All about great medical discoveries.* New York: Random House.

History of Western Medicine and Surgery 1989
   http://lib-sh.lsumc.edu/fammed/grounds/history.html

Lesson 14

Dietz, D. (1960). *All about great medical discoveries.* New York: Random House.

Lesson 15

The Battle Of Gettysburg: July 1st–3rd 1863
   http://members.aol.com/acw6165/index.html

Lesson 16

Dold, D. (1998, September). Needles and nerves. *Discover, 19,* 58–63.

PRE-ASSESSMENT

Goals Addressed: Goals 1 and 3

Content Goal	Concept Goal	Process Goals

Instructional Purpose

1. To administer a pre-assessment of student fluency with process and content goals.

Materials

Pre-assessments 1 and 2

Activities and Questions

1. Distribute pre-assessment 1 (content pre-assessment)

   ✓ The instrument will measure student fluency with the content presented in the unit.

   ✓ The pretest will present general background information and then ask students to provide information on certain topics to be covered in the class.

   ✓ Give students 40 minutes to complete the assessment.

2. Distribute pre-assessment 2 (process pre-assessment)

   ✓ The instrument will measure student fluency with Paul's reasoning model.

   ✓ The pretest calls for analysis of a primary source document.

   ✓ Students are provided a scaffold that roughly outlines the model.

   ✓ Give students 40 minutes to complete the assessment.

Assessment

1. Based upon performance on pre-assessment instruments. (See "Notes to Teacher.")

Notes to Teacher

1. Data from the content pre-assessment can be used to determine the amount of enrichment to be pursued by each student. Although the lessons are already prepared, the level of sophistication with content to be displayed by each student should be adjusted according to performance on the assessment.

2. Data from the process pre-assessment can be used to determine student fluency with Paul's reasoning model. Although students will most likely not be familiar with the model, they should show some ability with critical analysis. The degree of fluency displayed on the pre-assessment should help to determine the pace through which students will explore the eight facets of the reasoning model. It should also serve as a benchmark with which to compare the final assessment.

PRE-ASSESSMENT 1: THE EVOLUTION OF MEDICINE

Directions: Read the following introduction to the unit and complete the rest of the activity.

Medicine began in the days of the cave dwellers of the Old Stone Age. It is easy to see why this was so. The cave dwellers were faced with dangers on all sides. They might be clawed by a wild beast or bitten by a serpent. They might break an arm or leg in a fall from a cliff. A broken bone or a wound inflicted by a wild animal called for prompt attention. And so we may be sure that even in prehistoric times crude methods of accident surgery were developed. Some individuals were more skillful than others at binding up a wound or setting a broken bone. They became the world's first surgeons. But there were fevers and other illnesses that were completely mysterious, since the cave dwellers could see no cause for them. Why did his head begin to ache? Why did she tremble from a chill? Why did his skin break out in a rash?

Long before the dawn of written history, people turned to magic to deal with these mysterious ailments. We still find such magic practiced by the medicine men of primitive tribes in remote parts of the world. These tribal medicine men, or witch doctors, wear fantastic costumes and terrifying masks. They utter loud cries and perform weird dances to impress the gods and drive out the demons of disease. Perhaps the medicine men of the Old Stone Age did the same thing. Prehistoric cave dwellers developed one very strange practice. Many skulls found in all parts of the world have round holes drilled in them. We know that the individuals survived the operation because the edges of the holes show evidence of healing and the growth of new bone. Why was this done? We can only guess that it was to cure such diseases as epilepsy and migraine headaches by letting out the demons that were thought to be causing the disease.

In the spaces provided below write as much as you know concerning medicine and the following topics.

1. Ancient Egypt

_____

_____

_____

_____

_____

_____

_____

_____

_____

(If you need more space, you may write on the back.)

2. Ancient Greece

_____
_____
_____
_____
_____
_____
_____
_____
_____
_____

(If you need more space, you may write on the back.)

3. Ancient Rome

_____
_____
_____
_____
_____
_____
_____
_____
_____
_____

(If you need more space, you may write on the back.)

4. The Middle Ages

_____

_____

_____

_____

_____

_____

_____

_____

_____

_____

(If you need more space, you may write on the back.)

5. The causes of disease

_____

_____

_____

_____

_____

_____

_____

_____

_____

_____

(If you need more space, you may write on the back.)

6. Alternative (homeopathic) medicine

_____

_____

_____

_____

_____

_____

_____

_____

_____

_____

(If you need more space, you may write on the back.)

PRE-ASSESSMENT 2: THE EVOLUTION OF MEDICINE

Directions: Read the following information and excerpts about the meat industry during the early 20th century.

In the early 20th century, several American writers published detailed accounts about political corruption and improper business practices. Theodore Roosevelt nicknamed such writers "muckrakers," because he considered some of their accounts to be exaggerated. Sometimes the muckrakers' efforts led to government reforms. One of the leading muckrakers was a socialist and writer named Upton Sinclair. His novel *The Jungle* (1906) exposed filthy and dangerous conditions in Chicago's meatpacking plants. The exposé stirred public concern, prompting President Roosevelt to appoint a commission to investigate the meat industry. The first excerpt below is from Sinclair's novel. The second is from the commission's report. Both sources helped to convince Congress to pass the Meat Inspection Act of 1906, which mandated procedures to ensure proper sanitation in food preparation.

I. *Viewed by a Novelist*

There was never the least attention paid to what was cut up for sausage; there would come all the way back from Europe old sausage that had been rejected, and that was moldy and white—it would be dosed [doused] with [the chemicals] borax and glycerine, and dumped into the hoppers [tanks], and made over again for home consumption. There would be meat that had tumbled out on the floor, in the dirt and sawdust, where the workers had tramped and spit uncounted billions of consumption [tuberculosis] germs. There would be meat stored in great piles . . ., and thousands of rats would race about on it. It was too dark in these storage places to see well, but a man could run his hand over these piles of meat and sweep off handfuls of the dried dung of rats. These rats were nuisances, and the packers would put poisoned bread out for them; they would die, and then rats, bread, and meat would go into the hoppers together.

II. *Viewed by a Federal Commission*

Meat scraps were also found being shoveled into receptacles [containers] from dirty floors, where they were left to lie until again shoveled into barrels or into machines for chopping. These floors, it must be noted, were in most cases damp and soggy, in dark, ill-ventilated rooms, and the employees in utter ignorance of cleanliness or danger to health expectorated [spit] at will upon them. In a word, we saw meat shoveled from filthy wooden floors, piled on tables rarely washed, pushed from room to room in rotten box carts, in all of which processes it was in the way of gathering dirt, splinters, floor filth, and the expectoration of tuberculous and other diseased workers.

We saw a hog that had jut been killed, cleaned, washed, and started on its way to the cooling room fall from the sliding rail to a dirty wooden floor and slide part way into a filthy men's privy (toilet). It was picked up by two employees, placed upon a truck, carried into the cooling room and hung up with other carcasses, no effort being made to clean it.

Based on the readings, use the graphic to identify the issue, purpose of the writing, points of view expressed, evidence presented, inferences made, assumptions and concepts underlying the reasoning, and potential implications and consequences of the writers' work.

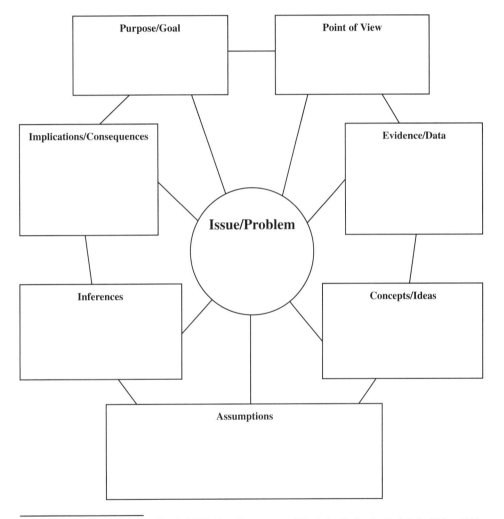

From *The Miniature Guide to Critical Thinking Concepts and Tools* (p. 2), by R. Paul & L. Elder, 1999, Dillon Beach, CA: Foundation for Critical Thinking, www.criticalthinking.org, cct@criticalthinking.org. Adapted with permission.

LESSON 1

Goals Addressed: Goals 1 and 2

Instructional Purpose

1. To introduce the basic structure of formal logic.
2. To reveal the pervasive nature of logic in modes of inquiry.
3. To display the fundamental role of logic in the process of human understanding and the collection of knowledge.

Materials

Syllogism quiz

Vocabulary

Induction: The process of deriving general principles from particular facts or instances

Deduction: The process of reasoning in which a conclusion follows necessarily from the stated data

Premise: One of the propositions in a deductive argument

Inference: The act or process of deriving logical conclusions from premises known or assumed to be true

Syllogism: A form of deductive reasoning consisting of a major premise, a minor premise, and a conclusion

A priori: Proceeding from a known or assumed cause to a necessarily related effect

Epistemology: The branch of philosophy that studies the nature of knowledge, its presuppositions and foundations, and its extent and validity

Empiricism: The view that experience, especially of the senses, is the only source of knowledge

Activities and Questions

✓ Presentation of the forced-choice psychic three book trick—a performance in which the teacher uses the concept of forced choice to manipulate students into believing he or she is psychic.

    Description of the trick: The teacher selects a book from a classroom bookshelf before class begins and memorizes a phrase on a specific page. In class, the teacher tells a made-up story about attending a psychic workshop and prepares the class for what they believe will be a psychic experience. The teacher says he or she will randomly choose three books from the bookshelf, and then selects the book from which he or she memorized and two others. The teacher says he or she will now "psychically divine" the phrase that a student will soon read from one of the three books, thinks for a moment, writes the previously memorized phrase on a sheet of paper, and asks a student to hold onto the paper. Then, the teacher asks a student to choose one of the three books. If the student selects the book from which the teacher memorized earlier, the teacher puts the other two books aside. If that book is not selected, the teacher picks up the book the student chose and asks him or her to choose again. The objective is to manipulate the student into selecting the book with the memorized phrase. After the student has the correct book in hand, the teacher pretends to randomly flip to the predetermined page number in one of the other books and asks the student to turn to the same page number in the book he or she holds. The teacher asks the student to read the phrase on the page (e.g., the top two lines) and then asks the student holding the message to read the "psychically divined" phrase aloud. The class should be amazed at the teacher's psychic ability.

✓ The teacher asks doubting students to explain their doubts. The class then discusses the trick and votes on the validity of the teacher's psychic claim. After some discussion, the teacher asks the class to reach agreement on a basic description of the trick.

✓ Starting from the basic description, the teacher constructs a syllogism that passes judgment on the trick. (A brief explanation of syllogisms may be necessary.) For example:

> Mr. Fischer knew what would be on page "X" of the book. Student "X"
> chose the book that contained the message Mr. Fischer wrote. Therefore:

✓ The teacher asks the students to discuss possible endings for the syllogism. The teacher then explains that more information is needed to complete the syllogism and reveals that he or she has no psychic ability and that no other class member was in on the trick. The class rewrites their syllogisms taking into account the new information.

✓ The teacher next reveals that he or she looked in a book earlier and memorized a specific page. The students again rewrite their syllogisms. (The teacher instructs the students not to blurt out the explanation of the trick when they figure it out but to write it down and wait until the end of the activity.)

✓ The teacher continues revealing facts about the trick until the majority of the students figure it out.

✓ The teacher explains that the class just went through the logical process of induction. He or she defines induction, drawing examples from the previous activity.

✓ The teacher asks, "Why weren't you able to figure out the trick from the first syllogism or immediately after the trick?" He or she draws out the point that induction (logic) is only as good as the premise upon which it is based. (The teacher may need to provide an explanation and definition of "premise.")

✓ The teacher conducts a brief lecture concerning the pervasiveness of logic and facilitate a class interactive discussion of how all academic disciplines (e.g., math, history, science) and many other activities (e.g., setting an alarm clock, using sunblock, the breaking of codes during wartime) use induction.

✓ The teacher conducts a simple science experiment (the inside-out balloon experiment) that demonstrates the use of induction to establish scientific laws.

Description of the experiment: The teacher performs an experiment that demonstrates how heat affects air pressure. The experiment requires a glass jar (jelly jar or similar size), a medium-sized balloon, and matches. The teacher places the balloon over the jar and asks the class why the balloon just hangs on the jar. He or she writes the students' suggestions on the board. Then the teacher asks what might happen if a fire were inside the jar and places a lighted match in the jar. The balloon should be sucked into the jar. Next, the teacher asks the students to explain the experiment in syllogism form and records the ideas on the board. This should lead the discussion to the differences in air pressure.

The point of this exercise is to emphasize the importance of observation in inferring scientific principles. As the class works through the discussion, the teacher reminds the students to use basic descriptions of what occurred to make probable assumptions about the causes until they have adequately explained the experiment. Afterward, the teacher asks, "Why weren't people able to explain air pressure thousands of years ago?"

✓ The teacher next explains the role of induction in the study of history. He or she begins by making the claim, "The pyramids were built by ancient aliens." The teacher then leads students in a discussion, reminding them to begin with the basic premise that solid proof of aliens visiting Earth has yet to be found. The class uses the syllogism to conclude that aliens did not built the pyramids. The teacher facilitates the discussion by correcting misconceptions and untrue statements the students provide. He or she discusses with students possible better explanations for the building of the pyramids. The class then talks about the difference between the historical discussion and the scientific experiment. The teacher helps the students to understand that history cannot be immediately observed and thus is subject to a fair amount of skepticism.

✓ The students participate in a discussion of the following questions:

— How is induction used during your everyday lives? How is deduction used?
— Which do you think is used more?
— Which is more reliable? More likely to be valid?
— Why did Aristotle formalize logic? Why didn't some other Greek discover it? What motivated Aristotle to think about logic enough to formalize it? (This discussion will lead to the introduction of the Aristotle assignment.)

✓ The students work in a group to develop a list of examples in which induction is used in their everyday lives.

✓ The students complete a syllogism quiz.
✓ The teacher assigns vocabulary words for students to define for homework (taken from the list at the beginning of the lesson).

Assessment

Score on syllogism quiz

Notes to Teacher

Practice the psychic trick several times before you perform it in front of the class. It's great at parties!

Homework

Aristotle assignment

Homework vocabulary

Syllogism Quiz

Read each syllogism and explain the logical sequence that results in the given answer.

1. Aristotle was born in Stagira.
   Stagira is in Greece.
   Therefore . . . Aristotle is from Greece

2. Aristotle attended the Academy in Athens.
   Plato founded the Academy.
   Therefore . . . Aristotle knew Plato

3. Aristotle left the Academy in 315 B.C.E.
   Plato died in 315 B.C.E.
   Therefore . . . Aristotle left because Plato died

4. Aristotle left the Academy in 315 B.C.E.
   The Lyceum was founded in 315 B.C.E.
   Therefore . . . Aristotle founded the Academy

5. Inference is a method of formal logic.
   Aristotle discovered inference as a method of formal logic.
   Therefore . . . Aristotle discovered formal logic

LESSON 2

Goals Addressed: Goals 1 and 2

Instructional Purpose

1. To identify various types of knowledge.
2. To examine the use of different types of knowledge in inductive and deductive thinking.
3. To identify real-world relevance to inductive and deductive thought.

Materials

"Inductive, Deductive, or Both" quiz; "types of knowledge" notes; Mastermind board game and rules

Activities and Questions

✓ The students are given a five-question quiz focusing on the difference between inductive and deductive thinking. The quiz is graded upon completion, and the answers are reviewed.

✓ The teacher discusses and collects the student assignments from Lesson 1. In the discussion, the class analyzes employed (inductive or deductive).

✓ The teacher conducts a discussion concerning the different types of knowing. The students are asked to analyze statements such as the following that are examples of the different types to identify what kinds of knowing are described:

— I know student "X." **Thinking/Sensing (recognition/familiarity)**
— I know how you feel. **Sensing (empathy)**
— I know who George Washington was. **Thinking (familiarity/recognition)**
— I know how to ride a bike. **Thinking (familiarity)**
— I know I'll be granted my birthday wish. **Believing (anticipatory)**
— I know it's raining outside. **Thinking/Believing/Sensing (anticipatory)**

✓ The students take notes outlining the difference between "knowledge how" and "knowledge that" and the difference between a priori and a posteriori knowledge.

— "Knowledge How" is described as procedural knowledge. It is the knowledge displayed in riding a bike, threading a needle, or tying shoes. It is the knowledge exhibited, for example, by a mentally challenged child who is a champion swimmer but cannot explain the strokes to you.

— "Knowledge That" is described as knowledge asserting that something is true or that something has happened or is going to happen. It is the knowledge exhibited, for example, by a teacher who has written many books and articles on swimming techniques but cannot swim.

— "A priori knowledge" is defined as knowledge derived by reasoning from a known or assumed cause to a necessarily related effect. This type of knowledge is based on theory rather than experience.

— "A posteriori knowledge" is defined as knowledge derived by reasoning from an observed effect to a related cause. This type of knowledge is based on observation.

✓ The students participate in a discussion of the following questions:

— What are some examples of these four different types of knowledge?

— Why is it important to know the difference between types?

— What sorts of professions would use each?

— Which is more important or useful?

— Are *a priori* knowledge and *a posteriori* knowledge mutually exclusive?

✓ The teacher distributes instructions for playing Mastermind, a game that employs inductive and deductive thinking. The students analyze the instructions and determine the type(s) of thinking involved in the game.

✓ The whole class participates in a Mastermind tournament. (The teacher pairs students in a tournament similar to the pairings in the NCAA basketball tournament.) After the teacher makes the tournament assignments, the students play one practice game. The students then commence the Mastermind tournament. The tournament consists of a winners' and losers' bracket and ends with the winner receiving some sort of award.

Assessment

Student ability to relate content of lesson to the concepts of the Mastermind game.

Extension

For extra credit, the students can design a game that will hone inductive or deductive thinking skills.

LESSON 3

Goals Addressed: Goals 1 and 3

Instructional Purpose

1. To examine the use of deductive and inductive thought in the creation of theories.
2. To identify the difference between validity and reliability and its relevance to critical thought.
3. To critically analyze pseudoscientific phenomena for types of thought and knowledge.

Materials

Scientific American video "Beyond Science?"; "Critical Thinking/Logical Thinking" sheets for dowsing and graphology; student journals; Assignment 3; types of knowledge quiz

Vocabulary

Validity: Containing premises from which the conclusion may logically be derived
Reliability: Capable of being relied on; dependable; precise

Activities and Questions

✓ The teacher conducts a class discussion reviewing different types of knowledge ("knowledge that," "knowledge how," "a priori knowledge," "a posteriori knowledge")
✓ The students take notes concerning the difference between validity and reliability. A statement or issue is described as valid if it is true or accurate. A test or experiment is valid if it measures what it is supposed to measure. A statement is reliable if it is consistent with known facts. A test or experiment is reliable if it produces the same results every time it is conducted.
✓ The teacher conducts a discussion concerning why it is important to be aware of the various types of knowledge and thinking. Students should arrive at the conclusion that being aware of the type of information they have and the type of thinking used to produce it will help them to better judge its validity. The teacher can use the following questions to guide the discussion:

 — Should you believe everything you read?
 — Should you believe everything your teacher tells you?
 — Are your parents or teachers sometimes wrong?
 — Why are they wrong? (misinformation, fallacious logic, self-delusion)

— Why should you question authority figures? Should you always question authority figures?

— Are you sometimes wrong? Why? (misinformation, fallacious logic, self-delusion)

— What steps could you take to reduce fallacious logic and self-delusion in your thinking?

— How can you reduce the amount of misinformation you receive?

— What can you do to reduce the amount of misinformation you accept as true?

✓ The teacher introduces the concept of pseudoscience.

✓ The students view the first portion of the segment on dowsing in the Scientific American video "Beyond Science" (6:45–9:15). Afterward, they are polled about their belief in dowsing and their interpretation of the segment. The teacher asks the following questions:

— What kind of knowledge is employed in dowsing? (Students identify the type of knowledge and match it with the details of the segment.)

— What kind of thinking do dowsers employ with this knowledge? Why is it important to know?

— What kind of thinking can you employ to figure out if dowsing is valid? How could we test this proposition? What types of knowledge would be involved in such a test? Why is it important to know if dowsing is valid?

✓ The students view the second portion of the dowsing segment (9:15–9:48). The teacher then distributes the "Critical Thinking/Logical Thinking" sheets and asks students to complete the section on dowsing. The teacher briefly goes over the sections that require students to diagram the knowledge and thinking employed in dowsing and to write a syllogism that describes their conclusions about dowsing's validity based on the information they received from the video. The students then complete the sheet.

✓ The teacher asks students to share their syllogisms and briefly reviews the sheet.

✓ The students view the first portion of the segment on graphology in the Scientific American video (39:40–41:15). Afterward, they are asked to complete the first portion of the "Critical Thinking/Logical Thinking" sheet on graphology. It requires them to diagram the type of knowledge and thinking involved in graphology.

✓ The students are asked to describe a way they might test the validity of graphology. They are also asked to describe the type of knowledge and thinking involved in such a test.

✓ The students turn in their work and watch the last portion of the graphology segment. (41:15–47:28).

✓ The teacher defines pseudoscience and conducts a discussion concerning why people believe weird and not-so-weird things such as pseudoscientific phenomena are true. To guide the discussion, the teacher asks, "Why do people believe things that are not valid?" He or she draws out that they may believe the source is reliable, want to believe the thing is true, or defer to what they perceive is a higher authority.

✓ The teacher provides an explanation of journaling assignments with words such as the following:

> From time to time I will ask you to write in your journal about something we've talked about in class. Journal entries contain your personal anecdotes, opinions, or thoughts on an issue. There are no right or wrong answers in journal entries. You should simply respond to the journal prompt provided. Write as much as you need to write to respond to the prompt. The evaluation is based upon whether you add superfluous, irrelevant information and whether you actually respond to the prompt. A good rule of thumb for length is about 3/4's of a page.

✓ The students are then asked to respond to the following journal prompt: Think about a time when you believed something that was not true or was at least questionable (it does not have to be a pseudoscientific phenomenon), and explain why you believed it and how you came to see that it was false or not totally a sure thing. An example would be your belief in Santa Claus.

Homework

The teacher distributes the following assignment:

Choose one of the following three phenomena to investigate: astrology, clairvoyance, or alien abductions. Research the common theory explaining that phenomenon. As we did in class, identify the type of thinking and knowledge employed in developing the theory that supposedly explains the phenomenon. Design and describe an experiment to test the theory's validity. Then write a prediction or hypothesis describing how you think the theory will change or develop 50 to 100 years from now.

You will be evaluated according to the following rubric:

Score

4   Accurately and in detail identifies the type of knowledge and thinking employed in the theory. Designs an experiment that successfully measures the validity of the theory. Describes the evolution of the theory in a way that is relevant and insightful. Your prediction or hypothesis includes original thought and considers circumstances that may alter the future development of the theory.

3   Accurately and in detail identifies the type of knowledge and thinking employed in the theory. Designs an experiment that *may* measure the validity of the theory. Provides a prediction or hypothesis that is relevant to the future development of the theory studied.

2   Accurately identifies the type of knowledge and thinking employed in the theory. Designs an experiment that attempts to measure the validity of the theory. Describes the future development of the theory.

1   Mistakenly identifies the type of knowledge or thinking employed in the theory. Designs an experiment that is not relevant to testing the validity of the theory. Provides an irrelevant prediction or hypothesis about the future development of the theory.

(*Note to teacher:* The students may ask their parents for help. They are not expected to write a novel. The length of the written explanation should be only as long as necessary to fulfill the requirements laid out by the rubric. Students should include only relevant information.)

Assessment

See rubric.

LESSON 4

Goals Addressed: Goals 1 and 2

Instructional Purpose

1. To introduce and develop the concepts of knowledge and evolution with an emphasis on evolution.
2. To introduce Egyptian medical practices and their origin in superstition.

Materials

Reading on ancient Egyptian medicine (Woods, G. (1998). *Science in ancient Egypt.* New York: Frankin Watts. Pages 46–55.); Venn diagram sheets

Vocabulary

Information: Knowledge derived from study, experience, or instruction
Development: To bring from latency to or toward fulfillment
Parameter: A factor that restricts what is possible or what results
Myth: A fictitious story, person, or thing

Science: The observation, identification, description, experimental investigation, and theoretical explanation of phenomena

Change: To cause to be different

Spectrum: A broad sequence or range of related qualities, ideas, or activities

Activities and Questions

✓ The teacher defines knowledge and evolution and identifies terms associated with the two concepts (see vocabulary list). Then, in pairs, students develop definitions for the following terms based upon previously existing knowledge: information, development, myth, parameter, science, change, and spectrum.

✓ Students create two lists: one of examples of things that develop and one of examples of knowledge. The teacher instructs them to delete items from their lists that do not evolve, reminding students of the definition of evolution. Students then share their lists with the class, and each pair of students explains at least one of their examples. Finally, students list examples of things that do not evolve and that are not knowledge.

✓ Students are asked to diagram how they think something evolves. They are to choose a topic or object and describe the steps in its evolution. The students should be reminded that their work is not expected to be 100% correct and that they are simply forming a hypothesis. (If necessary, the teacher should complete an example.) When they finish the activity, students are asked to hypothesize about the future evolution of their topic or object.

✓ The students participate in a discussion of the following questions:

— What is knowledge?

— How do people come to know things?

— How is knowledge like a living organism?

— Why does knowledge change?

— Are there limits to knowledge?

— How are myth and science related?

— Is change always for the better?

— Is evolution always an improvement?

— What are some examples of how knowledge has evolved? Devolved?

✓ The teacher explains what a generalization is and provides an example from one of the students' evolution hypotheses. An example of such a generalization might be "Knowledge is not static but changes." Students work in groups to come up with generalizations about knowledge based on their discussion.

✓ The teacher presents the unit generalizations:

1. Logic is only as good as the premises it is based upon.
2. Knowledge evolves by building upon existing knowledge.
3. Knowledge evolves through a process of eliminating prior misconceptions.

4. Misconceptions, when recognized, are positive building blocks toward understanding.
5. Knowledge is not static but changes.
6. Knowledge is subdivided into specific academic disciplines where it develops unique tools, approaches, standards, and traditions that contribute to the deep understanding of the discipline. This deep understanding leads to application in interrelated disciplines.

The students write the unit generalizations in their notebooks for future reference. The teacher asks the students to compare their generalizations to the unit generalizations.

✓ The students complete the reading on ancient Egyptian medicine and list 12 facts from the reading. They then fill in a Venn diagram outlining those practices that are useful today, those that were harmful, and those that were neither. Students also complete Venn diagram outlining practices that were based on science (observation), those that were based on myth, and those for which the basis is hard to determine. The students will observe that the practices that were harmful are frequently the same as those that were superstitious.

Assessment

Based upon ability to develop concept generalizations, participation in class discussion, and performance on extension activity.

Extension

Students research early medical scientists and outline how they changed the understanding of medicine in their time. Each student researches one scientist.

LESSON 5

Goals Addressed: Goals 1, 2, and 3

Instructional Purpose

1. To develop the concepts of knowledge and evolution.
2. To introduce the Hamburger model of persuasive writing; critical thinking; and Paul's reasoning model.
3. To develop understanding of ancient Egyptian medicine, its foundation in superstition, and its development of physiology.

Materials

Reading on ancient Egyptian medicine from Lesson 4; category chart rubric and butcher paper; Hamburger model diagram; persuasive writing example; unit generalizations

Activities and Questions

✓ Students complete the reading on ancient Egyptian medicine and enumerate 12 facts from the reading.
✓ Students complete a Venn diagram outlining those practices that are useful today, those that were harmful, and those that are neither.
✓ Students will then complete another Venn diagram outlining practices that were based on science (observation), those that were based on myth, and those that are hard to determine.
✓ The students combine into groups and share their lists of facts about ancient Egyptian medicine from the previous lesson. They delete duplicates and group the remaining facts into four categories of their choosing. They then create a poster of their categories and facts on butcher paper and include at least one generalization for each category they develop. Assessment is based upon the following rubric (Rubric 5.1):

Score

4   Identifies four novel categories, places relevant facts into categories, develops generalizations that are relevant, insightful, and important to an understanding of ancient Egyptian medical practices

3   Identifies four categories, places relevant facts into categories, develops generalizations that are relevant to ancient Egyptian medical practices

2   Identifies four categories, places facts into categories with some rational flaws, develops generalizations that are mostly relevant to ancient Egyptian medical practices

1   Identifies four categories, places irrelevant facts into categories with many rational flaws, develops generalizations that are irrelevant to ancient Egyptian medical practices

✓ The students participate in a class discussion of the following questions:

— Why did so much superstition surround Egyptian medicine?

— If Imhotep had never lived, how might Egyptian medicine have been different? What about Greek medicine?

— Why was so much superstition associated with medicine?

— How would science (especially the introduction of the microscope and the development of a more complex understanding of the various systems of the human anatomy) have changed ancient medical practices?

— How do the generalizations on your chart compare with the generalizations for the unit? How do they compare with others' generalizations?

— Did ancient Egyptian medicine evolve? If so, explain how in terms of the unit generalizations.

✓ The class is divided into three groups (based on students' ability to deal with the issues and concepts of the unit, as well as their fluency of information, knowledge, and the critical thought they employed during the class discussion) for the following tiered activity: Students in the lowest proficiency group will complete Assignment 1, those in the middle group will complete Assignment 2, and the highest proficiency group will complete Assignment 3.

Assignment 1. Imagine that you are Imhotep. You have just come from a medical conference in Stagira and are very aggravated because of the meddling of high priests in your medical practice. You feel like they are always interfering. First, they insisted that they be able to use their potions and amulets before allowing you to perform your real medicine. Now, they want you to stop performing surgery altogether. You will not stand for this. You have decided to use your influence with the pharaoh. You will write a letter to the pharaoh in an attempt to persuade him to block the priests' intentions.

Assignment 2. You are Notooswifto, an Egyptian high priest and the founder of the movement to ban all surgeries. You caught wind of Imhotep's plan to block your movement and will write a letter persuading the pharaoh to ban surgery.

Assignment 3. You are the pharaoh. Make a decision regarding the issue. Write a letter persuading the losing side to accept it.

Assessment will be based on the following rubric (Rubric 5.2):

Score

4   Addresses the issue in the assignment and the assigned point of view. Identifies at least three reasons that are original and display knowledge of historical content. Elaborates on at least three reasons using historically accurate evidence that supports a point of view. Includes an introduction and conclusion that are consistent with the Hamburger model and are grammatically correct.

3   Addresses the issue in the assignment and the assigned point of view. Identifies two or three reasons that display knowledge of historical content. Elaborates on two or three reasons using evidence that supports a point of view. Includes an introduction and conclusion that are consistent with the Hamburger model and are grammatically correct.

2   Indirectly addresses the issue in the assignment and the assigned point of view. Identifies at least one reason that supports the point of view. Elaborates on at least one reason using evidence that has some factual inconsistencies. Includes an introduction and conclusion that are consistent with the Hamburger model and are grammatically correct.

1   Vaguely addresses the issue in the assignment and the assigned point of view. Does not identify any reasons to support the point of view. Offers no evidence that supports the point of view. Introduction and conclusion are not evident, or the format is not consistent with the Hamburger model and/or the introduction and conclusion are not grammatically correct.

After the assignments are distributed, the students will discuss what it means to write persuasively. The teacher will display an example of good persuasive writing concerning the evils of the Internet and will introduce the Hamburger model of persuasive writing and analyze the model and the example with the class. The students will then have 15 minutes to complete the assignment.

Assessment

Based on students' ability to develop concept generalizations (see Rubric 5.1), participation in class discussion, and persuasive writing ability and fluency of critical thought (see Rubric 5.2).

Notes to Teacher

To best group students for the tiered assignment, be sure to note their participation during the class discussion. Students who are not assertive should be called upon to allow for assessment of their knowledge. You may find it helpful to plot data on a sociogram or simply to take notes on student fluency with content and comfort in discussing the generalizations. After students are ability grouped for the tiered assignment, differentiation in product and teacher assistance with the assignment should be observed.

Homework

Students should list 10 modern customs or comforts that evolved from superstition.

Principled Leadership (LESSONS 1–5)

Ninth and Tenth Grade

Diann Drummond
Center for Gifted Education
College of William and Mary

INTRODUCTION

This unit is designed around the idea that leadership should be governed by the universal principles of justice, which espouse the equality of human rights and respect for the individual. Understanding one's strengths, the needs and viewpoints of others, problem solving, global issues, and group processes through an examination of developmental theories and analysis of moral dilemmas will lead the student to develop "habits of mind" conducive to principled leadership. In addition, students will develop the skills of metacognition (thinking about thinking), cooperative communication, and decision making. The activities of this unit will engage students in an examination of their own thinking patterns and those of famous leaders and will provide opportunities for literature and historical analysis simulations, writing, and role-playing.

RATIONALE

Leadership curriculum should allow the student to develop the learned leadership of parliamentary procedure, cooperative communication, decision making, and time management. Additionally, it should provide an opportunity for students to develop the more innate, less tangible qualities of a responsible and ethical leadership. This unit provides those opportunities through an interdisciplinary study of the thinking and actions of great leaders and the practice of effective leadership skills.

CURRICULUM FRAMEWORK

Concept Goal and Outcomes

Goal 1: To understand the concept of justice and develop an understanding of the principles of the equality of human rights and respect for the individual

The student will be able to:

1. Understand that the quest for justice is eternal and universal.

2. Illustrate how justice changes over time in relationship to individuals and society.
3. Categorize justice, given several examples.
4. Evaluate a moral decision/judgment in literature using Nash's "12 Questions."
5. Demonstrate an understanding of the viewpoints and needs of people from different cultures, genders, and races and their basis for determining what is just.
6. Identify and analyze global issues dealing with human rights and the dignity of the individual.

Process Goals and Outcomes

Goal 2: To develop and demonstrate metacognitive skills across disciplines

The student will be able to:

1. Analyze, evaluate, and judge the efficiency of the steps and strategies used to solve a problem in history or literature.
2. Identify a real-life problem and develop a plan to solve it.
3. Monitor the progress of strategies used to solve a real-life problem and develop new strategies to overcome obstacles.
4. Assess the efficiency of a plan used to solve a real-life problem.

Content Goal and Outcomes

Goal 3: To develop leadership skills

The student will be able to:

1. Define a real-life problem of a global nature and explore solutions during a simulation.
2. Analyze and develop an understanding of group processes.
3. Use effective cooperative communication skills.
4. Demonstrate the use of parliamentary procedure.
5. Demonstrate the use of decision-making skills in solving a real-life problem.
6. Demonstrate the use of effective time-management skills.

Goal 4: To understand the role and characteristics of a principled leader

The student will be able to:

1. Analyze theories of moral development to formulate ideals of leadership.
2. Identify his or her own strengths and recognize potential for leadership.
3. Analyze historical and current leaders for characteristics and effectiveness.
4. Contrast and compare theories of leadership.
5. Identify and compare characteristics of principled (just) leaders and immoral (unjust) leaders.

GIFTED LEARNERS AND LEADERSHIP

Gifted learners have the cognitive ability and potential for emotional growth that, if guided, can progress toward greater self-actualization and leadership roles.[1,2] Dabrowski's levels of positive disintegration specifically addressed the gifted learner's capabilities of living a life in service to humanity.[3,2] Maslow developed a theory of self-actualization in which many of the characteristics, including the following, were similar to the characteristics of gifted children: advanced awareness and perception, greater autonomy and self-direction, intrinsic motivation, task commitment, intensity in sensory experiences (emotions, empathy), capability of intense concentration and periods of isolation for deep reflection, creativity, sense of humor, and a continuous curiosity about life.[1] This unit addresses the need of gifted learners to recognize their present developmental stage and develop and understanding of their strengths and weaknesses so that they can move along the road to self-actualization (i.e., to being the best they can be).

Through examination of theories of development, gifted learners will use their advanced skills of perception and awareness to identify their strengths and weaknesses and evaluate their level of development. The exploration of their metacognitive processes will require intense concentration and solitary reflection, a gifted learner trait. The analysis and evaluation of moral dilemmas will address the gifted learner's intense empathetic and emotional capabilities.

Gifted learners exhibit different traits, and this unit provides opportunities for the practice of traits already present and the development of new ones. Through this unit, the gifted learner will experience a multidisciplinary approach to developing and practicing leadership and metacognitive skills in simulated and real-life situations on a local and global scale.

CONTENT OUTLINE

Lesson 1: Introduction and Pre-Assessment
Lesson 2: The Concept of Justice
Lesson 3: Examining a Moral Dilemma
Lesson 4: Types of Leadership
Lesson 5: An Analysis of Leaders
Lesson 6: Metacognition
Lesson 7: An Analysis of the Declaration of Independence
Lesson 8: Theories of Moral Development
Lesson 9: Guest Speaker

---

[1]Clark, B. (1997). *Growing up gifted.* (5th ed.). New York: Merrill.
[2]Silverman, L. K. (1993). *Counseling the gifted and talented.* Denver, CO: Love Publishing.
[3]Piirto, J. (1999). *Talented children and adults: Their development and education.* (2nd ed.). Upper Saddle River, NJ: Merrill.

Lesson 10: Decision Making
Lesson 11: Introduction of Process Project
Lesson 12: Time-management Skills
Lesson 13: Communication Skills
Lesson 14: Simulation of a Global Problem
Lesson 15: Analysis of *A Time to Kill*
Lesson 16: Presentation of Process Project
Lesson 17: Closing Discussion of Justice and Principled Leadership
Lesson 18: Post-assessment

LESSON 1: INTRODUCTION AND PRE-ASSESSMENT

Goals Addressed: Goals 1 and 4

Instructional Purpose

1. To introduce students to the topics of the unit.
2. To administer a pre-assessment of principled leadership.

Materials and Resources

1. Quotes on leadership from *Thoughts on Leadership: A Treasury of Quotations* by William D. Hitt
2. Pre-assessment of principled leadership
3. Rubric for pre-assessment
4. Readings on justice for this lesson and the next lesson (from *What Is Justice? Classic and Contemporary Readings,* edited by Robert C. Solomon and Mark C. Murphy, New York: Oxford University Press, 1990):

   ✓ *The Iliad, Book IV,* by Homer, pp. 15–16
   ✓ Leviticus 24:17–22
   ✓ *The Koran,* (pp. 49–53)
   ✓ *Nicomachean Ethics, Book V,* by Aristotle, pp. 39–40
   ✓ *Summa Theologica,* by St. Thomas Aquinas, pp. 54–55
   ✓ *On the Mind,* by Mencius, pp. 62–65
   ✓ *The Republic, Book IV,* by Plato, pp. 35–37
   ✓ *Discourse on the Origins of Inequality* and *Social Contract,* by Jean-Jacques Rousseau, pp. 115–116
   ✓ *Justice as Fairness,* by John Rawls, pp. 305–306
   ✓ *Anarchy, State, and Utopia,* by Robert Nozick, pp. 313–315
   ✓ "Justice and the Passion for Vengeance," by Robert C. Solomon, pp. 292–294

✓ U.S. Supreme Court, *Gregg v. Georgia,* Minority Opinion by Justice Thurgood Marshall, pp. 270–272
✓ *On the Genealogy of Morals,* by Friedrich Nietzsche, pp. 262–264
✓ *Wild Justice,* by Susan Jacoby, pp. 287–289
✓ *A Theory of Moral Sentiments,* by Adam Smith, pp. 164–167
✓ *Utilitarianism,* by John Stuart Mill, pp. 194–196 or 259–260

Vocabulary

1. abhorrence
2. acquisition
3. admonition
4. analogous
5. appetitive
6. approbation
7. attributes
8. censurable
9. countenance
10. deliberative
11. deserts
12. disapprobation
13. distributive
14. entitlement
15. epithet
16. euphemism
17. impropriety
18. pejorative
19. principles
20. rectification
21. rectitude
22. reparation
23. retribution
24. sojourner
25. sovereignty
26. supplicated
27. tacitly

Activities

1. Hand out the two quotes "What Is Leadership?" (Hitt, p. xxx, from J. M. Burns, *Leadership,* p. 1) and "Leadership Is Like Beauty" (Hitt, p. xxx, from N. Bennis, *On Becoming a Leader,* p. 1). Tell the students that in this unit they will be studying principled leadership. Ask two students to read the quotes aloud.
2. Hand out the pre-assessment. Give the students 30 minutes to respond to the pre-assessment essay question.
3. Collect the pre-assessment and then ask if anyone would like to share his or her definition of leadership and example of an effective leader.
4. Have the students brainstorm a list of characteristics of an effective leader. Write the list on the board.
5. Read aloud the following Machiavellian concept: *Effective leaders are power-wielders, individuals who employ cunning and subterfuge to achieve their own ends.* Ask the students if they agree or disagree with this concept. Then read the following John Gardner quote: *"In any community, some people are more or less irretrievably bad and others more or less consistently good. But the behavior of*

most people is profoundly influenced by the moral climate of the moment. One of the leader's tasks is to help ensure the soundness of that moral climate." (Hitt, p. 119). Have students categorize the list of characteristics into two lists: *effective leadership* and *principled leadership.*

6. Ask the students the following questions: Is principled leadership different from leadership? How? What are the necessary components of principled leadership? Have students share their lists of components and brainstorm additional characteristics and principles that a person would need to possess to be a benevolent *and* effective leader.

7. List the principles from the brainstormed list in the previous question on the board. Narrow the list down to the three most important principles. Justice should be one of these. Tell the students that they will now examine the concept of justice as a necessary component of a principled leader. Have the students identify examples of justice, and list them on the board.

8. Divide the class into groups of two or three students. Give each group copies of two of the readings on justice (each student should have his or her own copy). Allow the remainder of the period for the students to read the selections and, if time allows, to discuss them in their groups. Explain that the selections will be discussed in depth in the next class. Instruct the students to read them again before that class and to take notes on them.

Homework

1. Read the assigned selections and take notes.
2. Be prepared to discuss, compare, and contrast the ideas and concepts put forth in the readings.
3. Write briefly in your journals about whether you agree or disagree with the ideas in the readings, and why.

Teacher Notes

Rubric for Pre- and Post-Assessment and Other Writing Assignments

Score

0   No clear position, no data to support main idea or viewpoint, no elaboration

2   Position vague, poorly formed, minimal data to support main idea or viewpoint, minimal elaboration

4   Position is clear but not strongly stated: at least three pieces of relevant, supporting data; some elaboration

6   Clear and concise position; good detail; a minimum of three pieces of accurate, convincing data; complete and insightful elaboration

Pre-assessment: Principled Leadership

1. Define leadership.
2. Give an example of an effective leader. Support your example with the qualities you feel make that person an effective leader.

LESSON 2: THE CONCEPT OF JUSTICE

Goals Addressed: Goal 1

Instructional Purpose

1. To develop an understanding of the concept of justice.
2. To understand how perceptions of justice have changed and stayed the same over time in relationship to society.

Materials and Resources

1. Readings from *What Is Justice? Classic and Contemporary Readings,* edited by Robert C. Solomon and Mark C. Murphy, New York: Oxford University Press, 1990.
2. Students' thinking journals.

Activities

The students will have read and briefly discussed the readings in their groups and re-read them for homework.

1. Have the students get into their groups from Lesson 1 and brainstorm examples of justice according to their readings. Write the following questions on the board. Have the students discuss their responses in their groups:

    ✓ According to your readings, what is justice?

✓ Do you agree or disagree with the authors about this definition?

✓ Is there one justice for all or different types of justice? Does the meaning vary for different cultures?

✓ Is "doing the just thing" the same as "doing the right thing"?

✓ What do you think justice is?

2. Bring the groups together to share their ideas and categorize the ideas into groups. Tell the students that theologians and philosophers have been struggling with the definition of justice since Plato wrote *The Republic* in 380 B.C. The readings should have led the students to the following definitions of justice: revenge (Homer), limited vengeance (Leviticus, Jacoby, Solomon), merciful retribution (the Koran, Thurgood Marshall), equality as a personal virtue (Aristotle), "natural" or divine law, human nature (St. Thomas Aquinas), compassion and understanding (Mencius), social and psychic harmony (Plato), social contract—an artificial virtue (Rousseau), fairness in social institutions—liberty, equality, reward (Rawls), and entitlement (Nozick). Help the students to develop these ideas and categories in the discussion by asking the following questions:

✓ How can you categorize these ideas into groups?

✓ What label can you give to each category or group?

✓ Do all of the ideas belong to a group? Do any belong to more than one?

✓ What are some of the characteristics of justice based on these ideas?

3. Have the students return to their groups to brainstorm ideas of what justice is not. Many of the selections refute the definitions of other philosophers. At this point the students should be arriving at their own definition of justice, discarding ideas they do not believe in. Write the following questions on the board to help guide the group discussions:

✓ What are some ideas of what is not justice?

✓ How can you group these ideas?

✓ How are these ideas similar to or different from what justice is?

4. Bring the groups back together to share and discuss their responses. List their ideas on the board. During the discussion ask students to explain their reasoning. Try to come to a class consensus on what justice is and is not.

5. Make a time line on the board extending from 800 B.C. to the present. Ask the students where the different selections should appear on the time line, and list them by title, author, and the category or definition represented by that reading (see Activity #3). Help the students trace the definitions of justice across time by asking the following questions:

✓ How was society different at each point on the time line?

✓ How did the definition of justice change in relationship to society?

✓ When do you see a significant change toward a more political definition?

✓ What factors to you think have influenced society's beliefs about justice?

6. Based on the brainstorming activities and time line, have the students make generalizations about justice. Explain that a generalization is something that is always or almost always true. Then ask what generalizations they can make about justice. The students can work in small groups or individually to list generalizations. After they have completed their list, write the following list on the board. These are the core generalizations that will be used in this unit. Ask students to compare their list to these core generalizations. Following each core generalization are suggested discussion questions and possible responses.

✓ **The quest for justice is eternal and universal.** *(How long has the definition of justice been discussed by philosophers?* Since Homer, 800 B.C. *What cultures in your readings have struggled with the definition of justice?* American, British, Ancient Chinese, Scottish, Eastern European, Ancient Greek.)

✓ **The concept of justice reflects the wants and needs of society.** *(What ideas of justice support this generalization?* Social contract, vengeance, merciful retribution, free enterprise, and private property.)

✓ **The concept of justice determines the relationship between the individual and society.** *(Revenge*—the death penalty; *natural or human nature*—compassion, respect; *social contract*—laws, private property, free enterprise.

✓ **Justice is both natural (human nature) and artificial.** *(What is a natural occurrence of justice?* Respect for others, revenge. *Artificial?* Social contract, laws.)

✓ **Justice is related to equality among groups or individuals.** *(In what way is justice related to equality?* Equality as a personal virtue, equality as a social contract, equality of retribution, equality in social and psychic harmony, equality in social institutions.

7. Have students respond to the generalizations in their journals.

Assessment

Students' response to generalizations in their journals.

Homework

1. Choose one of the generalizations and write a five-paragraph essay explaining why it is true, giving supporting evidence from one of the readings. Include a minimum of three references to the reading.

Extension

1. Read all selected readings on justice.
2. Read additional selections from *What Is Justice?* by Solomon and Murphy.

Teacher Notes

LESSON 3: EXAMINING A MORAL DILEMMA

Goals Addressed: Goal 1

Instructional Purpose

1. To recognize the viewpoints and needs of others in a given situation.
2. To evaluate a moral decision.
3. To categorize a moral decision in accordance with a particular theory of justice.

Materials and Resources

1. "The Cole Equations," by Tom Godwin
2. Students' thinking journals
3. Copy of Nash's 12 Questions* for each student (template included with lesson) and written on several large sheets of paper with several questions per sheet
4. Copies of readings from Lesson 2
5. *The Crucible* by Arthur Miller, New York: Penguin, 1996

Vocabulary

1. inured
2. qualm
3. symbolic potential

Activities

1. Review the topic of the last lesson briefly: what justice is and the different theories of justice. Ask: Do you think the concept of justice is easy to define? Do you think the just thing to do is always clear-cut and an easy decision? Why or why not?
2. Post the large sheets of paper with Nash's 12 Questions on the walls around the room. Give each student a copy. Have the students read and discuss the questions. Ask: What do you think Nash means by symbolic potential? Can you give an example? Have you ever heard the expression "on the horns of a moral dilemma"? What do you think that means? Can you give some real or imaginary, current or historical, examples of a moral dilemma?

---

* Laura Nash is a senior research fellow at Harvard Business School. Prior to this position, she was visiting lecturer and program director of business and religion at the Center for the Study of Values in Public Life at the Harvard Divinity School. She is author of *Good Intentions Aside* and *Behaviors in Business* and past president of the Society of Business Ethics.

3. Have the students read the story "The Cold Equations" silently. Then instruct them to break into groups of two to three students and discuss how they would answer Nash's 12 Questions from the viewpoint of the pilot of the spaceship.

4. As a whole-class activity, have a representative from each group read aloud the group's answer to one of Nash's questions. Lead the class in a discussion of the content, perception, and accuracy of the answer, and solicit different answers. After the discussion, have the group's representative write the group's final answer on the large paper with that question on it. Ask the students: Do you think your perception of the problem is comprehensive and accurate? Have you considered all the information given? Do you think the pilot's decision was fair and just? Have the students write their responses and turn them in when they are finished.

5. Have the students discuss, as a class responses to Nash's 12 Questions from the viewpoint of the stowaway in "The Cold Equations." When they are finished, ask the following questions: Whom, in the story, do you empathize with the most? Can you think of another solution to the problem? How would you feel if you were the pilot? Stowaway? How do you feel about the idea of one sacrificing for the many? How does this relate to the theories and principles of justice we discussed in our last lesson? Would you always sacrifice one for many? Do you think a member of another culture would respond differently? Would gender be a factor? Give an example of when you might not sacrifice the one for the many. (An example might be the president of the United States or a ruler or diplomat from another country.) Did the stowaway's age or gender affect your decision or feelings? Have the students reflect on these questions in their journals. Allow the students to share their reflections.

Assessment

1. Participation in group discussion
2. Each group's answers to Nash's 12 Questions
3. Journal entry

Homework

1. Write a five-paragraph essay relating the decision in "The Cold Equations" to one of the theories of justice discussed in the last lesson.
2. Read *The Crucible* by Arthur Miller for next class.

Teacher Notes

If students raise the issue of the stowaway's viewpoint prior to Activity 5, you may wish to conduct Activity 5 at that time.

Nash's 12 Questions

1. Have you defined the problem accurately? *(students: define the problem)*

2. How would you define the problem if you stood on the other side of the fence?

3. How did this situation occur in the first place?

4. To whom and to what do you give your loyalty as a person and as a member of a particular organization?

5. What is your intention in making this decision?

6. How does this intention compare with the probable results?

7. Whom could your decision or action injure?

8. Can you discuss the problem with the affected parties before you make your decision?

9. Are you confident that your position will be as valid over a long period of time as it seems now?

10. Could you disclose without qualm your decision or action to your boss, the chairperson of the board, your family, society as a whole?

11. What is the symbolic potential of your action if understood? If misunderstood?

12. Under what conditions would you allow exceptions to your stand?

Source: Nash, Laura L. (1981). Ethics without sermons. *Harvard Business Review, 59,* 79–90.

LESSON 4: TYPES OF LEADERSHIP

Goals Addressed: Goal 4

Instructional Purpose

1. To explore the characteristics of different types of leaders.
2. To evaluate skills of different kinds of leaders.
3. To recognize how social leaders emerge in a group.

Materials and Resources

1. *The Crucible,* by Arthur Miller
2. Leadership Chart handout
3. Students' thinking journals
4. Four to five large pieces of paper and markers
5. *The Prince,* by Niccolò Machiavelli

Activities

1. Ask the class to brainstorm and form a consensus on which characters were leaders in the play *The Crucible.* (*Note to teacher:* Suggested leaders: Abigail Williams, John Proctor, Reverend Hale, and Judge.) Write the name of each leader the class identifies at the top of a large sheet of paper. Leave room to write the type of leader beneath the name later in the lesson. Post the sheets of paper on the wall at the front of the room. (*Note to teacher:* You may want to limit the number of names to four)
2. Divide the students into groups. Have each group determine the characteristics of each person identified that made him or her a leader and whether these individuals were effective leaders. As the students begin this activity, approach each group individually. Ask one group to choose a leader. In the next group, assign a leader. In the third group, appoint the person with the highest test score on the Leadership pre-assessment as the leader. In the fourth group, do not mention anything about a leader. (*Note to teacher:* After the leadership positions are assigned, you may wish to take several students aside, individually, and explain that this is an experiment and you'd like them to play a particular role in it. For example, a student could purposely be a poor leader or dominate a group to gain leadership.)
3. When the groups have completed their lists of characteristics, ask them to send a representative to the front of the room to write their lists on the sheets of paper posted on the wall. As each person completes a list, he or she moves to the next

piece of paper. Each person writes only characteristics not already listed for an individual.

4. Conduct a discussion of the characteristics written on each chart, and have the class come to a consensus on leadership traits. You might guide the discussion with questions such as these:

   ✓ What characteristics are present in each leader?
   ✓ What characteristics do they share? How were these leaders different?
   ✓ How effective were each of these people as leaders?
   ✓ Is there a correlation between the characteristics and effectiveness?

5. Have the students categorize the characteristics. Guide them to the following leadership types as the categories:

   ✓ Power—one who leads through coercion, brutality, and so forth
   ✓ Position—one who leads because of his or her position
   ✓ Personal or social—one who leads because of charisma, personal merit, or accomplishment

6. Distribute the Leadership Chart handout. Have students fill in the leaders' names and leadership types. Then, have the students break into groups. With the other members of their group, have them refer to their journals and notes to determine what definition of justice identified in Lesson 2 most fits the leadership style or type for each person listed on the chart. You may guide their work with questions such as the following:

   ✓ What definition of justice applies to the leadership style of each of these leaders?
   ✓ Which leaders would you say were just, and which were not? (*Note to teacher:* Examples: Abigail Williams—revenge; Reverend Hale—divine law, social contract laws; John Proctor—human nature, respect for others; Judge—social contract, laws.)

7. Bring up the topic of the leaders of each student group. Reveal the experiment of "planting" leaders in each group. Ask what their leadership styles were—personal, power, position? Together, complete a leadership chart for the group leaders. Have the students record in their journals responses they had to their group leaders. Allow time for students to share their journal entries. Before doing so, however, ask everyone to be sensitive to the feelings of the leaders.

Assessment

1. Journal entries
2. Charts

Homework

1. Read chapters XV–XIX and XXI of *The Prince,* by Niccolò Machiavelli.
2. Respond in your journal to the readings. Answer these questions:
   - ✓ What qualities does Machiavelli believe a prince should have?
   - ✓ How does Machiavelli's conception of leadership relate to the concepts of justice we discussed earlier?
   - ✓ What is your reaction to Machiavelli's ideas?
   - ✓ Do you feel he is describing a principled leader? Why or why not?

Teacher Notes

Leadership Chart

Leader	Leadership Type	Concept of Justice

LESSON 5: AN ANALYSIS OF LEADERS

Goals Addressed: Goals 1 and 4

Instructional Purpose

1. To analyze speeches, documents, and articles written by or about historical and current leaders.
2. To identify characteristics of principled leaders.

Materials and Resources

1. *The Prince* by Niccolò Machiavelli
2. Leadership chart
3. Networked computers. (*Note to teacher:* If you do not have access to the Internet in a classroom or lab setting, you can gather readings ahead of time from the Internet or library books or schedule time in the library for the students to do the research. If you provide the readings, be sure to select leaders of different genders, cultures, races, and venues (politics, arts, sciences, and so forth). This lesson will take two class periods unless you provide the names of leaders, limit their number, and provide the reading selections.
4. Suggested list of leaders: Chief Joseph, Marie Curie, David Duke, Mahatma Gandhi, Charlton Heston, Adolf Hitler, Jesse Jackson, John or Robert Kennedy, Martin Luther King, Jr., Ayatollah Khomeini, David Koresh, Margaret Mead, Golda Meir, Arthur Miller, Supreme Court Justice Sandra Day O'Connor, Georgia O'Keefe, and Franklin Delano Roosevelt. (*Note to teacher:* This is a suggested list. You may add or subtract names, but be sure to represent leaders from different fields, races, cultures, disabilities, and genders.)

Activities

1. Ask the students to open their journals to the entries they wrote about from *The Prince*. Ask for volunteers to share their reflections on the chapters. Allow several students to read their reflections and discuss their findings.
2. List on the board the qualities Machiavelli believed a prince should have. Have the students take out their lists of leadership characteristics from Lesson 4 on *The Crucible*. Ask the following questions:
   - ✓ What characteristics demonstrated by leaders in *The Crucible* were similar to or the same as the characteristics described by Machiavelli?
   - ✓ Who demonstrated those characteristics?

✓ Which characteristics would you categorize as principled leadership qualities and which as unprincipled leadership qualities?

3. Distribute the list of leaders to the students. Tell them they may work alone or in groups of two to research one person from the list. Write the following research questions on the board, and allow the students the remainder of the class to research answers to the questions.

✓ In what field or venue is this person a leader? Give a brief, one-paragraph biography.

✓ What is this person's leadership style or type?

✓ From speeches, documents, or articles written by or about the person, what leadership qualities or values do you think were important to this person?

✓ How did this person treat others?

✓ To what concept of justice do you think this person adhered?

4. When the students complete the research, ask them to share the information they found about the leaders they researched. On the board, list the leadership qualities and values each student offers.

5. Have the students categorize the qualities and values into two categories—principled and unprincipled. (*Note to teacher:* Suggestions of principled leadership characteristics and philosophies include the following: places others' interests before self-interest; gives needed meaning and significance to people's work lives; responds to the reality that emotions, values, and membership connections are important human motivators; unites people to a higher end; demonstrates moral responsibility, honor, integrity, tolerance, and mutual respect; trustworthy; fair; and visible.

6. Have students complete the Leadership Chart for the leaders researched. Review the chart with the students, examining the relationship between the types of leaders, their concepts of justice, and whether or not they are principled leaders.

7. Have the class work together to develop a statement that embodies "principled leadership." Write the statement on the board, and have the students copy it into their notebooks or journals. Ask for a volunteer or volunteers to create a poster of the statement to be displayed in the classroom.

Assessment

1. Research report—2–3 pages
2. Leadership charts

AUTHOR INDEX

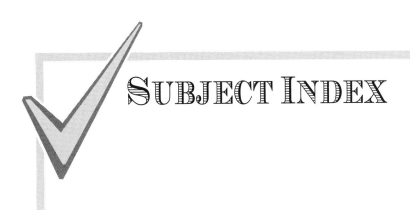

SUBJECT INDEX